PRE-MILLENNIUM SHAKE

IAN MOSS

EMPIRE PUBLICATIONS
1 Newton St., Manchester M1 1HW

Many thanks to my brother Neil for his organisational skills, his time and his infinite patience. His assistance in compiling this volume has been invaluable.

Foreword

The early 90's were a wild ride for me and my fellow bandmates in James, from the relative obscurity of *NME* curated Indie culture to regular performances on *Top Of The Pops* and *The Old Grey Whistle Test.* Two legendary BBC music programmes regularly watched with religious fervour by both the young Ian "Moët" Moss and me before discussing them at length the following day at school. One memorable occasion being Bowie's electrifying performance of 'Starman' in July 1972 which, I recall, blew us both away.

By the decade's end, my life had returned to relative normality thanks to an overdue return to education in order to study art and design. Unlike many of my musical heroes, who had gone to art school before joining a band... I'd done it all backwards!

I was in the same class at school as Ian, a thoroughly likeable and robust kid with a cocky smile who was blessed with an excitement for discovering new music that clearly eclipsed mine even then. Over the years, his knowledge, as you will discover in these very pages, has grown to be encyclopaedic.

It was from this same starting point of a nondescript northern secondary modern classroom that the pair of us set forth, like two music obsessed projectiles fired from a twin-barreled gun hurtling toward adult life; living parallel lives, neither converging nor diverging, destined to travel similar paths but ultimately to reach different targets.

Over the years our singular paths have crossed a few times and, when they did, we would share the journeys experienced since last we met. Meetings as dissimilar as 1979's 'Stuff the Superstars' gig at the Mayflower Club, where Moët was performing with his band The Hamsters whilst I soaked up the vibe, furthered my studies on how to be a good musician and, hopefully, score some illicit substances. Twenty odd years later, as the new millennium rapidly approached, I popped out to buy some potatoes only to discover that Moët was now the new owner of my favourite greengrocers!

On this particular occasion, we quickly adjourned to the nearest pub in order to celebrate our reunion and thanks to recent advances in mobile communication, we exchanged numbers and have since managed to stay in touch for which I'm very grateful.

Strongly opinionated, Moët always had a nose for eclectic musical excellence. It was no surprise for me to learn, many years after the fact, of his attendance at the legendary Sex Pistols gig at the lesser Free Trade Hall and to subsequently hear his many tales describing nights of excess with musicians, footballers, and boxing legends.

One of the beauties of reading the earlier books in this series is the way it has helped me (and anyone else who'd lived through those years) to retrace, recall, or revisit the events and music of the three decades covered, to happily make connections between them that we had forgotten or hadn't even realised at the time.

If, like me, music is a large presence in your life, or even your escape from its often grim realities, then you should find plenty to enrapture or inform you in this, the third instalment of Ian's journey.

Larry Gott

Introduction

I, like many others, was happy to kiss the 1980s goodbye. It had been a wearying experience as I'd felt constantly forced onto the back foot defending principles and core beliefs against the populism of Thatcher's war against working-class communities. I was also exhausted from arguing against American imperialism as they set themselves up as a gun-toting sheriff on the world stage. I was now in my early 30s; I had a little house and a mortgage around my neck, a steady job and a modest income – all in the vain hope that these acquisitions would somehow transform me into a more acceptable, well-adjusted, happier and all together more contented individual, that might feel at peace – a peace that my wild and free living had singularly failed to deliver. I was no longer in a band; the creative release that had always sustained me I now denied myself... what was the point of it? Where had it ever got me? I was through with devoting my energies into projects that came to nothing; "work comes first" became my mantra. I repeated it to myself so often that I nearly succeeded in making myself believe it.

In truth, I wasn't in a particularly healthy state. I would sit and ponder dark thoughts; whilst brooding, I would polish off a bottle of whisky or tequila on a regular basis. I'd also not lost my knack for getting involved in ultimately toxic relationships; I seemed to be a junkie for the unpleasant dramas that were a by-product of these dalliances. I kept up the appearance that everything was okay, but just below the surface was a simmering cauldron of deeply wounding discontent. The pre-millennium world outside my front door was also throwing up plenty of shocks and upheavals for me to digest. On the most superficial level, tastes would change... and mostly for the better. Sartorially speaking, things certainly improved – the mirrors that had seemingly been lost in the 1980s had thankfully been relocated.

Technological advancement continued at a dizzying pace; portable music players, cameras and camcorders all became smaller and sleeker; television sets and motor cars became bigger and brasher. We endured the first Gulf War; it was horrific, and yet only a prequel to the even more catastrophic second Gulf War. War was becoming just another reality TV show that desensitised viewers to the horror they were witnessing whilst sipping coca-cola and eating a slice of pizza. Europe, as well as the Middle East, once more became a theatre of war with the Bosnian conflict causing terrible sorrow, brought about via evil acts of genocide as concentration camps returned. This inhumanity was bloodily mirrored in Africa as Rwanda descended into a horrible, vicious civil war. We witnessed the rise of cable TV and the World Wide Web. Dolly the Sheep was huge news; an animal that had been cloned in a startling demonstration of chemical and biological engineering. Nelson Mandela was freed from jail and went on to lead South Africa, providing a powerful example of dignity and forgiveness to people around the globe. *Baywatch* and *The Simpsons* were American TV shows that were loved in the UK, as was the stunning *Twin Peaks*. Home-based successes included *Cracker*, *Absolutely Fabulous* and *Last of the Summer Wine*.

In UK politics, Thatcher would fall and perish due to her arrogant belief that she was always right – the wicked witch finally vanquished and replaced by a rather dull chap who, perversely, had run away from the circus in order to join the Conservative Party. John Major (for it was he) came and went and at last we had a Labour Government once again. Alas, before we got there, John Smith, a Prime Minister in-waiting, suffered a fatal heart attack and was replaced by Tony Blair, a deceitful, preening ponce who would re-brand the party and water-down its socialist content lest it upset his pop-star chums and the gutter press, run, as ever, by Rupert Murdoch who endorsed the premiership of this unprincipled lickspittle.

On the subject of pop-stars, Madonna endured and serenely flourished; Prince and Michael Jackson didn't fare quite as well. In their place came Mariah Carey, Whitney Houston and Simply Red. Additionally, hip-hop would increasingly be dominated by gangster rap and Scandinavia would birth death metal, where church burnings and murder became an unwelcome part of the scene. Punk and metal were melded in unholy alliance to spawn grunge, which provided the era's biggest star (and victim) in Kurt Cobain of Nirvana, and Britpop was big in the UK, even though essentially it was all about imitating The Beatles and The Kinks… really, really badly. More interesting were the different strands of dance music culture that pushed in all directions; acid-house, acid-techno, trance, drum & bass, trip-hop and big-beat were mere tips of a gigantic iceberg. My love for music was undiminished; I was not immersed in any scene or genre and not part of any particular tribe. I went wherever I felt like going and my tastes grew ever wider. Music still held huge power over me – it was the medicine that picked me up when spirits were low; it was the bandage when life left me feeling battered and bruised; it was the celebratory sound of little triumphs and the occasional days when I simply felt good to be alive. In reality, music was my everything. These pages are full of music; it's my music, it's your music and it's our music.

Come with me on a marvellous trip, hold onto your hat and enjoy.

I started the decade looking a little worse for wear, here in Philadelphia

1990

NOTABLE EVENTS

United States invades Panama deposing leader Manuel Noriega.

Soviet troops occupy Baku, Azerbaijan and kill 130 protesters who are campaigning for independence.

The American fast food chain McDonald's opens branches in Moscow and Shenzhen, China

In South Africa the African National Congress is legalised and Nelson Mandela is freed after 27 years imprisonment.

Mikhail Gorbachev is elected as First President of the Soviet Union.

Namibia gains independence from South Africa after 75 years of being ruled from Pretoria.

A massive anti-poll tax demonstration in London's Trafalgar Square erupts into a large scale riot as Thatcher's police force behave like storm troopers.

In Manchester, prisoners riot and take control of Strangeways prison for just under four weeks.

In what became known as the Singing Revolution, Lithuania, Latvia, and Estonia declare independence from the USSR.

The World Health Authority removes homosexuality from its list of diseases.

East Germany and West Germany begin the process of re-unification, which is completed by October. Helmut Kohl becomes the First Chancellor of Germany.

A stampede in a pedestrian tunnel leading to Mecca kills 1,426 people.

Iraq invades Kuwait leading to the first Gulf War.

Civil war in Sri Lanka sees massacres committed by both government forces and the opposing Tamil Tigers.

Pizza Hut joins McDonald's and KFC in opening outlets in Russia and China.

Tim Berners-Lee begins work on the creation of the World Wide Web.

Civil war begins in Rwanda.

Mikhail Gorbachev is awarded the Nobel Peace Prize for his efforts to bring an end to the Cold War and institute reform in the USSR.

Mrs Thatcher resigns her premiership and is replaced by John Major.

British and French workers on the Channel Tunnel meet 40 metres beneath the English Channel, establishing the first land contact between Britain and Europe for 8,000 years.

As communism crumbles, Albania announces free elections after mass protests by workers and students.

Alex Ferguson wins his first trophy as Manchester United manager, beating Crystal Palace 1-0 in the FA Cup Final replay. Another empire crumbles as Liverpool's title win is their last for 30 years.

NOTABLE BIRTHS

Laura Marling; Daley Blind; Kristen Stewart; Emma Watson; Dev Patel; David de Gea; Corey Anderson; Joe Root.

NOTABLE DEATHS

Terry Thomas; Barbara Stanwyck; Ava Gardener; Del Shannon; Keith Haring; Johnnie Ray; Ric Grech; Lev Yashin; Sarah Vaughan; Greta Garbo; Dexter Gordon; Sammy Davis Jr; Jim Henson; Rocky Graziano; Stiv Bators; Joe Mercer; Stevie Ray Vaughan; Leonard Bernstein; Art Blakey; Aaron Copland.

NOTABLE FILMS

Goodfellas; Miller's Crossing; Total Recall; *Home Alone; Edward Scissorhands; Wild at Heart;Tie Me Up Tie Me Down;Cry Baby;Arachnophobia; Teenage Mutant Ninja Turtles;Superstar: The Life and Times of Andy Warhol.*

NOTABLE BOOKS

Possession – A.S. Byatt

Rabbit at Rest – John Updike

L.A Confidential – James Ellroy

The Buddha of Suburbia – Hanif Kureishi

Use of Weapons – Ian M Banks
The Snapper – Roddy Doyle
Devil in a Blue Dress – Walter Mosley
Get Shorty – Elmore Leonard
Immortality – Milan Kundera
Age of Iron – J.M. Coetzee
Among the Thugs – Bill Buford

MY 1990

Here we were in a new decade, and here was I still plagued by dark depression and suicidal thoughts. To combat these destructive feelings and impulses, I was hell-bent on embracing orthodox normality. This implied a regimen that encompassed taking work seriously along with an acceptance of the concept of forging a career that would yield a satisfactory disposable income and desired material possessions. It seemed, from the outside, a way of life that made my peers happy – I determined to give it a good try; I would attempt to fit in; I would compromise in the hope that I might find contentment. My parents both reached the age of 65; I loved them dearly and wanted to be more supportive and less of a worry to them. Now that they had more time in their retirement, I drove them to the towns in the Midlands where my mother had been born and raised… she was able to visit friends and family whom she had not seen in years. I tried to take an interest in maintaining my house; I had quite extensive improvements made and dutifully redecorated the place. I was good at my job; I worked hard and knew that I was not just liked but respected. I had a wide circle of good friends but still life ailed me. I was a seemingly stable mature adult and yet the angst I had experienced as a troubled teenager had never dissipated; indeed, it had intensified. I felt detached and hollow as if I was simply going through the motions. I'd all but abandoned any dalliances with drugs but my drinking was ferocious. In my own mind I normalised this excessive consumption – after all, I could still function. I never missed work and even when I behaved like an asshole (which was frequently) people were quick to forgive me, even though I hated myself.

Football was one avenue of escape; I could immerse myself within a crowd of people, and although the sport itself was undergoing an existential crisis as it struggled to come to terms with the tragedies that had occurred at Hillsborough and Valley Parade, I was still able to give myself up to its rituals and feel a deep-rooted connection. I watched Manchester United play both home and away, as always. Even though I was engaged in shop work, the agreement with my employer was that weekends were my own. It was a strange season that began with a man called Michael Knighton agreeing in principle to buy the club from the clueless Martin Edwards, for the paltry sum of £20 million. Unfortunately for Knighton, he hadn't got and couldn't raise the cash; he and the club were a laughing stock. On the field the team were astonishingly abysmal and a collective air of despondency hung over everyone connected to the club. Somehow, in the FA Cup, a stumbling run was concocted that resulted in a trip to Wembley Stadium. After a 3-3 draw with Crystal Palace, notable for jittery goalkeeper Jim Leighton delivering yet another dreadful performance, a change of keeper and a 1-0 victory saw the team clinch the trophy.

Of course, music was another release, and my friend Marc Riley now worked as a record plugger for Tony Michaelides PR company. They worked on behalf of Factory Records, 4AD and other record labels of repute. I was a frequent visitor to the office and always left with an armful of albums that were generously gifted and gratefully received. Each weekend would find me watching bands at The Boardwalk – which was a club I loved – or Roger Eagle's promotions at The International 1, which had previously operated as a nightclub called Oceans 11, retaining much of that former club's decor and comfortable fittings. I liked much less the sister club, The International 2, which had once been The Carousel Club, a place where I had seen Gil Scott-Heron perform and also attended numerous Northern Soul all-nighters – all of the character had been ripped out and now it was a soulless dark bunker; I found the place depressing and, for the most part, I tried to avoid it. I was walking a tightrope with my sanity and I didn't want to tumble; it wasn't always easy, and I could be my own worst enemy, but I was at least seriously trying to sort myself out.

A NOTE ON THE NINETIES

The CD age was truly upon us and record companies were awash with cash; this led to a flood of releases. My research for this book allowed me to compile long lists of up to 500 singles per year that I considered truly representative of my tastes and worthy of inclusion. However, I must limit my choices to 100 per year or run the risk of wallowing in excess. To that end, I have restricted the number of entries by any particular artist to just one per year, though I will attempt to mention other notable singles that they released during the period. It must also be noted that it had become common practice by the 1990s to release singles in multiple formats; multiple mixes were often made available and B-sides and bonus tracks would often be changed on each version to appeal to completist collectors (and earn stacks of cash for stinking rich record companies too). I have no intention, nor desire, to detail this labyrinth of versions and shall content myself with simply writing about the featured track of each release. Entire books could be written about the various styles of music that proliferated during this decade. It can be fascinating to immerse oneself in the worlds of drum & bass, hip-hop, alt-rock or whatever your particular taste and affinities may be; that is not my purpose here. I have always liked variety in the styles of music I listen to; I have never wanted to attach myself to one particular genre and be consumed by it. I wouldn't want to eat beans on toast at every mealtime, so why would I subject myself to a diet of non-stop punk, jazz, or techno? This is too limiting, too constricting. I need a variety of sounds to stimulate, inspire and lift me. Welcome to my world…

My favourite gigs of the year included:

MC 900FT JESUS & DJ ZERO at The Boardwalk
MAZZY STAR at MCR University
THE MEKONS' 48 Hour Party at various venues, NYC

1990

100
ALL WOMEN ARE BAD
THE CRAMPS
ENIGMA
OTHER SINGLE 1990:
BIKINI GIRLS WITH MACHINE GUNS

A decade and a half into their career of chaos and confusion, The Cramps issued their 4th album *Stay Sick*. They had a new bass player in Candy del Mar which allowed Poison Ivy to take on the guitarist role vacated by first Bryan Gregory, and then Kid Congo Powers. Ivy also produced the album. Taken from it, 'All Women Are Bad' made a fabulous, though somewhat controversial single. The refrain that gave the song its title, would never sit comfortably in a climate where the appearance of being 'politically correct' was becoming increasingly important. However, anyone who looked closely would see that no sexism whatsoever existed in this band. Ivy, along with husband Lux Interior, was very much in control. Anyway, the song throbbed and shook in the way that only The Cramps could manage, and anyone who bothered listening to the lyric would find that the women portrayed in the song were tougher and smarter than their easily-duped male counterparts. In the world of The Cramps, women were not timid little creatures who liked to cook and clean, but strong, independent Amazonian warriors.

99
TECHNARCHY
CYBERSONIC
PLUS 8 RECORDS

'Technarchy' is an incredibly huge record; it is techno with an industrial edge that really stomps. The bass line is devastating and in just under 4 minutes duration, an awful lot happens… minimal it is not. The track powers its way into the consciousness and, as if to hammer home the message, the only lyric is delivered via a spooked sounding male voice saying "it's a state of mind", whilst heavenly female voices offer up a dream-like counterpart. Created by techno wizard Richie Hawtin, in collaboration with John Acquaviva and Daniel Bell, this was just awesome.

98
I GOT THE GROOVE
LEE 'SCRATCH' PERRY
MANGO

In 1977, at the famed Black Ark studio, Lee 'Scratch' Perry had re-purposed Gamble and Huff's Philly-soul classic and transformed it into a deeply beautiful, hypnotic slice of sublime reggae magic; it was sung by Horace Faith and played by crack musical force The Upsetters. After burning down his studio in the early 1980s, Perry was cut adrift – but after connecting with Adrian Sherwood and Mad Professor in London, his confidence was restored and the muse returned. 'Scratch' was now as sharp as a needle; he ceased to use alcohol and herb and let his playful personality run riot through his music. He re-cut 'I Got the Groove', this time featuring himself as vocalist; he merrily chants and chunters in a most eccentric manner. Meanwhile, the groove is uptempo and it runs like celestial clockwork.

97
HOUSE
BABES IN TOYLAND
SUB POP

Babes In Toyland were formed in Minneapolis in 1987 by guitarist/vocalist Kat Bjelland, drummer Lori Barbero and bassist Michelle Leon – though there are claims that Courtney Love (Barbero's house-mate) was also tried out as bassist too. 'House' was the band's second single; it was limited to a pressing of 3,500 copies…1,500 for Sub Pop's singles club and 2,000 pressed-up on yellow vinyl for shops. 'House' flies out of the traps fast and furious, and Kat Bjelland spits out the impressionistic lyric with venom. The song slows to walking pace, speeds up again, faster than before, and then slows once more as the vocal crawls and slurs. When it finally stops, the listener has been given a very severe jolt.

96
DIFFERENT DRUM
THE PASTELS
K RECORDS

'Different Drum' was written by a pre-Monkees Mike Nesmith in 1964. It was offered to the makers of The Monkees TV show, but rejected. In 1967, The Stone Poneys, featuring Linda Ronstadt on vocals, had a U.S. hit with a version of the song. It has subsequently been covered regularly by a variety of artists. In 1990, for instance, both The Lemonheads and The Pastels released the song as a single; while the former gave the song a smooth and sweet treatment, The Pastels take is much less so – in fact it is gloriously ramshackle and sounds all the more heartfelt for it. The music, played on banjo with a lovely steel-guitar interlude, has a spritely, exuberant quality, and while Stephen Pastel's rather flat vocal performance is something of an acquired taste, fortunately it suited mine just fine.

95
MERRY GO ROUND
THE REPLACEMENTS
SIRE

'Merry Go Round' was a song written by Replacements lead singer Paul Westerberg, about his relationship with his younger sister. It came from the group's seventh album *All Shook Down*, and was the lead-off single. This was the most successful of all The Replacements singles and it spent a month at number one on the American 'Modern Rock Tracks' chart. The track featured Charley Drayton on drums; he had played with the likes of The Rolling Stones, The B52s and Neil Young… suffice to say that he added immeasurably to the groove of the record. Guitars are used like scalpels and the sound is redolent of a band strutting with a confident swagger. There are memorable hooks to hold the attention and Westerberg delivers an eloquent, downbeat lyric via and a highly-impassioned vocal.

94
THE POWER
SNAP
ARISTA

'The Power' was a monstrously catchy European hip-house track. At its core there is a juggernaut riff, but equally there is enough unhurried space to add an emotional rollercoaster feel to the track. The record was mired in litigation because the original release featured multiple uncleared samples. This forced a complete re-recording of the song which nevertheless shot to the top of the charts in the UK and several other European countries, as well as reaching number two in the USA. The deeply-soulful female vocal, aligned to a male rap, in combination with its machine generated beat all came together exquisitely well to make this record an inescapable pleasure.

93
BABY STONES
ROBERT FORSTER
BEGGARS BANQUET

With the retirement of The Go-Betweens, following the serial disappointments that dogged and cursed that most sublime of bands, Robert Forster relocated from Australia to Germany to be with his future wife Karin Baumler, who appears on this record alongside Bad Seeds members Hugo Race, Thomas Wydler and Mick Harvey – the latter of whom also produced the track. The song is written from the perspective of a man seeking a binding, faithful love, whereas his prospective beau seeks a looser, less tying arrangement. The song was recorded quickly and the spontaneity is evident and refreshing. Robert Forster sing/speaks his poetic ode in customary style and with perfect enunciation; it was a fine opening introduction to his solo career.

92
AMERIKKKAS MOST WANTED
ICE CUBE
4TH & BROADWAY
OTHER SINGLES 1990:
WHOS THE MACK?;
ENDANGERED SPECIES;
JACKIN' FOR BEATS

After the acrimonious, bitter split from NWA, rapper Ice Cube was keen to get back to work. His NWA bandmate Dr Dre was set to take the producer's chair, but band/label politics scuppered the plan and Ice Cube turned instead to the Bomb Squad from New York's Public Enemy. They produced a sample-laden track that was rich and irresistible; it contained multiple samples from the likes of James Brown, The Lost Poets, Cerrone and comedian Richard Pryor. Over this backdrop, Ice Cube raps hard and fast; his passion is palpable and the sap is rising as he spits out the way life on the streets is lived in ghetto communities, and speaks of the harshness of being raised in the projects. He is unsentimental; he simply throws his truth into the face of polite society, as if to say "you created the problem, you'd better find a solution".

91
UNBELIEVABLE
EMF
PARLOPHONE

Insanely catchy, 'Unbelievable' was hard not to love; it was driven by adrenaline and infectious good humour. EMF was an acronym of *Epsom Mad Funkers*, a title taken from a fan club of Manchester band New Order… though it should be noted that there is an alternate reading of the acronym – namely *Ecstasy Mother Fucker*. They were clearly influenced by the Manchester sounds, not only New Order, but also The Stone Roses/Happy Mondays axis. To this blueprint they added a zany pop twist, and 'Unbelievable', their first single which went as high as number 3 on the UK chart, displayed this to the maximum. It has a lolloping bass, pounding beats, an immense riff and vocal samples of interjections from comedian Andrew Dice Clay, as well as a member of The

Black Panthers exclaiming "what the fuck!". EMF add their own exuberant shouted choruses, and you quickly realise that resistance is futile; a place in your heart must be located for this record.

90
I GOT DRUNK
UNCLE TUPELO
ROCKVILLE

Country music had long been unfashionable, but as this decade continued there would be a huge upsurge in interest in the roots of American rock, and the alt-country scene would become vibrant and popular. Some credit must go to The Mekons from the UK, whose embrace of the form sowed the seeds of this revival. One of the first American bands to head firmly in this direction were Uncle Tupelo, who featured both Jeff Tweedy (later to lead Wilco) and Jay Farrar (who would go on to form Son Volt). 'I Got Drunk' is a vigorous and rowdy rumination on the affects of alcohol – "I got drunk and I fell down" is the hard hitting, straight-to-the-point confessional chorus. The sad irony was that a division within the band resulted from Tweedy's hard-drinking lifestyle; it resulted in pushing the sober Jay Farrar away from his erstwhile colleague.

89
EASY LIFE
CABARET VOLTAIRE
PARLOPHONE

Cabaret Voltaire had a streak of aggression in their band chemistry, which generally manifested itself as the dissonant noise which seemed to be an integral part of their music. Here though, on 'Easy Life' (and the album it came from, *Groovy, Laid-Back and Nasty*) the nastiness and noise were absent. Rather than find themselves stuck in an easy to define rut, the Cabs had travelled to Chicago to work with house music maestro Marshall Jefferson. Their sound on 'Easy Life' is bright and accessible; it is a mid-paced instrumental track that twists and turns. It feels like the kind of music one might listen to whilst wandering through a run-down and derelict neighbourhood full of ghosts – it was a prime example of musical hauntology.

88
THE GHETTO
TOO $HORT
JIVE
OTHER SINGLE 1990:
SHORT BUT FUNKY

Crime, crack addiction, shootings and prison are just some of the true-to-life issues that Too $hort raps on in his lazy sounding, conversational drawl (much copied by the more successful Snoop Doggy Dogg). He is accompanied by the heavily sampled Donny Hathaway song of the same title. The problems in his Oakland, California home-town are laid bare, but his message is tempered by the love that he expresses for his fellow citizens; this underpins the song and ultimately makes it an uplifting listen.

87
SHE COMES IN THE FALL
INSPIRAL CARPETS
MUTE
OTHER SINGLE 1990:
THIS IS HOW IT FEELS

The Inspirals were nice; they inspired affection. Certainly, around Manchester, everybody seemed pleased that they had become successful. I, for one, had no reason whatsoever to feel any negativity towards them. Late one drunken night, I had a minor disagreement with singer Tom Hingley. A week later, his bandmate Clint Boon sought me out to apologise on his colleague's behalf. It was a classy gesture that I was impressed by… they were good people. On the whole though, as much as I tried, I just couldn't like much of their output. I went to see them and was bored. Their style came across as being too twee for my taste. Happily, there are always exceptions, and 'She Comes In The Fall' is a very good example of this. Here, they sound less rinky-dinky, and altogether tougher; the drumming is exceptional and the verses are dark swirls that give way to a bright, chiming Byrds-like chorus, where the band harmonise quite wonderfully.

86
PSYCHOBILLY FREAKOUT
THE REVEREND HORTON HEAT
SUB POP

The Reverend Horton Heat were a rock & roll group who came with a significant degree of kitsch attached; the very much in-on-the-joke band were self-aware enough to accentuate this to the full… and even allow it to brim frothily over the top. 'Psychobilly Freakout', and its parent album *Smoke 'Em if you Got 'Em*, were recorded live in the studio, directly onto two-track tape, which generated a loose, raw feel. The band are captured perfectly; the guitar wrangling that takes place is frankly astonishing, the vocal is feverish and frenzied, and the rhythm section hard and primal. This is brash, noisy, dumb pop music of the highest order.

1990

85
DON'T BE CRUEL
THE RESIDENTS
RALPH

If you have never been in fashion, it follows that you can never be out of fashion, so the niche status enjoyed by The Residents meant that the individualistic seam they mined was always a haven for broad-minded music lovers who could dip in and out of the band's repertoire to enjoy many different flavoured refreshments. Here, the mysterious San Franciscans were exhuming the song book of Elvis Presley; they forensically deconstructed his songs before reassembling them in Residents style. A full album titled *The King and Eye* was released, and from it 'Don't Be Cruel' was issued as a single. It jerks rather than swings, and is taken more slowly than the familiar version. Also, Presley's smooth singing style is ditched in place of what sounds like a deranged hill-billy howling at the moon. My boat was well and truly floated by these free spirits and I sailed away with a smile on my face.

84
THIEVES IN THE TEMPLE
PRINCE
PAISLEY PARK
OTHER SINGLE 1990:
NEW POWER GENERATION

After providing the soundtrack for the hugely successful *Batman* movie, Prince set about recording another soundtrack album – this time for his own film *Graffiti Bridge*. 'Thieves in the Temple' was the final song recorded; the shining jewel on the album, it was duly released as a single and went into the top 10 of the charts both in the UK and USA. The track is undoubtedly one of the high-points from Prince's 1990s output. It begins quietly with a keyboard and vocal cloaked in echo, only to be suddenly transformed as drum machines and a pulsing, synthesised bass-line kick in. Middle-Eastern melodies give the song an 'Arabian Nights' flavour as Prince sings in a highly emotional and accusatory manner about deception and lies, about being wronged by an unfaithful lover. A sampled harmonica solo adds further excitement to proceedings and the layered backing vocals are impeccable. A guitar is briefly used as a flame-thrower and then the song stops dead… it is quite simply audacious and brilliant.

83
DOIN' OUR OWN DANG
JUNGLE BROTHERS
ETERNAL
OTHER SINGLE 1990:
WHAT U WAITIN' 4

This collaboration was a summit meeting of some of the mightiest talents from the *Native Tongues* collective; De La Soul and Monie Love contribute to the writing and performing, whilst Q-Tip also co-writes and produces. The old adage about too many cooks spoiling the broth is not applicable here – egos are sat upon and the collective flow harmoniously and joyfully. Bob Marley's reggae classic 'Jamming' is referenced in the intriguing lyric, and 'Doin' our Own Dang' shares a similarly bright, uplifting vibe.

82
HYSTERIA
MARK STEWART & THE MAFIA
MUTE

With the musical muscle of *The Mafia* to the fore, Mark Stewart's voice is mostly buried deep in the mix by producer Adrian Sherwood. The sound is dense, thick as treacle, dark and dangerous. The groove, created by Messrs Wimbish, LeBlanc & McDonald, is pummelling and brutal; phrases occasionally cut through the maelstrom where Stewart, a wired presence at its centre, rages incandescently.

81
THE ONLY ONE I KNOW
THE CHARLATANS
SITUATION TWO
OTHER SINGLES 1990:
INDIAN ROPE; THEN

My Friend, Russ Wilkins, had relocated from Mold in North Wales to the great Mancunian metropolis; he set up a record store in the foyer of Manchester University which I often frequented. We would chat – or rather I would listen to Russ enthuse – about new bands. One band he advised me to listen to were The Charlatans, who he described as a pack of Midlands scooter-boys playing updated mod anthems. Before I'd even had the chance to act upon his words, The Charlatans were in the charts, reaching number 9 with 'The Only One I Know'. It was a driving slice of soul-infused garage rock, in the style of The Spencer Davis Group, that cheekily pillaged both The Byrds and Deep Purple – the former lyrically, and the latter for the Hammond organ sound. Despite, or maybe because of, its prominent 1960s influences, it chimed perfectly with the times. It mixed the past and present into a delicious cocktail. The floppy-fringed front man sang angelically, the band were tight as a nut and The Charlatans were clearly a force to be reckoned with.

80
THAT IS WHY
JELLYFISH
CHARISMA
OTHER SINGLES 1990: THE KING IS HALF UNDRESSED; BABY'S COMING BACK

Jellyfish were a band from Los Angeles and they were power-pop incarnate. They dressed themselves, and their records, in bright, garish, day-glow colours whilst projecting a happy, smiling image. They were a perfect example of 'right band, wrong time'. In the mid- to late-1980s, they might have been accepted by the *Paisley Underground* scene; later in the 1990s, their brand of tunefulness was back in vogue… but in 1990 the world was gearing itself up for grunge. It was choosing to dress down in workers' clothes rather than look like psychedelic refugees. The world looked away and missed a real treat. 'That is Why' was perfect pop in the manner of *Revolver*-era Beatles. The band's harmonies are gorgeous and the guitar playing is Harrison-esque. In writers Andy Sturmer and Roger Manning they had a duo with the knack of creating fabulous, melodic, hook-laden tunes that were on a par with those of ELO and Fleetwood Mac.

79
THE FORMULA
THE D.O.C.
RUTHLESS RECORDS

'The Formula' was the fourth of five singles extracted from the Dr Dre produced debut album *No One Can Do It Better*, which seemed all set to propel The D.O.C. to international success. He was an affiliate of NWA, and had contributed lyrics to their *Straight Outta Compton* album. Here, on 'The Formula', over a jazz/blues vibe provided by a manipulated sample taken from Marvin Gaye's 'Inner City Blues', The D.O.C. lets his 'rhythmic American poetry' flow smoothly as he proclaims and demonstrates his skills; this was classic West Coast rap. But then The D.O.C. fell asleep at the wheel of his car, under the influence of alcohol and cannabis; he crashed and was catapulted through the windscreen, face first, into a tree. His injuries were extensive and initially his voice was lost; after six weeks it returned… but much changed. He went on to co-found *Death Row Records* with Dr Dre and Suge Knight, and he wrote for Dre, Easy E and Snoop Dogg amongst others. In 1997 he returned with a new solo album, but his best work is found here, at the very start of his career.

78
LFO (THE LEEDS WAREHOUSE MIX)
LFO
WARP

LFO were teenage duo Mark Bell and Gez Varley, who first met in Leeds. They had a shared enthusiasm for dance music and had been playfully recording tracks in their bedrooms while still at school. They took the name LFO from the initials commonly used for the synthesiser function *low frequency oscillation*. Their first track, the eponymous 'LFO', was well received and often played in clubs; this led to an official release deal with Sheffield label Warp. So, despite being recorded more for pleasure than commercial aspiration, they landed themselves a number 12 hit on the UK pop chart. 'LFO' was a real standout, raw and bleep heavy. Equally though, it was spacey and melodic, and this contributed to helping Sheffield join the likes of Detroit and Berlin as important techno music breeding grounds.

77
HOW WAS IT FOR YOU?
JAMES
FONTANA
OTHER SINGLE 1990:
LOSE CONTROL

Momentum was with James; their last two singles on the Rough Trade label had been huge independent hits. Now, on a major label with major label money behind them, it was time to deliver; the national chart was the target. 'How Was It For You?' was indeed a modest hit – it reached number 32 – but just as importantly, it was a record that enjoyed significant airplay. Its sexually suggestive theme and catchphrase chorus was cheeky enough to titillate, yet ambiguous enough not to offend. The band had never sounded so tough and tight as here, helped immeasurably by the recruitment of Dave Baynton-Power, a new and very solid drummer. The song is anchored on a memorable guitar riff from Larry Gott, and a prominent cowbell percussion part. It's actually rather redolent of 'Start Me Up'-era Rolling Stones, although the clever lyric and arch delivery of front man Tim Booth take it into completely different territory.

76
TOMORROW NEVER KNOWS
DANIELLE DAX
SIRE
OTHER SINGLE 1990: BIG BLUE 82

Another independent music stalwart to be wooed and seduced by a major label was Danielle Dax, once a member of the fondly recalled Lemon Kittens. Dax had it all; the talent, the charisma and the voice were all present and correct… as were the looks and striking image. That Sire failed to make her a household name was totally down to their own mismanagement. Musically, the relationship started well; Dax was paired with Smiths producer Stephen Street, and this magnificent re-interpretation of the Lennon & McCartney classic 'Tomorrow Never Knows' was released as a single. The psychedelia is ramped up by use of Indian instrumentation and the rhythm track uses house music beats and piano along with subtle electronics. Dax is in fine voice – she enunciates clearly and with great character.

75
CRACKDOWN
PSYCHE
TRANSMAT

Carl Craig was the leading light in the second wave of Detroit techno artists. His albums *The Secret Tapes of Doctor Eitch* (under the pseudonym Paperclip People) and *More Songs About Food and Revolutionary Art* would, later in the decade, mesmerise and educate me. Here though, at the start of his career, he issued 'Crackdown' under the assumed name Psyche. It is majestic and symphonic sounding, featuring a drum track created with care and precision. A female voice, whispering in French, is an almost ghost-like presence and at the mid-point of the track, a bass is introduced that seriously grooves; then, without changing tempo, the track somehow moves into a higher gear. This is an addictive listening experience.

74
TIMELESS MELODY
THE LA'S
GO DISCS

'Timeless Melody' was the single that preceded The La's much anticipated debut album, on which a different recording of the song appeared. It was another golden pop nugget from the pen of Lee Mavers, whose songs never seemed to be even the slightest bit forced, almost as if they had simply dropped from his imaginative mind, into the fingers and then onto the fretboard of a guitar – the man was a simply a natural with music flowing through him. This track has a Beatle-esque *Revolver*-era feel to it. The song shimmers and builds inexorably up to a guitar solo that can only be described as an eruption.

73
MANSION ON THE HILL
NEIL YOUNG & CRAZY HORSE
REPRISE

Neil Young's album *Ragged Glory* continued his artistic re-awakening, after an early- to mid-1980s slump. Young and Crazy Horse cranked up the amps and blasted through the songs with wild abandon. 'Mansion on the Hill' (not to be confused with a Hank Williams song of the same name, which incidentally was a song Neil Young had once covered) is lyrically quite a slim song that speaks of an ageing man reflecting on himself and his life, before deciding to retreat from the public eye to a place of privacy. Here, unreformed and unrepentant of his lifestyle, his passions can be indulged in secrecy. "Psychedelic music fills the air" wails Young during the frequent choruses, which are played as ramped-up primal stomps accompanied by paint-stripping guitar mayhem.

72
WINDOWPANE
COIL
THRESHOLD HOUSE

'Windowpane' was a seventeen-minute-long track on the album *Love's Secret Domain*. The title of the track alludes to the square shaped, thin gelatine strips impregnated with LSD that were readily available, and the subject matter is a lyrical description of the transformative effect of ingesting the aforementioned hallucinogenic drug. The song was edited down to a more immediately digestible five minutes and issued as a single. Musically, it is repetitive and electronic, incorporating expanding voice echoes, as John Balance delivers his vocal in a ritualistic, chanted manner. The whole piece is hypnotising, trance-inducing and highly seductive.

71
BIG
NEW FAST AUTOMATIC DAFFODILS
PLAYTIME
OTHER SINGLE 1990: FISHES' EYES

Although lazily lumped into the 'Madchester' category, The New Fast Automatic Daffodils shared none of the laddishness inherent in that scene – only geographical proximity linked them. Although not at all po-faced or obscure, the band were an altogether more artistic proposition than most of their peers. 'Big' perfectly captures what they are all about; it is a combination of tribal polyrhythms, African-style horns, scratchy guitar, funk bass and blurred vocals. It works on a cerebral level, but also as a great dance track as well.

70
BUKE E KRIPE NE VATER TONE
3 MUSTAPHAS 3
GLOBE STYLE

For five years, 3 Mustaphas 3 had amused, educated and confused us. They were a six-piece band who featured the talents of ex-Magazine guitarist Ben Mandelson, along with former member of The Damned and P.I.L. (besides being current member of The Mekons) Lu Edmonds. Elaborate mythology was spun, pseudonyms adopted and the 6th of August given as the birthday of each member. They played a wired brand of Balkan folk music, utilising authentic instruments of the region. Often the sound was celebratory, but here on 'Buke E Kripe Ne Vater Tone', the group's final single, it is sombre and mournful before, during the last section of the song, becoming lighter and more high-spirited. Possibly the track references a funeral and the wake that follows? Of course, I don't really have a clue… but I can conclude that this is a splendid record.

69
SHINE ON
HOUSE OF LOVE
FONTANA

House of Love had been formed by vocalist Guy Chadwick and guitarist Terry Bickers. The combination of Chadwick's pop classicism and Bickers' at times untethered and highly-psychedelic guitar sound, earned them a deal with Creation Records – and a sizeable audience; it seemed inevitable that they would go on to achieve mainstream success. Following the release of four singles, which sold well, they signed to Fontana; it was a mistake… they were paired with unsuitable producers who didn't understand what was good about the band. Instead, they accentuated the 'trad rock' aspect of the band's DNA and made them sound dull. The one thing they did get right was to re-record the band's original Creation single, 'Shine On'. It was rhythmically taut and the drums powered the track; the guitar shimmered majestically and then soared during a startling solo. Chadwick sang with an authoritative ease while the song itself is strong and the choruses hook the listener. In short, the record sparkled and the band had the hit they deserved, reaching number 20 on the pop chart. Sadly for The House of Love, that was as good as it got.

68
NOVEMBER SPAWNED A MONSTER
MORRISSEY
HMV
OTHER SINGLE 1990: PICCADILLY PALARE

For this single, which was a stand out in his solo career, the ex-Smiths vocalist had a new songwriting partner in producer Clive Langer, the former Deaf School mainman. Also featured on bass was Morrissey's one-time band mate Andy Rourke, and vocals were added courtesy of genius figure Mary Margaret O'Hara. Here, the lyric challenges the listener to examine their attitudes toward the disabled and to forsake any prejudice. It aims to disturb and discomfort those harbouring any notions of body fascism.

67
YOU'RE NEVER ALONE WITH A CIGARETTE
SUN CITY GIRLS
MAJORA

Sun City Girls came from Phoenix, Arizona. They were experimental and highly prolific, issuing in the region of seventy album length releases. 'You're Never Alone with a Cigarette' was a single that did not feature a song of that title; the A-side contained '100 lbs of Black Olives' and the B-side featured 'The Fine Tuned Machines Of Lemuria'. The niceties of commercially-targeted recording technology are completely absent here; the band are raw, wired, loose and free-form. They use conventional rock music instruments but approach them in a most un-rock manner. If one can imagine jazz masters Albert Ayler and John Coltrane transposing their approach to saxophone onto electric guitar, bass and drums, you will have a near perfect sound picture of this record.

66
THE DEVIL MADE ME DO IT
PARIS
TOMMY BOY

Banned by MTV, this was an angry, political and highly provocative rap, which attacked systems and institutions that are full of bigoted, institutionalised racism. Paris is revealed to be every bit as militant and hard-hitting as Public Enemy. The beats are pristine and polished, and his rapid fire delivery is unswerving, revealing a mind that is just as sharp as his tongue. He was dropping bombs that made some people squirm, but his motives and integrity were beyond reproach… and even if the social content of the record is disregarded, this was still a sonically thrilling record.

65
SPIKE CYCLONE
ROYAL TRUX
VERTICAL RECORDS

Once Neil Hagerty had left Pussy Galore in favour of Royal Trux, thereby pursuing a more wayward musical path in conjunction with his girlfriend Jennifer Herrema, any notion of orthodoxy was discarded and a thrilling adventure began. 'Spike Cyclone' was the lead track on a double 7" single. At this relatively early stage in the band's career, their sound was dense and atonal. The duo were devotees of New York's eccentric electronic band Suicide, and here the influence shows; there is no semblance of a verse, chorus or middle-eight structure. Jennifer's singing voice challenges conventional tastes, while the drums, guitars and bass are all playing relatively orthodox parts… except that there is no attempt whatsoever to make them gel into a cohesive whole. The song, indeed the band's whole approach, is a radical experiment in pushing at the boundaries; it is wonderful.

64
OCEAN TO OCEAN
MODEL 500
TRANSMAT

Juan Atkins was to techno what James Brown had been to funk and Chuck Berry to rock & roll; he was the figurehead, the influencer, the leader. This latest issue, under his Model 500 alias, illustrated the point precisely. Strings were added by Martin Bond and mixed together with a sublime bass part and drumming that just epitomised propulsion. By this point, Atkins had been doing the business for a decade, and this was yet another record that sounded like music from the future.

63
D.O.A.
DEAD MOON
TOMBSTONE

Dead Moon were a garage/punk band from Portland, Oregon; at this point, they were almost unknown in their homeland but had a strong European fanbase. 'D.O.A.' is an anguished cry on the subject of loss. Singer Fred Cole has a rasping voice that is as real as it gets; musically, there is a slight trace of country – which, after all, is a genre infused with pain. Sadness and desperation are so eloquently expressed that the song sends shivers down my spine in precisely the same way that Iggy and the Stooges did with their immortal 'Gimme Danger'.

62
YOU PLAYED YOURSELF
ICE T
SIRE
OTHER SINGLES 1990:
DICK TRACY;
MIND OVER MATTER

Tracey Lauren Marrow had a turbulent upbringing. He was orphaned in his early teens and affiliated to 'The Crips' whilst still in high-school. This led to involvement in serious violent crime, drug dealing and pimping… in short, he was not a very nice person. His machismo led to him enlisting in the U.S. army where, somewhere along the way, he picked up the nickname of Ice T because of his love of the novels of Iceberg Slim – passages of which he would learn by heart and recite to friends. Hip-hop gave him the possibility to change his life for the better; after hearing The Sugarhill Gang single 'Rappers Delight' he bought turntables and began to DJ – only to discover that his raps were better received than his mixes. He began recording in the mid-1980s and by the time 'You Played Yourself' was issued, he was a high-selling artist of international renown. 'You Played Yourself' takes a sample of 'The Boss' by James Brown as its musical base; it sounds very cool indeed. Atop the track, Ice T tells a story in 3 parts; it is a cautionary tale of men who allow their egos to become so big that they trip over them and fall into the dirt… as Ice T emphatically states, "it ain't nobody else's fault". This was a man who had learned life's lessons the hard way; he was worth listening to.

61
DE-LUXE
LUSH
4AD

'De-Luxe' was the lead track from the e.p. *Mad Love* that saw Lush paired with Robin Guthrie of Cocteau Twins, who produced and helped develop the band's trademark ethereal sound of textured guitars and almost indecipherable vocals, an idiosyncratic and individual approach that remained forever intact. 'De-Luxe' was punchy in the extreme; the rhythm was akin to riding a rollercoaster as the song rose and fell, only to rise, fall and swerve once again. This was breathless stuff, and with the addition of heartbreakingly angelic voices emanating from the centre of the sound landscape, it was a truly wonderful piece of music.

60
SILVER
NIRVANA
SUB POP

Between the reputation making album *Bleach*, and the supreme and iconic *Nevermind*, came the single 'Silver'. It was recorded in the interregnum period when Nirvana were lacking a full-time occupant of the drum stool – for this session, Dan Peters of Mudhoney was used. It is a very literal and simple song about a boy who is dropped off and placed under his grandparents' supervision whilst not wanting to be there. This is also the moment when everything began to change for Nirvana – a hitherto only hinted at pop sensibility is clearly revealed. Although much of the song is hammered hard and Kurt Cobain sings in a throat-shredding growl, the melodic finesse that underpins the song is obvious. A genius of pop music was beginning to show his hand; soon he and his bandmates would change the face of the cultural scene for evermore.

59
BLUE SAVANNAH
ERASURE
MUTE
OTHER SINGLE 1990:
STAR

As befits a song describing savannah, this is a beautiful, lush and sweepingly atmospheric musical piece; every aspect of the track is handled with subtle precision. Vince Clarke plays with the usual formula here, and back references his original musical inspiration – Kraftwerk are evoked by use of the 'motorik' rhythm track. Elsewhere, a piano sparkles like cut crystal. Andy Bell sings with delicious restraint; his voice simmers with emotion. This is a romantic, melodic tour-de-force… a pop gem that charted at number three in the UK, and despite its low-key feel, still managed to double as a dance-floor smash as well.

58
BEEN CAUGHT STEALING
JANE'S ADDICTION
WARNER BROTHERS
OTHER SINGLES 1990:
STOP; THREE DAYS

I saw these disreputable, clearly degenerate and dissolute people at The Apollo, round about the time of this release. I'd been attracted by 'Been Caught Stealing' which had been a number 34 hit single here in the UK; I hoped that more of their material would match this smart and sharp piece of rock-pop that reminded me very much of the early Alice Cooper group. Sadly, it didn't; the rest of the band's repertoire resided in that dull place where hard rock and heavy metal converge. Nevertheless, 'Been Caught Stealing' was a treasure. It was cheerfully subversive in subject matter – the use of acoustic guitar and the playful vocal from Perry Farrell (along with his dog Annie's barking cameo) displayed great panache and lightness of touch. Throw in an incendiary guitar break from Dave Navarro and you have a latter-day rock classic.

57
MY DEFINITION OF A
BOOMBASTIC JAZZ STYLE
DREAM WARRIORS
4TH & BROADWAY
OTHER SINGLE 1990
WASH YOUR FACE IN MY
SINK

Dream Warriors were King Lou and Capital Q from Toronto. This slice of alternative hip-hop was their debut single and it put them into the number 18 chart position in the UK. Musically, it is created via a sample of 'Soul Bossa Nova' by Quincy Jones, well-known to these two native Canadians as the theme tune to a popular TV game show called *Definition*. The piece is an affectionate parody, repurposed to allow the wit and wisdom of the rappers to be good-naturedly peppered across the track. It is finger-clicking good stuff.

56
BLUES FOR CEAUSESCU
THE FATIMA MANSIONS
KITCHENWARE

A momentous riff underpins this six minutes of savagery, during which drums pound, bass rumbles and cutlery rattles. The architect of this musical carnage is a man – a very angry man –

whose name is Cathal Coughlan, and he is unleashing a barrel-load of bile in the direction of Nicolae Ceaucescu and other tin-pot, despotic autocrats of his ilk. However, it is not solely these cruel dictators who are under fire; Coughlan also rails against the immorality and stupidity of mankind which allows these evil people to seize power. (From recent history, see also Vladimir Putin, Donald Trump and Boris Johnson as examples of this moral vacuum).

55
I.C. WATER
PSYCHIC TV
TEMPLE RECORDS

Genesis P-Orridge claimed to be a confidant of Ian Curtis, and suggested that the pair were planning a collaborative venture that would have seen Curtis leave Joy Division. As fanciful as that sounds, it is not difficult to imagine the pair being drawn towards each other and engaging in dialogue. Here, Genesis delivers a musical memorial to the deceased singer and icon. The single was packaged in a sleeve which bore an image of Ian Curtis, and his voice was sampled during the songs intro. This track bears no stylistic resemblance at all to 'Godstar', where Psychic TV had eulogised another fallen icon… in that case Brian Jones. There, the song lyric had been accusatory towards Jones's old bandmates in The Rolling Stones. Here, there is no finger pointing, and the only motive seems to be payment of a sincere and genuine tribute to a man who died tragically… and tragically young. Psychic TV were under the musical direction of Fred Giannelli, and his restrained techno stylings offer a suitable soundscape for the sing-speak utterances of Genesis P-Orridge.

54
NOT GIVEN LIGHTLY
CHRIS KNOX
FLYING NUN

Chris Knox was a major part of the Flying Nun Records story. For example, it was his four-track machine that was used to record most of the labels early singles, and his adherence to an unpolished, lo-fi sound was also highly influential. Knox was one half of the quite wonderful Tall Dwarfs, but his prolific songwriting also prompted him to begin releasing solo records. 'Not Given Lightly' is his undisputed, utterly fabulous classic; it is a sweet and tender song with a jaunty lilt, written for Barbara, his then partner, and it contains the beautiful opening line "This is a love song for John and Leisha's mother". The main refrain and title of the song is a direct lift from 'Venus in Furs' by The Velvet Underground, but it is borrowed and re-used in a totally different context – in The Velvets' hands, the phrase is a signifier of darkness, whereas here, Chris Knox suffuses the words, and indeed the whole of this song, in bright and brilliant sunshine.

53
TOM'S DINER
D.N.A. FEATURING SUZANNE VEGA
A&M

Suzanne Vega had written and released 'Tom's Diner' as an *a cappella* piece in 1987; it was a clever observational song about sitting in a cafe, which turned this everyday experience into a fascinating narrative, drawing the listener into another person's world. At this point, Vega was at the height of her success; her album *Solitude Standing* and single 'Luka' had both been huge. D.N.A. were an anonymous British production team who decided to cut up Vega's vocal and turned her ad-libbed outro (Da da duh doo, da da duh doo) into a hook of gigantic proportions that ran throughout the song; then they added a dance beat from Soul to Soul's 'Keep on Movin''. Their version was then pressed up as a low-key, white label release, and it was made available to club DJ's without seeking permission from either Suzanne Vega or her record company. Fortunately for D.N.A., after hearing what had been done she was impressed; so, rather than begin litigation against the re-mixers, A&M struck a deal to release the track themselves. This proved to be beneficial all round – the song became a radio staple and a number two chart hit – everyone was happy.

52
STREETS OF NEW YORK
KOOL G RAP & DJ POLO
COLD CHILLIN'

Given the opportunity to do some recording by DJ Marley Marl (with results that clearly impressed him) the duo of Kool G & DJ Polo were taken under his wing and they duly became members of The Juice Crew. They released a debut album in 1989 and a year later came the album *Wanted Dead or Alive*, from which 'Streets of New York' was taken. The single was striking and bold, adorned as it was by distinctive piano and saxophone samples taken from The Fatback Band. This infusion of funk was the perfect platform for Kool G; he tells vividly of the social issues that blight the inner city ghettos he knew all too well. Homelessness, alcohol and drug abuse, corrupt police officers, gambling, prostitution and violence are all depicted in this aural noir. His style and delivery, along with the choice of subject matter, marked Kool G out as a special talent. His influence was subsequently felt in the works of Nas and The Notorious B.I.G.

51
HURDY GURDY MAN
BUTTHOLE SURFERS
ROUGH TRADE

Butthole Surfers didn't often record versions of other people's songs, but on the evidence of The Guess Who's 'American Woman' and Black Sabbath's 'Sweet Loaf' (re-titled 'Sweat Loaf') when they did, the Buttholes could be considered to be excellent interpreters of other writers' work. Here, Donovan's 1960s hit 'Hurdy Gurdy Man' gets an irreverent going over; Paul Leary and Gibby Haines hysterically voice the whimsical lyric and really ham it up – simpering, hiccuping and exaggeratedly mimicking Donovan's fey style of singing. The band psychedelically enhance the strongly melodic tune without taking any liberties with its structure. They breathe new life into the old chestnut by warping and bending it from the inside; it's a whole lot of fun.

50
VOGUE
MADONNA
SIRE
OTHER SINGLES 1990: JUSTIFY MY LOVE;
KEEP IT TOGETHER;
HANKY PANKY

Yet another international chart topper for Madonna, who continually kept on evolving and improving. 'Vogue' was a brilliant track, co-written and co-produced with Shep Pettibone. It is an uplifting, anthemic, house-styled track, specifically saluting and inspired by the Vogue dancers of Harlem's drag ball culture… but in a wider sense, it also celebrates dance as an expressive form of escapism from societal constriction. The song features a middle section where Madonna name-checks movie icons including Greta Garbo, Marilyn Monroe, James Dean and Fred Astaire, all of whom inspired look-a-likes at the drag balls. Madonna introduced into the mainstream a hitherto marginalised culture, whilst simultaneously creating a brilliant dance record that held universal appeal.

49
SPEEDING MOTORCYCLE
DANIEL JOHNSON & YO LA TENGO
SINGLES ONLY LABEL

Daniel Johnson first released a version of 'Speeding Motorcycle' in 1983; now, with the aid of Yo La Tengo, it was re-visited. Daniel Johnson's off-kilter take on pop classicism and untutored singing is, I acknowledge, an acquired taste… and yet, when one opens the heart to his simplistic style, one is struck by the purity of his work and world-view – 'Speeding Motorcycle' is no exception to this rule. Yo La Tengo don't attempt to polish or professionalise Johnson's music; instead, they adapt to the needs of the song and offer empathy and support. This is a wonderful record… it's as simple as that.

48
HEAVENLY POP HIT
THE CHILLS
SLASH
OTHER SINGLES 1990:
PAST PART FICTION;
THE MALE MONSTER FROM THE ID;
THE ONCOMING DAY

For The Chills, tucked away in Dunedin, New Zealand, influences were untainted by the concept and conceit of coolness, and here, the configuration of punk and pop result in something very special indeed. After a decade of excellence, The Chills gained their first UK hit as the sublime 'Heavenly Pop Hit' climbed to number 97 on the chart. It features a riff dominated by a Farfisa organ sound borrowed from The Nuggets era of 1960s garage rock. Martin Phillipps sings like a sad choirboy surrounded by angelic harmonising, and the wonderful verses lead to a chorus that is just sublime.

47
CRAZY
SEAL
ZTT

This debut single from Seal was a deserved international hit; it was an excellent song, sung superbly, and sonically it broke new ground. Seal wrote the piece in the aftermath of the Tiananmen Square massacre in Beijing and the fall of the Berlin Wall – these upheavals happening on a global scale felt profound. Production duties were handled by the rightly acclaimed Trevor Horn, who spent two months working on the track, incorporating ambient sounds amidst the bass-heavy rhythm, swirling keyboards and wah-wah guitar provided by Kenji Suzuki of Simply Red. The result of all this attention to detail meant that although the track dutifully satisfied the needs of a club dance-floor, equally importantly, it also managed to transcend the whole dance music genre.

46
LOOK LIKE A GIRL
THE SERVANTS
PAPERHOUSE

The Servants were a very English, anti-rock four piece band who formed in the mid-1980s around the songwriting talent of singer David Westlake. They also featured Luke Haines on guitar and backing vocals, better known as front man for The Auteurs. The sound on 'Look Like A Girl' is brittle; as sharp and angular as a Bauhaus designed structure. This is art-rock with the art part very much to the fore; they play minimally and without fuss. Melody is provided by the bass guitar and vocal, which is delivered in a detached and neutral tone.

45
ALL MY SENSES
GRANT HART
SST

The friction between Grant Hart and Bob Mould, caused by a desire to dominate the songwriting, led to the demise of Hüsker Dü. However, the work ethic of Hart continued unabated and the quality of his music remained extremely high. He had been the hippy-haired, barefoot drummer in the band, and the hardcore leanings of Hüsker Dü had always been somewhat alien to his true self. With 'All My Senses' he cools down the tempo and distances himself from the frenzy of yore. He serves up a floating, organ-led meditation on his feelings about chemically-enhanced detachment. Hart is reaching deep into his soul for the song and his singing clearly reflects this; he reveals himself to be a person of warmth and great sensitivity.

44
RETARDED
AFGHAN WHIGS
SUB POP
OTHER SINGLES 1990:
SISTER BROTHER;
MY WORLD IS EMPTY
WITHOUT YOU

Packing a mightily impressive punch here, the funk/R&B influence that was very much a part of Afghan Whigs' DNA means that, although they rage and roar whilst singer Greg Dulli screams out his self-lacerating pain over guitars that are cranked-up high, the band still swing and groove. Self-loathing and weakness of will provide the stimulus for the lyric that crests this juggernaut of sound, where everything is executed with hard-hitting precision.

43
ONLY LOVE CAN BREAK YOUR HEART
SAINT ETIENNE
HEAVENLY
OTHER SINGLE 1990: KISS AND MAKE UP

Saint Etienne's first single was this re-interpretation of Neil Young's early 1970s classic, 'Only Love Can Break Your Heart'. It took all of two hours to record and featured a vocal by Moira Lambert. The plan, simply put, was to mix up the culture of a past era with a modern dance sound. To that end, a piano driven house track was incorporated while Lambert delivered a fresh and ultra-natural performance… it was a wonderful pop record. A further mix was undertaken by Andrew Weatherall that emphasised the dub reggae bass lines and added melodion to the instrumentation, thus taking the song even further away from the preserve of student bed-sitting rooms and onto the nation's dance floors.

42
JUST TO GET A REP
GANG STARR
CHRYSALIS
OTHER SINGLE 1990:
JAZZ THING

Gang Starr, comprising MC Guru and DJ Premier, had an influential fan in film director Spike Lee; he had them record the track 'Jazz Thing' for the soundtrack of his film *Mo' Better Blues*. This exposure earned them a contract with Chrysalis Records and they soon served up the album *Step in the Arena*, which is regarded as one of the finest ever records in the hip-hop genre. The first single released from the album was 'Just To Get A Rep'. Whereas many of their peers engaged in the dangerous and stupid glorification of gang life and violent crime, Gang Starr tear that posturing attitude to pieces. Guru deadpans his vocal, which adds power to his words and DJ Premier provides a restrained, neo-psychedelic soundscape for his partner's rhymes. This is by no means a dull, preachy polemic; this is brilliant, essential listening that remains highly relevant today.

41
SUMMER IN SIAM
THE POGUES
POGUE MAHONE

As a band, the Pogues were in their death throes; inspiration and commercial success were slipping away from them. 'Summer in Siam' was taken from the Joe Strummer produced album *Hell's Ditch*, which sadly captured the group – who had been so vivid and full of life – at their most insipid and forgettable. Fortunately, 'Summer in Siam' was the one moment that evoked past glories. It is a fragile, piano-led piece that drifts like an untethered boat on a gentle tide. A tired sounding Shane McGowan sings a very slight lyric, almost as a mantra, evoking a calmer, quieter place that is preferable to the place he was in his life. The piano brings to mind the ripple of water as it moves steadily and irreversibly, just like time itself.

40
TASTE
RIDE
CREATION

Ride came from Oxford and they perfectly suited the times; four earnest, handsome young men playing jangling, dreamy guitar pop. They were immediately labelled as a 'shoegaze' band and compared to My Bloody Valentine. As it was, Ride wished to emulate the likes of Sonic Youth and Dinosaur Jr, and they were blessed with two writers possessing fine melodic sensibility. Their debut album, *Nowhere*, yielded 'Taste' as a promo only, though fairly widely-available single. It was written and sung by the floppy-haired, doe-eyed Mark Gardener… and it really kicked; drums were hit hard and the bass runs were fluid, nimble and exemplary. This rhythm then became a perfect launch pad for the twin guitars of Gardener and Andy Bell to twist and twine, while the lyrics and vocal are used wisely as yet another musical flavour. All in all, It was a very cool record…

39
HEY VENUS
THAT PETROL EMOTION
VIRGIN
OTHER SINGLES 1990.
SENSITIZE
TINGLE

With principal songwriter John O'Neill having quit, drummer Ciaran McLaughlin stepped up to the plate to provide new impetus for the band. His composition, 'Hey Venus', was a joyous, punkish gem, and in terms of pure effervescence, it brought to mind T. Rex during their imperious 1970s stage of pop perfection. The song has a scalpel-edged, see-saw riff and a ping-pong bouncing rhythm. It is sung with a smile by a jubilant Steve Mack and the only fault is the record's relative brevity… the enjoyment it produces ends much too soon.

38
100 MILES AND RUNNIN'
N.W.A.
RUTHLESS

This was the first N.W.A. release since the departure of Ice Cube and Arabian Prince due to financial discrepancies. DJ Ren comes to the fore, stepping into the space vacated by Ice Cube; his rhyming is on-point and his delivery is calm and authoritative. However, it is Dr Dre's verse that fanned the flames of a feud between N.W.A. and Ice Cube, as accusations of treacherous behaviour are aired. Notwithstanding the contentious lyric, this is a hugely-accomplished track; the production is outstanding, capturing all of the band's fiery rhetoric in full flow, with a rhythm track that is a thrilling and adventurous musical ride.

37
DUBS BE GOOD TO ME
BEATS INTERNATIONAL
GO BEAT

After The Housemartins had called it a day (and half a decade before he would adopt the Fatboy Slim moniker) Norman Cook formed Beats International and earned himself a UK number one single. The track itself, a funk and dub hybrid, consisted of a fairly faithful version of The S.O.S. Band's 1983 hit 'Just Be Good to Me', sung here by Lindy Layton, which was matched with the sampled bass line of 'Guns of Brixton' by The Clash, along with the memorable harmonica part from Ennio Morricone's theme for *Once Upon a Time in The West.* Drums were sampled courtesy of 'God Make Me Funky' by Herbie Hancock's jazz fusion outfit The Headhunters, and finally DJ Deejay added a spoken introduction and outro. This was an intoxicating mix of familiar sounds coming together to create a fresh cocktail of sweet music.

36
ENJOY THE SILENCE
DEPECHE MODE
MUTE
OTHER SINGLES 1990
WORLD IN MY EYES;
POLICY OF TRUTH

To their great credit, Depeche Mode refused to stand still – instead, they constantly opened out their sound. Here, on what could be considered amongst their finest singles, they transform an already deeply affecting ballad by introducing a ringing guitar motif and a house-style rhythm track; these additions enable this melancholic song to spread its appeal to the dance-floor. Dave Gahan sings superbly; hc inhabits the soul of the song and interprets Martin Gore's profound lyric with deep, knowing solemnity. Paradoxically, a hymn-like quality seems to hang over the track, even as it simultaneously displays the masterly knack of creating highly affecting pop music.

35
IT'S GRIM UP NORTH
JUSTIFIED ANCIENTS OF MU MU
KLF COMMUNICATIONS

Don't ask me how a track as downright weird and subversive as 'It's Grim Up North' somehow became a top-ten hit; these were stranger times than even *I* thought. The harsh environment and mind-numbing labour of mill and factory is successfully evoked here, with a backdrop of churning, industrial techno and what sounds like steam-valves straining under pressure as machines grind and malfunction. Over this musical concrete mixer, a list of northern towns is recited… this constitutes the lyric; it is spoken in a monotone and brings to mind a Tannoy announcement at a wet and windy rugby league stadium. Orchestrated passages of the hymn 'Jerusalem' are also segued into the mix – so simple and yet it makes me feel emotional; a curious mixture of pride and sadness. It conjures up for me, in some abstract manner, the innate dignity of the region's downtrodden working class.

34
LOOKING AT THE FRONT DOOR
MAIN SOURCE
WILD PITCH
OTHER SINGLE 1990:
WATCH ROGER DO HIS THING

Main Source consisted of MC/Producer Large Professor and twin DJs k-Cut and Sir Scratch; they had true musical chemistry and Large Professor was a profoundly brilliant lyricist.

Here, 'Think Twice' by Bobby Byrd is sampled, and a very tasty groove is created. Large Professor examines a troubled relationship; he displays empathy and insight but cannot reconcile himself to the pain he feels and therefore sees no other solution than to walk away… he's literally 'Looking at the Front Door'.

33
FREEDOM 90
GEORGE MICHAEL
SONY

Although 'Freedom 90' is a deeply cynical song – it rails against the pin-up image that gave George Michael so much success and a devoted audience – it came in such an attractive musical package that it was still a top ten hit. The pressure of fame had sickened him so much that Michael now seemed intent on undermining his own celebrity; he wanted to be judged on his music alone. The shallow bubble of stardom was to be exploded and this was the song that stated his case. It was given an uptempo treatment – the beat came from a sample of 'Funky Drummer' by James Brown, and the lead instrument was a jangling, dancing piano. There were elements of structure directly traceable to Bo Diddley and a hugely catchy chorus… but soaring above everything was the distinctive voice of the song's creator, who had served up yet another gem.

32
DREAMTIME
THE HEART THROBS
ONE LITTLE INDIAN
OTHER SINGLE 1990: I WONDER WHY

The Heart Throbs were once label-mates of mine when they, and I, both released music on Marc Riley and Jim Kahnbatta's In-Tape label. Later on, they had flourished, enjoying a significant degree of success whilst signed to Rough Trade. Now, from their debut LP (produced by Martin Hannett) came this excellent single that mixed pop and dance influences with a shadowy, spooked-sounding guitar. Singer Rose Carlotta sings of disharmonious, emotional turmoil in a moody, low-register voice, as all around her the music swirls.

31
EVERYTHING FLOWS
TEENAGE FANCLUB
PAPERHOUSE
OTHER NOTEWORTHY SINGLES 1990: EVERYBODY'S FOOL; GOD KNOWS IT'S TRUE

'Everything Flows' was the debut

single of Teenage Fanclub, and therefore it was the beginning of a journey that has been accompanied by a liberal sprinkling of classic records along the way. They opened their account with this excellent release. It is raw, guitar-based rock/pop that sounded more American than Scottish – in fact, it could easily have been mistaken for an unheard track from Big Star. The punchy tunefulness marked it out as special, along with Norman Blake's yearning vocal as he sings of life changes bringing uncertainty and self-doubt.

30
ONE WORD
BRIAN ENO & JOHN CALE
OPAL
OTHER SINGLE 1990:
SPINNING AWAY

In the early- to mid-1970s, after Eno's departure from Roxy Music, he and John Cale had assisted each other at various points. They had also been the "C" and "E" of the *A.C.N.E.* album and live shows that featured Kevin Ayers and Nico as well. Now, Cale proposed a full-scale collaboration between the pair which would necessitate Eno returning to vocal performance for the first time in more than a decade. By all accounts, their working relationship became extremely fractious, and yet, out of the unpleasantness came the album *Wrong Way Up* which was amongst the best records that either had ever made. For the most part, songs were sung by one or the other, but on 'One Word' – which is based on an entertainingly fidgety rhythm – the pair join voices in an intricate, interwoven harmony, before bouncing off each other in a merry call and response during the choruses – truly a thing of beauty.

29
LET THE RHYTHM HIT 'EM
ERIC B AND RAKIM
MCA
OTHER SINGLES 1990:
MAHOGANY;
IN THE GHETTO

There was no reason at all for Eric B & Rakim to change their *modus operandi*; they had achieved a kind of signature-style perfection in a manner comparable to The Ramones or Barry White. Wisely, they did not follow new trends in hip-hop, but simply serve-up here an absolutely killing rhythm of dizzying bass and crunching drums that gave Rakim – in a lower register than heard before – a perfect platform to unleash a torrent of rhymes in a smooth flow. 'Let The Rhythm Hit 'Em' was yet another sure-footed, extremely satisfying single from the pair.

28
TRUTH IS OUT OF STYLE
MC 900 FT. JESUS & DJ ZERO
NETWERK
OTHER SINGLE 1990:
UFO'S ARE REAL

DJ Zero scratches over a looped jazz sample and MC 900 Ft. Jesus raps the lyric; but this is a hip-hop styled record that isn't really hip-hop at all. There is no attempt to ape the authenticity of the likes of Ice Cube or Snoop Dogg; in fact MC 900 Ft. Jesus's storytelling manner is more akin to Cab Calloway or Spike Jones. He whines in a deeply sarcastic style, incorporating dark humour into his narrative on the insincerity of that age… and nowadays, in the era of Donald Trump and Boris Johnson, this sounds highly prophetic. 'Truth Is Out of Style' is therefore another inversion, because despite the humour in the lyrical skits about aliens and Shirley MacLaine, at its heart, this is a song that is virulent and angry.

27
BIG CITY
SPACEMAN 3
FIRE

Spaceman 3 had been brought to a close, their sonic explorations ceased. But, as a sweet kiss goodbye, this posthumous single was released and actually charted – albeit at a lowly number eighty-eight position. The title was taken from the opening lyric of Dandy Livingstone's 1970s reggae with synthesisers hit; but the song itself simply fixes on a blissfully beautiful groove that just rolls and rolls, with minimal repetitive vocals delivered in a reassuringly gentle tone. It is spacey, trippy music, and with writer Pete Kember's permission, it featured in a *Simpsons* episode where Homer embarks on an LSD trip.

26
ENERGY FLASH
JOEY BELTRAM
TRANSMAT

From Queens, NYC, Joey Beltram was just 19 years old when he released this propulsive, moody single that remains to this day one of the absolute, definitive peaks of techno music. Fat bass sounds and crisp percussion lead us into the track proper; once there, manipulated sounds twist and mutate before strings swoop like ravens, and the whispered, single word lyric of "Ecstasy" feels like an instruction on how to unlock and access the deepest, darkest, secret depths of this rave culture classic.

25
BLUE FLOWER
MAZZY STAR
ROUGH TRADE

Mazzy Star were a band formed by David Roback (ex-Rain Parade and Opal) and the distinctively-voiced Hope Sandoval, who had been in a folk duo named Going Home; this was their first single. It is a song originally recorded by Slapp Happy, but here it is given a garage rock makeover with Roback playing a filthy-edged guitar riff that wheels and circles. By contrast, Hope Sandoval sings with purity; she is clear and strong with an air of insolence in her delivery. A guitar solo with a Velvet Underground sensibility is dropped into proceedings and then the song closes. It's short, it's sweet… and it's near perfection.

24
CUBIK/OLYMPIC
808 STATE
ZTT
OTHERSINGLES 1990:
THE EXTENDED PLEASURE OF DANCE;
THE ONLY RHYME THAT BITES (MC Tunes v 808 State);
TUNES SPLITS THE ATOM (MCTunes v 808 State)

808 State didn't re-invent the wheel; their sound owed much to Detroit's techno pioneers – however, it did come with a different sensibility that owed much to the group's Mancunian upbringing. 'Cubik', which opens with a wigged-out guitar that wails in the style of Funkadelic in their prime, is a brutal mix of massive riffs, dropped like concrete blocks, and percussion breaks that are mixed with avant-garde noise. 'Olympic' is pretty much the opposite in form and sonic intent; it is serene and majestic, and its beautiful tones and melodies are palate-cleansingly fresh.

23
HEAVEN OR LAS VEGAS
COCTEAU TWINS
4AD
OTHER SINGLE 1990:
ICEBLINK LUCK

A pinnacle of perfection in the sound-sculpture mini-epics released by The Cocteau Twins, 'Heaven or Las Vegas' is a slow-burning piece of bittersweet aural magic. It is blessed with a tune that is instantly memorable, from a place where pop and art become entwined. This music stirs the emotions and stimulates feelings… musical notes cascade, shimmering from the instruments like pearls sparkling on a necklace. A drum machine is the foundation of this music, and above its throb, bass and guitar mesh. In the midst of it all is Elizabeth Frazer with a voice like no other voice; she is singing meaningless, made-up words, and yet she makes sounds that are transportive and awe-inspiring. Nobody had ever sounded like The Cocteau Twins previously – and although some have tried, nobody has ever managed to sound like The Cocteau Twins since.

22
FOURTH OF JULY
GALAXY 500
ROUGH TRADE

Galaxy 500 were breaking up when they recorded this track; pretty soon afterwards, Dean Wareham would call time on the band, but on the evidence of 'Fourth of July' there was still plenty of creative juice inside the band. The piece is given a sympathetic production by Shimmy-Disc main-man Kramer. The band sound expansive and unconstricted, pushing at limits and rattling along in a manner that resembles the Doug Yule-era Velvets; the lyric, sung by Wareham is abstract and intriguing. To these ears, it sounds as if the band were having fun, although apparently that was definitely not the case…

21
LAST TRAIN TO TRANSCENDENTAL (Live From the Lost Continent)
THE KLF
KLF COMMUNICATIONS
OTHER SINGLE 1990: WHAT TIME IS LOVE
(Live at Trancentral)

This was not released as one unique single, but as a series of singles with radically different mixes, and this particular version yielded a UK number two hit record. This mix was the latest in the so-called *Stadium House* series in which Messrs. Cauty and Drummond abandoned all notion of restraint, instead creating a gigantic beast of a song with thunderous dance beats and hooks at every turn. Genre-fixated purists could scoff all they wanted – this track showed that the lunatics had been given the keys to the asylum, and had begun to re-build it very much in their own image.

20
BEING BORING
PET SHOP BOYS
PARLOPHONE
OTHER SINGLE 1990:
SO HARD

This song, one of the very best that The Pet Shop Boys ever wrote, was only a relatively minor hit for them. The lyric consisted of tiny vignettes from writer Neil Tennant's life – from the wide-eyed expectations of youth in Newcastle, through to adulthood where success was mixed with doubt and painful loss, as AIDS claimed close friends. The music is completely in tune with the lyrical sentiments; the beat delivers a sense of motion while the rest of the instrumentation remains subdued, with only occasional swells for emphasis. A wah-wah guitar hides just below the surface, adding texture, and the intermittent trills of a string section add more than a dash of drama.

19
HIGH TENSION LINE
THE FALL
COG SINISTER
OTHER SINGLES 1990:
POPCORN DOUBLE FEATURE; WHITE LIGHTNING

With a title that nods toward composer La Monte Young's minimalist piece 'The Second Dream of the High-Tension Line Stepdown Transformer', and a record company reluctant to release a fourth Fall single within twelve months, it was little wonder this this track, most unfortunately, fell through the cracks. The typically-cryptic lyric by Mark E. Smith, seems, at least in part, to be a mockery of people who, in the midst of a mid-life crisis, dress-up in gaudy clothes and seek to exploit the housing market! The music, meanwhile, though mixed into a slightly distant fog, is nonetheless a speedy concoction with a definite air of threat in its rumbling undercurrent.

18
LITTLE FLUFFY CLOUDS
THE ORB
BIG LIFE

There was a long period of hesitation before the public at large took 'Little Fluffy Clouds' to its collective heart – indeed it was 1993 before it charmed its way into the UK top ten. The piece came into being after Jimmy Cauty departed from The Orb. The remaining member, Alex Paterson, began to work on the track with ex-Killing Joke bassist Martin "Youth" Glover. The initial inspiration for the record came from a cassette that was sent in by a fan of The Orb; on one side, the cassette contained an interview with Rickie Lee Jones, and on the other was 'Electric Counterpoint', a piece written by Steve Reich and played on guitar by Pat Metheny. Samples from both sides formed the basis of the piece, with further samples from Ennio Morricone's soundtrack for *Once Upon A Time In The West* adding a very distinctive flavour. The drum track was another sample taken from Jim Gordon's performance on Nilsson's 'Jump In The Fire', slowed down from 45 to 33rpm. When everything got put together, the result was stunning; it was blissful and elegant, and as gorgeous a piece of ambient dance music as had ever been created.

17
(What Will We Do To Become)
FAMOUS AND DANDY
(Like Amos and Andy)
THE DISPOSABLE HEROES OF HIPHOPRISY
WORKERS PLAYTIME

'Famous and Dandy' was a signature song for The Disposable Heroes of Hiphoprisy; it rails against stupidity and explicitly references Amos & Andy, white men who performed in blackface. Negative racial stereotypes are used to highlight identity crisis confusion as a cause of the low expectation and self-esteem typical within a black community battered by such propaganda disguised as entertainment. Over head-nodding beats and an electrical soundtrack (a work of art in itself) Michael Franti, uses a rhythmic, spoken-word style, to turn the stereotyping on its head with his intelligent lampooning of the situation.

16
THE WAGON
DINOSAUR JR
BLANCO Y NEGRO

Bang! Without any fanfare whatsoever, we are hurled into a whirlwind of drums and guitar; despite the departure of Lou Barlow, Dinosaur Jr sounded as fresh and ebullient as they ever had. 'The Wagon' is an exhilarating rush of adrenalised tunefulness, containing a whole clutch of masterful pop hooks. J Mascis sings in his trademark whine, and also throws in a fabulously textured guitar solo. Nirvana were eagerly poised to make melodic guitar pop/rock a sound revered by the masses… but make no mistake, Dinosaur Jr were every bit their equal.

15
KILLER
ADAMSKI
MCA
OTHER SINGLES 1990:
N-R-G; THE SPACE JUNGLE;
FLASHBACK JACK

Adamski had a track called 'The Killer' which he imagined to be the cinematic soundtrack to a murder scene. Seal had been a singer in various blues bands but had undergone an epiphany and was now embracing rave culture. The two came together and Seal came up with a lyric about overcoming the fears that prevent people from achieving their true potential. When this was combined with Adamski's backing track, which included an absolutely pulverising bass riff, synergistic magic somehow occurred. In the midst of the buzzing, hypnotic hip-house sounds – which on their own are dramatic and edgy – Seal's smooth vocal adds disorienting strangeness; he sounds bewildered and uncomprehending. This is a mesmerising record; it was a UK number one single and a hit across much of the world too.

14
DIG FOR FIRE
THE PIXIES
4AD
OTHER SINGLE 1990:
VELOURIA

This great record was scathingly dismissed by its creator, Black Francis, who said of 'Dig For Fire' that it was "a bad Talking Heads imitation" – I totally disagree with him. 'Dig For Fire' may share a structural similarity with certain Talking Heads songs, but whereas that band performed with ironic intent, the sound of The Pixies is fired-up with blood and guts, and here the switch from spoken introduction, into the song proper, hits like a punishing uppercut delivered to the solar plexus. This is as lyrically oblique as most other Pixies' songs, but here the intensity of the delivery makes the words sound like vitally important communiqués sent in a frustratingly indecipherable code. As for the sound, it is the typical Pixies loud/quiet, soft/hard routine, but performed with exquisite panache.

13
SOON
MY BLOODY VALENTINE
CREATION

Released as both a stand-alone single and as part of the *Glider* EP, we find MBV leader Kevin Shields expanding on the possibilities of what could be done with a guitar to devastatingly brilliant effect. The song rests upon an intermittent keyboard pattern, buried ethereal vocals and swathes of heavily-treated guitar noise that are magisterial and awe-inspiring, hitting us like a gigantic series of tidal waves. The ever busy Andrew Weatherall also produced a re-mixed version of the track, emphasising the rhythm and beats, and this too was issued as a single which itself is a wonderful record… and yet the care and attention put into the Shields-produced original ensures that it remains the definitive article.

12
MOST OF THE TIME
BOB DYLAN
COLUMBIA

In 1990, Dylan re-located his muse; as a highly interested observer, he had attended sessions for The Neville Brothers album *Yellow Moon*, produced by Daniel Lanois. Dylan asked Lanois to produce his own next album using the same techniques employed on *Yellow* Moon, and so *Oh Mercy* was recorded in New Orleans. Of all the songs on the album, possibly the strongest was 'Most of the Time', so it was inexplicable when a brand-new version was recorded for a video / single, utilising a completely different band of musicians, and this time produced by Don Was. This second attempt was inferior on every level to the *Oh Mercy* version, but thankfully that too was included on the single in both full and edited lengths. 'Most of the Time' is a wonderful song; in some ways it is a distant cousin of The Velvet Underground's 'Sweet Jane', but taken at a somewhat more stately pace. Dylan adopts the role of a man attempting to fool himself that he has gotten over the pain of a broken relationship; he is in denial about his true feelings and so he candidly states his case that the hurt has been put behind him – only then to utter the contradictory line of the song's title, "Don't even remember what her lips felt like on mine… most of the time'. This is a wonderful encapsulation of the difficulty in navigating matters of the heart.

11
KINKY AFRO
HAPPY MONDAYS
FACTORY
OTHER SINGLE 1990:
STEP ON

The Happy Mondays had reached that imperious stage where their sound, though much imitated, was never replicated with as much style and swagger as when in their own hands.'Kinky Afro' reached number five in the charts and, along with 'Step On', it was one of the band's two biggest hits. It was also something of an artistic peak – it plays by its own rules, goes at its own speed, and refuses to go any faster. The groove is slow, contagious and devastatingly brilliant. Mark Day's circular guitar part is an ear-worm in itself and Shaun Ryder's lyric, along with the relaxed and ever-so-easy delivery, is in itself a thing of near genius. He looks, with an unsentimental eye, upon the travails of parenting a child when a degree of reluctant commitment is present. His bass playing brother Paul presumed that it was he who was the subject of the song, whereas Tony Wilson guessed it was about Derek (Sean and Paul's father) who was a party-loving member of the band's road crew. Maybe the truth is that (like most great writers) Shaun was really analysing himself in his work.

At Haverford College with Tom and Jon of The Mekons

10
DIRTY CASH (MONEY TALKS)
THE ADVENTURES OF STEVIE V
MERCURY

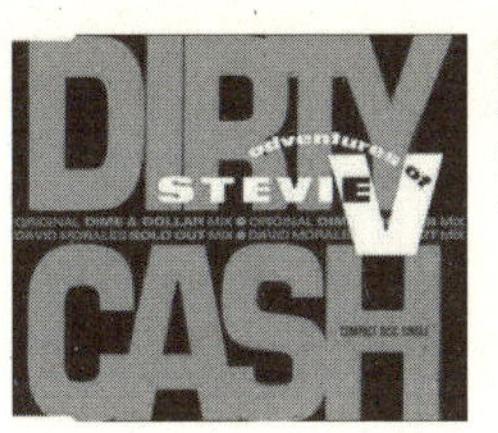

The sacrifice of pride and principle, drug use and the exploitation of sexual favour, are all examples offered up here to illustrate the power of money in the capitalist society in which we live. 'Dirty Cash' is just one of many songs that explain the truth of the saying that "money is the root of all evil" but interestingly, *this* song does not adopt a moralistic point of view, but instead takes a tongue-in-cheek, satirical look at the lust for those almighty green bills. The record was by a hitherto unknown British dance act composed of writer/producer Steve Vincent and co-author Mick Walsh. They found the soulful vocalist they needed for the song in Georgia-born music teacher Melody Washington; her voice added sweetness to the harshness of the rough-edged and raw hip-house backing track. A male-voiced rap section adds contrast and the song's hooks and magnificent chorus made this a huge commercial success; it was only denied a number one spot by Adamski's iron grip on that position with 'Killer'.

9
FALLING
JULIE CRUISE
WARNER BROTHERS

Like a frosted cake made for a wedding that never takes place, 'Falling' is beautiful yet sad, eerie and unsettling… and yet it is difficult to fathom the reason why. Is it the solitary repeating guitar figure amidst the lushness of the orchestration? Is it the forlorn quality embodied in the heavenly, brittle voice of Julie Cruise? To me, her vocal feels like a whispered secret;–I'm drawn towards it instinctively and inexplicably. The music was composed by Angelo Badalamenti, and the lyric by David Lynch; it was used as the theme song for his acclaimed TV series *Twin Peaks*, where music and visuals combine to provide a masterclass of hauntology.

8
THE STORM
WORLD OF TWIST
CIRCA

World of Twist were the hottest band in Manchester. They were a must-see act who blended a love of psychedelia, northern soul, 1960s pop and acid house… along with visuals that displayed a degree of absurdist humour and a fondness for the kitsch. Everybody turned out for their gigs; they were big events and special occasions. Indeed, I remember incredulously bumping into, and having a most convivial chat with, Joey Santiago of The Pixies at one of their shows. Single-wise, 'The Storm' was World of Twist's opening salvo; it almost took them into the UK top 40 where they very much deserved to be. It was magnificent, swirling and stirring; an evocation of one of nature's outbursts. But this track referenced both an electrical storm and an intense emotional storm, as from the midst of the track came the voice of Tony Ogden expressing deep pain as he called out for shelter.

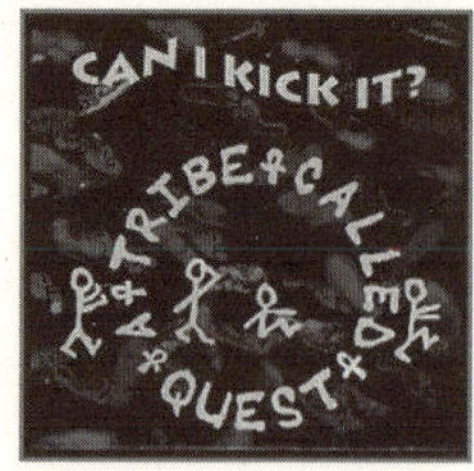

7
CAN I KICK IT?
A TRIBE CALLED QUEST
JIVE
OTHER SINGLE 1990:
BONITA APPLEBUM

As per usual, this is a cheerful and cheering dose of positivity from ATCQ. They create a slinky, elasticated groove from a variety of unusual samples; Lou Reed's 'Walk on the Wild Side' bass part is featured, as well as samples from Ian Dury & the Blockheads, Dr Buzzard's Original Savannah Band, Dr Lonnie Smith and even 'Dance of the Knights' by Russian composer Sergei Prokofiev. Combining these disparate elements, they achieve a rare alchemy and the call and response chant-a-long vocal is a sheer delight.

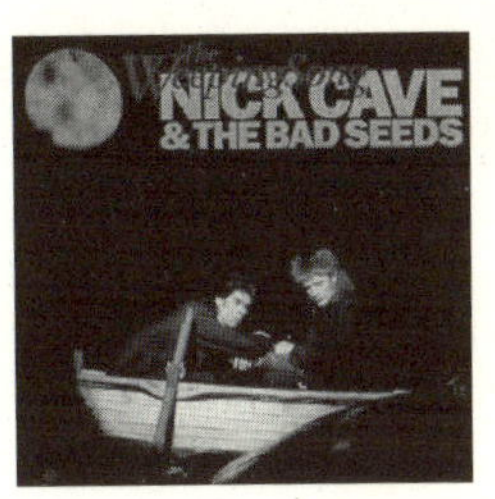

6
THE WEEPING SONG
NICK CAVE & THE BAD SEEDS
MUTE
OTHER SINGLE 1990:
THE SHIP SONG

Religious overtones abound in this lyric concerned with the sorrow that each of us carries through life, and the way in which we must unburden ourselves through the act of weeping. But this mournfulness is somewhat offset by an uptempo arrangement and the unholy relish with which Cave and Blixa Bargeld duet, becoming positively unruly at points. The rocking motion of the music, which rests heavily on a chiming vibraphone part played by Mick Harvey, is also perfectly simpatico.

5
LOADED
PRIMAL SCREAM
CREATION
OTHER SINGLE 1990:
COME TOGETHER

To state that producer/remixer Andrew Weatherall was the principal architect in the making of this single is simply a statement of fact that should in no way denigrate Primal Scream; after all, they instigated the collaboration in the first place, and it was them, when presented with an earlier "too reverential" re-mix of the track 'I'm Losing More Than I'll Ever Have', who had the conviction and integrity to reject it. In the words of guitarist Andrew Innes, they gave Weatherall *carte blanche* to go and "fucking destroy" the source material. In fact, Weatherall did exactly that; he came back having salvaged a mere seven seconds from the original recording. What he now presented was introduced via a sample of Frank Maxwell and Peter Fonda from the film *The Wild Angels*, where they jive on hedonistic freedom and state the intention to get 'Loaded'. From that beginning, a dance-friendly drum loop acts as the base for a vocal sample from soul outfit The Emotions, with Bobbie Gillespie adding a line from Robert Johnson's 'Terraplane Blues'. Maracas were then shook, a house-style piano was prominent and horns and guitars both acted as fanfares; the track grooved and snaked quite incredibly. As a whole, the piece is infused with magic - it has an amazing, uplifting feel. This single transformed the perception of Primal Scream from the status of "ok indie band' into that of respected sonic pioneers; it put them into the top twenty as well, which was the least they deserved, because this was a very bold artistic statement.

4
DAYDREAMING
MASSIVE ATTACK
WILD BUNCH RECORDS

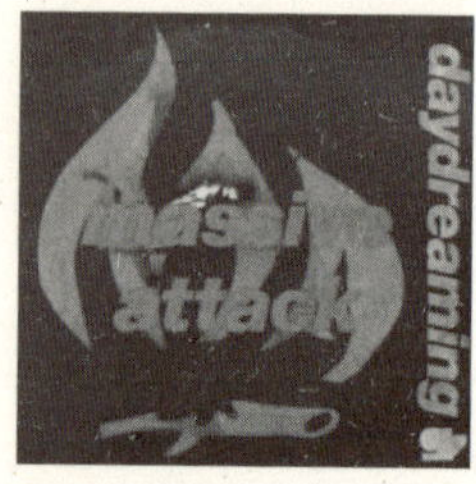

Six months prior to the release of *Blue Lines*, their groundbreaking and seminal, debut album, this single was dropped to prepare the way and spread around some cool vibrations. It only attained a number 81 chart placing, but amongst the cognoscenti it was spoken of in reverential tones. The track featured Shara Nelson on otherworldly lead vocals, whereas raps came from the rest of the crew, including Tricky, who was then the wild-card in the pack. Incorporating a prominent sample from 'Mambo' by Wally Badarou, the sound was lean; it shuffled along with machine-like rhythm and further instrumentation was sparingly used. The overall effect was truly mesmerising – I played it for my friend Derek and he was bowled over. From that day onwards, Massive Attack were a shared enthusiasm; together, we never failed to see their always thought-provoking shows whenever they came to Manchester, and when Derek died in 2021, the sounds of Massive Attack were an essential part of his funeral service.

3 (Joint)
WELCOME TO THE TERRORDOME
PUBLIC ENEMY
DEF JAM
OTHER SINGLES 1990:
ANTI-NIGGER MACHINE; 911 IS A JOKE; PUBLIC ENEMY NO 1; BROTHERS GONNA WORK IT OUT; CAN'T DO NUTTIN' FOR YA MAN

This is genuine high-energy on plastic; turn it up loud and feel the bone-crunching power. The Bomb Squad were at their highest peak of musical creativity – the abstract expressionism was simply awesome – and Chuck D was able to match them every step of the way with his lyrical prowess and capacity to reel-off rhyme after rhyme, without ever coming up for air. 'Welcome to the Terrorzone' succeeds on every level; not only was it anti-authoritarian and insurrectionary, but it was also eloquently delivered and highly intelligent.

3 (Joint)
KOOL THING
SONIC YOUTH
DGC

'Kool Thing' was a Kim Gordon song inspired by a meeting she had with LL Cool J – she was a fan of hip-hop in general, and his music in particular, but she found him to be narrow-minded as regards musical taste and misogynistic in attitude. However, she transformed this negative encounter into a quick-witted observation of power, gender and racial stereotyping… including her own entrenched, right-on beliefs. The song was played with much gusto, incorporating, as it does, a riff that is practically an instruction to dance, and Chuck D of Public Enemy makes a spoken-word cameo appearance mid-song.

2
NOTHING COMPARES 2 U
SINEAD O'CONNOR
CHRYSALIS
OTHER SINGLES 1990:
I AM STRETCHED ON YOUR GRAVE;
THE EMPEROR'S NEW CLOTHES;
THREE BABIES

The insecurity and loneliness felt in the aftermath of a broken relationship had never been expressed with such sincerity and clarity as when Sinead O'Connor took 'Nothing Compares 2 U' – a song that Prince, its composer, hadn't quite got to grips with – and turned it into an emotional tour de force. The song had first been issued in 1985 by The Family as an album track; this relative obscurity was where it was seemingly destined to languish, until O'Connor and producer Nellie Hooper re-shaped and re-modelled the song. They ironed out the creases to create an elegant, slow-moving, haunting and rather ominous piece of music, which served as the perfect canvas for O'Connor's extraordinarily soul-baring voice. Somehow she managed to grasp the emotional heart of the song so completely that she entirely owned it. This was a record that could not be ignored, such was its power to affect the listener… and even if that was not yet sufficient, there was, in addition, the accompanying video which captured a tear running from the eye of the singer – this too became iconic. Surely nobody with a beating heart would ever be churlish enough to deny the true classic status of this amazing record.

1

GROOVE IS IN THE HEART

DEEE-LITE

ELEKTRA

OTHER SINGLE 1990: POWER OF LOVE

Deee-Lite were a trio who emerged from the underground New York dance scene. Their first ever release, 'Groove Is In The Heart', was the record that will always define them because it completely captured the zeitgeist. The piece was a combination of 1970s funk, 1990s slinky house grooves, smooth rap and a multitude of other ingredients that made this the tastiest track to hit the turntables in what was a golden age of dance music. 'Groove Is In The Heart' leaps out of the speakers and spreads joyously good vibrations; it is cheeky, sassy and extremely smart. The groove comes primarily from a sample of Herbie Hancock's 'Bring Down the Birds' from the film *Blow Up*, and its genius drum part comes courtesy of 'Get Up' by Vernon Burch. Lead vocalist Lady Miss Kier was incredible, but taken as a whole, Deee-Lite sounded compellingly larger than life. Throw-in the contributions made by Parliament/Funkadelic legend Bootsy Collins on bass and vocals, and the superbly judged rap from Q-Tip (A Tribe Called Quest) and this amounted to a party invitation that only an unmitigated fool could refuse to accept.

1991

NOTABLE EVENTS

In Haiti, the Tonton Macoute, a paramilitary force led by the country's former dictator Jean-Claude Duvalier, fail to stage a coup d'état against the democratically-elected government.

Iraq refuses to withdraw its troops from Kuwait, and in January the UN-backed Operation Desert Storm commences; the Gulf War had begun – it lasts from January 16th to February 27th.

The Provisional IRA launches a mortar attack on 10 Downing St as a government cabinet meeting takes place. Two weeks later they explode bombs at Paddington Station and Victoria Station in London.

A video capturing the beating of black motorist Rodney King by four white police officers in Los Angeles sparks civil unrest and protests against the inherent racism within the city's police department.

After spending sixteen years in prison for an IRA bombing that they did not commit, six men (known as The Birmingham Six) are released when a court rules that the evidence used to convict them was fabricated by the police.

Germany becomes independent again when the four post-war occupying nations (France, USA, USSR and UK) formally relinquish rights to the country.

Civil War begins in Sierra Leone.

Georgia votes for independence from The Soviet Union

A tropical cyclone in Bangladesh kills over 138,000 people.

Following votes for independence in Croatia and Slovenia, both countries leave Yugoslavia.

In South Africa the last legal foundations of the apartheid system are repealed.

Boris Yeltsin is elected as President of the Russian SFSR.

Serial killer Jeffrey Dahmer is arrested after the remains of eleven male victims are found in his apartment in Milwaukee.

Ukraine, Moldova, Azerbaijan, Kyrgyzstan, Uzbekistan, Kazakhstan, Turkmenistan, Armenia, Tajikistan and Belarus declare independence from The Soviet Union.

Serbian forces attack the Croatian town of Vukovar; when the town falls, more than 260 prisoners of war are executed.

Macedonia declares independence from Yugoslavia.

American journalist Terry Anderson is released after seven years of captivity as a hostage in Beirut.

Croatian forces kill eighteen Serbs and a Hungarian in the town of Paulin Dvor.

Mikhail Gorbachev resigns as president of the Soviet Union.

The Soviet Union is dissolved.

Manchester United lose The League Cup Final to Sheffield Wednesday, but win The European Cup Winners' Cup by defeating Barcelona in Rotterdam. Arsenal win the league, Tottenham the FA Cup.

NOTABLE BIRTHS

Ed Sheeran; Tyler the Creator; Travis Scott; Azealia Banks; Ben Stokes; Jedward

NOTABLE DEATHS

Margot Fonteyn; Serge Gainsbourg; Doc Pomus; Leo Fender; Aldo Ray; Graham Greene; David Lean; Steve Marriott; Johnny Thunders; Gene Clark; David Ruffin; Stan Getz; Peggy Ashcroft; Lee Remick; Frank Capra; Klaus Barbie; Miles Davis; Gene Roddenberry; Mort Shulman; Robert Maxwell; Tom of Finland; Klaus Kinski; Freddie Mercury;

NOTABLE BOOKS

American Psycho - Bret Easton Ellis

Regeneration- Pat Barker

The Famished Road - Ben Okri

The Firm - John Grisham

Wild Swans - Jung Chang

The Beauty Myth - Naomi Wolf
Generation X -Douglas Coupland
The Birthday Boys - Beryl Bainbridge
Times Arrow - Martin Amis
Wilderness Tips - Margaret Atwood
The Unbearable Peace - John Le Carre

NOTABLE FILMS

Cape Fear; Boyz N The Hood; Beauty And The Beast; The Commitments; Barton Fink; JFK; The Silence Of The Lambs; Thelma And Louise.

MY 1991

As the map of the world was being re-drawn by political upheavals that were, by turn, fascinating, frightening, sometimes inspiring but always compelling, for the most part I kept my destructive urges at bay and threw myself into work. I was earning more money than I had ever done before and it was refreshing not having to struggle and save for the smallest things; I could dress myself in new clothes rather than charity shop hand-me-downs. I kept a well-stocked supply of liquor at home – which frequently needed replenishment – and I bought records at a prodigious rate. At weekends, my house often functioned as a social hub and I enjoyed these late-night soirees. During the football season, I travelled a lot watching a much-improved Manchester United team that both entertained and won more frequently; this culminated in a glorious, rain-soaked night in Rotterdam, when the mighty Barcelona were defeated in the European Cup Winners Cup, thanks to Mark Hughes scoring two goals and Clayton Blackmore making a match-saving goal-line clearance. Despite the club's despicable attempts to block independent travellers (they only favoured those who booked packages directly with the club) between 30,000 and 40,000 Mancunians swamped the Feyenoord stadium to alternately serenade the teams with raucous renditions of 'Always Look On The Bright Side Of Life' and 'Sit Down' by James; football was definitely developing a somewhat surreal edge…

I also took another trip to New York with my friend Wayne Edwards, who was a great travel companion. We stopped with the near legendary music obsessives Dennis and Lois, who were saluted in song by the Happy Mondays on their album *Thrills Spills and Bellyaches*. Whilst there, we saw several gigs and experienced the delights of the famed Halloween Parade. I was running on alcohol and adrenaline; I loved New York and treated it with a devil-may-care attitude that was, on more than one occasion, reckless and foolhardy. I got myself into dangerous scrapes as I treated the place like a giant adventure playground; I had a gun pulled on me in the infamous Limelight Club, was gently mugged in a bar as I lay drunkenly snoozing, and was discovered unconscious on the pavement one night by a pair of generous and caring girls who dragged me back to their apartment where I awoke to the smell of strong coffee and a picture-postcard view of the Empire State Building.

Among the memorable gigs I saw in 1991 were:

CITIES IN THE PARK – this was a weekend festival of music at Heaton Park in Manchester. Among the multitude of acts who performed were The Fall, Happy Mondays, De La Soul, Cath Carroll and Cabaret Voltaire.

BERNIE WORREL of Funkadelic, in a small Manhattan basement club.

LAIBACH at the Limelight Club, Manhattan.

THE MEKONS at Maxwell's, Hoboken, with Gibby Haines of The Butthole Surfers guesting on vocals; on the mini-bus ride back to Manhattan, Gibby amazed me with a strange and brilliant stream-of-consciousness rap.

GODS AND MONSTERS at Tramps, Manhattan. Gary Lucas (formerly Captain Beefheart's guitarist and manager) had asked me along to see his new band; once I saw and heard the young singer in the group, I didn't need anybody to tell me who he was – he looked like his father, he sang like his father and he was incredible. Of course, he was Jeff Buckley, the son of Tim Buckley. Gary fetched him over for a chat; we were both wearing Sex Pistols t-shirts and laughed about it. I mentioned how impressed by his performance I had been and he blushed a little; he seemed shy and a really nice kid. I wished him well for the future – he was the real deal…

100
THE WARMING
HELIOS CREED
AMPHETAMINE REPTILE

American guitarist Helios Creed had been one half of seminal proto-industrial band, Chrome. When that band ended in the mid-1980s, he began a solo career that could accurately be described as heavy metal for people who don't like heavy metal. That suited my taste perfectly, and with 'The Warming' he truly struck a chord with me. The sounds are heavily mutated and mangled, the vocals are treated and distorted, and although the drums remain rock-solid, space noise winds around the beats. If someone created a new genre of sci-fi rock, this record would define it.

99
LOOSEN UP YOUR MIND/
THE PLANET
A CERTAIN RATIO
ROBS RECORDS

This was a double-dose of goodness from the Mancunian institution that was, and remains, A Certain Ratio. The 'Loosen Up Your Mind' side of the record was a slow and slender bubbling groover that featured the soulful vocals of the late, great Denise Johnson. 'The Planet', meanwhile, returned the band to the artiness of their early days and it was a wonderful, creeping slice of dislocated cosmic funk.

98
NEON ZEBRA
SHONEN KNIFE
SUB POP
OTHER SINGLES 1991: SECRET NO 712; SPACE CHRISTMAS

When describing the effect on him of witnessing Shonen Knife live for the first time, Kurt Cobain said that these charming girls from Osaka turned him into "a screaming nine-year old girl at a Beatles concert". Here, with 'Neon Zebra', they display the full panoply of their panache and punk-rocking prowess. The lyric concerns a zebra which is abducted from a zoo and turned into a wonderful multi-coloured creature! With a story like that, and Shonen Knife's enthusiastic knack for ramshackle punk/pop tunes that are on a par with Buzzcocks, who could fail to fall in love with this?

97
SPLOOSH!
OZRIC TENTACLES
DOVETAIL RECORDS

The Ozrics were from Somerset; at first, a somewhat marginal band, they became festival favourites by playing a brand of progressive space rock that seemed, on the face of it, to be terribly dated… but word of mouth approval had somehow pushed them towards the fringe of the mainstream. They have released scores of albums but only a handful of singles, and 'Sploosh!' was the first – it was well-timed. Acid house had built up a receptive audience for trippy, repetitive music that grooved and gave off a good vibe, and this track certainly did the business in that respect. The band, without changing or compromising, had managed to chime with the times, and this delicious slice of instrumental, space-rocking boogie was a winner.

96
HOW I COULD JUST KILL A MAN
CYPRESS HILL
RUFFHOUSE
OTHER SINGLES 1991: THE PHUNCKY FEEL ONE; HAND ON THE PUMP; PIGS

Chunky and funky, brutalist beats and an inventive use of Lowell Fulson's 'Tramp' (along with a whole range of other samples) this was a triumph of invention over the lo-fi technology available to them at the time; by means of this debut single, Cypress Hill introduced themselves to the world. There are seemingly reckless breaks in the flow of the song where the group seem to jump off a metaphorical cliff, and lyrics that speak truly of how life was on the streets, all rapped in a weed-influenced, slow and idiosyncratic style.

95
NOT SUPERSTITIOUS
LEATHERFACE
ROUGHNECK RECORDING COMPANY
OTHER SINGLES 1991: I WANT THE MOON

Leatherface were a band from Sunderland who played a brand of ferocious punk-rock in a style that owed rather more to Hüsker Dü than to The Clash. Here, a wall of guitar noise fails to disguise a melodic undercurrent in the deep heart of the song, and the vocals are roared out in throat-shredding style by Frankie Stubbs – but, as they are deliberately placed low in the mix, they become an added texture within the song, rather than being the focal point.

94
WEAR YOUR LOVE LIKE HEAVEN
DEFINITION OF SOUND
CIRCA

Definition of Sound were a dance act from London who put this 1967 hit by Donovan back into the charts via the ingenious device of pairing Donovan's lyric with the irrepressible rhythm of 'Let It Out (Let It All Hang Out)' by Memphis band The Hombres (written, incidentally, by B. B. Cunningham Jr., a friend of mine whom I met when he was part of Jerry Lee Lewis's band. Sadly, he was killed by gunfire whilst working as a security guard in 2012). Definition of Sound give their track a smiling face, and they dress it up in bright, gaudy colours; it was great pop music.

93
TASTY FISH
THE OTHER TWO
FACTORY

Named with delicious irony, The Other Two consisted of Stephen Morris and Gillian Gilbert, the two members of New Order who the media were least interested in. They began this group during a New Order hiatus and initially recruited Kim Wilde as singer, before realising that Gillian was, in fact, perfectly suited for that role. 'Tasty Fish' was their first release and it reached no. 41 on the UK chart. There is an obvious similarity with the parent group's work – the mix of melody and dance groove is potent – although Gillian's vocal is perhaps more reminiscent of Tracy Thorn from Everything But The Girl.

92
I WON'T TRY
MIDWAY STILL
ROUGHNECK RECORDING COMPANY
OTHER SINGLES 1991: WISH

'I Won't Try' was a glorious helping of tunefulness served-up in a punk/pop style from Kent band, Midway Still. Guitars are wrangled purposefully and the harmonies are quite heavenly; when all is said and done, it makes me happy.

91
PLAYING WITH KNIVES
BIZARRE INC
VINYL SOLUTION
OTHER SINGLES 1991: BIZARRE THEME / X-STATIC

'Playing with Knives' mixes an energetic, quick-tempo house groove with piano, a wailing female vocal, acid-laced keyboard effects, disco strings and industrial noise… in other words, it is jam-packed, but never feels cluttered or clunky. The hooks have talons and, along with the frenetic pace, they make this a raver's staple that had enough crossover appeal to reach the masses and deservedly yield a top five chart placing.

90
MISSING THE MOON
THE FIELD MICE
SARAH

Although The Field Mice were lazily lumped in with the fey and jangly C86 indie scene, it was not a particularly justified or accurate categorisation. From their earliest inception the group had experimented with samplers and sequencers, and for this, their swansong single, they destroyed all preconceptions; 'Missing The Moon' is a seven minute excursion into dance/pop. This is a sequencer-led piece with alternate male and female voices used in an undemonstrative and highly un-rock manner. There is also a magnificent guitar lick, sparingly used, which adds a dramatic feel to the song, and the bass-driven conclusion nods unmistakably toward Peter Hook's work in New Order.

89
RUBBERBANDMAN
YELLO
MERCURY

By this point, Yello were veterans of the electronic wing of the music scene; however, the Swiss duo still sounded fresh and their sense of humour remained intact. 'Rubberbandman' has a sparse electronic groove and a rude-sounding rhythm, embellished by neo-Spaghetti Western interludes and a house-style piano playing a tasty motif. Meanwhile, in a ridiculously exaggerated baritone, Dieter Mejer serves up a vocal that elsewhere might seem ludicrous, but within the context of this particular song is absolute perfection. Always tongue-in-cheek, never po-faced and never a novelty act either, Yello had unquestionable artistic integrity.

88
APPARENTLY NOTHIN'
YOUNG DISCIPLES
TALKIN LOUD

Acid jazz had a cool sound, a cool look and a cool scene; it was rare though that the music ever had anything more than minority appeal until British/American band Young Disciples managed to buck the trend with the infectious 'Apparently Nothin''. Fronted by Carleen Anderson (god-daughter of James Brown) they took this chunky groover onto daytime radio and then into the hit parade. The drum track provides the song with the legs that it uses to progress in a slow, strutting style. Luscious velvety bass, muted horns, wah-wah guitar and organ add a 1970s funk vibe, and Carleen Anderson sings phenomenally well; gospel-infused, her voice slips and slides across the rhythm with immaculate timing and feel.

87
TOKYO XXX
SOICHI TERADA
BPM

The young Japanese student Soichi Terada, already proficient on keyboards, travelled to New York in the mid- to late-1980s and was introduced to house music and synthesisers – it was the start of a love affair. He began to make his own music and on 'Tokyo XXX' we hear his very dramatic and individualistic take on house. He employs clean, lean sounds with a martial rhythm and savage stabs of machine noise that ramp up the tension. Voices wordlessly wail, a piano is introduced and the rhythmic flow becomes intensified; it is no surprise at all that Terada eventually became best known as a composer of music for video games.

86
GIRL FROM 62
THEE HEADCOATS
REGAL SELECT RECORDS
OTHER SINGLES 1991:
SOMETHING WENT WRONG;
HATRED, RIDICULE,
CONTEMPT; SHOULDN'T
HAPPEN TO A DOG;
CAVERN BY THE SEA

When it came to the music of Thee Headcoats, we knew exactly what we were going to get – primitive garage rock regardless of the fashions of the day. The group was one of several monikers assumed by Billy Childish in order to release his very regular messages to a largely apathetic world. Here, sounding like a mash-up between The Troggs and Hamburg-era Beatles, we have a two-minute lightning storm with a shouted-out chorus that adds just a little touch of sweetness to proceedings.

85
SUBSTANCE ABUSE
F.U.S.E.
PLUS 8 RECORDS

F.U.S.E. is an acronym for Futuristic Underground Sound Experiments, and it was an alias used by Canadian techno legend Ritchie Hawtin. 'Substance Abuse' is an absolute classic of the genre that was a massive floor-filler in discerning clubs – it is a dark and heavy trip; spiralling, squelching and sucking us into its orbit. At one point, there is a heavily-distorted voice repeating the word "overdose"; that is the only vocal… and it speaks volumes.

84
I'M GOING SLIGHTLY MAD
QUEEN
PARLOPHONE
OTHER SINGLES 1991: INNUENDO; THESE ARE THE DAYS OF OUR LIVES

Freddie Mercury would die this year, but he continued to work until the end, and this single from the album Innuendo was a delight. Though treated in light-hearted fashion, the song dealt with the mental decline the singer was suffering due to the effects of AIDS. The lyric was put together by Mercury and his friend Peter Straker, inspired by the tongue-in-cheek witticisms of Noel Coward. Played predominantly on a wonky-sounding keyboard, with lovely guitar touches by Brian May, this is sung brilliantly by Mercury, whose bravery and sense of humour in coping with his illness remained steadfast until his eventual, sad passing.

83
ENDLESS ART
A HOUSE
SETANTA

In a declamatory fashion, over a repetitive guitar motif, vocalist Dave Couse runs through a list of both highbrow and lowbrow artistic figures; he states name, year of birth and year of death. Sid Vicious, Oscar Wilde, Jackson Pollock and Mickey Mouse all feature amongst a multitude of others. This leads into a chorus that quotes musically from Beethoven's Fifth Symphony – as Couse states, "all dead but still alive, in endless time and endless art". Simple, beautiful and memorable.

82
CAN YOU DIG IT?
MOCK TURTLES
SIREN

When Martin Coogan was asked which song would be used as a B-side for the forthcoming single 'Lay me Down', he replied 'Can You Dig It?', simply because he had been watching the film The Warriors in which the phrase was featured extensively. Only then, with the title decided, was the song actually written and released on independent label Illuminated. Later, when the Mock Turtles signed to Siren Records, it was decided that

'Can You Dig It?', with its gorgeously sunny sound, should be released as a single proper. As a result, a little more guitar was added; and so, with the baggy beat, luscious, layered guitars over a 1960s-style organ and gently sung verses followed by a sparkling chorus, the band achieved a top-twenty hit that was replicated twelve years later when Fatboy Slim came up with a re-mixed version.

81
GO
MOBY
INSTINCT

Moby properly announced himself, and his talent, with the release of this single. He took vocal samples from English goth band Tones on Tail, and soul singer Jocelyn Brown; he then mixed-in some of the Laura Palmer Theme (composed for TV series Twin Peaks by Angelo Badalamenti) and twisted these disparate elements into the shapes he required. Finally, after contributing his own rhythms and further musical elements, all he had to do was… and please pardon the pun… sit back and watch it 'Go'. This was a huge dance-floor smash, and the success was replicated in sales terms as the record catapulted Moby into the UK top-ten.

80
ME IN TIME
THE CHARLATANS
SITUATION TWO
OTHER SINGLES 1991:
OVER RISING

'Me In Time' saw a change in The Charlatans line-up as John Baker was replaced as guitarist by Mark Collins. Whether coincidental or not, the band's sound also changed considerably; Hammond organ had been the principal featured instrument on previous releases, giving the group a somewhat dated, neo-mod sound. But, on 'Man In Time', the guitar is much the most conspicuous instrument – there is now a lighter touch. With the departure of the dense Hammond sound, rays of sunlight are able to filter through the song which leans more for inspiration to 1967 San Francisco rather than Wardour Street in London. All in all, this is vaguely psychedelic and highly refreshing; the band had successfully stepped out of their comfort zone.

79
FATS HUSTLES THE PROS AND CONS
CC SAGER
SACRED HEART

Delving into the deep and murky soundscape of the delta blues, whilst utilising dadaist imagery, Gareth Sager (once of The Pop Group, Rip Rig + Panic and Head) wasn't a million miles away, stylistically, from Nick Cave & The Bad Seeds. His delivery is reminiscent of an old style preacher, possessed, and raging at his flock. The music has an untamed edge; it jerks and spasms like a wounded animal as sparks fly from the guitar and the drums give an impression of hammer striking anvil.

78
RHYTHM IS A MYSTERY
K-KLASS
DECONSTRUCTION

K-Klass met at The Hacienda – two of them were in the Manchester band Interstate whereas the other two were comparative novices from North Wales. They put their ideas together, recorded some tracks and took them to Eastern Bloc, the record shop that was pivotal in Manchester's embrace of electronic music. Impressed by the demo, the shop had white labels pressed up of the tracks, and K-Klass were up and running. After a debut EP, along came 'Rhythm Is A Mystery', which, after an unsuccessful initial release, was re-issued and became a number three hit record. Featuring a vocal by Bobbi Depasosis that had stacks of character, the track mixed up garage house styles with a European disco sensibility. If the aim was to make people feel good and get their feet onto the dance floor, they succeeded with ease.

77
KISS THEM FOR ME
SIOUXSIE AND THE BANSHEES
POLYDOR
OTHER SINGLES 1991: SHADOWTIME

For Siouxsie and the Banshees this was a sonic departure, bordering on re-invention. They chose to work with producer Stephen Hague, who dusted away the cobwebs and gothic detritus, and gave them instead a pristine, dance-pop makeover combined with Eastern-style instrumentation that was used in a highly effective manner, adding further delicious flavours to the musical palette. Lyrically, the song concerned Hollywood star Jayne Mansfield, and it refers to her heart-shaped swimming pool, party-loving nature and her very grisly end in an automobile accident.

76
WE ARE BACK
LFO
WARP

The lyric, delivered in robotic voice, says "There are many imitators, but we are the true creators, we are back, we are back". This is a serious claim to make, but LFO back it up with a superb, idiosyncratic brand of techno excellence that is dance-floor friendly and massively entertaining. One gets the feeling that, in Paris, Guy-Manuel de Hormem-Christo and Thomas Bangalter, who, in 1993, would go on to form Daft Punk, were paying very close attention and experiencing a collective light bulb moment.

75
COAST IS CLEAR
CURVE
ANXIOUS

Both Toni Halliday and Dean Garcia were in Eurythmics orbit; she was signed to Dave Stewart's Anxious Records and he was a backing musician for Eurythmics. Stewart made the introductions and, after following an elaborate route, they formed Curve. For this single, they built-up an impressive bass and beat-heavy wall of sound, and over the top scrawls a brilliantly simple guitar motif. Toni Halliday sings with authority and assurance, completely owning the lyric, which could be interpreted to be apropos of a child's sense of abandonment and lack of parental love.

74
PEARL
CHAPTERHOUSE
DEDICATED

'Pearl' is a song that shimmers; it is trance-like and the waves of titanic guitar put it in the same aural arena as, for example, Ride or My Bloody Valentine. The vocals replicate the soft focus used by other bands of the era, and yet… there is more going on here than first meets the ear. At the foundation of the piece is a shuffling dance beat, helped along by the sampled power drumming of John Bonham. Then, as the song reaches a crescendo, the introduction of a female harmony vocal has an unequivocally awe-inspiring effect.

73
BRENDA'S GOT A BABY
2-PAC
JIVE
OTHER SINGLES 1991:
TRAPPED

Taken from debut album 2Pacalypse Now, the young rapper looks compassionately at teenage pregnancy and the plight of impoverished, poorly-educated children growing up in the ghetto neighbourhoods of American cities. The song's lyric was based on a newspaper article that 2Pac had read concerning the case of a twelve-year old girl who had given birth to her cousin's baby, and then threw the infant into a rubbish compactor. Pertinent to this horrific incident, in his lyric, 2Pac raps about a child called Brenda who manages to disguise her pregnancy and gives birth to a baby that she disposes of in the trash. She is from a poor family; her father is a drug addict and she has received virtually zero education. Ashamed of herself, she leaves home and is forced into prostitution just to survive, before eventually meeting a violent end. The sad fact is that this tale resonated so much because the listener realises that this is no sensationalised fantasy, but rather an accurate and astute social commentary. Society in general, it is pointed out, simply closes a collective eye to what is really happening to its most vulnerable citizens.

72
SO AND SLOW IT GOES
WIR
MUTE

Drummer Robert Gotobed had left Wire, and so, slimmed from a 4- to a 3-piece, the band decided to shave a letter off their name to become Wir. Their intriguingly abstract approach was evident with this single too; it is a beautiful, hypnotising piece of music, with the customary hard to fathom, though deeply-intriguing lyric. As the title suggests, it is played, and sung, slowly… ever so slowly.

71
STARS
SIMPLY RED
EASTWEST

Simply Red were uncool; they were derided as purveyors of bland slickness. However, the situation was remedied to a large degree by the single 'Stars', along with much of the album it was taken from. It was, I was delighted to say, a superb song that displayed a new found maturity. Superbly arranged, produced and performed, Mick Hucknall gave a fabulously warm and nuanced vocal performance that expressed hope, tempered by fatalism.

70
MENTASM
SECOND PHASE
R&S RECORDS

Second Phase comprised Joey Beltram and Mundo Musique, and 'Mentasm' was an inescapable rave anthem that is dark and foreboding. There is an unrelenting "in ya face" aggression, and sounds are twisted and distorted. This was techno with a serious confrontational edge; energy, excitement and anxiety all come together and combine to quite devastating effect.

69
SON OF MUSTANG FORD
SWERVEDRIVER
CREATION

Out of the ashes of Oxford band Shake Appeal came Swervedriver. They recorded a demo of 'Son of Mustang Ford' and gave it to Mark Gardener of Ride. He, in turn, played it to Alan McGee, who immediately flipped upon hearing the fiery guitar riffery, and he instantly signed the group to Creation Records. They went back into the studio with ex-Vibrator turned producer Pat Collier, and soon 'Son of Mustang Ford' was soundtracking life in students' Halls of Residence all across the UK. Although Swervedriver would be lumped into the shoegaze scene, their sound, as revealed here, owed much more to USA bands such as Dinosaur Jr and Sonic Youth. They were much harder hitting than many of their British contemporaries; drums were pounded and guitars cranked high in the mix. Admittedly, the lyrics were pure juvenilia, but no matter – they were sung with gusto and relish and it was very much rock & roll.

68
FAME GOES TO YOUR HEAD
BLACK A.G.
DARN GOOD

Along with Quicksilver Cooley – his producer sidekick – the rapper Black A.G. was responsible for attracting attention to the hitherto unheard Chicago hip-hop scene, when a video that was attached to the b-side of this single ('No Typa Drugdeala') gained national exposure via a phone-in request channel called The Box. As for 'Fame Goes To Your Head', it was a grooving slice of head-nodding funk that featured the obligatory James Brown drum sample, as well as a vocal sample of Jean Carb's 'Don't Let it Go To Your Head' and an assured rap from Black A.G on the corrupting influence of hollow fame.

67
EVERYBODY IN THE PLACE
THE PRODIGY
XL

'Everybody In The Place', with its mixture of breakbeats, fairground organ and techno, sounds exactly like the corkscrew roller coaster that was pictured on the single's sleeve. It's a superb, high-energy evocation of doing something, rather than merely observing, and there were plenty of takers who were willing to throw themselves into the excitement of this world that The Prodigy stood at the very centre of. The record was a huge hit, only failing to top the charts because of the re-release of 'Bohemian Rhapsody' following the death of Freddie Mercury.

66
OPTIMISTIC
SOUNDS OF BLACKNESS
A&M

Written and produced by Gary Hines, alongside the formidable pair of Jimmy Jam & Terry Lewis, this track is taken from debut album The Evolution of Gospel. Religious content is combined here with contemporary and urban secular sounds, and the results are simply awesome. As one might expect, the voices are strong and deeply soulful; the message thoughtful, inspirational and uplifting, but the beats and rhythms are most certainly aimed at enjoyment below neck level. Here is gospel music that broadens the scope and reaches out to the souls who populate the dance-floor.

65
SHOVE
L7
SUB POP

Forcefully lambasting – amongst others – sexists, air polluters and the unthinking, blind patriots who blight our society, L7 are a riot of fuzz guitars and snarled vocals, with enough sticky sweet pop flair and a grasp of take-it-to-the-brink dynamics to make 'Shove' a deliriously good time record.

64
THE FLY
U2
ISLAND

Having taken their anthemic, big rock sound as far as it would go – admittedly, they were very good at it – U2 were now confronted with the need for radical change; it arrived with 'The Fly' and its parent album Achtung Baby. In came syncopated dance beats, industrial noise, experimentation with distorted guitar sounds and a lyric that alludes to a telephone call from a man in hell… and then come the choruses which are counter-intuitive in their heavenly beauty. U2 were refreshed, rejuvenated, and had never sounded as intriguing as they did at this moment in time.

63

111
ORBITAL
FFRR

'111' was the title of a three-track e.p. by Orbital, containing the tracks 'Satan', 'Belfast' and 'LC1'. Opening with a sample from 'Sweat Loaf' by The Butthole Surfers, this is a launch pad for some sonic malevolence and mischief. 'Satan' is dance/techno in attack mode, while 'LC1' is a science-fiction soundtrack which makes good use of a spoken word sample of TV presenter Fred Dineage reporting on an alleged alien abduction, as well as boasting the Hartnoll brothers' full repertoire of spacey sounds. However, the absolute stand-out track is 'Belfast', which is a blissful, aural adventure over crisp beats and the soprano voicings of Emily Van Evera.

62
FEEL EVERY BEAT
ELECTRONIC
FACTORY
OTHER SINGLES 1991: GET THE MESSAGE

A crunching guitar riff from Johnny Marr opens the song, giving way to house-style piano and a lush, synthesised backing. Donald Johnson, the ace drummer of A Certain Ratio, provides a bracingly wonderful beat and Bernard Sumner raps (yes, raps!) a vocal about the injustice of criminalising rave culture, all before we reach a quite lovely, reflective and melodic chorus. The eccentricity of the songs construction was most definitely a strength, displaying a resolute refusal to play it safe.

61
TEENAGE WHORE
HOLE
CITY SLANG
OTHER SINGLES 1991: DICKNAIL

This is music to exorcise a festering, open sore; a howl of anguish and defiance from a young woman whose self-image has been destroyed by criticism from her disappointed, prim and proper mother. She turns the negativity into a weapon to strike back, taking the insulting label of 'Teenage Whore' and flaunting it, wearing the abusive tag with an insolent, angry pride. Courtney Love sings with dead-eyed assurance, completely inhabiting the soul of the song while musical carnage is committed everywhere around her; the sound is all feedback and fuzz, and the drums hit as hard as coffin nails.

60
PAPER DOLL
PM DAWN
ISLAND
OTHER SINGLES 1991: SET ADRIFT ON MEMORY BLISS; A WATCHER'S POINT OF VIEW

Because their sound was as smooth as silk, New Jersey's PM Dawn were a hard sell to hip-hop purists. As a source of influence and musical template, they harked back to soft soul rather than hard funk, and their sample-laden music referenced acts such as Spandau Ballet and The Doobie Brothers, acts who were perceived to be highly uncool. However, in the UK, PM Dawn did briefly achieve a measure of success, precisely because they sounded a little bit different. 'Paper Doll', whilst being only a minor hit, is a perfect example of their sound; it is lush and sensuous, with a beat that is baggy and fun. The song's lyrics, alluding to deeply spiritual thoughts, are gentle, unthreatening and certainly very unusual, and the whole package is wrapped in a bright and appealing sunshine pop style that has much more in common with The Mamas & the Papas than The Last Poets.

59
NOT TOO SOON
THROWING MUSES
4AD

Most of the music made by Throwing Muses came from the fertile mind of Kristin Hersh, but here, Tanya Donnelly (her equally talented half-sister) composes the song and takes the lead vocal in a fascinating and furiously strummed piece which observes the interaction between a predatory male and an intrigued, but ultimately uninterested female. The guitars sound bright, and along with the bass, they weave a most arresting pattern. As for the drums, they are huge, in the manner of Phil Spector-produced 1960s girl group singles. Donnelly sings, with brilliant impudence, in a feigned coquettish manner; it is a magnificent vocal and a quite superb single.

58
NUFF RESPECT
BIG DADDY KANE
SOUL
OTHER SINGLES 1991:
GROOVE WITH IT; THE LOVER IN YOU; SMOOTH OPERATOR

'Nuff Respect' was taken from the soundtrack of the crime/drama film Juice, and it teamed Big Daddy Kane with Public Enemy's production team The Bomb Squad. This high-octane combination of talents fuels the track as it moves along at a cracking pace. Kane raps impeccably; his flow is fast and smooth and his words are clever and laced with an undercurrent of humour.

57
RUN
SPIRITUALIZED
DEDICATED

Driven by a motorik rhythm, as patented by Neu, and incorporating elements of both The Velvet Underground's 'Run Run Run' and J.J. Cale's 'Call Me The Breeze', this debut single by Spiritualized saw Jason Pierce expanding on the work he had done as one half of Spaceman 3 by moving into a more subtle and substantial area of music making. The feel of the song is strongly suggestive of movement itself, but also the exhilaration that accompanies this movement. The blur of images and the sense of wind against skin are very convincingly conveyed.

56
THE WHISTLE SONG
FRANKIE KNUCKLES
VIRGIN

'The Whistle Song' was initially created by Eric Kupper (a studio collaborator of Frankie Knuckles) who made a demo of the track after finding inspiration in a DJ set performed by Knuckles, before passing it onto the DJ himself the very next day. Frankie Knuckles began playing the untitled demo at The Sound Factory and his audience began to refer to it as 'The Whistle Song'. More work was then undertaken on the track by Knuckles, Kupper and John Poppo, and this single version was then released. The record is a true classic of the house genre; the beat is mid-tempo and unhurried, opening with flutes that eventually give way to a whistling section. The whole piece is as light as a feather which gets carried away on the groove; it is a track that makes people feel good, brings people together and contains highly enjoyable magic.

55
MY LEGENDARY GIRLFRIEND
PULP
FIRE
OTHER SINGLES 1991:
COUNTDOWN

With 'My Legendary Girlfriend', Pulp showed for the first time the aces that had previously remained hidden in their hand. Over a propulsive disco beat and repeated piano figure, Jarvis Cocker whispers a long introduction. He is role-playing, inhabiting the personality of the song's utterly confused and frustrated narrator. Soon, Cocker becomes louder and more demonstrative – at this point, finding his own style rather than borrowing from Mark E. Smith of The Fall. The band add various flourishes to colour the song; a hint of Shaft-style wah-wah guitar, a touch of violin. Pulp had made good records before… but this was definitely the best yet.

54
FREQUENCY
ALTERN 8
NETWORK
OTHER SINGLES 1991:
ACTIVE 8; INFILTRATE 202

Hailing from Stafford, Altern 8 were a hardcore rave outfit notable for wearing chemical warfare suits and utilising ultra-heavy bass sounds. 'Frequency' is absolutely full on; it is fast and furious and samples of 1970s funk records provide the breaks between monumental slabs of noise that are used like a battering ram. The track absolutely bristles with energy; it is also extremely raw and immediate – and when it hits, it leaves an indelible mark.

53
FOR LOVE
LUSH
4AD

Sweetness and pain are entwined together in this song. It concerns a girl entranced by the illusion of idealised love, who ends up being hurt and disillusioned by the altogether grim reality she is faced with. The song is played mid-tempo and Rickenbacker guitar dominates the sound, jangling over a simple but solid drum beat. The lyric is sung with wonderful, angelic purity, but although the whole piece is very pretty indeed, the songs deep emotional heart is crammed full of desperate sadness.

52
OH CANADUH
NOMEANSNO
ALLIED RECORDINGS

Here, Canadians Nomeansno cover 'Oh Canaduh', which was originally released by Subhumans (CA), a Canadian punk rock band in 1978. Nomeansno absolutely blast through this anthem of dissatisfaction that rails against smug complacency – but although the band really do rage and convey fury, they nevertheless play with precision and economy; nothing is ragged and nothing is superfluous.

51
I'LL BE YOUR FRIEND
ROBERT OWENS
PERFECTO

In Chicago in the 1980s, in what was the golden era of house music, Robert Owens, along with Larry Heard and Ron Wilson, had released seminal records as Fingers Inc. Now, under his own name, he issued this expressive electronic meditation on the bonds of friendship to a community which, during the AIDS epidemic, was having to deal with loss on a titanic scale. This message of solidarity and reassurance is a sublime slice of house music, voiced to perfection as well as being both lean and funky. Emotion is palpable, but there is no egotistical showmanship involved, just a mournful trumpet solo which adds to the atmosphere of this highly impressive piece of work.

50
100,000 FIREFLIES
THE MAGNETIC FIELDS
HARRIET

The Magnetic Fields debuted with this remarkable single. It was written by Steven Merritt, the leader of the ensemble, but sung in a glass-shattering soprano by Susan Anyway. The lyrics are full of abstract imagery and display dark, wicked humour as they portray a relationship as a trap to be avoided. The music is trebly and sparse, consisting only of a painfully sharp keyboard pattern and a simplistic thudding drum. The overall effect is disturbing, unsettling and claustrophobic in the extreme.

49
A ROLLER SKATING JAM NAMED "SATURDAYS"
DE LA SOUL
TOMMY BOY
OTHER SINGLES 1991: RING RING RING (HA HA HEY); MILLIE PULLED A PISTOL ON SANTA

Something of a collaborative effort from the Native Tongues collective, this De La Soul single features Q-Tip (from A Tribe Called Quest) who raps the first verse, and R&B vocalist Vinia Mojica, who sings between verses. There are a multitude of samples incorporated into the track, but the main riff derives from 'Evil Vibrations' by The Mighty Ryeders. Thematically, the song is a celebration of the roller-skating craze of the 1970s, and the sheer joy of escape from routine that was offered by the weekend.

48
EASY COME EASY GO
G.W. MCLENNAN
BEGGARS BANQUET

The lyric here was clearly addressing the issues in McLennan's turbulent life since The Go-Betweens had split-up nine months previously. He had formed a new band, Jack Frost, and released a somewhat patchy album with them. Next came his solo album, Watershed, from which 'Easy Come Easy Go' was taken. In terms of sound, it harks back to the final Go-Betweens masterpiece, 16 Lovers Lane, i.e. deceptively simple guitar strumming from which gorgeous melodies emerge, along with self-reflective lyrics, sung in an unassuming manner and underpinned by fabulous, uplifting harmony vocals. McLennan's records never disappointed; this was no exception.

47
SOUND
JAMES
FONTANA

James had hit big the year before, with the re-recorded version of 'Sit Down'; it had given them the commercial breakthrough they deserved. They now followed up with 'Sound', which again went into the top-ten of the charts. Opening with a bass riff, before drums and guitar are added, the song has impressive momentum; it seems to prowl and there is an evident sense of restrained power throughout. Tim Booth sings, with great elan, an impressionistic lyric which I take to be about growing up and leaving childhood behind. His approach is similar to a method actor inhabiting a part, and the rolling of vowels to create the song's hook is highly impressive.

46
I'M FREE
MORGAN KING
BTECH

Morgan King had been the drummer in Manchester band Illustration, who had appeared on the Some Bizarre Album alongside such luminaries as Soft Cell, The The and Depeche Mode'. 'I'm Free' is an outstanding piece of progressive house, that drifts blissfully over a wonderfully funky drum loop. Lyrics appear at the mid-point of the eight-minute track and they are suitably consciousness expanding and uplifting. Akin to a gentle hallucinatory trip, these sounds were a delightful pleasure to immerse oneself in.

45
SAFESURFER
JULIAN COPE
ISLAND
OTHER SINGLES 1991:
BEAUTIFUL LOVE;
EAST EASY RIDER; HEAD

In this year, Julian released his sprawling magnum opus Peggy Suicide, which was an incredible artistic peak. The eight-minute epic 'Safesurfer' was the second of four fabulous singles extracted from the album. All remaining remnants of Julian's post-punk past were ripped to shreds and cast on the wind. Here, he took on the mantle of shamanistic cosmic explorer using prog-style guitar, stately piano, experimental electronic noise and a vocal that was an incantation rather than a sung lyric; it was unequivocally brilliant.

44
NOTHING CAN STOP US
SAINT ETIENNE
HEAVENLY

Sarah Cracknell made her debut appearance on a Saint Etienne record when she sang 'Nothing Can Stop Us'... and she was a perfect fit; her breathy vocal style gelled immediately with the song-craft of Pete Wiggs and Bob Stanley. This single displayed a pop classicism that gave the song a feeling of familiarity right from the very first hearing. There is more than a touch of Northern Soul in the pacing and chug of the track, and yet the utilisation of piccolos and flutes to enhance its lightness and brightness would be, most likely, never heard at The Twisted Wheel or Wigan Casino.

43
ENTER SANDMAN
METALLICA
ELEKTRA

Metallica had emerged in the mid-1980s (alongside Anthrax, Slayer and Megadeth) as leading proponents of thrash metal, but by the time they released 'Enter Sandman', they had modified their sound to create a heavy metal lullaby that utilised a single, mesmerising riff and which concerned itself with the nightmares of children. Without alienating their core audience, they now found favour amongst a broader demographic. My friend Marc persuaded me to go and see them in concert – I thought they were bloody awful... but I could never find fault with this quite excellent single.

42
VAPOUR TRAIL
RIDE
SIRE

'Vapour Trail' was Ride's ace-in-the-hole song; it was a track where everything that was good about the band came together and coalesced into something mightier than the sum of its parts. Although it was a US-only single – and an absolute failure in commercial terms – it was a complete artistic triumph. Written quickly by Andy Bell, there is an effortless, natural flow; the combination of two interlocking twelve-string guitars creates a trebly, buzzing sound and drones are also added to great effect. The drum beat is bold and distinctive and the vocal sits perfectly within the overall structure of the song. Finally, when the singing ceases, we enter a two-minute coda supplemented by a string quartet; sheer bliss.

41
IN YER FACE
808 STATE
ZTT
OTHER SINGLES 1991:
OOOOPS

A top-ten chart placing was 808 State's reward for this masterpiece, which has an anti-capitalist, anti-war, pro-environmentalist slant that is conveyed in the opening vocal segment. To intensify the lyric, the sound is magnificent, stirring techno with a glorious melody, aligned to simply brutal hip-hop beats. This was a euphoric club staple that managed to send a ripple of energy and adrenaline through everybody who listened to it.

40
CAR WASH HAIR
MERCURY REV
MINT FILMS

Written and sung by Johnathan Donahue, with Dean Wareham of Galaxie 500/Luna guesting on guitar, this debut release from Mercury Rev reveals the band – and their distinctive sound – to be pretty much fully-formed, even at such an early point in their development. 'Car Wash Hair' is gentle, dreamy, melodic, experimentally-edged, enigmatic, playful, intriguing, neo-psychedelia… and if that is not already more than enough for one record, it is also a quite wonderful listening experience.

39
KALTES KLARES WASSER
MALARIA
MOABIT MUSIK

Co-managed by my friend Mark Reeder, Malaria were an all-female band from Berlin, who, at this point, had already been releasing music for a decade. 'Kaltes Klares Wasser' (which translates into English as 'Cool Clear Water') showcases the band's amalgam of post-punk and electronic sounds. Also into the mix goes a distinct whiff of Weimar-era decadence, via a cascade of piercing piano notes and the sexually provocative lyric, sung with a devil-may-care and confident flourish.

38
THERE'S NO OTHER WAY
BLUR
FOOD

Blur's second single release propelled them into the top-ten for the first time, and 'There's No Other Way' was indeed a very good piece of pop, marrying a 1960s post-psychedelic sensibility with a more modern Happy Mondays baggy groove, complete with tambourine high up in the mix. It also features a trademark breezy vocal from Damon Albarn, although the real star of this record is Graham Coxon, whose left-field approach to guitar playing really lights up the song.

37
YOU AND YOUR SISTER
THIS MORTAL COIL
4AD

'You And Your Sister' is a song by Chris Bell, the one-time co-leader of Big Star (alongside Alex Chilton). It had previously been the b-side of Bell's only solo single, 'I Am The Cosmos'. Now, Ivo Watts (the head of 4AD records and initiator of This Mortal Coil) selected Breeders' band-mates Kim Deal and Tanya Donnelly to give voice to this delicate reading of the sweet and fragile love song. Their voices blend wonderfully over a repeated guitar figure as they exquisitely convey the song's bruised tenderness; then, as a cello is added to the sound, the sense of emotion and pathos rises to an almost unbearable degree.

36
PERPETUAL DAWN
THE ORB
BIG LIFE

This version of 'Perpetual Dawn' was a concise four-minute adaptation of the nine-minute track on the album The Orb's Adventures Beyond The Underworld. It is a breathtaking, flowing piece of sun-flecked reggae that features smooth vocals from Jeffrey Nelson and Shola. Audible in the mix is the sound of a cool, fresh-water spring bubbling up from its source… and just like spring water, this track is cleansing and refreshing.

35
SUPER ELECTRIC
STEREOLAB
TOO PURE

Stereolab, at this early point in their genesis, still contained elements of rock music within their sound; here, guitars compete with vintage synthesisers as the dominant instrument. Otherwise, Laetitia Sadier's sweet but emotionless vocal was strangely compelling; as she voiced the oblique lyrics, a tight and dense rhythmic interplay was firmly in situ. At the climax of the song, the instruments begin to drone, and Stereolab sound for all the world like spiritual heirs to The Velvet Underground.

34
WATERFALL
THE STONE ROSES
SILVERTONE

Two-years after the release of The Stone Roses debut album, it was still being mined for singles as the band struggled to write or record any new material. Fortunately, that album was blessed with lots of melodically strong, hugely appealing pop anthems, and so 'Waterfall' made for an excellent single. With a splendid guitar part to the fore, the genius rhythm section that gave the band its grooving element plays a faultless supporting role; and although, as a live performer the flatness of Ian Brown's voice was painfully obvious, with a little bit of studio help, here he sounded more than proficient.

33

YOU LOVE US
MANIC STREET PREACHERS
HEAVENLY
OTHER SINGLES 1991:
MOTOWN JUNK;
STAY BEAUTIFUL

Although a re-recorded version of 'You Love Us' became a big hit in early 1992, this less heralded original is the one that best captures the Manic's raging glam/punk spirit. The band were frequently derided as poseurs and fakes by the music press, so the title and chorus of this record was clearly a cheeky and ironic riposte to that negativity. The sound is thin and brittle and played at a whirlwind pace… but it is also thrilling, passionate and full of ideas. The breadth of the band's influences are displayed in the opening sample – taken from Penderecki's 'Threnody to the Victims of Hiroshima' – and the closing lift from Iggy Pop's 'Lust for Life'. This track also displays the band's considerable knack for creating highly tuneful hooks, a talent that would contribute greatly to the band's longevity.

32
DOMINATOR
HUMAN RESOURCE
80 AUM

Human Resource were a Dutch electronic act, and 'Dominator' was their first single. It broke into the UK chart, and a re-mixed version of the track, by Joey Beltram, became a huge ravers' favourite. "I'm bigger and bolder and rougher and tougher", goes part of the lyric, and sound wise, it does indeed live up to that boast. This is dark and epic, conjuring up images of the power-mad, destructive lunatics who have littered human history, all of whom believe themselves to be "the only dominator".

31
PLANET OF SOUND
PIXIES
4AD
OTHER SINGLES 1991:
ALEC EIFFEL;
LETTER TO MEMPHIS;
HEAD ON

Kim Deal's bass playing leads us into this song, which is driving and unrelenting. Joey Santiago then hits his guitar strings and summons forth a tidal wave of electrifying noise. Holding these elements together is David Lovering, who anchors proceedings with a solid drum pattern. Above the mayhem, Black Francis narrates; he whoops, hollers and rants a science-fiction themed lyric about an alien discovering Earth and hearing music… a unique occurrence in an otherwise silent galaxy – hence 'Planet of Sound'. Utterly bonkers of course, but all the better for it; another fabulous single by The Pixies, and one that always makes me smile.

30
TIME
WOLFGANG PRESS
4AD

Wolfgang Press had previously made records that were both interesting and intriguing, but the missing ingredient was fun. They had hitherto been a deadly serious proposition… but by listening extensively to De La Soul, they were duly inspired to alter their music. 'Time' is an idiosyncratic and funky Pink Floyd sampling gem; fuller sounding than previous releases, this transformed the group from one that you would stand and nod your head to, into one you would now happily dance to.

29
ALONE
DON CARLOS
CALYPSO

Pure and blissful Italo-house with a distinctly jazz flavouring, this is music that combines a pumping bass line, strings, thrilling piano, raw saxophone and deep, deep emotion. In short, perfect music for watching awestruck as the sun rises – and consequently, this became something of a classic on the Ibiza rave scene.

28
ROCKIN' BACK INSIDE MY HEART
JULEE CRUISE
WARNER BROTHERS

'Rockin' Back Inside My Heart' was taken from Julee Cruise's album Floating in the Night; it was composed by Angelo Badalamenti with lyrics by David Lynch. The song was performed by Cruise in an episode of Twin Peaks, and it will forever be associated with that show – but mere nostalgia for an iconic TV series is not what makes this such a memorable record. 'Rockin' Back Inside My Heart' is, on the surface, sweet, gentle and dreamy; conventional instruments are used and it is played pretty straight with few conspicuous flourishes. Of course, Julee Cruise sings beautifully, with an ache evident in every line, and space is utilised to great effect. The whole piece is saturated with echo to a point where the song begins to feel ghostly, other worldly and touched by death… this really is highly potent music.

27
SUMMER BABE
PAVEMENT
DRAG CITY

Pavement's first release was 'Summer Babe', a spidery sprawl of loud guitar and drums bashed like dustbin lids. The bass meanders and the singer alternates between drawling and yowling as he speaks the thoughts inside the mind of a male observing and obsessing over a female he desires. This guy is creepy, watching her every move and gesture; she, however, is oblivious to his presence, and even if she did notice him, there would be no interest – but still he watches…

26
JEALOUSY
PET SHOP BOYS
PARLOPHONE
OTHER SINGLES 1991:
WHERE THE STREETS HAVE NO NAME (I CAN'T TAKE MY EYES OFF YOU);
DJ CULTURE

'Jealousy' was one of the first songs written by Pet Shop Boys – dating from as far back as 1982 – but it had never been recorded because the duo hoped to persuade Ennio Morricone to score an orchestral arrangement. After nearly a decade of waiting, it was eventually given over to Harold Faltermeyer to fulfil the task. Elegant and melancholy, the song concerns the titular green-eyed monster eating away at a relationship from the inside, a relationship infected with suspicion and paranoia. Neil Tennant narrates the calamitous tale, calmly accompanied by stately piano, before the orchestrated grand finale, where all the emotional turmoil is unleashed in a titanic swell of strings.

25
HUMAN NATURE
GARY CLAIL
PERFECTO
OTHER SINGLES 1991: THE EMOTIONAL HOOLIGAN

Gary Clail had initially been encouraged to perform by Mark Stewart, and had subsequently become an integral part of Adrian Sherwood's incredible On-U Sound roster of renegade artists and visionaries. With 'Human Nature', all the faith that had been placed in him was vindicated; this was a masterful record, uncompromising but accessible – it spoke harsh truths but was also musically attractive. The track was simply a dance-floor bomb; the combination of piano and electronics was perfectly judged, and the main vocal is cut-up, adding resonance to each phrase that Clail throws-out, partly to challenge the apathetic way in which social issues are viewed, and partly to warn of the consequence of this apathy. Finally, my old friend Lana Pellay (a former Mancunian resident) adds a diva touch to the chorus, giving a perfect juxtaposition to the verses.

24
NEAR WILD HEAVEN
R.E.M.
WARNER BROTHERS
OTHER SINGLES 1991: LOSING MY RELIGION; SHINY HAPPY PEOPLE; RADIO SONG

'Near Wild Heaven' was an unusual R.E.M. single insofar as it was sung by bassist Mike Mills, who had co-composed the lyric with regular lead vocalist Michael Stipe. This was the third single to be extracted from the monumentally successful album Out of Time, and lyrically, it is a somewhat foreboding song about the imperfections of a failing love affair. Despite this dour subject matter, the song is played in a brisk, sunny manner with a luscious bass sound and chiming guitars; the lovely Beach Boys-style harmonies then provide both the icing and cherry on this very palatable cake.

23
LOOSE FIT
HAPPY MONDAYS
FACTORY

'Loose Fit' captures The Mondays at their peak; here, they were ably assisted by production pair Paul Oakenfold and Steve Osborne, who shrewdly added session singer Roweta into the musical mix, giving the band the final essential ingredient in their evolution from ne'er-do-well chancers to respected musical innovators. With 'Loose Fit', they manage to locate a slinky but deadly groove, adorned with a delicious guitar lick that tickles the ears. Shaun Ryder, with his conventionally unlovely (but perfect for the Mondays) sing/speak vocal style, imparts a coded manifesto on his life values – and when the band hit the chorus, Roweta's rich and powerful voice gives the track the wings on which it soars.

22
HIGHER THAN THE SUN
PRIMAL SCREAM
CREATION
OTHER SINGLES 1991: MOVIN' ON UP; DON'T FIGHT IT, FEEL IT

'Higher Than The Sun' is an ode to Ecstasy, the acid-house drug of choice. Produced by The Orb, it attempts to capture the loved-up, euphoric effect of the drug. Bobby Gillespie gently sings of the positive experiences and enlightenment that he encounters whilst under its influence, and, for the most part, the song is soft and soothing. Moving slowly over a subtle beat, with a sample from 1970s funksters Young Holt Unlimited, this is captivating, calming and pretty tranquil. On the whole, a quietly confident artistic statement and very much a resounding success.

21
FINALLY
CE CE PENISTON
A&M
OTHER SINGLES 1991: I LIKE IT

'Finally' was the first song written and released by the twenty-one year old American CeCe Peniston. Her potential had been spotted when she provided backing vocals on a session for female rapper Overweight Pooch; the power of Peniston's performance convinced the producers that she might be capable of creating something special herself, so they worked with her on a self-written poem and the end result was 'Finally', a spine-tingling, fizzing and joyous celebration. In the lyric, she expresses her happiness at locating Mr Right, while musically we hear a delicious amalgam of house and pop, with a fabulous R&B-style vocal from CeCe, whose verve and vigour added an electric current to the already exceptional, feel-good classic. This record propelled the previously unknown young singer to the number two position in the UK chart.

20
WHEN YOU SLEEP
MY BLOODY VALENTINE
CREATION

Trying, and failing, to record a definitive vocal, Kevin Shields hit upon the idea of mixing the dozen or so different takes all together; it sounded fantastic. The words became indistinct but the vocal was no less appealing; the human voice had simply become just one component of the overall sound. Shields plays all the instrumental parts himself, and he somehow created a piece of music that is both grandiose and mischievous at the very same time. Considering the somewhat avant-garde creative process (which, by all accounts, was torturous in its laborious repetition) this is fabulous pop and a unique, shining jewel of a record.

19
LOVE TO HATE YOU
ERASURE
MUTE
OTHER SINGLES 1991:
CHORUS; AM I RIGHT?

With their album Circus, it was evident that the intention was a toning down of their glorious, over-the-top camp, as Erasure presented to the world a more measured and mature face. The one exception was this track; 'Love to Hate You' was a stomper that was fierce and unapologetic in its fabulousness, harking back to the hedonistic days when disco reigned. It rides in upon a synthesised Georgio Moroder beat and references the melody of Gloria Gaynor's 'I Will Survive', whilst Andy Bell sings with strutting self-confidence and audibly unrestrained power.

18
CAN'T TRUSS IT
PUBLIC ENEMY
DEF JAM
OTHER SINGLES 1991: SHUT EM DOWN/BY THE TIME I GET TO ARIZONA

Another year, and another masterful Public Enemy single, with huge power and swagger as well as having plenty to say for itself. For this track, The Bomb Squad create a staggered, funky groove from a tapestry of samples which include 'Slave' by James Brown, along with vocal parts from Malcolm X and Ofra Haza. The lyric is concerned with the way that the corporate world (which controls the media) generates a negative stereotyping of black people; this, in turn, denies equal opportunity because of either white prejudice or black inferiority complex. Chuck D is a master lyricist, provocateur and committed exponent of black rights; his perfect flow and gritty vocal style mark him out as a spiritual heir to Otis Redding or Levi Stubbs. In essence, 'Can't Truss It' was a new kind of soul classic.

17
DIAMONDS AND PEARLS
PRINCE AND THE NEW POWER GENERATION
PAISLEY PARK
OTHER SINGLES 1991:
GETT OFF; CREAM

Prince had enjoyed a massively successful year, where mostly he displayed his mastery of sleazy, innuendo-laden funk; but when he dropped 'Diamonds and Pearls' into our midst, he turned that stylistic uniformity well and truly on its head, because this lavish ballad was chocolate-box sweet and as magical as a fairy tale. Fortunately, the innate fine taste that Prince possessed ensured that this confection stayed safely on the right side of schmaltz. It is a song of pure romance, sung as a duet with New Power Generation member Rosie Gaines. The track alternates between delicacy and grand flourish; it is playful, beautifully melodic and a great pop record.

16
GOODBYE HORSES
Q LAZZARUS
ALL NATIONS

Q Lazzarus, a struggling singer from New Jersey, was driving a cab; one of her fares was film director Jonathan Demme, who heard the demo tape she was playing as she drove him to his destination. Subsequently, he took her to Hollywood to promote her career, but they received little encouragement from record companies who seemed to view her as unmarketable. Nonetheless, 'Goodbye Horses' was cut and included in Demme's 1988 film Married to the Mob. Three years later, Demme again turned to the song for use in a crucial scene in his iconic film The Silence Of The Lambs; its pulsing dark wave/ post-punk electronic backing and the husky contralto voicing of Q Lazzarus fitted the film's mood perfectly, and this new exposure resurrected interest in the song, which finally gained an official UK release. For Demme's next film – Philadelphia in 1993 – Q Lazzarus recorded a version of the Talking Heads song 'Heaven', and played lots of shows in New York clubs and galleries, before disappearing completely from the public eye in 1996. In 2018 she was eventually tracked down and revealed to be working as a bus driver on Staten Island.

15
AFTER THE FLOOD
TALK TALK
VERVE

'After the Flood' was taken from the final Talk Talk album Laughing Stock, and it is as far removed from the band's synth-pop origins as it is possible to be. This is a gossamer thin tone poem built from church organ, a single drum and an electronic wash of sound. The slim lyric contains biblical allusions and is sung in a deathly croak by Mark Hollis, who, by this stage of his career, was operating in uncharted, uncompromising and very uncommercial territory. Much like the later works of Scott Walker, this is highly satisfying and deeply moving music, that definitively demands the abandonment of all preconceptions.

14
JAZZ (WE'VE GOT)
A TRIBE CALLED QUEST
JIVE
OTHER SINGLES 1991: CHECK THE RHIME

The album *The Low End Theory* was a marvellous, groundbreaking release; 'Jazz' was lifted from it, and is a brilliant single. Before recording, Phife Dawg had been diagnosed as diabetic and was considering leaving the group; instead, he was persuaded to stay and take an even more prominent role. This worked out brilliantly for ATCQ since Phife revelled in the responsibility, and thus the group now had a seriously impressive duo of rappers as he traded verses with the already highly renowned Q-Tip – they each have distinctive styles, yet both flow equally well. The lyrics are smart and poetic, the beat is steady and the sounds are silky smooth. Hip-hop had originated on the street but had never wanted to remain in the gutter… ATCQ were aiming for the stars.

13
JUSTIFIED AND ANCIENT (STAND BY THE JAMS)
KLF
KLF COMMUNICATIONS

In its original form, this song had appeared on the album 1987 (*What The Fuck Is Going On?*), but the potential had not been fully realised; the KLF knew that something was missing… a female voice perhaps? Confusing his country music divas, Jimmy Cauty suggested Tammy Wynette – although in his mind, he visualised Dolly Parton. However, Bill Drummond thought that Tammy would be perfect, so she was duly contacted and, amazingly, agreed to the collaboration, whereupon Drummond flew out to Nashville to supervise the recording of vocals. The track abandoned the Stadium house style of recent singles, and a more conventional structure was adopted… that is, if a song with house rhythm, employing Jimi Hendrix riffs and subtle, country flavoured pedal steel guitar colourings can ever be considered conventional. Add to the mixture a lyric that references Tammy Wynette's signature song, 'Stand By Your Man', whilst concerning itself with the mythical Mu Mu Land, and one has to conclude it is pretty strange. Still, everyone was happy; it was a fabulous pop single that was a huge hit, and, as Tammy herself remarked, "Mu Mu Land seems a lot more interesting than Tennessee".

12
DRESS
PJ HARVEY
TOO PURE

The genius that is PJ Harvey launched her career with this single. From the very first hearing, one sensed that this artist, in the decades to follow, would go on to become the major figure that she has proved herself to be. The lyric is concerned with a woman who is putting on a dress that she is uncomfortable wearing; she chose it to woo a man, but gets rebuffed and humiliated. This is an awkward, discomforting song, and the music reflects this; we hear a series of stuttering, staccato guitar riffs undercut with a mournful, scraped violin part as Harvey lives out the lyric with a desperate, out-on-the-edge sounding vocal.

11
D
CODEINE
GLITTERHOUSE

'D' was the opening track on Codeine's debut album Frigid Stars and it set the template for all their subsequent releases i.e. slow, sad guitar music, sung despondently over crushing waves of guitar. The lyrics are abstract and seem to act as a smokescreen for something unsaid; "D for Love" and "D because you're heaven sent" we are told. Somehow, we sense the hidden truth that just maybe 'D' is for darkness, desperation or depression.

10
GONNA MAKE YOU SWEAT
(EVERYBODY DANCE NOW)
C+C MUSIC FACTORY
COLUMBIA

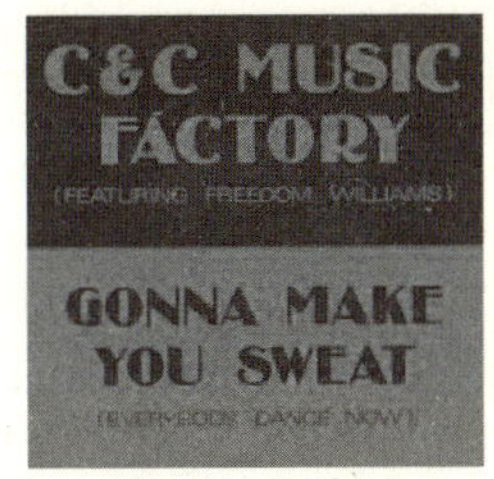

Producer Robert Clivillés created an instrumental version of 'Gonna Make You Sweat' and offered it to the vocal group Trilogy, who declined to record it. Instead, he chose to use the track for C+C Music Factory, a project he was working on with David Cole. Ex-Weather Girls singer Martha Wash was recruited to supply a vocal that was steeped in soul and gospel. Alongside her, they placed rapper Freedom Williams, and the combination was irresistible. The track is a juggernaut of guitar-fuelled house rhythms and hip-hop drumming, with the X-factor addition of a spine-tingling vocal performance from Wash – who urges everyone to dance – expertly balanced out by the cool flow of Williams's rapping.

9
KILLER INSIDE ME
MC 900 FT JESUS
NETWERK EUROPE

As literature, The Killer Inside Me was a classic piece of noir from pulp crime writer extraordinaire Jim Thompson. The central character is named Lou Ford, a small town policeman, who hides his murderous darkness behind a facade of niceness, good manners and a cloak of outwardly perceived simplicity. For this excavation into the mind of a psychopath, MC 900 ft Jesus inhabits the character of Ford, who goes about his everyday routine wearing a smile that conceals the devil in his heart. In a poetic rap style, the persona of Lou Ford is portrayed to perfection; the delivery of MC 900 ft Jesus is incredible as we feel this individual's inner contempt for others and his inflated sense of self-confidence in believing that he is cleverer than everybody else. The electronic musical accompaniment hums and rattles like moving traffic and the Dragnet-style horns add a twist of cinematic suspense. In short, a masterful, superb single.

8
MIND PLAYING TRICKS ON ME
GETO BOYS
RAP A LOT

Inspired by his grandmother's use of the phrase, Geto Boys member Scarface wrote much of 'Mind Playing Tricks On Me'. He intended to use it for a solo release, but he was persuaded that it would be more valuable as a Geto Boys single to enable the Texan rap act to make a commercial breakthrough. As it turned out, the track would prove to be one of the greatest ever released in the hip-hop genre. Written from the perspective of a successful, affluent street gangster – and violent hoodlum as well – it deals with the demons that prey upon him because of his chosen lifestyle… paranoia, stress, distrust, loneliness and thoughts of suicide all torture his mind. In order to maintain his lofty position, he must appear at all times to be strong and commanding, although inside he is vulnerable and fragile. This macabre morality tale is played out over a funky beat and a very appropriate repeating guitar lick that is sampled from Isaac Hayes's soundtrack for the 1974 film Tough Guys. So, tough guys indeed… here was a track that very perceptively revealed the fact that even those who seem to be the biggest and the baddest can still break down due to problems of mental health.

7
THE CONCEPT
TEENAGE FANCLUB
CREATION

Teenage Fanclub have always been the choice of the connoisseur, because somehow their brand of gorgeous guitar pop has managed to remain, to the public at large, somewhat beneath the radar. 'The Concept' is a lovely, tongue-in-cheek character study of a woman who is resolutely part of a dated music scene; she is dressed head-to-toe in denim and she buys records by Status Quo. But the song has an innate warmth; it is neither judgemental or cynical. The sound owes a considerable debt to the guitar jangle of Big Star and The Byrds – with a dollop of Monkees-style bubblegum thrown in for good measure.

6

JESUS BUILT MY HOTROD

MINISTRY

SIRE

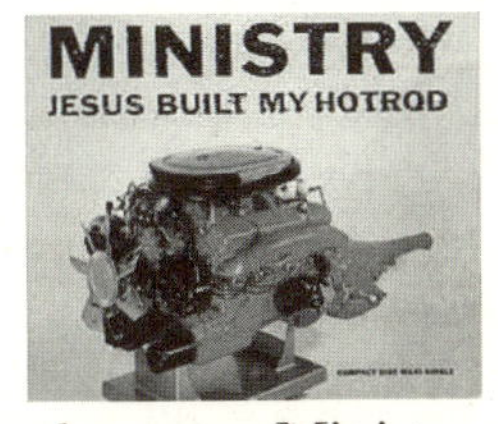

'Jesus Built My Hotrod' was the unholy alliance between Ministry, Al Jourgensen's industrial metal outfit (who play furiously and very fast) and a very drunk Gibby Haines of The Butthole Surfers, who scat sings a lyric about drag racing in the style of The Trashmen's 'Surfin' Bird'. Samples were added from cult films Wise Blood and Blue Velvet, along with drag racing sound effects and a relentless, polyrhythmic percussion track which propels this titanic track screeching around the turntable. Although it is absolute dynamite, this wonderfully unhinged record was very reluctantly released… and only then because they had nothing else to issue. Jourgensen didn't particularly like it, and the record company hated it. Notwithstanding this, 'Jesus Built My Hotrod' was adored by the public and it sold by the shedload.

5

SONS OF THE STAGE

WORLD OF TWIST

CIRCA

'Sons of the Stage' is a song about the euphoria of live performance, when music creates a connection that both the audience and those on stage can equally share… when barriers are broken down and removed… when everybody is lost amidst the joyful noise. The track is played over a northern soul beat; a serpentine guitar coils and uncoils, the bass pumps and synths gurgle, while Tony Ogden provides a breathless vocal that captures the wonderment of standing right in the middle of this mind-blowing, epic sound.

4
HALLELUJAH
JOHN CALE
COLUMBIA

Leonard Cohen had written and released 'Hallelujah' on his 1984 album Various Positions and there it languished – an unpolished gem, an over-long and overly complicated, synth-driven dirge. Enter John Cale, the iconoclastic former Velvet Underground man, who was a great admirer of Cohen's work. Cale was asked to contribute a track to a Cohen tribute record called I'm Your Fan, and so he contacted the composer and asked him to send over the lyric. Cale's fax-machine duly spewed out reams and reams of paper containing the fifteen verses that Cohen had written. As he felt that they wouldn't suit him, Cale elected to discard the verses with a religious theme and only retained – as he put it himself – the "cheeky ones". Then, he created a new piano-based arrangement for the song, and when, in his rich baritone, he sang Cohen's words, the whole thing took on new life. Immediately the piece was transformed from the original burial hymn into a glorious thing of great beauty that soared, cathedral-like, with a divine and heavenly trajectory.

3
BLIND WILLIE McTELL
BOB DYLAN
COLUMBIA

Bob Dylan recorded 'Blind Willie McTell' in 1983, during the sessions for his album Infidels, but inexplicably, it was to remain unreleased until 1991. I use the word inexplicably quite deliberately, because this is a song, and performance, that ranks in the highest echelons of Dylan's artistic achievement; it is nothing short of a masterpiece. Played as a slow blues lament, and loosely based upon the standard 'St James Infirmary Blues', the instrumentation is sparse – Dylan plays piano and Mark Knopfler, acoustic guitar. Like many of Dylan's greatest songs, this contains multiple, entwined themes; one is the religious conversion of the titular great bluesman, who abandoned his secular and sinful career to thereafter only ever perform unrecorded gospel music. Another theme is a sort of time-travelling documentary through moments of America's inglorious past – the flip-side of the American dream – making reference to the history of slavery and the Civil War. Dylan's spellbinding performance expertly leads us through verse after riveting verse, emphasising key phrases with all the skill of a master storyteller.

2
SMELLS LIKE TEEN SPIRIT
NIRVANA
GEFFEN

'Smells Like Teen Spirit' is a track which somehow manages to be greater than the sum of its parts; the fiery performance of the band, Kurt Cobain's sweetly sung, and then raging vocal, the soft and hard dynamics within the song, and its irresistible chorus, they all combine to make this an indispensable and iconic record. But its origins are surprisingly humble and prosaic; the starting point was a phrase scrawled on the wall by Cobain's friend, Kathleen Hanna of Bikini Kill. She wrote "Kurt smells like Teen Spirit" – 'Teen Spirit' being a popular brand of spray-on deodorant. Being blissfully unaware of this fact, Cobain interpreted it as a revolutionary slogan, which inspired him to write a song using the graffiti as a title. Borrowing a riff from 'More Than A Feeling' by rock dinosaurs Boston, and duplicating the loud/quiet style of The Pixies, he took his idea to a band rehearsal. Bassist Krist Novoselic thought the whole idea ridiculous, and he began to fool around by playing his part deliberately slowly. This led to drummer Dave Grohl playing a disco-style drum pattern to complement the bass... and all of a sudden, as if by magic, the song grooved. It was released as a taster single for the album Nevermind, with the plan that it would hopefully build interest in the next single, 'Come As You Are', which was thought to be the most likely to succeed. But 'Smells Like Teen Spirit' caught fire and then exploded; it became not only a huge hit, but a record that changed the face of music, changed fashion, spawned a whole new movement... and changed people's lives.

1
UNFINISHED SYMPATHY
MASSIVE
WILD BUNCH

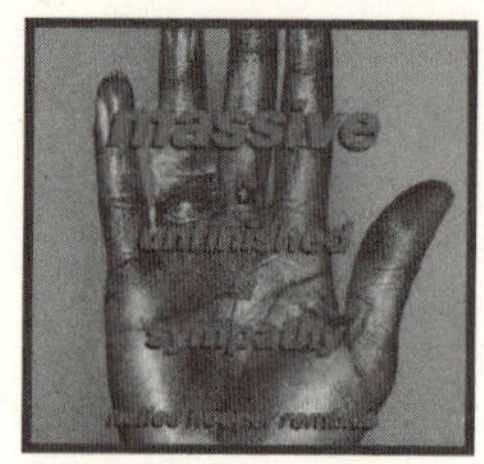

As the release of this single coincided with the Gulf War, it was considered that Massive Attack was a somewhat insensitive name, and so, for this record only, Massive Attack adopted the slimmed down and inoffensive title, Massive. Marketing strategies aside, the first point to note is that this single was incredibly bold and inventive; here, the group's artistic vision was fully realised without any hint of compromise. The song originated from an idea that singer Shara Nelson had been working on, with the provisional title of 'Kiss and Tell'; she was overheard humming the melody to herself during sessions for the Massive Attack album *Blue Lines*, and thereafter the piece was developed during studio jam sessions, where it was given the punning Schubertesque title 'Unfinished Sympathy'. The song was built up via drum machines, keyboards, scratches and samples, with Shara Nelson's heart-wrenching vocal highly prominent. What they created was an epic dance-floor ballad that carried a huge emotional pull. Still, something was missing… it was concluded that strings were required to add the necessary sweeping grandeur to the recording. The problem was that the recording was already over budget, and synthesised approximations sounded much too cheesy. Therefore, the band sold their car to raise funds to hire a string section. The song was now complete, and its diverse elements complemented each other to fashion a unique whole that was, without reservation, an unqualified success. Hip-hop roots were noticeably present, along with deep soul, courtesy of Shara Nelson, plus a melody worthy of Gershwin. The track was sassy, but elegant, and it represented the musical culmination of a decade of cultural cross pollination that had come about in Bristol. This had all started with The Pop Group, and then, along the way, Adrian Sherwood, Smith and Mighty, Neneh Cherry, Soul II Soul and several others had melded reggae, punk, jazz and hip-hop to forge a new type of British music, one of unashamed inclusiveness. 'Unfinished Sympathy' was its pinnacle and spearhead, as it stepped forth from the cellars and small spaces, out into the wider world and the future.

1992

NOTABLE EVENTS

Paul Simon tours South Africa after the ending of the cultural boycott.

As Federal Yugoslavia breaks up, Croatia and Slovenia gain international recognition as independent nations.

Boris Yeltsin announces that Russian nuclear weapons will no longer be aimed at US cities. In response George H.W. Bush announces that the US will stop aiming its own nuclear weapons at Russia. The pair meet and formally declare that The Cold War is over.

The Maastricht Treaty is signed and the European Union is formed.

Bosnia and Herzegovina proclaim independence. Bosnian Serbs rebel and the siege of Sarajevo begins.

Neil Kinnock's Labour party seem certain to come to power. Their complacency sees the Conservative Party, led by John Major, to win the general election.

The acquittal of four police officers who assaulted black citizen Rodney King leads to widespread rioting in Los Angeles. In six days over $1 Billion in damages and sixty-five deaths are recorded.

After singing a song on USA television program *Saturday Night Live*, protesting about child abuse within the Catholic church, Sinead O'Connor rips up a photograph of the pope.

Democratic candidate Bill Clinton becomes President of the USA defeating the Republican incumbent George H.W. Bush.

The Church of England votes to allow women priests.

The *Archives of Terror* are discovered; these detail the fate of thousands of people kidnapped, tortured and murdered by the security services of Argentina, Brazil, Bolivia, Chile, Uruguay and Paraguay, in what becomes known as *Operation Condor*.

Manchester United seem set to win the Football League title, but injuries and fatigue hamper them. A disastrous Easter period, during which the authorities forced them to play 4 games in 8 days, leads to a final day shootout against Leeds United, who manage to beat Sheffield United as United lose at Anfield - they finish second. Liverpool also win the FA Cup.

In November Eric Cantona, untrusted and unwanted by Leeds United, is signed for a bargain £1 million by Manchester United.

NOTABLE BIRTHS

Neymar ; Laura Kenny ; Sam Smith; Frances Bean Cobain ; Cardi B; Miley Cyrus; Jesse Lingard.

NOTABLE DEATHS

Willie Dixon; Alex Haley; William Schuman; La Lupe; Arthur Russell; Isaac Asimov; Frankie Howerd; Benny Hill; Satyajit Ray; Francis Bacon; Marlene Dietrich; Robert Morley; Albert Pierrepoint; Mary Wells; John Cage; Anthony Perkins; Eddie Kendricks; Denholm Elliott; Willy Brandt; Hal Roach; Larry Levan; Albert King; Eddie Hazel.

NOTABLE FILMS

Benny's Video; *Man Bites Dog*; *The Crying Game*; *Glengarry Glen Ross*; *Lessons of Darkness*; *Unforgiven*; *Bad Lieutenant*; *Malcolm X*; *Reservoir Dogs*; *Hard Boiled* ; *Twin Peaks: Fire Walk With Me.*

NOTABLE BOOKS

The Pelican Brief – John Grisham
The English Patient – Michael Ondaatje
All The Pretty Horses – Cormac McCarthy
South Of The Border, West Of The Sun – Haruki Murakami
Fever Pitch – Nick Hornby
Lost Souls – Poppy Z. Brite
The Wild Iris – Louise Gluck
Strange Pilgrims – Gabriel Garcia Marquez
Black Dogs – Ian McEwan
Never Mind (Patrick Melrose) – Edward St. Aubyn

MY 1992

I was now thirty-five and yet fulfilment, contentedness and stability were alien concepts to me – although I had grown quite adept at concealing my vulnerabilities. I ping-ponged both emotionally and behaviourally; on the face of it, I was urbane and relatively sophisticated – I read prodigiously and took regular trips to the cinema and theatre. On the other hand, my drinking was hugely excessive; tequila was my drink of choice – which I consumed by the bottleful – and under its pernicious influence my behaviour was, on occasions, utterly abominable. I could be boorish, argumentative and attention-seeking; I got myself into trouble when boarding a flight home from the Isle of Man because I drunkenly made my way to the cockpit, brandishing a child's plastic sword, and demanded to be flown to Cuba. In New York I careered around like an out-of-control dodgem car, and ended up being barred from several hostelries as a result. In the *Corner Bistro* in Greenwich Village I got into a violent argument with an expat Irishman about politics and Oscar Wilde which was only halted by the barman slamming a baseball bat onto the bar between my adversary and I.

As ever, music and football were my twin passions; I watched Manchester United home and away and was thrilled at the way Alex Ferguson had built a team that played expansive, attacking football, and I also loved the camaraderie I experienced with my travelling companions. I was earning a reasonable wage, going to numerous gigs and buying lots of records. In New York, I was able to feed my fascination for all things Velvet Underground; bootleg records and books were eagerly sought and purchased in large amounts. The single best thing that happened to me during the year was when my good friend Eddie Fenn (formerly a member of Tools You Can Trust and The Creepers) invited me into a recording studio he had installed in the cellar beneath his house; in order to try his equipment out, we wrote and recorded a track together. I'd not made music for a number of years, and it was a wonderful feeling to be creative again. I was, however, very low on confidence… but it was most gratifying just to have been asked. Eddie thought our track was pretty good; he played it to John Gill, a bass player and studio wizard who worked with The Mekons. John liked it too, and proposed that we work as a trio on a recording project. I agreed, but my lack of confidence was an issue that needed to be addressed. John took it upon himself to help; he was highly intelligent and academic, but also blessed with the common touch. He talked to me, nurtured and encouraged me, pointed out my strengths and effectively rebuilt me. We set about recording songs every Sunday and we called our unit The Stepbrothers.

Some of my favourite gigs this year included:

SONIC YOUTH/SUN RA – a July 4th free concert on the Summer Stage of New York's Central Park; the sun shone brightly and the music was excellent.

BELLY at The Academy – Marc Riley and I went along, and at some point we were joined by a polite young bunch of barely known musicians, for whom Marc had obtained guest list places; these guys turned out to be Blur. After the excellent gig by Belly, Marc and I headed just down the road to The Polytechnic, to watch Blur performing the songs that would feature on their album *Modern Life Is Rubbish*. I was stunned; they were spectacularly good, and easily the most vibrant stage band I'd seen for years.

100
SUL-E-STOMP
SUNS OF ARQA/ASTRALASIA
MAGICK EYE

I'd met Michael Ward (aka Wadada) through his other group, the lesser-known Sprout Head Uprising. I'd assisted them when they encountered a spot of bother in a bikers' bar in Ashton-Under-Lyne. Chatting to the grateful Wadada afterwards, he gifted me an album by his main group, Suns of Arqa. It was a most unusual listen; very dubby, but equally very dada. I was immediately hooked, and remain to this day fascinated by it. To the best of my knowledge, this single is a re-mix of a track by Astralasia, though I have absolutely no idea who Astralasia are, or even if they ever really existed. In any case, this is a dance track of somewhat left-field variety, incorporating, as it does, a hard trance rhythm alongside the pipes and fiddles of traditional Irish music, playing jigs and reels that are highly effective in this surprising contextual re-alignment.

99
PERCOLATOR
CAJMERE
CAJUAL
OTHER SINGLES 1992:
BRIGHTER DAYS; CHIT CHAT

Cajmere (who also recorded extensively as Green Velvet) was, in reality, Curtis Alan Jones, who hailed from Chicago. He had been a fan of rock and jazz music, but, in the mid-1980s, he heard house and began recording at home on cheap equipment. The DIY spirit was obvious in both his music and in the fact that he formed his own record label to release it. 'Percolator' is eccentric and inventive; Cajmere offers us a rhythmic re-creation of the sound of a frantically-bubbling coffee-making domestic appliance, as, completely deadpan, he chants the words, "It's time for the percolator". We then move on to a quickstepping beat, accompanied by occasional whistling sounds which act as a warning that either he – or his machine – is getting close to boiling point.

98
MURDER SHE WROTE
CHAKA DEMUS & PLIERS
MANGO

Chaka Demus & Pliers were cheerful raga practitioners, with a patois-heavy, Jamaican-accented, rapid-fire delivery. To the uninitiated, this was difficult to comprehend, but they nevertheless managed to score an unlikely major hit with this song, which discusses the unwanted pregnancy of a promiscuous woman. The success was doubtless due, in no small part, to the familiarity of its catch-phrase chorus of "Murder She Wrote", which was the title of a hit whodunnit television show staring Angela Lansbury. Of course, there was also the effervescent and highly infectious 'Bam Bam' rhythm of the track, borrowed from the 1966 Toots & the Maytals number, which would become a staple rhythmic ingredient in a huge number of Jamaican dance-hall recordings.

97
FIRE IN THE WESTERN SKY
DEAD MOON
TOMBSTONE

Unfairly underrated at the time, Dead Moon play hard-edged, psychedelic-tinged rock, and they do it with gusto. They sound like a consummate bar-band; spirited, gutsy and tuneful, with guitar blasting, drums pounding and the singer hollering for all he's worth.

96
FREE YOUR MIND
EN VOGUE
EASTWEST
OTHER SINGLES 1992: MY LOVIN'; GIVING HIM SOMETHING HE CAN FEEL; GIVE IT UP, TURN IT LOOSE

En Vogue were the uber-successful and acceptable face of pop/r&b, and their second album, *Funky Divas*, drew huge critical acclaim. 'Free Your Mind' was taken from the album and it thoroughly subverted the group's image and turned any preconception about how they should sound completely on its head. This is a ferocious hard rock track, with a head-spinning guitar solo and a lyric which attacks prejudice and the perniciousness of racism, sexism and other bigotry. It is a strutting, swaggering and extremely confident record, which clearly nods toward the influence of Funkadelic, but also brings to mind Ike & Tina Turner or Betty Davis at their full-throttled peaks.

95
WEEKENDER
FLOWERED UP
HEAVENLY

Although Flowered Up were signed to London Records, their label would not countenance the release of a thirteen-minute drug-fuelled odyssey which advocated hedonism for the masses. Therefore, to facilitate a single, previous label Heavenly stepped into the breach and 'Weekender' was allowed to spread like a virus, scattering seeds of sedition and infecting listeners with a twisted, rebellious spirit. Fusing mod with rave culture, the song opens and closes with dialogue from *Quadrophenia*; in-between, the track becomes distinctly spacey, displaying a clear Pink Floyd influence. If this gives the impression that everything is rather too nice, the vocal quickly corrects such a notion; it is pure aggression and belligerence as part-time weekend ravers are sarcastically castigated for their failure to fully embrace the alternative lifestyle that they flirt with. "Weekender fuck off and die", snarls vocalist Liam Maher, with gleeful malevolence, before trumpet fanfares and heroically wrangled guitars send the track hurtling skywards, to infinity and beyond.

94
STELLA
JAM & SPOON
R&S

Jam & Spoon were from Frankfurt, Germany, and although they were practitioners of pre-existing techno and house styles, they were not mere followers – in fact, quite the reverse, they were forward thinking and individualistic. 'Stella' induces feelings of pure bliss; it is a classic dance track, chock full to the brim with well thought out and distinct flourishes that perfectly combine to stimulate the senses.

93
JIMMY JAMES
BEASTIE BOYS
CAPITOL
OTHER SINGLES 1992: PASS THE MIC; SO WHAT'CHA WANT; GRATITUDE

'Jimmy James' is the Beastie Boys tribute to the culturally immortal Jimi Hendrix. The track was originally released on the album *Check Your Head*, but it was in a compromised form due to the refusal of the Hendrix family to licence samples that the Beasties wished to use. However, shortly after the album's release, the family relented and so this single version was recorded which extensively used the music of Hendrix, along with other prominent samples taken from Mantronix and The Turtles. The track is supremely funky and guaranteed to leave any right-minded soul feeling positively uplifted.

92
PLASTIC DREAMS
JAYDEE
R&S

'Plastic Dreams' is a house music classic by Dutchman Jaydee; it became a hit in the USA that was afforded just as much respect as tracks originating in Chicago. This is a piece of work that has never faded away, such is its potency; each year seems to herald a re-mixed/re-issued version of a record that never fails to pull people inexorably onto the dance floor. With its hypnotic grooves, hard beats, droning synths and cascading organ riffs, there is a jazz feel akin to mod-era classics by the likes of Jimmy Smith – and at ten minutes long, it is a piece of music that can really entrance the listener.

91
BOB'S YER UNCLE
HAPPY MONDAYS
FACTORY

Beginning with a sensuous, Latin-tinged rhythm, this was another seriously good single taken from the album *Thrills Pills and Bellyaches*; it displayed the depth of the Monday's musicality and their willingness to think outside the box. With a flute-driven melodic hook and chattering percussion, this could easily have been an early 1970s Gil Scott-Heron masterpiece… apart from the blindingly obvious fact that Shaun Ryder hardly writes in the style of the politically-driven American. In fact, on this occasion, Ryder uses a group-sex situation for lyrical inspiration, and whilst the subject matter is undisguised, it is handled with a fair degree of subtlety – although Rowetta's purring vocal part is very steamy and highly suggestive.

90

DEMON'S THEME
LTJ BUKEM
GOOD LOOKING

With the incredible track 'A Couple Of Beats' on the b-side, this release is pure nirvana for junglists. 'Demon's Theme' features exotic bird noises, pipes and chanted vocals (sampled from Malcolm McLaren's 'Double Dutch') along with frenetic beats, and it feels akin to journeying up the Mekong River for a date with destiny and a meeting with Colonel Kurtz from Coppola's *Apocalypse Now*. On the flip-side, 'A Couple Of Beats' is stripped back, gum-chewing raw energy, pressed decisively into vinyl grooves.

89
DROWN
SMASHING PUMPKINS
EPIC

Taken from the soundtrack to the Cameron Crowe film *Singles*, and only released as a promo-only single, 'Drown' nonetheless gained a considerable amount of radio airplay and earned Smashing Pumpkins the exposure they had never previously had. There is an attractive, rolling riff, and the piece is sung with great delicacy by Billy Corgan. It is quite haunting, though it signals that it may explode at several points, without actually doing so… until boom! … at the least expected moment, the song erupts and startles us, before subsiding into a gentle, feedback-laden finale.

88
THE WAY I MADE YOU FEEL
ED KUEPPER
HOT

Formerly of The Saints and Laughing Clowns, Ed Kuepper is a giant talent – 'The Way I Made You Feel' was extracted as a single from his punningly titled album, *Honey Steel's Gold*. As I listen to this song, the riff ricochets around my head; it is so exquisitely played. Overall, an intensely oppressive atmosphere is captured, as Kuepper sings about a destructive, obsessive relationship, in a humble and understated manner.

87
WAITING FOR THE SUN
JAYHAWKS
DEF AMERICAN

The Jayhawks were leading lights in the alternative country-rock movement, and here, on 'Waiting For The Sun', their finely honed songcraft is well in evidence. The song concerns a man who has encountered pain in his relationships, but has not yet lost hope that his situation might change, and the metaphorical sunshine may still, one day, warm his soul. Sung in plaintive high-register over a fractured guitar riff and gospel-style organ, this was an eminently easy to love sound.

86
GREY MATTER
DIVINE STYLER
GIANT

Divine Styler is an alternative hip-hop artist from New York, and

'Grey Matter', taken from the album *Spiral Walls Containing Autumns Of Light*, is freaky sounding and wildly experimental. Soundwise, it is warped and almost psychedelic, but, as if to offset this, Divine Styler raps hard on the subject of thinking before acting, and his Muslim faith is referenced too (as indeed it was on much of this album). For anyone who dug Kool Keith's work as Dr. Octagon – which arrived a few years later – Divine Styler is a simply must-hear artist.

85
I LOVE YOU
ELECTROTETE
APOLLO

In 1991, 'I Love You' had appeared as part of the EP *Sonar* on Rave Age Records; it now re-appeared, in several quite different mixes, as a stand-alone single. This is a gorgeous piece of creative trance; its electronic soundscapes are married to a perfect rhythm track and a vocal sample which is taken from a scene in *Twin Peaks* where the hospitalised Shelly says "I Love You" to Bobby…

84
FEAR LOVES THIS PLACE
JULIAN COPE
ISLAND

Julian Cope, by this time something of an elder statesman, steadfastly refused to go away. Fortunately, this made the world a nicer place to live in because here, from his album *Jehovahkill*, came 'Fear Loves This Place'; at the core of the song we get stumbling, low-key rock riffage, along with pearls of wisdom, half-sung, half-spoken by the druid dude, as the song wanders off in a different direction, leading inescapably to an immense chorus that never fails to elevate the spirit.

83
MY PIECE OF HEAVEN/ONLY TIME WILL TELL
TEN CITY
EAST WEST

Ten City were a trio of musicians (Byron Stingily, Byron Burke and Herb Lawson) from Chicago; they were practitioners of deep house music who were compellingly augmented by production legend Marshall Jefferson. In a sense, they were worthy inheritors of the mantle left by Earth, Wind & Fire because they shared the ability to create superbly sung dance classics with genius harmonies that were both passionate and soulful. This single served-up precisely those appetising ingredients.

82
WORKOUT
FRANKIE KNUCKLES FEATURING ROBERTA GILLIAM
VIRGIN

'Workout' is all about optimism and positivity; lyrically, it is couched in simplistic terms which allude to the way that mood can be lifted on the dance-floor. Just as the great disco records had always done, this track aims to empower listeners with its uplifting message and inclusivity. Here, Frankie Knuckles combines his talents with re-mix master Todd Terry and the imploringly voiced Roberta Gilliam to produce a record that really bounced. This was energy exemplified; a harbinger of better days ahead and a Haçienda floor-filling favourite.

81
LOVE OF LIFE
SWANS
YOUNG GOD

Like a pendulum, the music of Swans swings between dark and light, between good and evil. Rarely dull, their music is often full of drama… and this is exactly the case with 'Love of Life', which is huge and surging. The bass and drums are high in the mix, creating a thrilling sound; on this occasion, an arms wide, reaching for the light sort of sound – an overture to the heavens, if you will. I intentionally use the word "overture", because there is a neo-classical element present here; the soundscape is immense and the female voice almost operatic. One section of the track is spoken by a child, and, bucking a well-established trend, the fact that this is neither cloying nor cute has to count as something of an achievement in itself!

80
WOULD I LIE TO YOU
CHARLES AND EDDIE
CAPITOL

Serving up a slice of retro-soul, which nevertheless had enough modern R&B stylings to make this delicious record contemporary, previously unknown New Yorkers Charles and Eddie managed to hit the pinnacle of the UK pop chart. 'Would I Lie To You' was a sumptuous duet from a pair of smooth-voiced soulsters; close your eyes and this could have been Marvin Gaye and Al Green combining talents and entwining voices. Supported by a grooving bass, drums, piano and sweet-soaring harmonies, this was irresistible – the string-driven hook of the chorus will remain forever firmly locked inside my mind.

79
STAY
SHAKESPEARE'S SISTER
LONDON

Taking inspiration from *Cat-Woman of the Moon* – a 1953 B-movie – the female duo who comprised Shakespeare's Sister intended to come up with a suite of songs all written from the point of view of various characters in the film; 'Stay' came out of this process and it was written by Siobhan Fahey, her then husband Dave Stewart and Marcella Detroit. It is a ballad of epic proportions, concerning the alien Cat-Woman's love for a human, and it walks a fine line between feelings of tenderness and obsession. Mostly sung by Marcella Detroit, her voice angelic and tinged with melancholia, there is a devotional, almost gospel quality to the piece, though at the mid-point of the song, Siobhan Fahey enters proceedings and, accompanied by crashing heavy percussion, she provides a rough and tough counterpoint. The drama is immense, daring and chilling, transforming what could have been a conventional ballad squarely into the realms of dark theatricality.

78
MINDSTREAM
MEAT BEAT MANIFESTO
PLAY IT AGAIN SAM
OTHER SINGLE 1992:
EDGE OF NO CONTROL

By this point in time, Meat Beat Manifesto was simply a name attached to the solo work of Jack Dangers, who had steered away from harsh, industrial electronica, into a more palatable dance-centric approach. 'Mindstream' underlined this change of direction and showcased an eccentric melodicism and adherence to song structure which had not previously been apparent. Featuring floor-friendly rhythms, Hawaiian guitar and a charmingly restrained vocal, 'Mindstream' was rather excellent.

77
QUESTIONS IN A WORLD OF BLUE
JULEE CRUISE
WARNER BROTHERS

This year saw the release of the movie *Twin Peaks: Fire Walk With Me*, and in turn, that meant we were gifted this delicate, desolate sounding torch song from the pens of David Lynch and Angelo Badalamenti. Heartbreakingly sung by Julee Cruise, this is a gossamer thin piece of music which floats, ghost-like, into our ears, yet the ethereal majesty and deep emotion invested into the performance make this a most remarkable record.

76
IF MY HOMIE CALLS
2PAC
INTERSCOPE

The incredibly mature 2Pac was a mere twenty-years old when he wrote and recorded this track examining the bond between true friends, the loyalty that is a given and the responsibility of being ready and willing to help a friend in need. Delivered in a straight and serious manner, and accompanied by a lean, mean and rocking rhythm, he spoke his truth without compromise, and manifestly displayed his boundless potential to grow as an artist.

75
CONFETTI/MY DRUG BUDDY
LEMONHEADS
ATLANTIC
OTHER SINGLE 1992: IT'S A SHAME ABOUT RAY

Evan Dando was the troubadour of choice for the grunge era – his generation's James Taylor, if you like. His band, Lemonheads, filled a lemon-sized hole in the scene by providing easy-on-the-ear, jangly guitar pop, with a hint of sensitivity thrown in. This double A-sided single contains a pair of their finest ever moments; 'Confetti' is Badfingeresque power-pop, with a lively guitar solo to considerably raise the temperature, whilst 'My Drug Buddy' borrows a groove and an atmosphere from The Band's *Music from Big Pink* era, in a sincere salute to the camaraderie that exists between stoners.

74
OUTER SPACE
3DS
FLYING NUN

The startling flow of genius records released by Flying Nun Records – from the tiny New Zealand city of Dunedin – was simply not abating, and noise pop practitioners The 3Ds were the latest in a long line of bands to fill my ears with fantastic and energetic left-field pop. They display a distinct debt to The Pixies, although the vibe is cheerful rather than intense. Vocals are gleefully chanted, and the guitar, right upfront in the mix, exemplifies a beautiful, childlike playfulness with its nursery rhyme rhythm riffage.

73
ALL IN MY MIND
THE VERVE
HUT

'All In My Mind' was the first single released by The Verve. This band from Wigan were totally immersed in the sounds of deep, dark, consciousness expanding psychedelia. Here, guitarist Nick McCabe spins a spider's web of sound that shoots off at spiky angles, while the singer, known as Mad Richard, whispers and squeals his doom-laden, cosmic lyrics. It would have been easy to scoff at such a retro concept, but the band delivered with such steadfast conviction and sincerity that it was hard not to be impressed.

72
CLUB LONELY
LIL LOUIS
FFRR

Lil Louis was a big part of the Chicago house movement; he had deejayed, run his own club (called *The Future*) and collaborated with Marshall Jefferson on production work. In 1989, his single 'French Kiss' had been a massive hit… but to his credit, he did not churn out safe soundalikes. 'Club Lonely' heralded a stylistic departure towards a jazz sound; he used live musicians on the track, rather than pure electronics, and had Joi Cardwell provide a peerlessly cool and sophisticated vocal. The track is one of unadulterated joy; it pops, snaps and it is fleet-footed. The entirety sounds effortless in every respect, and yet this record bump-started an evolution in the house music genre.

71
WHAT YOU DO TO ME
TEENAGE FANCLUB
CREATION

With its sub-two minute playing time and repeated, minimalist lyric, this could be considered a somewhat insubstantial single. But countering that is the big warm-heartedness of Norman Blake's vocal performance and the hugeness of the guitar riff that underpins the song, which is epic and melodic in equal measure.

In my lifetime, I have not heard too many songs that can fill me up with a golden glow in the way that 'What You Do To Me' does.

70
PRETEND WE'RE DEAD
L7
SLASH

As vocalist/guitarist Donita Sparks adopted a stance of "fierceness and humour over vulnerability"; here, with 'Pretend We're Dead', she put that credo to good use in her songwriting. Having split-up with a boyfriend, she discovered that, for her, the best way of dealing with the fallout was to pretend that he was dead. Produced by Butch Vig – who gave the band a similar sonic pop/punk punchiness to that he had provided for Nirvana – L7's power is channelled into a rolling and churning riff; the guitar solos are clean and melodic, and the lead vocal is performed devoid of emotion, whilst around it, other voices chatter excitedly like those of a nagging conscience.

69
YA MAMA
THE PHARCYDE
DELICIOUS VINYL

The Pharcyde were from Los Angeles, and they debuted with this incredible sounding single that pushed the envelope in alt-hip-hop further and further away from orthodoxy. The beats they employed were spacey and sparse, and from that launchpad, they rapped a series of jokey putdowns with impressive rhythmic and poetic skill.

68
NEXT IS THE E
MOBY
INSTINCT

Here we have the original title of the single on its American label; in the UK, due to the (correct) assumption of "E" referring to the drug ecstasy, the song was re-named 'I Feel It' and released by Equator Records. The track is a riot of uptempo house piano, chattering techno beats, a speeded-up male voice and a dramatic female vocal performance. All-in-all, this brilliantly captures the feeling sweeping through the rave scene… a complete euphoric rush.

67
WHERE'S ME JUMPER
SULTANS OF PING FC
DIVINE
OTHER SINGLES 1992: STUPID KID; VERONICA

Named after, with sacrilegious glee, 'Sultans of Swing' by Dire Straits, this band from Cork dropped this abstract and absurd anthem that was a haphazard juxtaposition of weedy Adam and the Ants drum beat, AC/DC power chords and a whining, juvenile Mark E. Smith soundalike, mouthing the meaningless, but very amusing lyric. It was fabulous!

66

BLUE ROOM

THE ORB

BIG LIFE

OTHER SINGLE 1992: ASSASSIN

With a running time of thirty-nine minutes and fifty-seven seconds, 'Blue Room' is the longest ever single to enter the UK chart, and it managed to reach number eight. The title of the track references Wright-Patterson Air Force Base, where supposedly, a "Blue Room" is used as a holding facility for UFO evidence. Be that as it may, this is a mind-trip of a record; an extra-terrestrial excursion into sound, both soothing and stimulating, that is an absolute pleasure to undertake.

65

SCENARIO

A TRIBE CALLED QUEST

JIVE

Life-affirming, joyful and playful music seemed to flow from the grooves of records by A Tribe Called Quest – and 'Scenario' had all of those qualities… and more besides. Insanely catchy, with plenty of bounce to the ounce, 'Scenario' was a posse cut incorporating members of rap group Leaders of the New School, whose member Busta Rhymes first broke into the public consciousness with his show-stealing verse. To the eccentrically funky rhythm track, colour was provided via samples of 'Oblighetto' by Brother Jack McDuff, and 'Little Miss Lover' by Jimi Hendrix; the net result was a slice of rap that put a great big smile on people's faces.

64

A LOVE FROM OUTER SPACE

A.R. KANE

LUAKA BOP

At the time of its release, when Ibiza held sway as party-central and a lot of music was aimed specifically at that market, much was made of the Balearic flavouring of this track. Listened to now, when the cultural baggage has been removed and the music can judged on its true merit – rather than through a prism of fashionability – it is a lovely, tropical-tinged piece of dance pop. It displays a lightness of touch in both performance and production; there is no hint that any of the participants are trying too hard to please. On the contrary, it displays a spontaneity that is highly refreshing; it teeters on the edge of eccentricity and definitely adds a dash of brightness to the day.

63

KNOW THE LEDGE

ERIC B & RAKIM

4TH & BROADWAY

OTHER SINGLES 1992:
DON'T SWEAT THE TECHNIQUE; CASUALTIES OF WAR; WHAT'S ON YOUR MIND

Featured on the soundtrack for the film *Juice*, and also on Eric B & Rakim's album *Don't Sweat The Technique*, the duo used a highly distinctive bass line that was sampled from the Nat Adderley track 'Rise, Sally Rise'. Rakim, who largely instigated the track, then played live drums to create an original rhythm, over which he displays his rhyming ability as he shares a first-person narrative account of a neighbourhood thug who comes to realise the consequences of his violent and desperate lifestyle. The rhymes flow gracefully in tight combination with the killer rhythm. Here, Eric B & Rakim had created a slice of hip-hop noir storytelling that was worthy of Iceberg Slim himself.

62
STOCKHOLM
NEW FAST AUTOMATIC DAFFODILS
PLAY IT AGAIN SAM
OTHER SINGLE 1992:
IT'S NOT WHAT YOU KNOW

Manchester's New Fast Automatic Daffodils didn't fit into any little box. They were not easily categorised, but their idiosyncrasies made their music powerful and often fascinating; 'Stockholm' is both of those things and more besides. It has a gritty, insistent guitar phrase that gets under the skin, a funky bongo-driven beat, arresting sing/speak vocals from Andy Spearpoint, intriguing lyrics and a momentous hook that lands like a sucker punch.

61
A GOOD IDEA
SUGAR
CREATION
OTHER SINGLES 1992:
CHANGES; HELPLESS

Since the disbanding of Hüsker Dü, the more gentle and introspective sound of Bob Mould's solo career had yielded poor sales, leading to him being dropped by his record label. To survive, he undertook a nine-month tour of Europe where he wrote a bunch of songs that would suit a band, and sure enough, at the end of the tour, he formed Sugar, a high-powered but melodic rock trio. 'A Good Idea' shows the group off to perfection; there is an immediacy to their sound, an energetic rush that never becomes thrash but always retains a pop heart. Stylistically, it sits somewhere between Buzzcocks and Nirvana, which, of course, in terms of musical evolution, is precisely where Mould had previously been as part of Hüsker Dü. It is ironic that in order to re-energise, he found himself having to look backwards as a way of moving forwards.

60
IT'S A FINE DAY
OPUS 111
PWL INTERNATIONAL

Written by Edward Barton when he was living at Hulme Crescents in Manchester – a housing development which exemplified the phrase "planners dream wrong" – 'It's A Fine Day' was sung *a cappella* by Jane Lancaster (Barton's girlfriend) and released as a single in 1983, garnering much love and praise. Fast forward, and the song was picked up by Opus 111 who gave it a full instrumental backing, whilst using only the first verse and chorus. This new treatment was absolutely enchanting; it took the original version's feel of a child's lullaby, and married it to a superb house rhythm. It was shot through with rays of glorious sunshine, and the bird-like quality of Kirsty Hawkshaw's singing was just pure pleasure to listen to.

59
PEDOPHILE
THEE HEADCOATS
CLAWFIST
OTHER NOTEWORTHY SINGLE 1992: HAVE LOVE WILL TRAVEL; MY DEAR MR WATSON; HEADCOAT LANE

In the same way that Link Wray's 'Rumble' was the epitome of malevolence, this is a brooding and darkly violent slide-guitar instrumental piece that powerfully brings to mind the shadowy depths and depravity of the pedophile. The cover displayed a photograph of a man who was the childhood abuser of Billy Childish, plainly showing that this was a record that dared to bare its teeth and bite back; a record that demonstrates that, in this case, the child refuses to be the victim and is instead an unashamed survivor of adult evil.

58
CALL MR. LEE
TELEVISION
FONTANA

After being absent for more than a decade, Television – the most iconic of all the late 1970s CBGB's bands – made a welcome return, and here, on 'Call Mr. Lee', all the old magic is shown to be intact; the rhythm section is locked into a tight groove, providing a platform for the twin lead guitar excellence of Tom Verlaine and Richard Lloyd. The song itself twists and turns, coils and uncoils; it is sharp-edged but the heart is softer and quite playful. Verlaine's singing style is as nonchalantly cool as it ever was, as he pours forth a fantastical lyric that alludes to espionage and a communist dog. This is snappy, angular and abstract… and fully in keeping with the best moments of vintage-era Television.

57
SON OF SAM/BENT
JON SPENCER BLUES EXPLOSION
IN THE RED RECORDINGS
OTHER SINGLES 1992: SHIRT JAC/LATCH ON; RECORDED IN PERSON

After Pussy Galore splintered, guitarist Jon Spencer played short-term stints with Gibson Brothers, Boss Hog and The Honeymoon Killers. In the latter band, he encountered Judah Bauer and Russell Simins; the three musicians enjoyed playing together and so The Blues Explosion was formed. This early single has one side devoted to the serial killer *Son of Sam*; it is unhinged and ferocious, boasting a raw, rockabilly rhythm and Stooges-style saxophone sprayed across its surface as Spencer rages hoarsely in quasi-demented style. On the flip-side, 'Bent' is more of the same, but played in an even wilder style, reminiscent of Sonny Burgess, whose nearly forgotten 1950s singles for Sun Records had been a benchmark in untamed, raw talent.

56
GASOLINE MAN
YOUNG GODS
PIAS
OTHER SINGLE 1992: SKIN-FLOWERS

The Swiss band Young Gods created music that combined industrial/metal with techno beats and a very European sensibility; however, here on 'Gasoline Man' – produced by Roli Mosimann – they turn their gaze towards America and play the kind of bar-room boogie that we associate with the mid-west, and they sing about that most holy of American totems… the gas-guzzling automobile. This is a very successful melding of two cultures, and the differing musical approaches of the two continents combine to provide a foot jammed on the accelerator ride, that is pulsating and exhilarating.

55
HALCYON
ORBITAL
FFRR

Using a prominent, back-tracked sample from 'It's a Fine Day' by Opus111 as a base, a further sample from 'Leave it' by Yes is then introduced. These play out over a repetitive drum-machine beat that is so light it feels as if it could simply float away… only the mechanised rhythm anchors the piece, which evokes a kind of *Groundhog Day* horror, a quiet suburban nightmare that Paul Hartnoll imagined his mother was locked-into when she became addicted to the prescribed tranquiliser Halcion (Triazolam). Hartnoll dedicated the record to his mother, and the video (which depicted Kirsty from Opus111 as a lost housewife, oblivious to the mundanity of her semi-detached existence) made the meaning of the track entirely explicit.

54
ONE
U2
ISLAND
OTHER SINGLES 1992: WHO'S GONNA RIDE YOUR WILD HORSES; EVEN BETTER THAN THE REAL THING

As U2 were recording the album that would become *Achtung Baby*, tensions were rising and tempers fraying. This disunity could very easily have led to the group calling it a day; but instead, out of an improvised guitar piece, this song was built. With a lyric concerning the conflicts within the band – and finding the resolve to work through them – the song gradually took shape. Played at mid-tempo, with an abundance of added layers and textures grafted onto the bare bones, 'One' becomes a quite fascinating listen. Released as a fund-raising single to benefit research into the AIDS virus, this was a record that straightened-out all the wobbles in U2's ranks, and proved what a vital and essential unit they still were.

53
RHYTHM IS A DANCER
SNAP
ARISTA

'Snap' were a German Euro-house outfit who had scored a major hit with 'The Power'... and then had all but disappeared; 'Rhythm Is A Dancer' soon put an end to that. It was a monumental and inescapable anthemic hit that delivered with a mighty wallop from the opening, dancing synthesiser pattern, through a science-fiction themed lyric to the almost melancholic piano outro. Fronted by the American pair, singer extraordinaire Thea Austin – whose performance was a masterclass of powerful soul – and rapper Turbo B, who delivered his lines with liquid smoothness, this record was as sweet and frothy as a cascading soda-pop fountain.

52
TIMEBOMB
808 STATE
ZZT

A creepy voice utters a single word... 'Timebomb'... and then 808 State serve up an electrical storm over hip-hop beats; this is spine-tingling stuff, uptempo and full of zest. Vocoder voices hark back to the New York electro of the early-1980s that had so inspired 808 State, although in this single they act as no more than a nod of recognition in what is otherwise a track that is absolutely jam-packed with ideas and daring.

51
STRAIGHT TO YOU
NICK CAVE AND BAD SEEDS
MUTE
OTHER SINGLES 1992:
I HAD A DREAM JOE; WHAT A WONDERFUL WORLD (WITH SHANE MACGOWAN)

Deep, dark and totally arresting, every word and every sentence an arrow to the heart – nothing here is wasteful. The imagery conjured up is captivating, and the craftsmanship of the songwriting is immaculate. Musically, there is nothing overly complicated going on; it is a basic blues/gospel piece, with swells to accentuate certain parts of the song, and a thin, reedy organ that is akin to a constant itching of the skin, preventing any listener from getting too comfortable and imagining that this is entering MOR territory. Cave's baritone, which carries the fire and brimstone of a Baptist preacher, is an expression of latent power which simmers with concealed emotion.

50
SENSE
THE LIGHTNING SEEDS
VIRGIN
OTHER SINGLE 1992: THE LIFE OF RILEY

Written by Ian Broudie with ex-Specials and Fun Boy Three frontman Terry Hall (who also makes a vocal appearance) 'Sense' has a northern soul vibe with baroque flourishes. There is a wistfulness about the song that strikes an emotional chord, and the harmonica solo, at the mid-point of the song, sounds like the devastating torment of a broken heart.

49
MOTHER EARTH
UNDERWORLD
TOMATO

During the late 1980s, 'Underworld' had been a funk/electro band who had released a pair of rather unremarkable albums. In 1991, following the disbandment of the original group, Karl Hyde and Rick Smith recruited DJ Darren Emerson, and, using the incognito names Lemon Interrupt and Steppin' Razor, they released several tracks and also undertook some re-mix work. Amidst this activity, the Underworld name was re-adopted and they transitioned their sound in a techno/dance direction; the metamorphosis was first unveiled with 'Mother Earth'. It was futuristic, clean sounding, attractive and accessible, and with the poetic lyrics of Karl Hyde utilised as a prominent feature, the trio had an indelible uniqueness at a time when other artists were sacrificing their own individuality in an attempt to fit into a compartmentalised box.

48
THE ONLY LIVING BOY IN NEW CROSS
CARTER THE UNSTOPPABLE SEX MACHINE
CHRYSALIS
OTHER SINGLES 1992:
R.U.B.B.I.S.H.; DO RE ME SO FAR SO GOOD;
THE IMPOSSIBLE DREAM

With a title that cheekily parodies Simon & Garfunkel's 'The Only Living Boy in New York', this tale of the marginalised people in society who are forced to live in low-rent misery in an unlovely London suburb put this pair of crusty stalwarts into the UK top-ten. Performed with feeling and empathy for the poor souls depicted in the lyric, the song rattles along briskly on a rhythmic electronic base, with guitars sprayed all over the surface. Actually, it resembles a scruffier, more down-at-heel track by the Pet Shop Boys, which is a great compliment to Carter's impressive tunefulness.

47
REAL COOL WORLD
DAVID BOWIE
WARNER BROTHERS

On what was supposed to be a temporary break from his group Tin Machine, to record a track for the soundtrack of the film *Cool World*, there was a reunion with *Let's Dance* producer Nile Rogers. Although the fruits of their labour couldn't replicate Bowie's former glory, it showed that while he may no longer have been ahead of the curve, he was not lagging too far behind it either. 'Real Cool World' was a dance/ rock hybrid of chattering electronics, wailing guitar, honking saxophone and Bowie's magnificent tenor voice. After a decade of much mediocrity and lack of direction, this single was a clear signpost towards the great man's artistic resurrection.

46
CONNECTED
STEREO MC'S
ISLAND
OTHER SINGLE 1992: STEP IT UP

With relationships between people being severed, and tolerance fast diminishing, 'Connected' was a song which advocated a dismantling of the barriers erected between different races and creeds. It was set to a shuffling, lolloping rhythm that pulls, pushes and ultimately entrances the listener. This is a very persuasive dance-floor invitation that is slightly retro in its use of funky horns, chanted female backing vocals and rapped lyrics, and yet the mix of hip-house stylings and electronic Euro-pop somehow sounded fresh and life-affirming. This earworm seemed to be playing each and every time I climbed into my friend Derek's car as we went to a football match together; it remains forever lodged inside my head.

45
THE CITY SLEEPS
MC 900 FT JESUS
NETTWERK EUROPE

In the city of Baltimore, 'The City Sleeps' caused considerable controversy when an arson spree was attributed by outraged citizens to be a direct result of radio play of the song. Although that explanation was highly unlikely, in the lyric to this single, MC 900 Ft. Jesus (named after a TV evangelist who claimed that he received messages from a giant-sized Jesus figure) does indeed explore the twisted thoughts of a pyromaniac; however, the writing here is pure poetry and the words are delivered in a creepy whisper, accompanied by a down-tempo and jazzy hip-hop track. In summary, a record that is eerie and chillingly atmospheric.

44
OUT OF SPACE
THE PRODIGY
XL
OTHER SINGLES 1992: FIRE/ JERICHO; WIND IT UP (RE-WOUND)

'Out of Space' was an early career highlight for The Prodigy, created by looping a sample of Max Romeo singing 'Chase the Devil' (with The Upsetters) and incorporating a crazed, speeded-up lift from Ultra Magnetic MCs track 'Critical Breakdown'. Then, they married the above to the musical equivalent of riding the waltzers on the fairground to produce a dizzying experience that is just a whole lot of fun.

43
TRIGGER CUT
PAVEMENT
BIG CAT

This quintessential 1990s indie rock

displays Pavement at their finest. Scuzzy guitar and biscuit-tin drums dominate the sound, while Stephen Malkmus sings unfathomably but still manages to evoke something disconcerting and carnivalesque. A sweet chorus of "la-la-las" punctuates the lyrical flow, and then a heavily distorted guitar solo is introduced – charmingly it seems to be no more than an afterthought, though it still sits very well amidst the ramshackle clatter. Eventually, the whole thing comes to a stop before a decidedly odd coda is enigmatically appended to this fabulous, fabulous record.

42
BORN OF FRUSTRATION
JAMES
FONTANA

James were at the peak of their popularity; in this year they headlined a show at Alton Towers to a sold-out crowd of 30,000 people. On the other hand, there were signs that the group was somehow losing its way… losing the subtlety they had once possessed and substituting for it with bombast; thankfully, 'Born of Frustration' displayed the band at their melodically strong and quirky best. With mariachi-style trumpets used as a herald, in comes Tim Booth who sings – with wonderful purity – a parable on the Buddhist principle of suffering originating from desire. "La-la-la" hooks add a soupçon of sweetness, and finally, my old school chum Larry Gott plays a coruscating guitar outro to bring the song to a most dramatic close.

41
SET YOU FREE
N-TRANCE
WHITE LABEL

'Set You Free' was a real DIY success story. The song was inspired by a sweaty night out at The Haçienda in its packed-out, glory days. N-Trance member Kevin O'Toole was passed a pint of water by a woman whose heartbeat could be felt through her top. He and fellow member Dale Longworth searched for a singer and were hipped to Kelly Llorenna, a sixteen-year old college girl, and a bedroom recording subsequently took place. 'Set You Free' opens with a dramatic thunderclap effect followed by a powerful and uplifting vocal; then the song simply hurtles along, a high-tempo rave tune that is hands-in-the-air euphoric. This irresistible track was already well-known by the time it was officially released (in 1994) when it crossed over from clubland to become a huge, mainstream hit.

40
MEDICATION
SPIRITUALIZED
DEDICATED
OTHER SINGLES 1992:
RUN; I WANT YOU

Jason Pierce was attempting to meld a whole raft of influences as he sought to create a psychedelic music that wasn't simply an imitation of 1960s sounds… psychedelia for a post-rock age, no less. On the eight-minute plus 'Medication' he takes a giant leap forward; there is a strong gospel element in the introduction, but as the track moves along there are elements of free-jazz mixed in with the kosmische of early 1970s German music, as well as blazing guitars while Pierce narrates a tale describing the hell of medication addiction.

39
THE LIGHT THAT WILL CEASE TO FAIL
STEREOLAB
BIG MONEY INC
OTHER SINGLES 1992: HARMONIUM/FARFISA; LOW FI

Packing rather more muscle than usual, this is the sound of Stereolab locating a groove and driving along it – at full-throttle – to quite exhilarating effect. Add in the cool sounding, but impossible to decipher musings of the angelic voiced Laetitia Sadier, and what results is wonderful pop that has been touched by magic.

38
POPPA LARGE
ULTRAMAGNETIC MCs
MERCURY
OTHER SINGLE 1992: TWO BROTHERS WITH CHECKS

Here we have abstract raps over classic hip-hop beats; this is cram-packed with quotable lines that reference cultural figures and notorious characters such as Prince, Michael Jackson, John McEnroe, Son of Sam, Gary Gilmore and Dracula. The word-flow from Kool Keith is phenomenal, and the entire track is almost bursting at the seams with barely contained raw energy.

37
CHASING A BEE
MERCURY REV
COLUMBIA

Mercury Rev present us with a stinging (ouch!) and highly boisterous single – one part pure child-like simplicity, one part psychedelic chaos – and yet somehow, in aggregate, the track seems to wear a cloak of profound sadness as the meaning of the song is revealed. The subject matter is unhealthy, compulsive behaviour and an inexorable descent into madness… hence the allegorical chorus which concerns 'Chasing a Bee' inside a jar. This is a very disturbing song, but it is made more palatable, indeed, highly appealing, by the sheer loveliness of the arrangement and execution.

36
PROTECT YA NECK
WU TANG CLAN
LOUD

'Protect Ya Neck' is a catchphrase used to advise somebody to be careful and to recognise any potential danger, and it was very effectively used on this debut Wu Tang Clan single, produced by RZA, which brought together eight of the original members of the Clan. Right from the kick-off the group were blazing as the mic gets shared, moving from one distinctive voice to the next, with each one attempting to continually up the ante. This was a hard-hitting rap masterclass, performed over a fantastically lean and mean production.

35
POPSCENE
BLUR
FOOD

Moving away from the generic "baggy" sound of much of their first album, this one-off, stand-alone single showed that Blur were becoming a more confident and individualistic band who were able to express themselves more appropriately, without sacrificing their pop hooks. Here, they bare their teeth and re-position themselves outside the "indie" band herd, who they summarily dismiss as "insignificant". 'Popscene' is louder, rougher, more sarcastic and more daring than we might previously have imagined Blur to be; brass instruments bolster the already powerful chainsaw guitar riffs, while the bass runs amok and the drums, though hit hard, remain nimble and nifty.

34
PAPUA NEW GUINEA
FUTURE SOUND OF LONDON
JUMPIN' & PUMPIN'

Coming from a different perspective than many electronic dance acts, Future Sound of London had revered post-rock Factory Records acts such as ACR and New Order, rather than hip-hop or funk. This led to the group utilising rather unusual resources in the creation of 'Papua New Guinea'; the bass line is sampled from 'Radio Babylon' by Meat Beat Manifesto, and the perfectly chosen vocal sample is Lisa Gerrard from Dead Can Dance's 'Dawn Of The Iconoclast'. This unorthodox approach lends an air of the exotic to proceedings, and 'Papua New Guinea' is a sumptuous record that takes the mind on a trip, far away from mundanity and into lush and warm tranquility.

33
GIRLS ON MY MIND
DAVID BYRNE
LUAKA BOP

David Byrne's first single following the dissolution of Talking Heads offered no radical sonic departure from his last half-decade inside the band; it is extremely catchy and it successfully straddles the line between dumb and smart with typical adroitness. Byrne adopts the language of middle American frat boy turned advertising executive, whose lustful feelings are only barely suppressed. He lampoons his subject's immature obsessiveness as he sings over a bed of Latin-style percussion that adds freshness and rhythmic bounce to what is a superb pop record.

32
HAZY SHADE OF CRIMINAL
PUBLIC ENEMY
DEF JAM
OTHER SINGLES 1992:
LOUDER THAN A BOMB;
THE CURE

By now, we knew exactly what to expect from Public Enemy, but the all-out assault on the senses that was the band's signature style still gave a powerful jolt, still pinned us up against the wall, and still made us pay attention to the litany of grievous injustice and pertinent questions that constituted a Public Enemy lyric. 'Hazy Shade of Criminal' showed the group to be as sharp, poetic and provocative as ever; there was no compromise in terms of sound either – this was most definitely funk with ferocity.

31
BABIES
PULP
GIFT
OTHER SINGLES 1992:
COUNTDOWN;
O.U. (GONE GONE)

Pulp had been inching towards maturity, but with 'Babies', the recognisable and quintessential Pulp sound was finally arrived at in what constituted a great leap forward. The song was initiated by drummer Nick Banks who was playing a riff on Jarvis Cocker's guitar; this inspired the lyricist to create a piece which concerned the misadventures of a boy who hides in the wardrobe of a friend's sister as she engages in sexual shenanigans. Adopting a lighter, poppier and altogether more idiosyncratic sound than ever before, this was a brilliant subversion of the pop form – Pulp had well and truly arrived.

30
DIDGERIDOO
APHEX TWIN
R&S
OTHER SINGLE 1992: XYLEM TUBE

Richard D. James *is* Aphex Twin, but that is only one of many aliases he has adopted in order to release music. His work has been experimental and highly pioneering – right from the very start of his career – and 'Didgeridoo' was the first of his tracks to catch my ear. In fact it had been issued during the previous year (on the *Analog Bubblebath Vol. 2* EP) when it was called 'Aboriginal Mix', but now, with a new title, it was back again. This is a piece of simple perfection; the drone of the didgeridoo is recreated electronically… it relentlessly hums, hisses and buzzes. The track hammers away at an utterly furious tempo, unambiguously capturing the dangerous atmosphere of the Australian outback; it is edgy, frightening and fierce.

29
SHOWGIRL
THE AUTEURS
HUT
OTHER SINGLE 1992:
SHE MIGHT TAKE A TRAIN

A "greed is good" frenzy had taken hold; it reflected what a decade of Mrs Thatcher's Conservative government had done to the principles of the nation's youth – and, of course, the backward-looking Britpop brigade gleefully embraced it. Thank goodness then that along came The Auteurs, led by singer/songwriter Luke Haines. His brand of misanthropically-laced classic pop was the perfect antidote to the cheeky laddishness of many of his peers; his bile a welcome respite from the faux do-gooders who populated the very lucrative music scene. 'Showgirl', the band's first single, was a wonderful mixture of chiming guitars and bittersweet observations on the disappointment lurking beneath the glossy veneer of idealised romanticism. Delivered in a sneering, couldn't-give-a-toss tone that was totally at odds with prevailing trends, The Auteurs had arrived… Praise the Lord!

28
KEROSENE
BIG BLACK
SOUTHERN

Big Black, a group who split up in 1988, recorded and released 'Kerosene' in 1986 on the album *Atomizer*; it became their most iconic song… their equivalent of The Stooges' 'I Wanna Be Your Dog' or Led Zeppelin's 'Kashmir'. In 1992, a handful of twelve-inch single test-pressings somehow reached the public, presumably to tie-in with retrospective album *Pig Pile*. Whatever the provenance, 'Kerosene' certainly deserved a single release and it definitely merits its place in this book. It is, at the same time, the most hypnotically compelling piece in Big Black's oeuvre as well as being one of the bleakest and most chilling songs ever written. It is also wonderfully sung, by a seemingly out-on-the-edge Steve Albini who adopts the mindset of a man looking at life and finding it to be utterly sterile. For something interesting to do, he chooses self-immolation; he chooses death as a preferable option to the continuation of a senseless and futile existence.

27
RELEASE THE PRESSURE
LEFTFIELD
HARD HANDS

It may seem pretty obvious now, but when Leftfield first created this stylistic mash-up between dub reggae and techno, it was considered to be an unusual – if not unique – departure from orthodoxy. Featuring the voices of reggae/ragga singers Earl Sixteen, Papa Dee and Cheshire Cat resonating inside a spacey dub construction, the words co-exist harmoniously with the techno beats to yield a track of vast, luminescent quality.

26
MR WENDELL
ARRESTED DEVELOPMENT
CHRYSALIS
OTHER SINGLES 1992:
TENNESSEE;
PEOPLE EVERYDAY;
REVOLUTION

Arrested Development were a band from Atlanta, Georgia and they reacted against the negativity of the popular gangsta-rap style by featuring a non-macho spirituality and positivity in their music. 'Mr Wendell' was typical of the sensitivity that was an inherent quality of the group; it concerned a homeless man, and the lyric pointed out the finer qualities that he possessed, along with others in his position… the non-materialistic lifestyle and hard-won wisdom are celebrated as an example to follow. Fabulously catchy and bright, with a sample of Sly and the Family Stone's 'Sing a Simple Song' used in a brilliantly creative way, 'Mr Wendell' was a record full of love; it was gentle, compassionate and quite beautiful.

25
MOTORCYCLE EMPTINESS
MANIC STREET PREACHERS
COLUMBIA
OTHER SINGLES 1992: SLASH 'N' BURN; LOVE'S SWEET EXILE

Going somewhat easier on the throttle than was usual, Manic Street Preachers presented us with this luscious single which is concerned with the hollowness of life controlled by capitalist dogma and its self-perpetuating reliance on consumerism. Using imagery inspired by *Rumble Fish* (the S.E. Hinton novel that spawned Francis Ford Coppola's film about biker gangs) 'Motorcycle Emptiness' rides on a rock-solid drum track, tuneful lead guitar lines and even plucked violins. Alongside this newfound grandiosity, James Dean Bradfield sings with confident accomplishment. This was an ambitious song for a young band to experiment with; the Manics pulled it off with aplomb, proving that they were more than just Johnny-come-lately punk-rock wannabes.

24
TWIN PEAKS THEME
ANGELO BADALAMENTI
WARNER BROTHERS

From the opening, ominous, naked guitar figure, to the mournful descending bass-line, this music has me ensnared, hook, line and sinker. Add to this the swell of the strings, and now I am entirely sucked into the weird, wonderful and fantastical world of David Lynch.

23
JUMP AROUND
HOUSE OF PAIN
TOMMY BOY

Using a beat created by DJ Muggs of Cypress Hill, who, at that point, declined to use it himself, House of Pain were the grateful beneficiaries. The song contains a series of great moments; from the opening horn fanfare taken from Bob & Earl's 'Harlem Shuffle', to the sixty-six separate occasions that a high-pitched squeal punctuates the track. The melding of rock and rap creates a high-energy feel, perfect for the rapidly delivered lyrics that are full of bravado and which lead into the big on bounce choruses – 'Jump Around' is unquestionably a sure-fire party starter.

22
MONEY DON'T MATTER 2 NITE
PRINCE AND THE NEW POWER GENERATION
PAISLEY PARK
OTHER SINGLES 1992: THUNDER; SEXY MF; MY NAME IS PRINCE

Here is Prince with something important to say, though he is unhurried and the tempo is kept slow. The smooth sound nods towards 1970s Philly-soul with its laid-back groove, and the gorgeous, melodic choruses provide a sweet sugar-coating too. All of this acts as clever counterpoint to the message concerning greed and poverty, and there is also a subtle reference to the horrors of the Gulf War written into the lyric as well. The singer handles the song with noteworthy restraint, although more emotional backing vocals do inject urgency and passion into proceedings. Amidst the magnificence of Prince's numerous hit records, this one is a grossly underrated jewel.

21
THEY REMINISCE OVER YOU (T.R.O.Y.)
PETE ROCK & C.L. SMOOTH
ELEKTRA
OTHER SINGLE 1992: STRAIGHTEN IT OUT

Mourning the tragic and accidental death of their friend, Trouble T Roy of Heavy D & The Boyz, Pete Rock & C.L. Smooth remember loved ones, and over bass and saxophone samples from Tom Scott's jazz/funk version of Jefferson Airplane's song 'Today', word pictures of growing-up are fondly related by C.L. Smooth, while Pete Rock provides the ad-libs. This is rightly considered to be a classic of 1990s hip-hop; 'They Reminisce Over You', whilst never resorting to sentimentality, still carries a huge emotional charge.

20
ONLY SHALLOW
MY BLOODY VALENTINE
CREATION

'Only Shallow' turned out to be the final single release from My Bloody Valentine; it was recorded over a two-year period, across several studios, and it was also the opening track on the album *Loveless*. This is a masterclass in sonic manipulation and dynamics; Kevin Shields does incredible things with his "Glide guitar" technique and controlled feedback between the verses, where Bilinda Butcher sings the mournful lyric with a sombre edge to her voice, as Colm Ó Cíosóig drums with precision and economy. The track perplexingly shifts in both volume and feel; it is disorientating as we are tilted from one extreme to another. This is a thoroughly exhilarating record that really sets the pulse racing.

19
START CHOPPIN'
DINOSAUR JR
BLANCO Y NEGRO
OTHER SINGLE 1992: GET ME

'Start Choppin'' is ultra-catchy guitar pop – the lead guitar line is a magnificent ear-worm, and as J Mascis delivers an audacious, but captivating vocal, he kicks convention well and truly in the teeth, singing in a much higher register than his voice is comfortable with… so even if the vocal does challenge orthodox notions of what is good and bad, the guitar playing is well beyond criticism; two intense, red-hot solos of great skill are just awe-inspiring, and they contribute hugely in making this a truly glorious record .

18
LANGUAGE OF VIOLENCE
DISPOSABLE HEROES OF HIPHOPRISY
4TH & BROADWAY
OTHER SINGLE 1992: LIVE TELEVISION

Written in an easy-to-follow narrative style, 'Language of Violence' tells the sad story of a boy being bullied at school; he is taunted with dehumanising insults – "faggot", "sissy", "punk", "queen", "queer" – until finally the mob physically attack him, and in the barrage of blows, with blood flowing, he dies. One of the mob is tried, convicted and sentenced to an adult prison; the tables are now turned and he has become the weak and vulnerable one who gets picked on. The insults he hurled at *his* victim are now used against *him* – the cycle of violence has revolved and so he must reap what he has sowed. There are no victors in this story; everybody involved is sucked into the violence and has to pay a heavy price. Michael Franti narrates with clarity and concision over an ominous electrical storm, that swirls round and around and around.

17
TWISTERELLA
RIDE
CREATION
OTHER SINGLE 1992: LEAVE THEM ALL BEHIND

This is a record dominated by thrilling guitars that almost seem to generate heat; the drums, equally magnificent, are matched by a superlative Motown-esque bass-line, and the singing is other-worldly and dreamy… just like a sugar-rush, this sweet confection makes me feel good. The title is a reference to a song that was featured in the 1963 film *Billy Liar*, and 'Twisterella' caught Ride at the very peak of their powers, before tensions between group members reared their heads and relationships began to sour.

16
DRIVE
R.E.M.
WARNER BROTHERS
OTHER SINGLE 1992: MAN ON THE MOON

If you like music to be understated, enigmatic, mysterious, and yet somehow poignant, 'Drive' should definitely be on your playlist; it is the opening track and first single taken from the album *Automatic for the People*. In the lyric there is a critical – albeit cryptic – reference to George W. Bush, alongside nods to 'Rock On' by David Essex. However here it is the ambience created by the musicians that is the outstanding feature of the track, as an almost folk-style guitar rides upon the dense and snaking rhythmic interplay between bass and drums.

15
DEEPER AND DEEPER
MADONNA
SIRE
OTHER SINGLE 1992:
EROTICA

'Deeper and Deeper' is a brilliant dance single that has genuine depth, alongside a raft of daring and unusual musical features. Lyrically the song deals – in first person narrative – with overwhelming sexual desire… and it contains hooks in the chorus that come with talons attached. Performed, for the most part, in a disco/house style, this is lively, uptempo and effectively irresistible, and the introduction of a bolero-style bridge, replete with flamenco guitar and castanets, is a truly audacious master stroke.

14
REVERENCE
THE JESUS AND MARY CHAIN
BLANCO Y NEGRO
OTHER SINGLES 1992:
FAR GONE AND OUT;
ALMOST GOLD

Banned from a slot on *Top Of The Pops* because of lyrics that were deemed to be offensive – "I want to die just like Jesus Christ" being the chief culprit – 'Reverence' displayed all the antagonistic devilment of former times; it returned the band's sound to the fractiousness of their early days, and it was unapologetically abrasive. However, underpinning the guitar noise here were programmed dance beats; the pop classicism remained intact because the Reid brothers had always been arch tunesmiths as well as sonic terrorists, but now, on top of those invaluable attributes, they really grooved too!

13
HALF TIME
NASTY NAS
RUFFHOUSE

Nineteen-year old Nas first revealed his precocious talent with this fast and furious rap, which was produced by Large Professor from seminal New York rap group Main Source. They cooked-up a track that was heavily percussive and clean – apart from some eerie horn flourishes – and Nas rapped over the beats, throwing down memorable line after memorable line, revealing in the process that (amongst others) he liked Marcus Garvey, Malcolm X and The

Jackson 5. His fondness for reefer is also stated, as is his self-confidence… and in my view, he quite rightly places great faith in his own abilities. This single showcased an undeniable talent, and two-years later the track was included on *Illmatic*, the first Nas LP, considered by many to be the finest hip-hop album of all time.

12
HARVEST MOON
NEIL YOUNG
REPRISE
OTHER SINGLE 1992: WAR OF MAN

Written in tribute to his wife Pegi, this lovely and loving song was a celebration of mature love and the longevity of relationships. Although it is somewhat artlessly presented, it is that very artlessness which adds to the feeling of sincerity within the lyric. Played on acoustic guitar, with brushed drums and pedal steel guitar adding further warmth to the track, Linda Ronstadt proves to be a perfect vocal foil for Young, contributing some quite beautiful harmonies. The song plays like a gentle, romantic waltz, and a bright, illuminating harvest moon is magically evoked.

11
FRIDAY I'M IN LOVE
THE CURE
FICTION
OTHER SINGLES 1992:
A LETTER TO ELISE; HIGH

In this period, The Cure were in one of their imperious pop stages, and they released a run of attractive and outstanding singles, of which this is the best. 'Friday I'm in Love' was a glorious, happy, unashamedly romantic and sweetly naive song… truly the icing on top of the cake. It is delicious, fizzy pop, and a jolly sing-along that was played in a more upbeat fashion than originally intended, gaining even further zip following a happy accident with a vari-speed recorder. For good reason, this is the Cure single that everybody knows and remembers.

10
VISIONS OF YOU
JAH WOBBLE'S INVADERS
OF THE HEART
OVAL

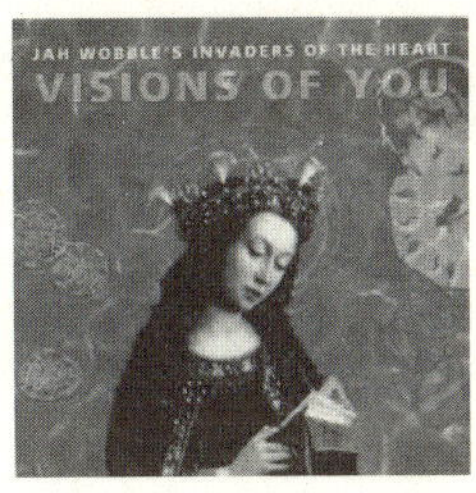

The world of music knows no boundaries, and so, on a sound journey through the imagination, we are transported to the foothills of the Himalayas, and, via the bass, we also travel to Kingston, Jamaica. In addition, downtempo western beats are incorporated too, and mellowness envelopes us like the effects of a narcotic. Wobble provides an elastic bass sound that underpins the record, as he sing/speaks lyrics of a spiritual bent, and his deadpan voice is sweetened by the presence of Sinead O'Connor as featured guest vocalist.

9
FREE RANGE
THE FALL
FONTANA/COG SINISTER
OTHER SINGLE 1992: ED'S BABE

The Fall were generally regarded as an album band, but although it is true that all of their LPs did contain gems, most were a little bit patchy. On the other hand, their singles tended to be consistently excellent, and top-forty hit 'Free Range' was quite superb. It was written by Mark E. Smith and drummer Simon Wolstencroft, though the sound was created by new keyboard-playing band member Dave Bush, who constructed a juddering and abrasive techno track, even daring to use previously forbidden click-tracks and sequencers, greatly against the better judgment of curmudgeonly band leader Smith who opted to retreat to the pub. Despite his fit of pique, Smith's lyric was prescient in predicting the coming war in Europe, as Yugoslavia began to disintegrate due to internal ethnic resentments, and his vocal performance was simply a masterclass of timing and understated ego-free reportage.

8
100%
SONIC YOUTH
DGC
OTHER SINGLE 1992:
YOUTH AGAINST FASCISM

'100%' is a song full of abstract imagery, difficult to fathom, but it relates to the senseless murder of Joe Cole, a friend of Sonic Youth and a roadie for Black Flag. It is loud, garage rock, with a prominent dumb – but great – guitar riff that is sleazily played with scuzz seeming to ooze out from the feeding-back amplifiers. Thurston Moore sings hoarsely, practically spitting out the violent lyric in order to properly emphasise the horror that he is verbalising.

7
JOIN OUR CLUB/PEOPLE GET REAL
SAINT ETIENNE
HEAVENLY
OTHER SINGLE 1992: AVENUE

After their record label refused to countenance the release of 'People Get Real' as a stand-alone single (on the grounds that it wasn't sufficiently commercial sounding), Saint Etienne cold-bloodedly set about constructing the most public-pleasing offering imaginable, and the result was 'Join Our Club', a delicious production that has a lyric full of lovingly placed references to favourite tunes; songs by The Flamin' Groovies, The Lovin' Spoonful, Nirvana and Jimi Hendrix are all seamlessly woven into place. With its frothy summer-flavoured sound, veering between twee 1960s pop and cutting-edge dance beats, 'Join Our Club' was irresistible – an ear-worm chorus, invitingly sung by Sarah Cracknell, made this an absolutely unstoppable hit.

6
THE DROWNERS
SUEDE
NUDE

OTHER SINGLE 1992: METAL MICKEY

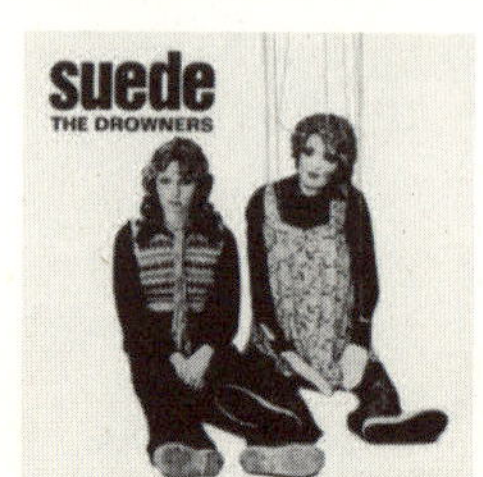

There was a whiff of sedition about Suede, as they emerged, fully-formed, with this debut single. It was not just the fact that they were stick-thin, or the pouting lips and razor-edge cheekbones, nor even the mix of grubbiness and grandeur… it was the way that this appearance fed into their sound. 'The Drowners' was a raucous melodrama, played out over Bernard Butler's re-appropriated glam-rock guitar riff that stung as well as it stuttered, while singer Brett Anderson channelled his inner Ziggy Stardust for a flamboyant crooning of sexually ambiguous lyrics. For a first single by a young band, this was staggering stuff; it had poise and it swaggered with a coquettish self-confidence. With 'The Drowners', Suede came, saw and conquered, and the UK musical landscape had to be re-drawn in their wake.

5

SHEELA-NA-GIG

P.J. HARVEY

TOO PURE

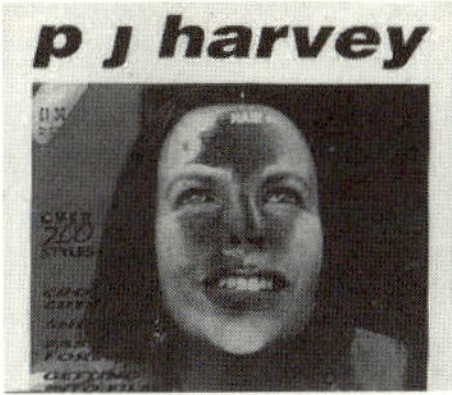

Written entirely by front person Polly Jean Harvey, this song references the grotesque Sheela Na Gig statues of naked women which are found on buildings all over Britain and Ireland. The image is compatible with the self-loathing felt by the song's narrator, who offers herself to a man, who in turn dismisses her as unclean and an exhibitionist. The disturbing nature of the song creates a crackling tension that is viscerally played-out with startling élan by Harvey, as she coos and whispers the verses, only to abruptly erupt in righteous fury as she hits the chorus. The vocal is amply matched by the dramatic music that surrounds it, veering from almost minimalist folk stylings to brutal guitar power-chords over a hard-driving rhythm. The intensity of this three-minute performance is utterly compelling.

4
CREEP
RADIOHEAD
EMI

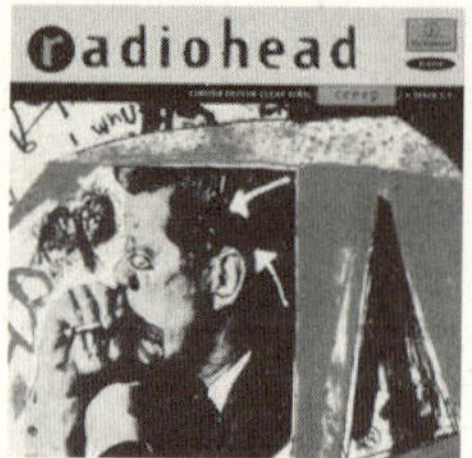

Famously, Radiohead don't like 'Creep'; for them, it became something of an albatross around the neck, so untypical of anything else they have done that its ultimate success created a burden of narrow expectation from people who urged them to replicate it. However I love the song; I remember buying it in a record shop in Hyde (Greater Manchester) purely on a whim – an unknown song by an unknown band. When I got it home, I played it, and then I played it again, over and over, again and again. The track was written by Thom Yorke in his student days, about a girl he was, initially, obsessed with, only to come to the painful realisation that they were incompatible, and even the places she liked to frequent made him feel ugly, out of place and uncomfortable. The piece is moody and it slithers along slowly, until we reach the chorus; now, Jonny Greenwood – who genuinely loathed the song – attempts to sabotage it with blasts of terrifying guitar noise. Ironically, this act of vandalism backfires spectacularly, as it proves to be the stunning counterpoint to the unsettling mawkishness of the verses.

3
SLOW DOG
BELLY
4AD

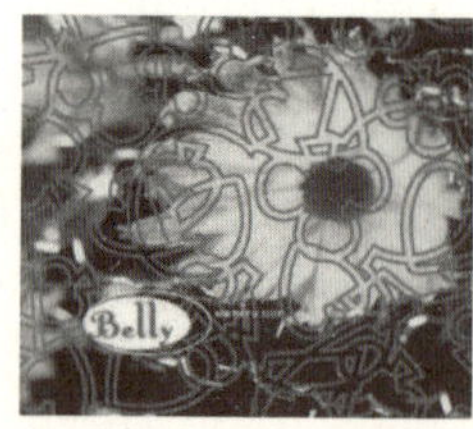

Tanya Donnelly was a member of The Breeders, along with Kim Deal, but the latter's commitments to tour with her other band (The Pixies) put The Breeders on hold. This unfortunate situation left Donnelly with a difficult choice to make; either wait and twiddle her thumbs for twelve months, or strike out on her own – she settled on the second option and subsequently formed Belly. Their first EP featured 'Slow Dog'; it was a stand-out song with a nagging and catchy guitar riff that skipped along quite joyously. Donnelly's voice perfectly matched the effervescence of the riff, being both strong and expressive. Her lyrics were also highly intriguing; they came from an old Chinese proverb that she had chanced upon, which told of the bizarre practice of hanging a dead dog around the neck of an adulteress until the animal decomposed. Interestingly, Donnelly chooses to view the subject in a positive light, seeing the metaphor of a decomposing dog as signifying an end to pain, and a step toward freedom and liberation.

2
COME AS YOU ARE
NIRVANA
GEFFEN
OTHER SINGLES 1992:
IN BLOOM; LITHIUM

The undeniable similarity of the main riff of 'Come As You Are' to that of 'Eighties' by Killing Joke, as well as 'Life Goes On' by The Damned, is the reason that Kurt Cobain was nervous about releasing it as a single; eventually though, he did see sense because the quality and commercial potential of the song was obvious to all. The song is clearly targeted at the sloganeering niceness of an idealised America – the bland insincerity of the invitation to 'Come As You Are' obviously irks Cobain because he knows that the seductive corporate voice tells lies… he knows that people like him are not really welcome to come at all. The verses are subdued and echoey, they draw the listener in to ponder the allegorical lyrics; some, such as "Come doused in mud, soaked in bleach" pertain to heroin addiction… others are simply empty clichés re-directed towards the people who use them as confusing double-speak. The song builds into the choruses when the volume reaches a maximum; the shifting dynamics add an edge that is further amplified by the repeated phrase "And I swear that I don't have a gun" – this is highly unnerving, almost as shocking perhaps as Johnny Cash's pronouncement "I shot a man in Reno, just to watch him die". Also noteworthy is the long guitar solo (played by Cobain) which is a brilliant melodic device, performed with elegance and grace.

1992

1

I DON'T WANNA GROW UP

TOM WAITS

ISLAND

OTHER SINGLE: WHO ARE YOU?

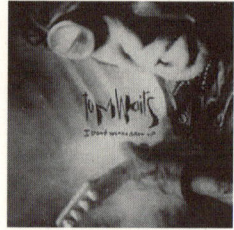

Following his 1987 album *Frank's Wild Years*, Tom Waits marked time for five years before returning to the recording studio to construct the bold and confrontational sounding *Bone Machine*. During the hiatus he had taken film roles and done some soundtrack work, but he had also clearly further honed his principal craft, sharpening his already considerable songwriting ability. 'I Don't Wanna Grow Up' was released as a single, and although it still resonates to this day, it wasn't even *nearly* a hit at the time, though it has since attracted scores of cover versions by a multitude of artists. On the face of it, this is merely a charming and simple song about childhood and innocence… but that is emphatically not the case. 'I Don't Wanna Grow Up' is a critique of society, and a rejection of the strictures placed upon the populace as we conform to a political and economic system that does damage to our souls. It is voiced by a disgruntled, disillusioned adult who has become wise to the true cause of his malaise; as a consequence he begins to tear up the rule-book and rebels against the burden of needing to act like a sensible grown-up. He feels trapped like a caged canary, and yearns for the feeling of freedom that he had during childhood. What a brilliantly written song this is; there is not a single word wasted, no fat to trim, scalpel sharp. An acoustic guitar is strummed with gusto, and Waits drums in a simple, untutored manner as he growls and states his case with wild abandon - it is marvellous stuff!

1993

EVENTS

Czechoslovakia ceases to exist – it splits into two countries, Slovakia, and The Czech Republic.

Bill Clinton is sworn in as the 42nd president of The United States.

Playwright (and fan of both Frank Zappa and Lou Reed) Václav Havel is elected as President of the Czech Republic.

In Waco, Texas, a siege involving a religious cult known as The Branch Davidians, led by David Koresh, ends in the violent deaths of 86 people.

Bombings in Bombay kill 257 people.

Tuberculosis is declared a global emergency.

Monica Seles, the World No. 1 female tennis player, is stabbed during a match in Hamburg.

Eritrea gains independence from Ethiopia.

In Somalia, the U.S. army conducts *Operation Gothic Serpent*; it leaves over 1,000 people dead.

British Rail is sold-off and privatised.

Columbian drug lord Pablo Escobar is shot dead by police.

All members of the Zambian national football team die in a plane crash en route to Senegal.

NOTABLE BIRTHS

Zayn Malik; Fred; Harry Maguire; Paul Pogba; Chance the Rapper; Ariana Grande; Stormzy;

NOTABLE DEATHS

Edwin Moss; Dizzy Gillespie; Rudolph Nureyev; Audrey Hepburn; Andre the Giant; Arthur Ashe; Bobby Moore; Lillian Gish;

Billy Eckstine ;Brandon Lee; Oliver Tambo; Mick Robson; Sun Ra; Conway Twitty; Arthur Alexander; Bernard Bresslaw; James Hunt; William Golding; GG Allin; Fred Gwynne; Stewart Granger; Vincent Price; Doris Duke; Federico Fellini; River Phoenix; Leon Theremin; Anthony Burgess; Albert Collins; Kenneth Connor; Frank Zappa; Danny Blanchflower.

NOTABLE FILMS

Cronos; *Menace II Society* ; *Farewell My Concubine*; *The Piano*; *Short Cuts*; *Groundhog Day*; *Schindler's list*; *Dazed and Confused*; *Carlito's Way*; *True Romance*; *Three Colours Blue*; *Naked* ; *Jurassic Park*;

NOTABLE BOOKS

The Shipping News – Annie Prouix

Trainspotting – Irvine Welsh

A Suitable Boy – Vikram Seth

Paddy Clark Ha Ha Ha – Roddy Doyle

My Mother, Demonology – Kathy Acker

Complicity – Iain Banks

Strange Pilgrims – Gabriel Garcia Marquez

The Black Book – Ian Rankin

In The Electric Mist With Confederate Dead – James Lee Burke

MY 1993

The year began well – I was fully immersed in creating music with The Stepbrothers and so every Sunday we would put in a shift at Eddie's studio. It was endlessly rewarding work, conducted in a friendly, civilised and highly positive manner. This was doing me a world of good; my spirits were lifted and my self-esteem managed to clamber up from off the floor. We finished our album in late summer; somehow, it had morphed into something bigger than the original electronics + vocal format, since we had now incorporated guitars, brass and sweet harmony vocals. The change in sound caused a loss of interest from record labels who had previously shown enthusiasm, but this was of little consequence because we were pleased with what we had achieved. The album was put to one side and we began recording some new, more experimental tracks. Tom Greenhalgh from The Mekons, and his bandmate Lu Edmonds (a former member of The Damned, 3 Mustaphas 3 and Public Image Ltd) spent a weekend working with us, and they contributed to a couple of tracks. I spoke to John Gill about the possibility of us performing live; it made sense, and so there was a real possibility that I would be returning to the stage. Football was also good; Manchester United had signed Eric Cantona, a footballing genius and true maverick. He galvanised a misfiring team and led them to the title; it was a euphoric time and Manchester was really rocking as most of its football supporting population celebrated. When the new football season began, Europe beckoned and Kispest-Honvéd were the first opponents. Hence, a trip with renegade travel company UF Tours was booked, and it was off to Budapest via a two day stop in Prague. This was quite hard on my liver, but it was a lot of fun… until it all went sour.

My dad, who had seemed to be indestructible, suffered a heart attack; he spent some time in hospital, but when he returned home he was clearly physically diminished and unwell. Typically, he put on a brave face, but my mum was clearly desperately worried by his condition. Shortly after this, I received a call to say that he was back in hospital – scar tissue from an old injury had flared up and his stomach was hugely swollen. He needed to have emergency surgery, even though it carried severe risk because of the recent heart attack. He came out of theatre alive, but in dreadful pain. I insisted that my mum go home, and I sat with him through a sleepless night, rubbing water onto his parched lips and calling for nurses when the dilapidated equipment that was meant to help keep him alive, kept breaking down. The staff were faultless; it was the Tory government who were starving the NHS of funds that were culpable. The morning eventually arrived, and with it the hope that the worst was over. My mother and brother then relieved my vigil, and I went home. I listened to *Low* by David Bowie and got some rest. By late afternoon, I was back at the hospital; my dad seemed to be a bit perkier, and even sang a verse of 'Waltzing Matilda' to cheer us up. However, he was clearly extremely tired and very uncomfortable; he asked me to help him change position. As I reached out to assist him, he smiled at me – I held him in my arms, and at that moment he had a fatal heart attack. Friends and colleagues were fabulously supportive, but I was very hurt indeed. Having had only one living grandparent when

I was born, I had never learned, on any level, how to come to terms with the death of a loved one. As raw as my grief was, it still paled in comparison with that of my mum; she was heartbroken, shattered and had very little will to go on. She, who had supported me so often, now needed my support. My routine changed; I needed to spend time with her – my Sundays now became dedicated to my mother… my music-making was over once again.

My favourite gig experience of the year was seeing Mazzy Star at Manchester University; they were intense and quite amazing. Iggy Pop at The Academy was pretty memorable too; after a splendid performance, Marc Riley and I were granted an audience with the man who had been a childhood hero of mine, as well as being highly inspirational as regards my general outlook on life. Almost inevitably, he was a let-down; although pleasant, he was impersonal and simply peeled-off well-practiced anecdotes in order to please his audience. Iggy had become a polished professional rather than the untameable free-spirit of legend.

100
WATER FROM A VINE LEAF
WILLIAM ORBIT
VIRGIN

Taken from William Orbit's album *Strange Cargo*, and featuring a vocal from frequent collaborator Beth Orton, this was a single that was genuinely atmospheric. Within its trance grooves there seemed to be unfathomable depths, and the impeccable production made for a lush and smooth trip through the seven-minute duration. Re-mixes by Underworld and Spooky beefed up 'Water From a Vine Leaf' and turned it into a more dance-friendly piece, but Orbit's original mix is the one I receive most pleasure from, touched as it is by exotica and graced with such an uplifting conclusion.

99
WHO IS IT
MICHAEL JACKSON
EPIC

Michael Jackson's imperious reign as the media-proclaimed "King of Pop" was over; he was knocked back by the first of a series of sexual misconduct allegations to be levelled at him. Furthermore, it was a plain fact that his records were just not as good as they had been a decade earlier. Still, 'Who Is It' was a very good single indeed; stylistically, it is extremely close to his earlier classic 'Billie Jean', both in structure and lyrical content, concerning as it does a lover's cruel act of betrayal. The track is rhythmically taut and seems to have a prowling quality, while Jackson sings superbly, capturing in his anguished performance all the bewilderment and pain of a wronged lover.

98
SHOT IN THE DARK
DJ HYPE
SUBURBAN BASE

Dark, moody and menacing, this features stretched drum beats, a Public Enemy vocal sample, insane scratching and an electrical storm of ominous, churning mayhem. DJ Hype succeeded in putting jungle into the charts, despite it being much too wild, wilful and hostile for daytime radio shows.

97
OHIO RIVERBOAT SONG
PALACE BROTHERS
DRAG CITY
OTHER SINGLE 1993: COME IN

Will Oldham's musical odyssey, incorporating multiple permutations of the Palace name – before abruptly becoming Bonnie Prince Billy in 1996 – starts right here with this debut single. Right from the off, it displays his out-of-step individuality; over strummed guitars and a single drum beat rhythm, Oldham plaintively sings a re-write of Scottish traditional ballad 'The Loch Tay Boat Song'. He sounds completely natural and untutored, and it resembles a newly discovered historical field recording; a really remarkable record.

96
MOVING ON UP
M PEOPLE
DECONSTRUCTION
OTHER SINGLES 1993:
ONE NIGHT IN HEAVEN;
DON'T LOOK ANY FURTHER

My old musical colleague, Tim Oliver (we had worked together in The DoDo's) had been a member of the fledgling M People, so even though Tim had subsequently moved on, I still had something of a soft spot for their brand of nu-disco. By this point, they had properly hit their stride and achieved their commercial peak, adroitly mixing up modern club sounds with elements of classic Motown-style soul. Here, on 'Moving On Up', an anthemic declaration of independence and self-empowerment, they served up a dance/pop masterclass. Throughout the verses, sung venomously by Heather Small, it was uptempo, defiant and sassy, setting us up perfectly for the hands-in-the-air euphoria of the titanic chorus.

95
AMERICAN JESUS
BAD RELIGION
ATLANTIC
OTHER SINGLE 1993:
STRUCK A NERVE

George H.W. Bush had effectively claimed that America could do no wrong in The First Gulf War because God was on their side; this record was a pointed response by Bad Religion to that ludicrous statement. With heavy lyrical irony, the song stretches such jingoism to laughter inducing extremes; the ridicule is well-aimed, touching on authoritarianism, famine, racism and all manner of other injustices where America has not exactly covered itself in glory. Buzzcocks-style punk rock guitar riffs dominate the sound, and disdainful vocals by Greg Graffin – with assistance from Eddie Vedder of Pearl Jam – make this a very listenable and forceful kick-in-the-pants for Bush and his White House cabal.

94
USE ME
R TYME
TRANCE FUSION

R Tyme consisted of Darryl Wynn and Derrick May; here, their music leans more towards house than the techno they are both normally associated with. 'Use Me' has a distinctive female vocal sample that runs over the top of a flawless mix of bass, synth strings and bright percussion; with radical mixes by Carl Craig included, this was dynamite material for clubbers.

93
THEME FOR DEREK JARMAN'S *BLUE*
COIL
THRESHOLD

This was released to commemorate the death of filmmaker Derek Jarman, in a limited pressing of 1,000 copies. Coil display a mastery of the ambient techno form; theme one is short… but not at all sweet in any conventional sense

– this particular shade of blue is dark-hued, dangerously deep and edging towards pitch black. Theme two runs to eleven minutes and it is a fascinating voyage into the depths… total submersion is utterly unavoidable. This music is certainly not comfortable or comforting, but it does possess a strange, incandescent beauty and luminosity.

92
LYOT RMX
BASIC CHANNEL
BASIC CHANNEL
OTHER SINGLES 1993:
PHYLYPS TRAK; Q1.1

Basic Channel comprise of Moritz Von Oswald and Mark Ernestus. They were based in Berlin, and were mostly a faceless operation who let their music speak for itself. 'Lyot Rmx' is typical of their work, both in structure and the idea that informs it; their music is always the same but always different. Here, they serve up eleven minutes and fifty-three seconds of minimalist, abstract techno with a dub tinge. Sure, it is highly repetitive, and yet the detours down various corridors of sound are ever fascinating and stimulating. If you have ever dreamed of trying to escape from an endless, desolate labyrinth, this could be the music that would soundtrack your wanderings.

91
BACK TO SCHOOL
ROYAL TRUX
DRAG CITY
OTHER SINGLES 1993:
STEAL YR FACE; CHAIRMAN BLOW; DOGS OF LOVE

Sludgy, lo-fi blues bemoaning the end of summer, this is shot through with wistfulness and aching nostalgia. 'Back to School' is a bumbling, stumbling delight as Neil Hagerty and Jennifer Herrema sound as if they are laying in a field, looking at the clouds, and recording the track in a lysergic haze. With a running guitar line that channels the gentle spirit of Jimi Hendrix, this is just blissful.

90
DREAMS
GABRIELLE
GO BEAT

'Dreams' was the debut single by Hackney-born singer Gabrielle. Back in 1991, she was a struggling nightclub singer who acquired her first studio experience when she helped out on a recording by her friend, Jackie King. The producer on the day, Tim Laws, was so impressed that he asked her to return alone, and when she did, she took along the lyric she had written for 'Dreams'. The words were a reminder to herself to keep her dream alive during the difficult times when it looked as if her career would never progress. Laws put her lyric to music, and a guitar sample from the Tracey Chapman song 'Fast Cars' was included. The finished track was superb; with its contemporary sound, adorned with retro-soul stylings, it managed to chime with the times. The song was highly melodic and in its heart-stopping chorus, there was an almost tangible aching quality. Gabrielle's voice was full of character and her performance was exceptional. One thousand five hundred copies were pressed-up, and they sold out before anybody realised that the 'Fast Cars' sample had been used without clearance… this, of course, meant that no further re-press could take place. But now fast-forward two years to 1993 – Gabrielle belatedly signed a recording contract and a new, sample-free version of 'Dreams' was cut; it had hit-record written all over it, and so it duly stormed to number one on the UK chart, and the fairy-tale ending of triumph out of adversity did finally come true for her.

89
BELIEVE IN ME
UTAH SAINTS
FFRR

Utah Saints were a dance act from Leeds, noted for their re-appropriation and re-contextualisation of mainstream chart hits into their own tracks; Kate Bush, Eurythmics and Gwen Guthrie were all extensively sampled on their singles. In this case, 'Believe in Me' is built around 'Love Action' and 'You Gave Me Love' (by Human League and Crown Heights Affair respectively) which are hurled with gay abandon into the midst of a frantic percussion and piano track. Utah Saints were described by Bill Drummond as the very first stadium house band, and that is a label which is perfectly applicable to this gigantic, good time raver.

88
MURDERER
BUJU BANTON
PENTHOUSE
OTHER SINGLES 1993: MAKE MY DAY; OPERATION ARDENT; DEPORTEE; VIGILANTE

In Jamaica, Buju Banton was a best-selling artist, and 1993 was the year that his talent became globally recognised, in no small part due to his song 'Murderer'. It was written as a reaction to the senseless and unsolved slaying of Pan Head, a fellow dancehall artist, who had been fatally shot in the head when leaving a venue in which he had performed. Buju Banton took Barry Brown's 'Far East' riddim and added his own lyric, questioning how a murderer can live with his conscience and how, in religious terms, a murderer must face the judgment of Jah. He talks of state-sponsored murder (which in Jamaica was very much a harsh reality) and in so doing, he bridges the divide between dancehall and cultural reggae… and he does it brilliantly.

87
LIQUID INSECTS
AMORPHOUS ANDROGYNOUS
ASTRALWERKS

Amorphous Androgynous was an

alias adopted by Future Sound of London, in order to release much more of the absolute flood of music that they were creating. 'Liquid Insects' is a sinister and atmospheric ambient/techno track, containing samples of the prowling alien from the movie *Predator*. Further musical samples of Tangerine Dream, Herbie Hancock and 808 State are used to stitch together a musical tapestry that is rich, dark and ominous. The track has the feel of a long journey, travelling through a series of dubby chasms before arriving at a point where machined percussion catapults it forward through a most weird and wonderful terrain.

86
ARE YOU GONNA GO MY WAY
LENNY KRAVITZ
VIRGIN

Too often for my liking the music of Lenny Kravitz seems derivative of others; a pale parody of John Lennon or Prince for example (NB: I have the same problem with Paul Weller's post-Style Council output). 'Are You Gonna Go My Way' didn't alter my perception of Kravitz one iota – here he was mimicking Jimi Hendrix, pure and simple. However, on this particular track, performed with huge panache, he somehow gets away with it. This is a hard-hitting, hard-rocking, funky jam with a monumental riff and an enormous, swaggering vocal performance. The rhythm section are locked into a killing groove, whilst Kravitz attacks the guitar so fiercely that the notes he produces seem to sting like swarms of bees.

85
SMOKEBELCH II
SABRES OF PARADISE
SABRES OF PARADISE

Sabres of Paradise were experimental electronic trio Andrew Weatherall, Gary Burns and Jagz Kooner. A series of re-mixes for other acts had built them an impressive reputation, but Smokebelch II was their own first single. It was rightly celebrated as a blissful and ethereal instant classic, although in fact it was not quite original. The origin of the piece was hidden away on the B-side of an obscure 1989 EP by L.B. Bad, where, buried within a suite of tunes entitled *The New Age of Faith*, we find the initial blueprint of the magisterial Smokebelch II.

84
MTV MAKES ME WANNA
SMOKE CRACK
BECK
FLIPSIDE
OTHER SINGLE 1993: LOSER

It is somewhat ironic that a future master of visual manipulation – via his carefully shot promotional films – should have launched his career with a single which lambasts MTV for its mindless, but addictive content. However, although the track is funny, it does make a good point and there is substantially more depth to the song than the throwaway title might suggest. There is also a strong autobiographical element, since it refers to the singer's doomed and soul-destroying stint working in a video rental store. The piece is played acoustically with harmonica embellishments, and Beck's voice is a harsh croak that curiously makes him sound like a slightly deranged Delta blues veteran.

83
CAMARGUE (RADIO EDIT)
CJ BOLLAND
R&S
OTHER SINGLE 1993: CAMARGUE (LIVE AT UNIVERSE); CAMARGUE THE REMIXES

At the age of three-years, CJ Bolland was transported from County Durham to Belgium, where his parents ran a nightclub in Antwerp (in which his mother was a DJ) and so was born his fascination with – and love of – dance music. Bolland was strongly influenced by the electro and EBM sounds that were popular on the Belgian underground scene, and these influences clearly feed into tracks such as 'Camargue', which is a brand of tuneful and trancey techno that is perfectly designed to cause mayhem on the dance floor, with its jackhammer rhythm and a vocal provided courtesy of younger sister Sian Louise Bolland.

82
KRAKPOT
PLASTIKMAN
NOVAMUTE

Since 1990, Richie Hawtin had recorded as both FUSE and States Of Mind, but with the release of 'Spastik', he first unveiled his Plastikman alias. That record was followed up by the quite marvellous 'Krakpot', which is a constantly evolving and bubbling mass of intense, acid-soaked sorcery – a demonic monster conjured up with only keyboard and kick drum. This is an insanely excellent track that is unbelievably good when heard through a high-quality club sound system, but it is also equally good to lie back at home, with the lights down low, and lose yourself inside its magick power.

81
SETTING YOU FREE
DAVID McCOMB
MUSHROOM

Here, David McComb, The Triffids main-man, steps out under his own name, backed by various members of The Bad Seeds and The Blackeyed Susans. 'Setting You Free' is a powerful, personal and passionate break-up song; it is fairly easy to imagine it being performed by Nick Cave or the post-Ed Kuepper version of The Saints… but surely, even those greats could not match the richness and drama of McComb's performance. His baritone voice never falters as he peels layers of hurt from the carcass of the disintegrating relationship which he describes so vividly, and the instruments are played with appropriate savagery by the musicians who are clearly in simpatico with the raw emotional needs of the song.

80
KINGDOM
ULTRAMARINE
BLANCO Y NEGRO

Ultramarine were a duo blessed with highly refined tastes; their music incorporated elements of ambient house, folk and the eccentricity of the late 1960s/early 1970s Canterbury art-rock scene. Here, on 'Kingdom', they are joined by iconoclastic musician/vocalist Robert Wyatt. The song is gentle and pastoral, but lyrically it rails against the inequalities that exist within society. Exotic sounding acoustic instrumentation lends the track a world music feel, which oddly counter-intuitive electronic bleeps somehow manage to complement, and Wyatt, as usual, expresses great wisdom and deep compassion in his plaintive singing.

79
MOVE
MOBY
MUTE

Moby was on an upward trajectory with each successive release; 'Move', his first record for new label Mute, put him once again into the UK top-twenty. It was an unstoppable, high-energy house anthem, peppered with idiosyncratic flourishes and a distinctly disco feel, courtesy of the vocal sample of 'Love Sensation' by Loleatta Holloway – her repeated cry of "You make me feel so good" brings an adrenalin rush of exquisite pleasure.

78
TIMEBOMB
CHUMBAWAMBA
ONE LITTLE INDIAN
OTHER SINGLE 1993:
ENOUGH IS ENOUGH

This is a brilliant, high-spirited pop single. With its joyous horns – more colliery brass band than Stax soul – the bright voices and the familiarity of the chorus (a straight lift from the Stephen Stills anti-Vietnam War song 'For What it's Worth') a strategic subterfuge is created which manages to place the group inside the heavily guarded walls of the system; in effect, 'Timebomb' is a Trojan Horse. This record was so ostensibly listener friendly that it was impossible to resist; it was Chumbawamba's passport into the inner sanctum of the music industry... once inside they could subvert to their heart's content; they themselves were the 'Timebomb'.

77
IN THE DEATH CAR
IGGY POP & GORAN BREGO-VIC
MERCURY

Serbian composer Goran Bregovic, and American "godfather of punk" Iggy Pop, teamed up to produce the score for the surrealist comedy film *Arizona Dream*. They seemed to inspire each other; Bregovic serves up an amalgamation of calypso, cocktail lounge jazz and oompah band horns, whilst Iggy voices his sad, kooky and ironic poetry in that gnarly but fruity baritone, dropping in references to

David Bowie's version of 'Wild is the Wind'… it is a magical combination.

76
PLAN 9
808 STATE
ZTT

With 'Plan 9', 808 State chose to show us a different weapon in their sonic arsenal; no sweeping grandeur or high-intensity here – instead, they offer up something altogether lighter and more relaxing. This was blissful, chilled-out stuff, with the guitars adding an almost Balearic feel to the track.

75
IF WE WAIT
GUIDED BY VOICES
ANYWAY
OTHER SINGLES 1993: THE GRAND HOUR; STATIC AIRPLANE JIVE

Robert Pollard's incredibly prolific Guided by Voices are the archetypal alt-rock band, and with 'If We Wait', they served up a quirky, tuneful, lo-fi gem. The sound is skeletal and the voice is natural and unforced. It is melodic, full of warmth, and it offers up not the slick sound of the west coast, or the studied cool of the east, but a music that represents the more rugged American heartlands.

74
ZEA
dEUS
BANG

dEUS were an art-rock band who ended up signing to Island Records where they enjoyed a degree of mainstream success – but this was their debut release. It opens with an homage to 'The Blimp' (a track from *Trout Mask Replica* by Captain Beefheart) before transitioning into a mid-tempo piece that rolls and swells into a full-blown epic. The piece is anchored by virtue of the calm voice at its centre (although the song *does* take a left-turn back into Beefheart territory before the conclusion) and it always manages to leave a satisfied smile playing on my lips.

73
BUENA
MORPHINE
RYKODISC

Hailing from Cambridge, Massachusetts, Morphine were a band who developed a sound drawing on jazz and blues influences, to create something that they termed "low-rock" – and 'Buena' is a stand-out track. The opening bars of the song are dominated by a deep and heavy bass, with softly played drums pattering beneath; writer/vocalist Mark Sandman, his voice a deep croon, sings of encountering the devil and a saxophone rips through the track. This highly unorthodox music is wired and spooky, thrilling and literally goosebump inducing.

72
MUSIC
LTJ BUKEM
GOOD LOOKING
OTHER SINGLES 1993: RETURN TO ATLANTIS; ATMOSPHERICAL JUBILANCY

LTJ Bukem made music that feels

multi-dimensional, and knowing that he was a classically trained pianist who was obsessed with jazz does help to explain this. 'Music' is, undeniably, a brilliant piece of drum & bass music – but it is much more than that. Lovingly crafted, it flows smoothly even as the mood of the piece changes; it is energetic and unhurried at the same time, with waves of sound that shimmer and mesmerise the entranced listener.

71
THE WOODEN SONG
BUTTHOLE SURFERS
CAPITOL
OTHER SINGLES 1993: WHO WAS IN MY ROOM LAST NIGHT?; DUST DEVIL

John Paul Jones of Led Zeppelin fame was hired to produce the Butthole's album *Independent Worm Saloon* – and he did an excellent job too. Much of the album saw the band delving into hard rock territory, but 'The Wooden Song' had a hummable, folky feel, and it made for an excellent single. In nursery rhyme style, Gibby Haynes sings a lyric that touches on darkness and danger, albeit with a surrealist edge; he proclaims that "Lately I've been dancing in ceiling fans". Overall, the track is jolly and quite light, although Paul Leary does contribute a face melting guitar solo, just in case some people were feeling a little bit too comfortable.

70
AFRO
JON SPENCER BLUES EXPLOSION
MATADOR

The Jon Spencer Blues Explosion had arrived at a point where their sound was fully evolved, and 'Afro' finds them playing with all the ferocity of a punk rock outfit, whilst simultaneously displaying the innate grooviness of a funk/soul band. Here, they are in possession of a riff to die for; however, said riff is absolutely pulled, pushed and pulverised, until it is left thoroughly battered and bleeding. Spencer hollers out his vocal whilst the guitar cuts like a scythe; the very epitome of wild, no-holds-barred rock & roll.

69
HEADLIGHTS
CAT POWER
THE MAKING OF AMERICANS

Charlyn Marshall adopted the stage name Cat Power, and immediately began to exhibit her considerable gifts with this debut single. 'Headlights' is written as a first person narrative which describes the aftermath of a car accident and a girl who is dying on the road. The song has a suitably sparse and haunting arrangement, utilising primitive guitar and drum. Additionally, there is an untuned violin sawing away that is prominent in the mix; this adds a desperate edge to what is already a sad, sad song. Marshall's voice is ragged and her performance harrowing, sorrowfully capturing the loneliness and helplessness of the girl as she faces her final living moments…

68
SHOW ME LOVE
ROBIN S
BIG BEAT

Robin Stone recorded and released 'Show Me Love' in 1990 on Champion Records; it was a moderate success, but nothing more. Three years later this version appeared, and it transformed latent potential into an enormous hit. Re-mixed by Swedish producer StoneBridge, the track had a more insistent drum beat and a distorted bass line that was not heard on the original. The changes and embellishments had created something very special, and 'Show Me Love' became a guaranteed floor-filler. Interestingly, Robin S had recorded her vocal whilst suffering from flu, and such was the raw, pleading quality in her voice, it sounds as if she had reached the very limit of her capabilities. As it was, this was just perfect for the darkness hidden inside this euphoric, house music classic.

67
GOODNIGHT MR SPACEMAN
TELEVISION PERSONALITIES
FIRE
OTHER SINGLE 1993: YOU, ME AND LOU REED

'Goodnight Mr Spaceman' finds Dan Treacy singing about his own mental health problems – and the alarming lack of success enjoyed by Television Personalities. This is a sad song disguised as a happy song, full of witticisms and pop cultural references, such as Slade, Suede and Edvard Munch. Unpolished but melodic, this is as tender a commentary on life for a troubled soul trying to exist at the margins of the music business, as one is ever likely to hear.

66
GREASE BOX
TAD
MECHANIC

Tad were a heavyweight – and very heavy – band from Seattle. In the wake of Nirvana's titanic success they were swept up in the "grunge" phenomenon, though in truth they had very little in common with the more accessible bands with whom they were compared. 'Grease Box' is produced by J Mascis of Dinosaur Jr., and he helps Tad create their definitive statement. The song is anchored by a dirty, thunderous bass riff and ultra-tight drums, while Tad Doyle summons from his gut a vocal that is an expression of deep pain. The guitar is played hard and choppy, ineluctably bringing to mind an axe being wielded by a madman.

65
YOU MAKE ME WANT TO WEAR DRESSES
LISA GERMANO
4AD

Brilliant satire unleashed by Lisa Germano; over what sounds like a country hoedown, featuring fiddles and bows, she sings about surrendering her power to a dominant male and adopting a traditional, subservient female role. Performed with sharp wit and subtle irony, this record had extremely sharp claws hidden beneath its outwardly cheerful surface.

64
POSITIVE EDUCATION
SLAM
SOMA QUALITY RECORDINGS

As promoters, DJs, record label founders *and* recording artists, Slam were a duo from Glasgow who spearheaded the Scottish techno scene. 'Positive Education' was a sublime piece of minimalism that totally rocks, before falling into pools of the deepest, dubby, bass, only to rise up again towards a spine-tingling, euphoric conclusion.

63
SHAKER
YO LA TENGO
MATADOR
OTHER SINGLES 1993: FROM A MOTEL 6; BIG DAY COMING

Yo La Tengo's output became increasingly dreamy and abstract, and 'Shaker' benefits greatly as a result. It is a slender but fascinating song, pretty much constructed on a single, jerky guitar riff. But underneath, the sound is layered; instruments entwine like a living, writhing, shape-shifting organism – it seduces the listener until it becomes impossible to ignore. In summary, this was a very cool record.

62
LEMON
U2
ISLAND
OTHER SINGLES 1993: STAY (FARAWAY SO CLOSE); NUMB

Stepping ever further from the big rock sound that made them seemingly omnipotent, U2 experiment with a bouncing and highly rhythmic disco sound, that manages to be funky too – this was a really radical stylistic departure. It features a lyric by Bono which concerns the use of film to preserve memories; it was inspired by a half-speed Super 8 reel of his twenty-four year old mother playing rounders whilst wearing a lemon coloured dress. Bono sang in an exaggerated falsetto that terrifically suits the warped eeriness of the track, and impressive backing vocals from The Edge and Brian Eno add texture. In place of stadium pleasing choruses, subtle hooks were used instead; 'Lemon' clearly revealed that a revitalised U2 were busily and successfully re-inventing themselves.

61
MARBLES
TINDERSTICKS
TIPPY TOE
OTHER SINGLES 1993: UNWIRED; A MARRIAGE MADE IN HEAVEN

Emerging from the ashes of a band called Asphalt Ribbons, this highly-refined group from Nottingham had a musical style that incorporated melancholy sounding orchestration, rather than using the ubiquitous guitar as principal instrument. 'Marbles' sounds as if it could easily have been taken from the soundtrack to an arthouse film; it sounds sophisticated and elegantly cool. Moreover, it is not difficult to imagine the expressive but puzzling lyric being voiced by Serge Gainsbourg rather than Tindersticks' own Stuart Staples.

60
POSITIVE BLEEDING
URGE OVERKILL
GEFFEN
OTHER SINGLES 1993: DROP-OUT; SISTER HAVANA

Urge Overkill were one of the era's must-see live acts; I was lucky enough to catch them several times, and I had 'Positive Bleeding' on heavy rotation in my car in the form of a cassette single. With members such as Nash Kato, Eddie "King" Roeser and Blackie Onassis, the band contained some larger than life figures; the image was strong and the music matched it. They played rock music with a pop sensibility, allowing a strong sense of enjoyment to be transmitted to the listener. 'Positive Bleeding' boasts a glorious guitar riff, gritty lead vocals with helium-filled harmonies, and a joyful release of entirely unrestrained energy.

59
SWEET HARMONY
THE BELOVED
EAST WEST
OTHER SINGLES 1993: CELEBRATE YOUR LIFE; OUTERSPACE GIRL

At this point, The Beloved consisted of husband and wife team Jon & Helena Marsh; they co-wrote 'Sweet Harmony' and it became a number eight hit single in the UK. The track is melodic, techno pop, with a spiritual message that advocates living together in harmony rather than the divisiveness which we can see all around. An unobtainable utopian ideal perhaps, but a genuinely uplifting message of hope for a better future.

58
BEAUTIFUL SON
HOLE
CITY SLANG

Courtney Love said that 'Beautiful Son' is a good example of her attempting to write more straightforwardly in an effort to uncomplicate her songs… and 'Beautiful Son' does have a simple purity. It contains a Nirvana-style riff that guitarist Eric Erlandson took issue with on the grounds that it sounded too similar to 'Smells Like Teen Spirit'. The lyrics are few but they succinctly convey a dedicated protective love, and Courtney howls them with heartfelt passion. The whole is a wonderfully liberating noise; a primal scream similar in intensity to Yoko Ono's early 1970s work with the Plastic Ono Band.

57
AIN'T NO LOVE (AIN'T NO USE)
SUB SUB FEATURING MELANIE WILLIAMS
ROBS RECORDS

Sub Sub consisted of Jim Goodwin and brothers Jez and Andy Williams, all later of Doves. Up to this point, they were creating instrumental dance music only… but then came 'Ain't No Love'. The bass line was abstracted from a recording of 'Good Morning Starshine' and transferred to keyboards, after which the majority of the track came together quite quickly. However, something was lacking… exceptionally, it was decided that a vocalist was required; enter Melanie Williams of soul band Temper Temper – the missing ingredient had been found. The track was already bursting with enthusiasm and energy; it was both retro and modern, incorporating disco strings and wah-wah guitar alongside up-to-date dance beats. But Williams, with a voice like honey, added the vital human element and the track suddenly combined dance-floor sassiness with radio friendliness – it justifiably became a huge hit.

56
THE GHOST AT NUMBER ONE
JELLYFISH
CHARISMA
OTHER SINGLE 1993:
NEW MISTAKE

'The Ghost at Number One' was released as a single in support of *Spilt Milk*, the second Jellyfish album. As expected from these classicists, it was a brilliant pop record that channeled the influence of Queen in the verses and *Pet Sounds*-era Beach Boys in the elongated bridge. Like a ray of sunshine on a gloomy day, this record is guaranteed to cheer the soul.

55
WHAT'S MY NAME?
SNOOP DOGG
DEATH ROW

Having featured as a guest artist on tracks by Dr Dre, the seemingly easy and lazy flow of Snoop was not new to our ears – but this debut single, taken from his album *Doggystyle*, created an immediate buzz. It was produced by Dre and we find Snoop immersing himself in P-Funk heritage; by using samples from the back catalogue of George Clinton, Funkadelic and Parliament, and then inserting his own quick-witted lines into the narrative of the aforementioned performers, Snoop made explicit the link between P-Funkers and hip-hoppers. He picked up the mantle of this neglected music and gave it new life by adding his own, very personalised twist.

54
ENFORCEMENT
CYRUS
BASIC CHANNEL

Monochromatic, harsh and brutal, there is no escape from these thirteen minutes of grinding hardcore Berlin techno. This is akin to taking a wild train ride through an endless series of dark tunnels at night, with only the occasional glimpse of moonlit scenery to indicate the slightly changing landscape. A cold warehouse was indeed the perfect place to hear this utterly unflinching track, as wound-up ravers chewed their own faces to this brain frying sound.

53
SOMETHING FOR JOEY
MERCURY REV
BEGGARS BANQUET
OTHER SINGLES 1993:
BRONX CHEER;
THE HUM IS COMING FROM HER

With 'Something For Joey', Mercury Rev offered up kaleidoscopic technicolor weirdness, with a beautiful twisted poppiness thrown in for good measure; restraint is thrown out of the window and subtlety is well and truly trampled on. It seems as if every single sound and idea from The Beatles flower-power epic *Sergeant Pepper's Lonely Hearts Club Band* has been mixed-up together and condensed into this four minute rampage of horns, flutes, drums, guitars and abstract thinking. This is vivid and pulsating stuff that only really obeys its own warped logic.

52
CHERUB ROCK
SMASHING PUMPKINS
VIRGIN
OTHER SINGLE 1993: TODAY

Because the impression was that they were too careerist and opportunistic, Smashing Pumpkins were always treated with a degree of suspicion on the independent scene. Now, on a major label, they *still* felt misunderstood since they were perceived as being something that they were trying very hard *not* to be… namely, a grunge band! An uncomfortable Billy Corgan plainly articulates the disdain he feels about his band being pulled and pushed about by attempts to commodify their music. 'Cherub Rock' is played aggressively, in an intense, hard rock style, over a searing riff; Corgan sings sweetly enough, but there is clearly an audible edge of contemptuous anger in his voice as he reaches the repeated refrain of "Let me out", which is delivered with distinctly heavy emphasis.

51
PETS
PORNO FOR PYROS
WARNER BROTHERS
OTHER SINGLES 1993:
CURSED FEMALE/CURSED MALE; MEIJA

Following the break-up of Jane's Addiction, band leader Perry Farrell and drummer Stephen Perkins formed Porno For Pyros, and 'Pets' became their first widely available single. The premise of the song is that mankind is in crisis – that following childhood we become increasingly fucked-up, until finally, in senility, we revert to a child-like state. The lyric goes on to speculate that aliens might make a better job of running the planet, and therefore the human race might be happier if we were treated as servile pets. Employing his one-in-a-million kind voice, Farrell sings, almost angelically, over a ping-pong rhythm that is embellished with acid-drenched guitar sounds.

50
MOMENTS OF PLEASURE
KATE BUSH
EMI
OTHER SINGLES 1993: RUBBERBAND GIRL; EAT THE MUSIC

At this point in her life Kate Bush was experiencing a good deal of painful loss; Alan Murphy, her favoured guitar player, had died and her mother Hannah, referred to in this song, would also soon be gone. Further loss occurred when her long-term personal relationship with bassist Del Palmer came to an end – and so 'Moments of Pleasure' is a salute to the spirits of the lost and departed. Strings swirl over a delightful piano melody, and Bush's voice is hauntingly beautiful; she sounds wounded and vulnerable, and her performance is genuinely moving as she sings "Just being alive, it can really hurt". The listener can't help but be touched by the naked emotion on display; this was a magnificent, artful, and heartfelt record.

49
IF
JANET JACKSON
VIRGIN
OTHER SINGLES 1993:
THAT'S THE WAY LOVE GOES; AGAIN

The ongoing partnership between Janet Jackson and producers Jimmy Jam & Terry Lewis had continued to flourish, and the material that resulted allowed Jackson to grow out of the shadow of her brothers to become a confident artist in her own right – one who was able to express a raunchy sexuality that was a world away from the squeaky-clean image projected onto her at the outset of her singing career. 'If' is uptempo and musically daring; it mixes various disparate elements together and manages to construct something that is rather startling. Hard-riffing industrial rock is combined with hip-hop beats and a filthy, funky bass to produce a full-on, highly frenetic fusion. Meanwhile, a helium-voiced Jackson pictures herself eying-up somebody else's man in a club, as she allows her x-rated imagination to run wild.

48
TILTED
SUGAR
CREATION
OTHER SINGLE 1993: JC AUTO

Bob Mould's first album with Sugar brought his greatest success; leapfrogging on the back of Nirvana's *Nevermind* (the album which created an audience for scuzzy noise rock with pop hooks aplenty) *Copper Blue* not only earned rave reviews, but it sold well too. Within months, it was followed by a mini-album called *Beaster*, described by Mould himself as "Copper Blue's evil-twin". That second record was a provocative, howling blast of difficult to digest, nerve-shredding guitar mayhem, the centrepiece of which was the positively ferocious 'Tilted'. The band play like wolves scenting blood… but from the midst of the carnage comes Mould's wounded, but beautiful voice. This was unquestionably a musical peak for Sugar; such a level of intensity could never again be replicated or sustained.

47
SLIDE AWAY
VERVE
HUT
OTHER SINGLE 1993: BLUE

'Slide Away' is epic in every way; it has the warmth of a narcotic embrace, and the liquid guitar sound achieved by Nick McCabe seems to seep into every single crevice of the song. Additionally, the rhythmic interplay between bass and drums is telepathic, and there is no hint at all of competition for space with the guitar – instead they complement it with subtlety and suppleness. Then, finally, there is Richard Ashcroft, in all-out sage mode, imparting his words as though their message is imperative, fully immersed and seemingly lost in a deep reverie.

46
CATCH A BAD ONE
DEL THE FUNKY HOMOSAPIEN
ELEKTRA
OTHER SINGLES 1993:
MADE IN AMERICA;
WRONGPLACE

Teren Delvon Jones (aka Del the Funky Homosapien) had appeared as part of Da Lench Mob on his cousin Ice Cube's *AmeriKKKa's Most Wanted* album. However, his own music was funkier, freakier and way more abstract than that of his more famous cousin. Del freestyles his lyrics, which are partly humorous but at the same time capable of revealing a rather sharp edge. The track is built around a sample of 'Mrs Parker of KC' by Eric Dolphy, displaying Del's taste for the exotic, to which he added his own amphetamine energy to the rhythmic push-and-pull of this see-sawing rap.

45
LOVE IS STRONGER THAN DEATH
THE THE
EPIC
OTHER SINGLE 1993:
SLOW EMOTION REPLAY

After the death of his younger brother, a grieving Matt Johnson sought therapeutic solace in writing, and although this song highlights the transience of our lives in a physical sense, it also speaks of an enduring love that survives and lives on. Despite emerging from a deep sense of sadness and loss, the song is ultimately uplifting and cathartic. The track features acoustic guitar, a solid drum track and bursts of spine-tingling harmonica. Johnson's vocal is then the icing on the cake; strong but sensitive, and perfectly pitched for this very moving elegy.

44
MISTRESS
RED HOUSE PAINTERS
4AD

Here we have beauty and despair wrapped up together; Mark Kozelek writes about an association that has become awkward and uncomfortable, with a mistress he no longer cares for. He has lost enthusiasm for the relationship and cannot just pretend to love her. Kozelek describes the pain of tangled emotions when long-standing ties need to be broken. This is a song full of mature wisdom, written by a lyrical master. Every phrase is loaded with meaning, whilst musically, Kozelek is surrounded by ethereal swells that are pierced by pin-pricking guitar notes.

43
KIMBLE
THE FALL
STRANGE FRUIT
OTHER SINGLE 1993: WHY ARE PEOPLE GRUDGEFUL?

The Fall managed to hit one of their periodic peaks during this period; their album *The Infotainment Scan* was quite wonderful. Preceding it, in 1992, was a session for DJ John Peel from which 'Kimble' was extracted as a single. In fact, this is a re-titled cover version of Lee Perry's 'Gut of the Quantifier', and The Fall prove themselves to be quite adept at interpreting reggae music. Perhaps this is not really surprising given that the internal logic of this wonderfully idiosyncratic band owed very little indeed to the dull conformity of rock orthodoxy. Here, Mark E. Smith sounds like he is thoroughly enjoying himself as he gleefully mangles the vowels in his inimitable style.

42
COME CLEAN
JERU THE DAMAJA
FFRR

Boasting a goosebump inducing beat from DJ Premier – undoubtedly one of the greatest in hip-hop history – 'Come Clean' was New Yorker Jeru's calling card to the world. His lyrical flow is immaculate as he deftly rhymes around the rhythm, displaying not just a mastery of vocabulary, but also a righteous soul into the bargain.

41
I FEEL YOU
DEPECHE MODE
MUTE
OTHER SINGLES 1993: CONDEMNATION; WALKING IN MY SHOES

'I Feel You' is a filthy blues track that features a memorable guitar hook, played by Martin Gore, and live drums, played by Alan Wilder. But it is the combination of these traditional instruments with deep and dirty synthesiser lines that gives the track its prowling momentum, as malevolent as it is sensual. This ambiguity lends great allure to the recording, and a titanic vocal by Dave Gahan adds even more richness to a truly heavyweight sound.

40
URANUS
SHELLAC
TOUCH AND GO
OTHER SINGLE 1993: THE RUDE GESTURE

'Uranus' was the title of this single by Shellac, although neither track on the record bears that name – the A-side being 'Doris' and the B-side 'Wingwalker'. Shellac were formed by Steve Albini and Todd Trainer, and when joined by bassist Bob Weston, they described themselves as a "minimalist rock trio". 'Doris' is a rhythmic tour-de-force with a sardonic vocal, deeply sarcastic lyric and savage, noisy interludes. 'Wingwalker' progresses with a churning bass riff and hammered drums, as guitar scorches across the track like a flame thrower, and a raw-throated voice howls at the moon. It is analogous to an aural action painting… abstract and gut-wrenchingly physical.

39
DELICATE
TERENCE TRENT D'ARBY FEATURING DES'REE
COLUMBIA
OTHER SINGLES 1993: DO YOU LOVE ME LIKE YOU SAY?; SHE KISSED ME; LET HER DOWN EASY

'Delicate' certainly lives up to its title; it was the crystalline jewel contained on Terence Trent D'arby's third album *Symphony or Damn*, and it is an elegant retro-soul smooch utilising exotic instrumentation and exquisite taste. The blending of Des'ree's rich and soulful voice, alongside D'arby's characterful purr, creates a feeling of intoxication which results in a majestically-paced record that is as smooth as velvet.

38
WILD AMERICA
IGGY POP
VIRGIN
OTHER SINGLES 1993: BESIDE YOU; LOUIE LOUIE

The *American Caesar* album briefly roused Iggy from his artistic torpor; he had been chasing sales and squandering his talent by releasing records unworthy of his exalted pedigree, but this album seemed to be much more heartfelt and thankfully much less polished. 'Wild America' was the stand-out track and most obvious single; it was loud and more than a little bit crazy. The lyrics were funny and they placed Iggy among the underbelly of society, for whom his empathy is natural and unforced. Henry Rollins supplied backing vocals, and there is a riff that never lets up apart for the intrusion of a sensational stun-gun guitar solo. Finally, there was the fabulous refrain of "exterminate the brutes", and all-in-all, this was a genuinely wonderful record by Mr Pop.

37
KEEP YA HEAD UP
2PAC
JIVE
OTHER SINGLES 1993: GOTTA GET MINE; I GET AROUND

'Keep Ya Head Up' was another

mature and compassionate track from the young Tupac. Here he casts an eye around his environment and takes a look at some of the problems and their causes, such as the issue of black women being mistreated and the stupidity of this misogynistic oppression. He also looks at poverty, and without resort to histrionics, makes the valid point that "they got money for wars, but can't feed the poor". His indignation is plain to hear as he rhymes conversationally over samples of 'O-o-h Child' by The Five Stairsteps and Zapp's 'Be Alright', which create a smooth soundscape to lure listeners in towards the harder to swallow, unsentimental truth of the track.

36
MMM… SKYSCRAPER I LOVE YOU
UNDERWORLD
JUNIOR BOYS OWN
OTHER SINGLES 1993: REZ; SPIKEE

'Mmm… Skyscraper I love You' relates to an observation of New York as seen from the sky; Karl Hyde jotted down phrases in a notebook, and then chopped them up to create the impressionistic lyric. This haunting and vaguely off-kilter track twists, throbs and pulsates, generating a distinct air of uneasy nostalgia.

35
SOMETIMES (LESTER PIGGOTT)
JAMES
FONTANA
OTHER SINGLE 1993: LAID

The famous jockey Lester Piggott gets name-checked in the title of this song due to the galloping acoustic guitar riff that dominates the sound. On this record, James were produced by Brian Eno, and he captured a lightness of touch and spontaneity from a band who were very much on a creative roll. The structure of the song is dramatic and Tim Booth's vocal is appropriately theatrical; colourful lyrical imagery deals with a swirling, inescapable turmoil, although the uplifting chorus suggests that there is at least some hope of redemption and peace.

34
LOS ANGELES
FRANK BLACK
4AD
OTHER SINGLE 1993: HANG ON TO YOUR EGO

'Los Angeles' was the first solo single by ex-Pixies main-man Black Francis, re-named as Frank Black; it pretty much picks-up where that band had left-off on their album *Trompe le Monde* – Joey Santiago remains on guitar, and the science-fiction theme is continued with a vision of a futuristic and dystopian Los Angeles. Opening acoustically with Black softly crooning, the track then springs to life as an electric guitar riff is introduced and a sense of urgency is injected into the voice. Keyboard string effects add an elegant touch until a dead stop, as the song concludes with the sound of whirring helicopter rotor blades.

33
LIGHTING FIRES
G.W. McLENNAN
BEGGARS BANQUET

This demonstration of supreme talent was taken from McLennan's second album *Fireboy*. The sound is crisp, the guitars are bright and a beautifully ornamental keyboard melody is picked out as a form of musical punctuation. McLennan employs flame-filled metaphor to deal with affairs of the heart, and his singing conveys an air of sadness which is cleverly juxtaposed with a bright female harmony. As co-leaders of The Go-Betweens, he and Robert Forster had been the Australian equivalent of Lennon & McCartney; it is a great tribute to the artistry of McLennan to note that the quality of his solo work did not slip from that lofty standard.

32
NICKEL BAGS
DIGABLE PLANETS
PENDULUM
OTHER SINGLE 1993: WHERE I'M FROM

Comprising of two men and a woman (named Doodlebug, Butterfly and Ladybug respectively) Digable Planets were a cosmic hip-hop group who advocated for political awareness and a higher state of consciousness. Influenced by bebop-era jazz, along with acts such as The Last Poets, they eschewed sampled sounds in favour of organic instrumentation. Here, over a laid-back groove, they rap about the music they love while ingeniously using drug terminology to emphasise the fact that music is their favourite drug – hence the desire to score "a nickel bag of funk".

31
LA TRISTESSE DURERA (SCREAM TO A SIGH)
MANIC STREET PREACHERS
COLUMBIA
OTHER SINGLES 1993: FROM DESPAIR TO WHERE; ROSES IN THE HOSPITAL

Written from the perspective of war veterans who are made to feel like undervalued embarrassments, 'La Tristesse Durera' (meaning "The sadness will last forever") took its title from the reputed last words of Vincent Van Gogh. Much of the album *Gold Against The Soul*, from which this single was extracted, was somewhat unfocused as The Manics searched for a way to move the band forward, but the exception was 'La Tristesse Durera', which was a breakthrough for them. Everything just seemed to come together; in particular the bass riff that is so important to the song is conclusively of the mutant funk variety. Beginning quietly, the song then explodes into life, devoid of bombast and cliché, and for the vocals, James Dean Bradfield combines in his performance melodicism, grit and passion. He was unmistakably shaping up to become an outstanding singer.

30
AWARD TOUR
A TRIBE CALLED QUEST FEATURING TRUGOY
JIVE

Following up the genius album *The Low End Theory* was not an easy task, and it took A Tribe Called Quest two-years to release *Midnight Marauders*, which proved to be yet another triumph. The lead-off single was 'Award Tour', which featured Trugoy on-loan from fellow Native Tongues outfit De La Soul. Jazz keyboardist and respected elder statesman Weldon Irvine is sampled, and he receives a co-writer's credit, whilst producer Q-Tip also borrows the bass line from Jade's 1992 R&B track 'Don't Walk Away'. The net result is that 'Award Tour' has such a fabulous feel-good vibe that it positively exudes both optimism and joy.

29
AFTERMATH
TRICKY
4TH & BROADWAY

Here, the wildcard collaborator of Massive Attack steps out of that group's shadow, and the result was strange and breathtaking music. 'Aftermath' is a deadly, slow blues with undercurrents of reggae and rock; this is music that seems to come from a half-conscious state, drifting in and out as thoughts change shape. The main vocal is handled by Martina Topley-Bird, a schoolgirl discovered by Tricky; she sings divinely, but in an emotionless manner, as Tricky mumbles and interjects some sleepy, stoned raps. This was intriguing and tricky (excuse the pun!) music to fathom – it felt like a jigsaw puzzle of sound where some of the pieces have been deliberately misplaced.

28
NEW RADIO
BIKINI KILL
KILL ROCK STARS

Turning completely on their head any imposed notions of the way in which women should behave and the language they should use, Bikini Kill revolt and subvert with panache and intelligence. Their sound is a howling punk thrash, turned up to maximum volume, and the lyrics are sharp and as pointed as needles. 'New Radio' is explicitly sexual, but it tramples all over gender stereotypes; this is messy, gritty, dirty and a real in-your-face statement of female sexual empowerment.

27
LIPGLOSS
PULP
ISLAND
OTHER SINGLE 1993:
RAZZAMATAZZ

Pulp were now on a major record label, and for them it was make-or-break time; they had decided that if this single – due to receive ample promotion – failed to find an audience, they would split. Thankfully 'Lipgloss' did give them a first hit, and albeit a very modest number fifty chart placing, this was still much higher than anything they had previously achieved. 'Lipgloss' details the travails of a couple going through the motions in a doomed relationship; it is about the disconnect that occurs when even language is deficient, and there is absolutely nothing left to say or do. The sound of the band is highly distinctive; their thrift-shop glam is evident as the guitar is tastefully fuzzy, the keyboards whirl and the vocal is unmistakably self-assured in its nuanced theatricality.

26
OPEN UP
LEFTFIELD–LYDON
HARD HANDS
OTHER SINGLE 1993: SONG OF LIFE

1992s Public Image Ltd album *That What Is Not* was a dull, hair-metal bore that seemed to suggest John Lydon had dried-up artistically... but his collaboration with Leftfield proved that he still possessed vitality and relevance when proper musical stimulation was available. 'Open Up' was constructed from impeccable, dubby trance dance beats, with a hint of malevolent dissonant spice added to the pot. Lydon rants and raves to the point of near hysteria – "Burn Hollywood burn" he wails maliciously. But really this is a collaborative affair that succeeds on every level, and both parties concerned certainly earned much deserved kudos.

25
STUTTER
ELASTICA
DECEPTIVE

Guitarist Justine Frischmann and drummer Justin Welch had been members of Suede when they were still an unknown band – but subsequently, after recruiting bassist Annie Holland and guitarist Donna Mathews, they formed their own group – Elastica – who looked like a fabulous, black-clad gang. 'Stutter' (along with superb B-side 'Pussycat') sounded just as good as they looked, and it came with substantive content too, incorporating a lyric concerned with male impotence as viewed from a female perspective. This was a boot-on-the-other-foot moment in pop history, as Frischmann offers up no sympathy whatsoever to her embarrassed and humiliated prospective lover, dismissing him instead with contemptuous short-shrift.

24
EGO TRIPPIN' (PART TWO)
DE LA SOUL
TOMMY BOY
OTHER SINGLE 1993: BREAKADAWN

The third De La Soul album, *Buhloone Mindstate*, maintained the high quality of its predecessors, as did the singles extracted from it – in particular 'Ego Trippin'', which is slyly satirical as it disparages the dubious motivations of many performers and the formulaic path pursued by many of De La Soul's hip-hop peers. Live instruments are mixed with sampled beats – something for which they received few accolades, even though musical progression was being prioritised over artistic stagnation – and they handle these mellow beats with huge virtuosity and finesse.

23
FOR TOMORROW
BLUR
FOOD
OTHER SINGLES 1993:
CHEMICAL WORLD;
SUNDAY SUNDAY

In 1992 Blur had toured in the United States; the antipathy shown towards them by grunge-obsessed crowds was reciprocated, and Blur had detested the whole experience. On returning home, they responded by writing a bunch of songs containing a deliberate and distinctly British sensibility, and 'For Tomorrow' was the most obviously commercial of these. It has a "La, la, la la" chorus, and an air of cheerful nostalgia as we are taken on a lyrical tour around London, including a drive along the Westway and onward to Primrose Hill and Emperor's Gate in South Kensington, where Damon Albarn had lived with his parents as a child (next-door-neighbours to John & Cynthia Lennon in fact). Strings are very effectively incorporated into the track – courtesy of The Duke String Quartet – and they add a lovely touch of melancholia to a beautiful song, which for Blur functioned as a refreshing new beginning.

22
YOU'RE IN A BAD WAY
SAINT ETIENNE
HEAVENLY
OTHER SINGLE 1993: HOBART PAVING/WHO DO YOU THINK YOU ARE?

'You're in a Bad Way' was written as a loving pastiche of innocent 1960s British pop – being a simple imitation of Herman's Hermits – and it was intended for use as a single B-side. Bob Stanley claimed that it took him just ten minutes to compose; nobody is contesting that claim, but somehow, the end result contained an unintended sprinkling of fairy-dust that made the song highly attractive. Opening with a sample from the 1963 film version of *Billy Liar*, the lyric goes on to describe a man who is feeling sorry for himself. Sarah Cracknell provides a perfectly pleasant girl-next-door vocal as she name-drops Bruce Forsyth and his TV show *The Generation Game*. With a galloping northern soul beat, a chirpy vibe and 'Telstar'-style sound effects, Saint Etienne were accidentally rewarded with an uncommonly memorable hit.

21
MAN SIZE
PJ HARVEY
ISLAND
OTHER SINGLE 1993:
50FT QUEENIE

Produced by Chicago noise-master Steve Albini, there is a deliberately crude and raw sound to this recording; the guitars bleed and the drums are so upfront they feel as though they are coming from inside your own head. Polly Harvey is a conduit for pure energy and the words seem to drip from her lips soaked in blood. She discusses gender roles and the power struggles which arise therein… but her meaning is ambiguous. On the one hand, she could be singing as a female who wishes to be perceived in a more masculine way so that society will confer a more valued status upon her, or, she could equally be singing from inside the mind of man, inhabiting his thoughts and exposing feelings of superiority over women. It doesn't really matter, because either way, this record is visceral and extremely potent.

20
FUZZY
GRANT LEE BUFFALO
SLASH

Led by vocalist/songwriter Grant Lee Phillips, here was a band who channeled old-style Americana into graceful melodic music full of gothic splendour. 'Fuzzy' was their first single and its haunting atmospherics made it an immediate ear-worm. Employing little more than a strummed acoustic guitar, with simple slapped rhythm in support, Phillips's voice takes the leading role – it is highly emotive, and at points it soars like a tortured angel as he sings of enduring a pained existence in a permanent state of indecision. A fuzzy guitar solo intrudes to break the reverie, adding a dash of colour to the sepia-wash of this entrancing and ghost-inhabited sound.

19
THE FUTURE
LEONARD COHEN
COLUMBIA

Recent world history had been turbulent: the fall of the Berlin Wall, the collapse of the Soviet Block, the Tiananmen Square massacre and riots in Los Angeles… all of these events inform this apocalyptic song. The biblical and the sexual, and the sacred and profane are placed side-by-side within a lyric that suggests we are in for an extremely bleak future. Of course, Cohen was both an arch-satirist and a wise Buddhist, so perhaps it is best to read this prophecy as a warning of what might happen if change is unforthcoming, rather than what will inevitably occur. The musical arrangement also supports the hypothesis that the singer is indeed putting us on – and wearing a wry smile as he does so – since it is an unholy cross-pollination between church spiritual and cheesy, middle-of-the-road lounge-bar schmaltz.

18
CAN YOU FORGIVE HER?
PET SHOP BOYS
PARLOPHONE
OTHER SINGLES 1993: I WOULDN'T NORMALLY DO THIS KIND OF THING; GO WEST

This has a title inspired by an Anthony Trollope novel, and a lyric that concerns a woman who accuses her boyfriend of retaining an unnatural love for a childhood friend; she publicly ridicules him, and his preference for disco over more 'masculine' rock music is used as a reason to undermine him. She is unprepared to share him with a memory that he holds dear, and so decides to "get herself a real man instead". Neil Tennant's conversational vocal is superbly employed in imparting these revelations; in his role of objective narrator, he is simply a neutral observer. For his part, Chris Lowe ads considerable oomph to his keyboard contributions, giving the overall track a trance style that is well complemented by orchestral stabs which add a dramatic emphasis to proceedings. An insistent chorus is the final cherry on top of this very sophisticated pop concoction that no-one other than Pet Shop Boys could ever conceivably have pulled off.

17
PASSIN' ME BY
THE PHARCYDE
DELICIOUS VINYL
OTHER SINGLE 1993:
4 BETTER OR 4 WORSE

Left-field rap with a jazzy twist, 'Passin' Me By' was such a wondrous sound. Jimi Hendrix, Quincy Jones and Weather Report are all sampled in the construction of this bittersweet, floating soundscape, with a sweet beat added so that one by one, Bootie Brown, Inani, Fatlip and Slimkid 3 can recount their feelings of heartbreak and inadequacy, as schoolboy crushes inevitably lead them to feelings of rejection and teenage angst.

16
NIGHTSWIMMING
R.E.M.
WARNER BROTHERS
OTHER SINGLES 1993: EVERY-BODY HURTS; THE SIDE-WINDER SLEEPS TONIGHT; FIND THE RIVER

R.E.M. had been touched by greatness and could do no wrong, either artistically or commercially, as they continued to convert rough half-ideas into era-defining songs. The genesis of 'Nightswimming' was a simple, circular piano riff that Mike Mills was playing. This was overheard by Michael Stipe who just happened to have a pre-written lyric concerning bonding and the making of friends whilst skinny-dipping. As if by magic, the song perfectly captured a time of innocence and wide-eyed wonder, that we as listeners can so easily relate to. A top-class string arrangement was then provided by ex-Led Zeppelin bass player, John Paul Jones, and when all the pieces were put together, R.E.M. had created, seemingly without great effort, a shimmering, serene song of exceptional beauty.

15
SUGAR KANE
SONIC YOUTH
DGC
OTHER SINGLE 1993: DRUNK-EN BUTTERFLY

'Sugar Kane' is upbeat, playful and it rocks! Sonic Youth certainly had undeniable chic appeal – no other band were cooler than they – but 'Sugar Kane' was fully inclusive and it could be enjoyed by anyone. This was simply a great guitar pop single from these denizens of New York's art underground. Although it is never made explicit in the lyric, 'Sugar Kane' is the name of the character portrayed by Marilyn Monroe in the film *Some Like It Hot*, so here we have yet another nod to the silver screen icon, following in the footsteps of the never cool Elton John.

14
LENNY VALENTINO
THE AUTEURS
HUT
OTHER SINGLES 1993: HOUSE-BREAKER; HOW COULD I BE WRONG

The opening guitar/cello riff pins you to your seat, and what comes afterwards offers absolutely no reprieve as an unflinching beat is used as a launch pad for a sneering and seething aural assault on the senses, the sort that forces the listener's neck to move in the manner of a nodding dog on the back-seat of an E-type Jaguar… it is spellbinding stuff. Luke Haines curls his lip and acid-flecked words drip from his tongue; this was brash, bold and bordering on genius. The Auteurs balanced the scales against a plethora of clueless, careerist British guitar bands – if they hadn't actually existed, it would have been necessary to invent them.

13
ANYONE CAN PLAY GUITAR
RADIOHEAD
PARLOPHONE
OTHER SINGLE 1993: STOP WHISPERING

Here, Jonny Greenwood plays guitar with a paintbrush, and everybody else in the studio was invited to pick up a guitar and make some noise for the record. This track is all about dismantling rock & roll pomposity and preening self-regard; it pokes fun at men who buy leather trousers in the belief that they somehow confer cool, and it highlights the fact that fretboard masturbation is mind-numbingly dull to absolutely everyone apart from the person who is actually engaged in the act of musical onanism. Sung by Thom Yorke with a sweetness that hides his deadly purpose, this very good single acted as a statement of intent for Radiohead; it strongly implied that they would not allow themselves to be turned into a clichéd and predictable brand, and indeed that proved to be the case. Eventually, Radiohead became a truly outstanding group and wrote much better songs than 'Anyone Can Play Guitar', but this was where their manifesto was first verbalised.

12
MIDDLE OF THE ROAD
DENIM
BOYS OWN RECORDINGS

After a period of reflection following the demise of Felt, Lawrence returned with another fabric-themed band called Denim. This new group embraced the sound of early 1970s glam rock, and although their song lyrics were sarcastic – often downright caustic – they also tended to have big pop choruses. 'Middle of the Road' has a chugging rhythm, over which Lawrence lists practically every credible musical artist of the post-war era, before declaring his antipathy towards them. Twee Scottish pop act Middle of the Road (remember the days of hot pants and tank tops!) have their number one smash hit 'Chirpy Chirpy Cheep Cheep' sampled as an anti-cool illustration that coolness is in itself naff, and therefore it is much more fun to dig mindless and cheap unfashionable pop.

11
FIVE STRING SERENADE
MAZZY STAR
ROUGH TRADE
OTHER SINGLES 1993: SHE'S MY BABY

Taken from their second album *So Tonight That I Might See*, 'Five String Serenade' was a loving interpretation of a song written by the legendary Arthur Lee of the band Love. Mazzy Star's version is stripped-back to its essential component parts; David Roback picks out the melody on acoustic guitar, and Hope Sandoval sings quietly… almost magnetically… her voice seemingly drawing us ever deeper into the song. A little touch of reverb adds atmospherics while a violin is sparingly used, its tone low and mournful. The net effect is spine-chilling; the strange beauty of this track possesses the power to send shivers rippling down my spine, just by thinking about listening to this magnificent record.

10

REGRET

NEW ORDER

LONDON

OTHER SINGLES 1993:

RUINED IN A DAY; SPOOKY; WORLD (THE PRICE OF LOVE)

It is a matter of public record that deep discord and acrimony existed between the members of New Order. They had been forced together to make the album *Republic* in the vain hope that they could save The Hacienda from closure – and, as a consequence, save themselves from financial ruin. Somehow, despite the circumstances, they conspired to make a good album from which this superb single was taken. 'Regret' is far less rhythmic and much less dance-orientated than their music had recently been, but melodically it is very strong. A distinctive and attractive guitar figure acts as a motif, whilst a propulsive bass line provides thrusting momentum. These two elements are perfectly balanced by drums and keyboards that are so unobtrusive you might not notice their presence unless they were taken away. Bernard Sumner's little-boy-lost vocals are also charming and help to make this wistful gem an unforgettable addition to the New Order catalogue of delights.

9

SHE DON'T USE JELLY

THE FLAMING LIPS

WARNER BROTHERS

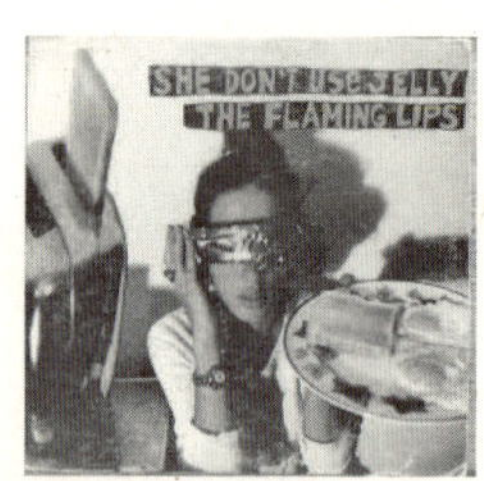

Nonsensical but joyous in its wide-eyed innocence, 'She Don't Use Jelly' was the moment of brilliance that The Flaming Lips had been threatening to produce. Here, everything just coalesces perfectly; all the disparate elements merge to create something greater than the individual parts would suggest. Pedal steel guitar features in the verses where weird but wonderful people are described, before giving way to outbursts of noise… a cheerful, harmonious kind of noise rather than the in-your-face variety. Somehow, Wayne Coyne manages to sing with childlike glee whilst simultaneously sounding like a mischievous, favourite uncle – surely nobody could possibly fail to love this record…

could they?

8
JENNY ONDIOLINE/FRENCH DISKO
STEREOLAB
DUOPHONIC

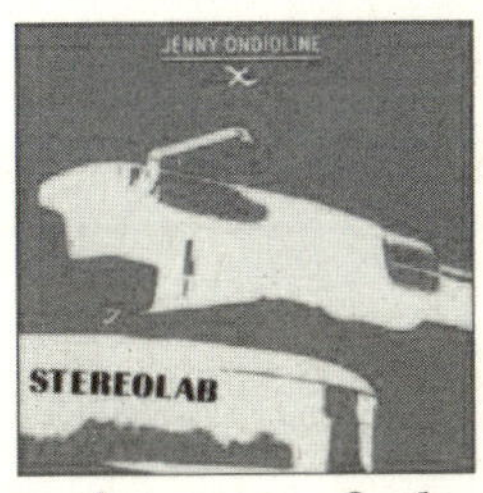

The Ondioline was an electronic keyboard predecessor of the synthesiser, invented by Georges Jenny… hence the title of the song. The track is heavily influenced by Neu's 'Hallogallo', sharing a rhythmic sensibility akin to travelling at high speed on a very long and clear stretch of road. The lyric admonishes all political creeds and doctrines. 'French Disko' is every bit as rhythmic, but more melodic, and it comes with a very tasteful guitar solo as well as some sonic dissonance. Lyrically, this song is concerned with achieving liberation from the absurdities of life, through free and independent expression. Totally anti-rock and unmistakably European, without even trying, Stereolab were the coolest band on planet Earth.

7
IN/FLUX
DJ SHADOW
MO' WAX

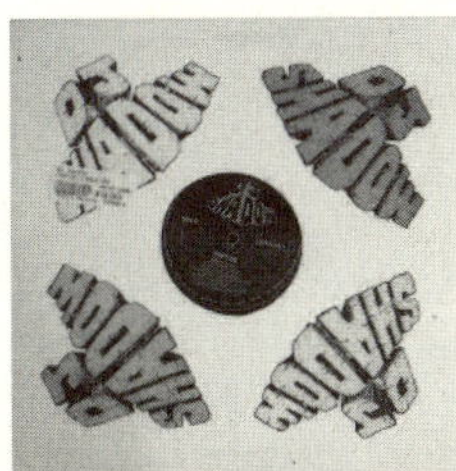

Mo' Wax was a London-based label run by James Lavelle, known for issuing records of dubious quality in the hipsterish soul/jazz genre that was rapidly becoming tiresome. But when Lavelle heard a dancey, breakbeat record that DJ Shadow had made with African group Zimbabwe Legit, it entranced him. He contacted Shadow and travelled to Los Angeles to meet him. As they were both unashamed record nerds, they got on like a house-on-fire, and Lavelle proposed that Shadow make a record for Mo' Wax. The resulting track was entirely assembled from bargain-bin record samples and it pushed at the boundaries of what hip-hop could be. In short, this was a masterful piece of work; intelligent dance music that was perhaps even better to hear through headphones, allowing it to seep into your soul, while undertaking the twelve-minute sonic journey entirely alone. Not many records can genuinely be considered truly groundbreaking… but In/Flux was undoubtedly one of the select few.

6

HUMAN BEHAVIOUR

BJÖRK

ONE LITTLE INDIAN

OTHER SINGLES 1993:

VENUS AS A BOY; PLAY DEAD;

BIG TIME SENSUALITY

Although we had heard her voice before, during her tenure as singer in The Sugarcubes the Icelandic vocalist extraordinaire still succeeded in stunning us with this debut solo single. She had teamed up with esteemed producer Nellee Hooper, who had been a member of pre-Massive Attack posse The Wild Bunch, as well as working extensively with Soul II Soul. Together they co-wrote 'Human Behaviour' and surrounded Björk's voice – already full of wonderment – with warm, sub-tropical jazz flavourings and a pounded kettle drum beat. This was already entrancing enough, but now factor in Björk's lyric (inspired by David Attenborough wildlife documentaries, where human beings are very unflatteringly viewed from the perception of wild animals) and one is inescapably forced to the conclusion that this single was just categorically magical.

5

ALL APOLOGIES/RAPE ME

NIRVANA

DGC

OTHER SINGLE 1993:

HEART SHAPED BOX

This was the final single released by Nirvana before Kurt Cobain's death, and both sides of the record featured on the Steve Albini produced album *In Utero*. 'All Apologies' was written in 1990 and had been demoed several times before release. It was also one of three tracks on the album re-mixed by Scott Litt, giving more prominence to the vocals. With its mix of acoustic guitar and cello – the latter playing a simple, but still potent melody – Cobain thought the song was peaceful and happy… although in truth, the lyric and his performance come across as an expression of sad and bitter resignation. 'Rape Me' had been written prior to the release of *Nevermind*; it has a sound and structure not dissimilar to 'Smells Like Teen Spirit', sharing the same loud/quiet pattern and containing a similarly rousing chorus. But lyrically, it steps into very dark and violent territory, being written from the perspective of a rape victim who is defiant in the face of the attacker, screaming "Rape me!" to deny him any power, and thereby refusing to play the role of victim.

4
ANIMAL NITRATE
SUEDE
NUDE
OTHER SINGLE 1993: SO YOUNG

'Animal Nitrate', with its punning title a reference to amyl nitrate, is a song about drugs and loveless sex, set in a seedy suburban scene; it hints at violence, disappointment and a longing to escape from an imprisoning world of mundane squalor. Originally the song had the working title of 'Dixon', because Bernard Butler used the theme tune from television series *Dixon of Dock Green* as the basis for the chorus. In fact, Butler plays up a veritable storm on this record; like a latter-day Mick Robson, he sets the guitar to stun and proceeds to combine powerful stomping riffs with dashes of vivid colour… it is a thrilling listen. Not to be outdone, Brett Anderson manages to match his bandmate with his vocal rendition, elongating his vowels with glee, and spitting out key phrases with disdain in a highly dramatic, but wholly appropriate performance. At this point, Suede seemed strange and interesting; they conveyed an air of androgynous bacchanal and seemed almost other worldly. Just three singles into their career and they were the most talked about group in the UK, because each one of those singles had been quite astonishing.

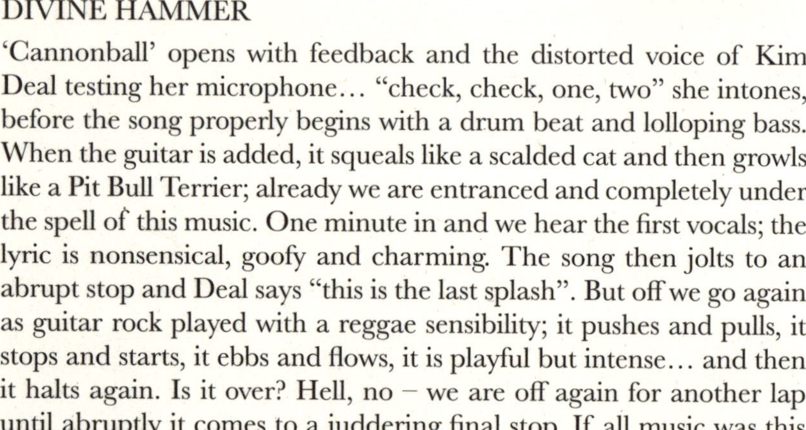

3
CANNONBALL
THE BREEDERS
4AD
OTHER SINGLE 1993:
DIVINE HAMMER

'Cannonball' opens with feedback and the distorted voice of Kim Deal testing her microphone… "check, check, one, two" she intones, before the song properly begins with a drum beat and lolloping bass. When the guitar is added, it squeals like a scalded cat and then growls like a Pit Bull Terrier; already we are entranced and completely under the spell of this music. One minute in and we hear the first vocals; the lyric is nonsensical, goofy and charming. The song then jolts to an abrupt stop and Deal says "this is the last splash". But off we go again as guitar rock played with a reggae sensibility; it pushes and pulls, it stops and starts, it ebbs and flows, it is playful but intense… and then it halts again. Is it over? Hell, no – we are off again for another lap until abruptly it comes to a juddering final stop. If all music was this unhinged and idiosyncratic, with this much bounce and high-spirits, good gracious, we would all be walking around unable to stop smiling.

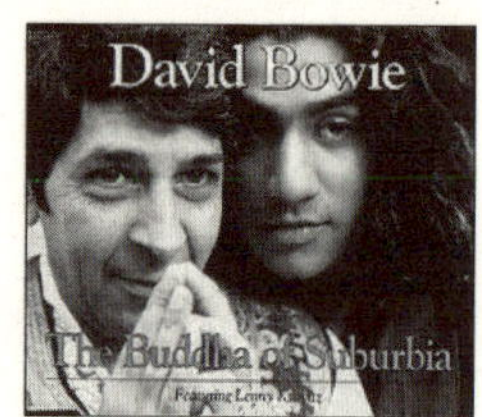

2
BUDDHA OF SUBURBIA
DAVID BOWIE
ARISTA
OTHER SINGLES 1993:
JUMP THEY SAY;
MIRACLE GOODNIGHT; BLACK TIE WHITE NOISE

David Bowie was doing the publicity round for his high-profile, very expensive and much vaunted comeback album *Black Tie White Noise*; as an album, it promised much but flattered to deceive… in fact it wasn't very good. However, whilst doing promotional interviews, Bowie found himself in conversation with British author Hanif Kureishi, whose 1990 novel, *The Buddha of Suburbia*, was to be adapted for TV. Bowie agreed to compose music for the series, which proved to be the wisest artistic decision he had made in two decades, as he re-located and re-discovered his mojo with this project. Choosing to work quickly, and at low budget, he found an able co-worker in Turkish multi-instrumentalist Erdal Kizilçay. A soundtrack album appeared and the title track was released as a single, which featured Lenny Kravitz. Inspired by Kureishi's storyline, Bowie saw clear parallels with his own youth, so he pastiches his own early 1970s sound and references in lyric and musical motif a number of his own songs such as 'All the Madmen' and 'Space Oddity'. A mix of synthesiser, guitar, percussion and trumpet are combined with Bowie's own prominent saxophone part, and he sings in a subdued and subtle manner, rather than at the top of his range. This was heart-warming music, and it was so pleasing to hear Bowie sound at his most vital since 'Absolute Beginners', way back in 1986.

1

JESUS' BLOOD NEVER FAILED ME YET

GAVIN BRYARS

POINT MUSIC

Gavin Bryars is an English modern classical composer and a founding member of The Portsmouth Sinfonia, an orchestra where musical competence was not a prerequisite of membership – Brian Eno was a fellow member. Commissioned to write a score for a documentary about street people in London, Bryars used a looped improvised stanza sung by an old homeless man to build a piece of music around, and in 1971, Eno released this twenty-five minute piece on his Obscure label. Since then, it has been re-recorded on several occasions, usually in much lengthier versions. In 1993, the advent of the CD saw a seventy-four minute version released with Tom Waits adding his voice to that of the unknown old vagrant; this was shortlisted for the Mercury Prize and from it, this single was released. The voice of the old man is emotionally devastating; it comes direct from his soul, ragged and imperfect, but full of faith and humility. The manner in which the sixteen words of the stanza are delivered is as eloquent a testimony as it is possible to imagine; he speaks nakedly and honestly, and hope is his only currency… he believes, with unshakeable inner conviction, that Jesus will be his salvation. Bryars orchestral swells, ebbing and flowing in accompaniment, are perfectly simpatico, creating a piece that truly inhabits the psyche; once heard, this is never to be forgotten.

Charles Atlas eat your heart out - on the beach at Montpellier, 1993

1994

EVENTS

Astronaut Valeri Polyakov begins a world record orbit of earth of 477.7 days.

US and Russian Presidents, Bill Clinton and Boris Yeltsin, sign the Kremlin accords, which stop the aiming of pre-programmed nuclear missiles at each other's countries.

The Bosnian Serb Army shell a marketplace in Sarajevo; 68 people are murdered and around 200 more are seriously wounded.

In Gloucester, Fred and Rose West are arrested for committing multiple murders.

Israeli terrorist Baruch Goldstein shoots and murders 29 Muslim worshippers inside the Cave of the Patriarchs in the West Bank; he is set upon and beaten to death.

The Church of England ordains its first female priests.

The Rwandan genocide begins.

Nelson Mandela becomes the first democratically elected President of South Africa.

The Channel Tunnel between France and England is opened.

The Flavr Savr – a genetically modified tomato – is declared safe and granted a licence for human consumption; it is the first genetically engineered food to be made commercially available.

Michael Jackson marries Lisa Marie Presley.

Former American Football star and Hollywood actor OJ Simpson goes on the run following the murders of his former wife Nicole Brown and her lodger Ronald Goldman. The man-hunt is screened live on TV and, when Simpson gives himself up, he is charged with their murders. The forthcoming trial would last a year.

Columbian footballer Andrés Escobar is shot dead after having scored an own goal at the World Cup in the USA.

Jeff Bezos founds Amazon.

The Provisional IRA announces a complete cessation of military operations.

Russia and China agree to end the targeting of each other with nuclear weapons.

The Taliban is formed in Kandahar, Afghanistan.

45 year-old George Foreman regains the unified WBA and IBF heavyweight boxing championships by knocking out 26-year old Michael Moorer; he becomes the oldest ever heavyweight champion.

Hurricane Gordon causes 1,152 fatalities when it hits the Caribbean and USA.

Sony release the PlayStation video game system.

Russia wages war in Chechnya, where the people seek independence from the Russian Federation.

Manchester United win the Premier League and FA Cup; they sign Roy Keane as a spiritual heir to captain Bryan Robson, who leaves to manage Middlesbrough. Brazil win the World Cup in the USA.

BIRTHS 1994

Harry Styles; Memphis Depay; Justin Bieber; Eric Bailly; Tom Daley; Victor Lindelof; Bruno Fernandes; Adam Peaty

DEATHS 1994

Cesar Romero; Harry Nilsson ; Matt Busby ; Telly Savalas ; Pierre Boulle; Joseph Cotton ; Derek Jarman ; Dinah Shore; Bill Hicks ; Jersey Joe Walcott; John Candy; Charles Bukowski; Fernando Rey; Dan Hartman ; Kurt Cobain; Richard Nixon; Ayrton Senna; John Wayne Gacy ; Jacqueline Onassis Kennedy; Erich Honecker; Dennis Potter; Henry Mancini ; Kristen Pfaff; Kim Il Sung; Peter Cushing; Lindsay Anderson; Billy Wright; Nicky Hopkins; Franco Moschino ; Robert Bloch ; Burt Lancaster; Carmen McRae; Cab Calloway; Jeffrey Dahmer; John Osborne;

NOTABLE FILMS

Serial Mom; The Crow; Interview With The Vampire; Bullets Over Broadway; Clerks; Natural Born Killers; Three Colours White; The Adventures of Priscilla,

Queen of the Desert; Forrest Gump; The Lion King; Léon: The Professional; The Shawshank Redemption; Shallow Grave; Three Colours Red; Chungking Express; Pulp Fiction

NOTABLE BOOKS

Midnight in the Garden of Good and Evil – John Berendt
Captain Corelli's Mandolin – Louis De Bernières
The Wind-Up Bird Chronicle – Haruki Murakami
Long Walk to Freedom – Nelson Mandela
Of Love and other Demons – Gabriel Garcia Marquez
Good Bones and Simple Murders – Margaret Atwood
East, West – Salman Rushdie
Dixie City Jam – James Lee Burke
Hollywood Nocturnes – James Ellroy
House of Splendid Isolation – Edna O'Brien
Rotten: No Irish, No Blacks, No Dogs – John Lydon
Faithfull – Marianne Faithfull

MY 1994

The death of my father at the end of the previous year had affected me greatly; I was depressed and withdrawn. I spent a considerable amount of time with my mother who was broken-hearted; I would take her for drives into the countryside, to the cinema, or indeed anywhere where her thoughts would be temporarily diverted from her loss. For me, the routine of work and its distractions was an escape; I drank to excess when alone, and in social situations. On the plus side, attending football matches brought pleasure and camaraderie with friends; there were two Wembley Cup Finals to attend this year – a loss in the League Cup, but a trouncing of the pre-dirty money Chelsea in the FA Cup. There was also a Champions League game in Barcelona, which was extended into an excellent week's holiday; what a marvellous city Barcelona is, even though the game itself resulted in a catastrophic 4-0 loss, accompanied by monkey noises from the Catalans every time one of United's black players touched the ball. The only good part of the evening was pre-match, when Mick Hucknall fetched over the suspended Eric Cantona for a brief hello and a handshake.

Back at home, I was persuaded that the purchase of a nice car would be beneficial to my equilibrium, and I succumbed to the temptation; £11,000 was spent on a brand-new vehicle… to this day, still the most money that I have paid for a car. Less than two weeks later, I had been out drinking on a Friday night; this continued until 4am back at my house, and then I made the ridiculous mistake of offering to give a companion a lift home. Fortunately, he was safely delivered to his door, but on the return journey I fell asleep at the wheel. I was jolted awake as my car hit a curb on the corner of a road; instinct made me pull on the steering wheel which had the effect of steering the offside of my car into a substantial wall. Without this instinct, I would have crashed head-on. I came to my senses immediately; miraculously, there was not a bump or scratch on me… although my lovely brand-new car was now a crumpled wreck and the wall I'd hit had been demolished by the force of the impact. I cursed my own reckless idiocy and waited for the Police to arrive, perfectly willing to accept the consequences of my actions; knowing that I could have killed either myself or somebody else, I had absolutely no excuse. The Police quickly arrived on the scene; I told them the truth about the extent of my drinking and how the crash had occurred. A breathalyser was produced and I blew into it… amazingly, the significant quantity of alcohol I'd consumed didn't even register. Perhaps because I'd been honest and was clearly contrite, the policeman smiled at me: "It's your lucky day" he said, "Get yourself home and get some kip". Incredibly, I had avoided criminal proceedings being taken against me; I had not lost my driving licence, or even accumulated any penalty points. Somehow I'd walked out of a severe car wreck physically unharmed; it was indeed my lucky day. Insurance assessors decided that my car had incurred £10,000 worth of damage and it was towed away. I learned a huge lesson that night, and never again have I driven under the influence of alcohol.

100
I'LL STAND BY YOU
THE PRETENDERS
WARNER BROTHERS

I had often quite liked singles by The Pretenders, without them truly moving me; I considered the execution of their music to be a little too traditional to truly cater for my tastes. However, 'I'll Stand By You' was somehow different; it was more emotional, warm and tender. As a somewhat embarrassed Chrissie Hynde later admitted, the song was written with the express purpose of scoring a hit. To that end, she collaborated with Tom Kelly and Billy Steinberg, the redoubtable songwriting duo who had helped Cyndi Lauper, Madonna and Whitney Houston to achieve career boosting success. 'I'll Stand By You' was a big ballad that communicated the message of keeping faith with a loved one through tough times. It was heart-stoppingly romantic – a grand gesture delivered with extraordinary panache by Hynde, over a reconstructed wall of sound.

99
LOVE SPREADS
THE STONE ROSES
GEFFEN

This is Led Zeppelin inspired blues/rock heaviness, with wailing guitars and a lyric about the Passion of Christ with a black woman in the role of Jesus. Bobby Gillespie of Primal Scream hailed 'Love Spreads' as "The greatest comeback single ever"; I have to say that I disagree with his level of hyperbole, but 'Love Spreads' was audacious, ambitious and as mad as a box of frogs – I certainly liked it.

98
BUG POWDER DUST
BOMB THE BASS
ISLAND
OTHER SINGLE 1994: DARK HEART

'Bug Powder Dust' references William Burroughs – and in particular his novel *Naked Lunch*. However, woven around the central theme are lots of other popular culture references, from *Twin Peaks*, The Beatles and *Apocalypse Now*, to Allen Ginsberg and *The Lulu Show*. Tim Simenon had teamed-up with the versatile Justin Warfield, whose rapped vocal is fast, furious and astonishingly good. The track itself is punishing, and set in motion by a bass sample (courtesy of ex-Weather Report member Alphonso Johnson) taken from the track 'Open Your Eyes, You Can Fly' by Flora Purim.

97
THROW
CARL CRAIG PRESENTS PAPERCLIP PEOPLE
OPEN
OTHER SINGLE 1994: REMAKE

For the cornerstone of this track, Carl Craig (under the Paperclip People moniker) takes a brief sample of Loleatta Holloway's disco number 'Hit and Run', and then does some rather wonderful things with it – in a supremely tasteful fashion – to bring forth this nine-minutes of techno excellence.

96
YOUR FAVOURITE THING
SUGAR
CREATION
OTHER SINGLE 1994: BELIEVE WHAT YOU'RE SAYING

Insecurity and desperation are forensically examined here, as a longing for attention and craving to feel special strips the pleading narrator of his self-respect. Soundwise, the band abandon the malice and sledgehammer attack they had so recently been pursuing, and they replace it with something altogether friendlier and poppier. Having said that, and remembering that this is Bob Mould and Sugar, the words "friendlier and poppier" are highly subjective, because 'Your Favourite Thing' is still the sonic equivalent of being kicked by a mule.

95
WILMOT
SABRES OF PARADISE
WARP
OTHER SINGLE 1994: THEME

Part tango, part dub reggae, part techno; when minds that are unbound by convention are allowed to run free, and when those same minds have been immersed in all genres of music that they love equally, then they can create their own absolutely brilliant music… and this is what it sounds like.

94
YOGA
THE PASTELS
DOMINO

Sounding a bit like a rough-around-the-edges version of Stereolab, this was more muscular than the normal shambolically reticent sound of The Pastels. The guitars are clipped and the drums are whacked with gusto as singer/bassist Annabel Wright (aka Aggi) performs admirably in the vocal department – albeit slightly out of tune – whilst simultaneously serving up a marvellously persistent bass line that drives the song along. This is great pop that pleasingly retains a very human touch.

93
GIVE IT UP
PUBLIC ENEMY
DEF JAM
OTHER SINGLE 1994: WHAT KIND OF POWER WE GOT?

In terms of hip-hop music, Public Enemy had been around a long time, and some critics thought they had become too old and out of touch to have any further relevance. Still, the public seemed to disagree, and 'Give It Up' was a top-twenty hit in the UK, as well as earning them their only ever top-forty placing in the US. Once again Public Enemy were encouraging people to maintain their own self-respect and, crucially, to treat others with equal respect… sentiments which saw them positioned in direct opposition to the negative self-serving attitudes expressed by many Gangsta Rap acts. As usual, The Bomb Squad deliver a masterful soundscape for Chuck D and company to paint their voices across; this time, it is a mellowish vibe of strutting funkiness, based around a sample of Albert King, Steve Cropper and Pop Staples performing 'Opus De Soul'.

92
SEA LIKE A CHILD
A.R. KANE
3RD STONE

'Sea Like a Child' is an oddly structured, but never awkward sounding, track; it simmers like a bubbling broth and is utterly gorgeous. A melody is picked out on piano, and the feathery vocals allow the Eastern flavours to bring a shimmering, ethereal quality, further enhanced by a cool jazz bass-line, which imparts a sinuous, time-stretching feel.

91
HOLD ONTO YOUR FRIENDS
MORRISSEY
PARLOPHONE
OTHER SINGLES 1994: THE MORE YOU IGNORE ME THE CLOSER I GET; INTERLUDE

A very beautiful and elegant guitar line underpins this understated song, which is concerned with the nature of friendship; the loyalty and mutual support that underpins feelings of true friendship are examined, as are the more disappointing aspects, such as when one feels a friendship is being taken for granted or abused. Played at walking pace and sung with aching clarity by the ex-Smith, 'Hold Onto Your Friends' was, for me, one of Morrissey's very best singles.

90
CHAMPION
BUJU BANTON
PENTHOUSE
OTHER SINGLES 1994: GOD MY SALVATION; TWIGGY – WANT IT; LOVING WAS A CRIME; RAMPAGE; OPERATION WILLY; MAN A LOOK YU

Funky Jamaica was represented by Buju Banton on this single – extracted from his classic *'Til Shiloh* album, on which he fused traditional sounds with the prevailing digital technology. For this track, he mixes a hip-hop rhythm with a reggae flavouring, and then vocalises with speedy finesse, in his deep, rasping style. 'Champion' is uptempo, uplifting, jubilant and positive.

89
STRESS
ORGANIZED KONFUSION
HOLLYWOOD BASIC

Organized Konfusion were a pair of lyrical wizards – Prince Po and Pharoahe Monch – from Queens, New York. Although largely self-sufficient, for 'Stress' they brought in outside help in the shape of future production heavyweight Buckwild. The piece is a dark, swampy and extremely funky creation of slowed down voices and beats, within a noir soundscape that features a Charles Mingus sample. Given such sonic splendour to work with, Po and Monch do not disappoint in either delivery or rhyme… a great example being "My perception of poetic injection is ejaculation… the immaculate conception". These outré hip-hoppers really were the bee's knees of lyricism.

88
SPACE COWBOY
JAMIROQUAI
SONY SOHO SQUARE
OTHER SINGLES 1994: HALF THE MAN

Jamiroquai were an acid jazz band built around Jay Kay, the writer/singer and famed hat-wearer. 'Space Cowboy' sees the band mining Sly and the Family Stone's *There's a Riot Goin' On* for heavy inspiration; it replicates Sly's slinky bass-led sound with impressive "bob and weave" results. Jay Kay sings in a friendly kind of way, using a high-register to give his vocal a floaty feel, as he trips the light fantastic and shares his inter-planetary good vibes with us more earthbound folks.

87
DEADLY DEEP SUBS
DILLINJA
DEADLY VINYL
OTHER SINGLES 1994: SOUTH SIDE; DEADLY CEREMONIES; YOU DON'T KNOW

Dillinja was a London-based record producer and a drum & bass DJ; being extremely prolific, he released music not just through recognised record labels, but also via numerous private pressings. 'Deadly Deep Subs' is an atmospheric track that utilises a haunting synthesiser sample from 'Just Want Another Chance' by Reese, plus drums from funk classic 'Think' by Lyn Collins, both of which help to create the thrilling and energetic bass heavy breaks that excite the listener throughout the duration of this track.

86
TRAIN #3 / TRAIN #1
JON SPENCER BLUES EXPLOSION
IN THE RED RECORDINGS

Two sides of primitive lo-fi garage rock, with dustbin lid drums at the front of the mix being hammered and clattered by a caveman, whilst the guitars are wrangled and choked until they spew out flurries of notes in agonised terror, and the vocals are shouted out in a throat-shredding frenzy. 'Train #3' is jarring and tough, and 'Train #1' is a white-knuckle ride without any brakes.

85
HOUSE A HOME
MARK LANEGAN
SUB POP

At this point Mark Lanegan was a notorious drug fiend deeply embroiled in his addictions; that issue, along with his touring commitments to the group Screaming Trees, meant that the album *Whiskey for the Holy Ghost* (from which 'House a Home' was taken) took a torturous four years to complete. Lanegan was unreliable and his life-style was violent and unattractive; however, his talent was real and it managed to keep offering him a shot at redemption. 'House a Home' is a lullaby-paced country blues piece with Celtic flavours added by prominent fiddles. Drummer Dan Peters (loaned from Mudhoney) lays down a sturdy foundation and Lanegan sings in his remarkable voice; though ravaged by crack pipe and whiskey bottle, he still convincingly conveys his deepest and darkest emotions, offering up a self-lacerating description of himself as a wrecking ball, unfit for normality and domestication.

84
FROSCH
MOUSE ON MARS
TOO PURE

'Frosch' was the debut single from German experimental duo Mouse on Mars; it is instrumental and fully electronic. Although somewhat harsh-edged, there is an attractive melodic heart, placing this more in the tradition of German groups from the 1970s such as Can and Cluster, rather than the more fashionable techno music of the day. There are also imperfections which reveal that the human element is still present and correct, along with a genial quality that makes this track very likeable indeed.

83
PAIN
2PAC (WITH STRETCH)
DEATH ROW

'Pain' was recorded for the soundtrack to the film *Above The Rim*, but was initially rejected as unsuitable by supervising producer Dr Dre, until it was re-cut with producer Isaias Gamboa. 'Pain' has a shimmering quality, along with a steady, relentless beat that is sweetened by female R&B harmony vocals. 2Pac and Stretch trade dense, articulate verses about the lack of opportunity that sucks the nation's youth into a negative cycle of crime, drugs and violence. Although both young men, their voices are street-hardened and old beyond their years, but they display wisdom and compassion as well as raw talent. All too soon, both would die from gunshot wounds, making 'Pain' something of a sorrowful self-fulfilling prophecy.

82
HAND GRENADE
TEAM DRESCH
KILL ROCK STARS

Self-styled "all dyke band" Team Dresch came from Olympia, Washington, and they were firmly rooted in the DIY punk/Queercore scene. 'Hand Grenade' is resolutely lo-fi, but despite the untidy edges, the pedestrian drumming and the painfully sharp guitars, it is also tuneful, high-spirited and wonderfully sung; in short, a fabulously joyful noise.

81
DO YOU TAKE THIS MAN?
DIAMANDA GALÁS WITH
JOHN PAUL JONES
MUTE

Diamanda Galás is capable of terrorising people when she unleashes the full fury of her incredible soprano sfogato voice; here, she largely keeps it under control, although she still sings with a dead-eyed conviction about spousal betrayal and the likely consequences of this abandonment of wedding vows. The music is a blues-shaped electrical storm, held together and dominated by a strident walking bass guitar masterclass from ex-Led Zeppelin man John Paul Jones.

80
THROB
JANET JACKSON
VIRGIN

Performed in uptempo house style, employing a repeated horn phrase over interlocking electronic beats, this is energetic and raunchy. Jackson is at her most sensuous… a veritable sex-kitten in fact; she purrs her way through the track, throwing in some seductive heavy breathing, as the music coils like a snake and – of course – throbs.

79
IN THE NEIGHBOURHOOD
SISTERS UNDERGROUND
JOY

Sisters Underground were a New Zealand duo comprising school friends Brenda Makamoeafi and Hassanah Iroegbu, and they recorded just one single before Iroegbu emigrated to America. 'In The Neighbourhood' was a complete departure for music from New Zealand, utilising as it did hip-hop beats and acoustic guitar. The sound is fresh and sun-dappled, with a nice, relaxed vibe that is complemented by the girls rapping about their lives. They may not have the drama of Compton or The Bronx to colour their lyrics, but they speak about the problems that people face in their own neighbourhood with refreshing candour – twee this is most certainly not.

78
BLUE
THE JAYHAWKS
AMERICAN

Minneapolis band The Jayhawks played a brand of alternative country music that was tuneful and plaintive. With 'Blue', the band's twin songwriters Gary Louis and Mark Olsen, deliver a slim, understated song, about loss, loneliness and longing, over a sympathetic minimalist backing. Their voices entwine as they harmonise on the chorus with heart-string pulling effect.

77
HERE COMES THE HOTSTEP-PER
INI KAMOZE
COLUMBIA

Mixing up hip-hop and dancehall, Ini Kamoze attained one-hit-wonder status with the highly infectious 'Here Comes The Hotstepper'. It bore a strong resemblance to Chuck Berry's 'You Can't Catch Me' channelled through The Beatles 'Come Together'. The track is catchy and extremely funky, so seasoned reggae star Kamoze rode the rhythm for all it was worth, proclaiming himself as the "lyrical gangster". The record was fabulous in any case, but the icing on top of this particular cake was the inclusion of the "Na-Na-Na-Na-Na-Na" chorus from the Wilson Pickett hit 'Land of a Thousand Dances'; it was this that turned the track into an impossible to stop dance monster.

76
CAN WE BE MATURE
THE DISMEMBERMENT PLAN
ALCOVE

'Can We Be Mature' was the thrilling recording debut of Washington post-punk act The Dismemberment Plan; it was a sharp-edged and joyfully propulsive noise created with guitar and drums. The ironic humour of the band was keenly evident in the lyric which concerns a baseball game that is forfeited because an irate spectator knees the referee in the balls, and poor "Timmy" has the shit beaten out of him for instigating the debacle in the first place!

75
I WANT YOU
INSPIRAL CARPETS FEATURING MARK E. SMITH
MUTE
OTHER SINGLE 1994: SATURN 5

No one could begrudge The Inspiral Carpets their success, because they seemed to be a genuinely nice bunch of people; that didn't make us all fans of their music, and I, for one, was usually unimpressed. On the other hand, Mark E. Smith was quite fond of them; he opined that they sounded like The Seeds. Despite this compliment, it still seemed unlikely that he would actually perform with them… but he did, and his presence seemed to energise the group – they sounded tougher, with drums and bass punching hard. Smith trades lines with Tom Hingley, and his uniquely cocksure vocal style adds a rebellious edge to proceedings, giving an extra buzz to this rattling, garage-rock homage.

74
JUICY
THE NOTORIOUS B.I.G.
BAD BOY
OTHER SINGLE 1994: BIG POPPA

'Juicy' is an autobiographical rags-to-riches rap that rides on a sample of sensual funk classic 'Juicy Fruit' by Mtume, with a chorus sung by female label-mates Total, along with Bad Boy boss Sean Puffy Combs. The Notorious B.I.G. details his early musical influences, giving due credit to the likes of Lovebug Starski and Mr Magic's *Rap Attack* radio show. He speaks of the poverty in which he grew up, and the way that this led him into drug dealing criminality, and he dispassionately details his rise to fame and fortune, and how those who had dissed him now seem to want to know him. He also touches on the lavish lifestyle he can now enjoy and share with his mother, but he is very matter-of-fact in his delivery; any self-glorification is tempered by the fact that he is using himself as an inspirational example of what can be achieved if we reach for the stars and refuse to be held down.

1994

73
GAME ONE
INFINITI
METROPLEX

Gold-standard Detroit techno excellence from the Godfather of the genre, the remarkable Juan Atkins under his latest alias Infiniti. This is a masterpiece of deep, echoey space with beats and a bass that really move and groove.

72
DISARM
SMASHING PUMPKINS
VIRGIN
OTHER SINGLE 1994: ROCKET

'Disarm' was a big hit in Britain, despite having being banned by the BBC because of the violent imagery used in the lyric. Billy Corgan reflects on a childhood ruined by abusive parents; he sings about attempting to disarm them by smiling, and his hopes that this would be enough to keep them happy. As an adult, he realises that the violent thoughts that consume him are a result of poor parenting, and he realises that if he lives out his violent fantasies, he will be perpetuating a tragic cycle of violence. Rather than soundtrack these words with aggressive music, subtlety is employed, and the pretty acoustic guitar track is made even more atmospheric with the employment of a complementary cello part, while the use of orchestral-type percussion adds considerable drama to the track.

71
FINLEY'S RAINBOW
A GUY CALLED GERALD
JUICE BOX
OTHER SINGLES 1994:
KICKING THE JUNGLE BEAT;
NAZINJI-ZAKA;
DARKER THAN I SHOULD BE

'Finley's Rainbow' takes a standard – in this case 'Sun is Shining' by Bob Marley – and casts it in an unfamiliar light, abstracting the original to create something entirely new, just as John Coltrane had done in jazz-style with 'My Favourite Things'. A sleepy, dream-like vocal from the pre-fame Finley Quaye, floats like an untethered balloon, gliding and bobbing across the elegant synths and chattering beats of Gerald's construction, and the overall effect is nothing short of magical.

70
CAUGHT BY THE FUZZ
SUPERGRASS
PARLOPHONE

This young, exuberant and energetic four-piece band from Oxford debuted with 'Caught By The Fuzz'; it was a song totally relatable to many teenagers, and also the young at heart, who unambiguously refuse to grow up. Written by singer Gaz Coombes, following an arrest for possessing cannabis, the recording was originally released on the independent Backseat label, but the song generated enough interest and enthusiasm to persuade major label Parlophone to sign the group. This is speedy and insanely catchy pop/punk; cheeky and irrepressible, Supergrass sounded like the spiritual heirs and naughty younger brothers of Derry's pop/punk legends, The Undertones.

69
GIT UP, GIT OUT
OUTKAST
LAFACE
OTHER SINGLE 1994:
SOUTHERN

The debut album '*Southernplayalistica-dillacmuzik*' had yielded a hit single in 'Player's Ball', but although 'Git Up, Git Out' didn't emulate that success, it was, nonetheless, an outstanding record. The track features a strong and positive lyric, offering encouraging motivational advice to seize and shape one's own destiny, rather than allowing circumstances to dictate the course in which one's life runs. This was very much a collaborative effort, spotlighting Goodie Mob members Big Gipp and CeeLo; every word of every rap counts, and the outstanding slow, funky beat is a perfectly judged accompaniment to the profundity of the song's message.

68
BRIGHT YELLOW GUN
THROWING MUSES
4AD

As a young girl Kristin Hersh was struck by a car whilst riding her bicycle; this led to periodic bouts of mental illness, and she was eventually diagnosed as having a dissociative disorder. The consequence of this was that she had an alternate personality, whom she christened "Rat Girl" and this persona delivered up songs all of her own. 'Bright Yellow Gun' alludes to the way in which Rat Girl's songs would arrive in a dream state in the middle of the night, leaving Hersh to piece them together in the morning. "I have nothing to offer but confusion, and the circus in my head", goes this fascinating and insightful lyric. The song is performed in hard-driven, power-pop vein, and it is sung with strength and conviction. It was tuneful too, and this killer combination actually propelled Throwing Muses into the USA Billboard Hot 100 singles chart.

67
NO GOOD (START THE DANCE)
THE PRODIGY
XL
OTHER SINGLE 1994:
VOODOO PEOPLE

Combining a sweet-as-sugar vocal sample, rough and tough beats, and a nagging ear-worm of a synth riff, the hit-making prowess of The Prodigy was assuredly displayed – and they sacrificed absolutely nothing in terms of credibility or integrity. The repeated vocal sample of Kelly Charles singing "You're no good for me" certainly did the trick of sticking in the head… but, it must be said, it did begin to grate after a while!

66
FEEL THE PAIN
DINOSAUR JR
BLANCO Y NEGRO

In much the same way you knew exactly what you were going to get with a single by Status Quo or The Ramones, there were no surprises from Dinosaur Jr. But that is not to say that their formula sounded tired; in fact, 'Feel the Pain' was fresh and immediate, due to the group's customary heavy reverb being eschewed in favour of a dry, in-your-face sonic attack. Beyond that, it was another track featuring an unbelievably brilliant guitar part from J Mascis, as he extemporised over a genius riff, making his guitar sound like liquid fire as he sings dolefully of crippling doubt and uncertainty; in short, classic Dinosaur Jr.

65
LIKE A MOTORWAY
SAINT ETIENNE
HEAVENLY

Combining the melody of 'Silver Dagger', an Olde English folk song, with precision Teutonic techno beat, à la Kraftwerk or Giorgio Moroder, and the polished, but girlish, vocals of Sarah Cracknell who sings a lyric concerning a woman who is suddenly deserted by a lover who had enlivened her life… a life which had previously been "Dull, grey and long, like a motorway". She now perceives the romantic phrases he had employed to be false in all respects and only said to please her. What a fabulously clever and brilliantly executed pop record this was.

64
DARK & LONG
UNDERWORLD
JUNIOR BOYS OWN
OTHER SINGLE 1994

Taken from the album *Dubnobasswithmyheadman*, and available in multiple versions, the Dark Train Mix became the best known of these following its use in the 1996 film *Trainspotting*, and also during the opening ceremony for the 2012 London Olympics. Typically (for Underworld) the track begins in very gritty fashion, with a rhythm akin to chattering teeth; a synth is then added to the urgent beats and a slow build begins. The track unfurls, moving from monochrome to technicolour, as a voice is introduced, repeating hypnotically "On a train, on a train", before the sound becomes even more expansive – whilst never for a moment faltering rhythmically – during this ten minutes of sheer techno excellence.

63
TIME'S UP
O.C.
WILD PITCH
OTHER SINGLE 1994:
BORN 2 LIVE

'Time's Up' became arguably O.C.'s most famous track, but originally its distinctive beat was earmarked – by producer Buckwild – for use with Pharoahe Monch, who at that point in time, was rapping as Organised Confusion. Somehow, the piece fell into the hands of O.C., who added a prominent sample from 'Hey Young

World' by Slick Rick, in lieu of a chorus. The tricky rhythm clearly poses some problems for the rapper, preventing his flow from becoming too smooth; however, this has the benefit of adding emphasis to some of the hard-hitting poetic lines that act as a kind of street-life manifesto from O.C.

62
MISS WORLD
HOLE
CITY SLANG
OTHER SINGLE 1994:
DOLL PARTS

On the outside, deceptively sweet and attractive… this is full of ugliness on the inside; such a description seems appropriate to represent the lyrical sentiments of 'Miss World' juxtaposed with the music, where an ever-so-pretty melody is used as a Trojan horse, to hide the darkness and self-lacerating pain lurking at the song's centre.

61
NASA-ARAB
COIL VS THE ESKATON
ESKATON

On the face of it, this single is a collaboration, but that is just a piece of mischief-making, because the credited "Eskaton" was, in fact, merely an alias that Coil used themselves (as well as also being the name of a record label they ran). 'Nasa-Arab' comprises eleven minutes of interlocking rhythmic patterns, engaged in a musical conversation; they seem to be seeking some sort of resolution, but that isn't easy to achieve. At the mid-point, a solid 4/4 drum beat is introduced, before we are sucked once again into the seething cauldron of competing rhythms, that wriggle and twist like electrified snakes.

60
LUCKY YOU
LIGHTNING SEEDS
EPIC

One imagines that 'Lucky You' must have been a huge hit, due to its bright, pop brilliance… but that wasn't the case, and in fact this single didn't trouble the UK Top 40 at all. The song was written by Ian Broudie, along with Terry Hall, the ex-Specials and Fun Boy Three singer. Although superficially the track is shiny and bouncy, with a chorus that hits hard and then sticks around, beneath the surface there is a hurt and very human heart. It would be a touch hyperbolic to compare Broudie's Lightning Seeds with Brian Wilson's, Beach Boys – but I think it perfectly fair to cast them as the 1990s equivalents of Jeff Lynne's Electric Light Orchestra…

59
FROM A MOTEL 6
YO LA TENGO
MATADOR

Yo La Tengo had always sounded good in a cosy, familiar kind of way; their huge debt to the Velvet Underground was undeniable. But here, they somehow hit upon a sound that was all their own, and, as a result, they suddenly became a very exciting prospect indeed. We hear a murky, dreamy pop sound that really grooves, and as the tension they create begins to mount, a screaming, trebly guitar cuts through the track, sounding like fingernails being dragged down a blackboard. For me, it never fails to bring goosebumps.

58
WE ARE NEVER TALKING
ROKY ERICKSON
TRANCE

'We Are Never Talking' finds Erickson singing a lament on the theme of disconnection, commenting on the way we often become too self-centred to show love to each other, or even communicate on any meaningful level. With his raw, but ever so real voice, Roky brings compassion and gravitas to the song; he seems otherworldly and sage-like. The track itself is a gentle acoustic strum, with elegant fills played by Charlie Sexton.

57
HYMN (THIS IS MY DREAM)
MOBY
MUTE
OTHER SINGLE 1994:
FEELING SO REAL

Each successive Moby single pushed at the boundaries of what was permissible within the techno genre, as each incorporated a sonic element from outside the sphere. 'Hymn' comes with stirring choral backing and a deadpan spoken vocal, and these are combined with hard techno beats. One may presume that this was Moby proclaiming his religious faith and performing for the glorification of his God… be that as it may, this was a fabulous record.

56
MASS APPEAL
GANG STARR
CHRYSALIS
OTHER SINGLES 1994: CODE OF THE STREETS; SUCKAS NEED BODYGUARDS

Poking fun at safety-first radio formatting, DJ Premier deliberately produced an ultra simple and catchy beat for 'Mass Appeal', whilst Guru details his dissatisfaction with the status quo demand that hip-hop be watered down and neutered in order to earn the radio play that is the stepping stone to success. He then goes on to chastise those artists who *allow* their music and message to be diluted in pursuit of the dollar – "Money's growin' like grass with the mass appeal", is the cutting chorus, rapped out in a deadly serious monotone.

55
TIED UP
LFO
WARP

With a brutal and distinctive beat, and a deep and sonorous bass line, an atmosphere of desperation is both created and sustained. LFO straddle the divide between techno and industrial music, and 'Tied Up' crunches along as it stalks the dark subconscious of our thoughts.

54
IF I ONLY HAD A BRAIN
MC 900 FT JESUS
AMERICAN RECORDINGS
OTHER SINGLE 1994: BUT IF YOU GO

The nearest MC 900 ft Jesus ever came to mainstream success was when the Spike Jonze directed video for 'If I Only Had A Brain' was memorably featured during an episode of *Beavis and Butt-Head*, in which Beavis mimics the impossible to ignore bass line from the track. The lyric here is caustic and simultaneously funny, with a style obviously influenced by hip-hop and electro, but also by the eccentric jazz of artists such as Slim Gaillard.

53
THE MOST BEAUTIFUL GIRL IN THE WORLD
PRINCE
EDEL
OTHER SINGLES 1994: SPACE; LETITGO

Prince – or "The artist formerly known as Prince", as he was now known – had his only UK No. 1 single with 'The Most Beautiful Girl in the World', a lush and romantic declaration of love, performed very much in the style perfected by Philly soul producer Thom Bell, whilst working with The Delfonics and The Stylistics in the 1970s. Prince sings with much passion, using his soaring falsetto voice, while a light-as-a-feather guitar line, played as sweetly as birdsong, complements the vocal. This luxuriant balladry definitively silenced any whispers that the purple one's masterful pop touch had somehow gone awry.

52
CONNECTION
ELASTICA
DECEPTIVE
OTHER SINGLE 1994: LINE UP

"If you are going to steal ideas, steal them from the best"... that seems to be have been Elastica's maxim, and following it through, they chose Wire as a source of inspiration, so tempting and potent was the source material. For example, the chorus of Elastica's previous single, 'Line Up', sounded suspiciously like 'I Am The Fly', and here on 'Connection', the main riff of 'Three Girl Rhumba' was much too distinctive for Elastica to convincingly disguise. That said 'Connection' was a great pop single, and it earned chart placings on either side of the Atlantic. Whereas Wire had displayed a chilly aloofness in their approach, Elastica were warmer and sinuous, they grooved while Wire jerked. As an aside, 'Connection' also gained an afterlife in the 2000s, when it was used as the theme music for comedy TV series *Trigger Happy TV*.

51
SICK AND TIRED
THE CARDIGANS
TRAMPOLENE
OTHER SINGLE 1994: RISE AND SHINE

The Cardigans were a Swedish pop group fronted by Nina Persson, whose beautiful, airy voice was perfect for the light and crisp music that the band created; in their own way, they were every bit the pop classicists that fellow Swedes Abba had been, albeit with an artier edge. 'Sick and Tired' is a brisk, hook-laden song, detailing the aftermath of a summer love affair, but strangely, the most striking feature of the record is the overall sound; it is uncommonly nice, polite and pleasant, similar to a 1960s children's television theme in its smooth and inoffensive charm, where soft guitar and flute combine to quite enchanting effect.

50
HYMN REMIXES
ULTRAMARINE
BLANCO Y NEGRO
OTHER SINGLES 1994: HYMN; BAREFOOT

Ultramarine were a duo from Essex, whose music could possibly be described as pastoral techno. Incorporating the jazz/folk elements found in the Canterbury scene of Soft Machine and Caravan etc, they struck up working alliances with important figures from that scene – Robert Wyatt, Lol Coxhill, Elton Dean and Kevin Ayers, and they released a splendid version of Ayers 1973 song 'Hymn' as a single. It was sung wonderfully well by David McAlmont, his voice soaring to almost heavenly heights. Simultaneously released were several remixes, one of which found Kevin Ayers reprising his vocal to the Ultramarine backing track; his vocal was more nuanced than that of McAlmont's... it was gentle, whispered and warm, and it fitted beautifully into the mix of electronics and ambient sounds provided by Ultramarine, to produce a truly heartwarming treasure of a track.

49
HOMOPHOBIA (SISTERS MIX) FEATURING THE SISTERS OF PERPETUAL INDULGENCE
CHUMBAWAMBA
ONE LITTLE INDIAN

'Homophobia' came from the album *Anarchy*, and this remixed version was issued as a single as an unambiguous message of support to the gay community. Performed as a beautifully sung, neo-traditional folk reel, the lyrics deal with ignorance, bigotry, violent homophobic attacks on defenceless victims and the indifference of the police and state to this vile persecution.

48
MURDER WAS THE CASE
SNOOP DOGGY DOGG
DEATH ROW
OTHER SINGLES 1994: GIN AND JUICE; DOGGY DOGG WORLD

'Murder Was The Case' was a track from Snoop's debut album *Doggystyle*, but it was remixed for this single version and used as part of the soundtrack for a short film (of the same name) starring Snoop Dogg himself. A chilling song, this metaphor for the heartlessness of the music industry details the selling of a soul to the devil by committing murder, and gaining, in return, huge success and a lavish lifestyle… the aftermath of which inevitably becomes a horrifying bad dream. The track is delivered at crawling pace, over a steady beat with attendant weeping and wailing; a very suitable sonic backdrop for this nightmare scenario.

47
PIECE OF CRAP
NEIL YOUNG
REPRISE
OTHER SINGLES 1994: SLEEPS WITH ANGELS; PHILADEL-PHIA; CHANGE YOUR MIND; MY HEART

In this year there was plenty of high-quality, thoughtful and intelligent work from Neil Young, but 'Piece of Crap' was undoubtedly the song best suited for single release. It is based around a Sex Pistols-style riff, played with the handbrake off. The vocal is a deliberately dumb call-and-response routine, with Young making serious ecological points, and attacking consumerism in as blunt and straightforward a way as possible. You can practically hear him cackling gleefully at his own continued ability to get right up people's noses and offend them, still stubbornly refusing to be typecast as the nice, sensitive, mature artist that the music industry desired him to be.

46
UNDONE – THE SWEATER SONG
WEEZER
DGC
OTHER SINGLE 1994: BUDDY HOLLY

Musically pitched at the mid-point between twin influences Metallica and The Velvet Underground, this debut single introduced Weezer as loveable, nerdy outsiders, who combined quirky humour with a fine melodicism. Whispered ad-libs pepper the song, and give the listener a sense of being alone in a room full of strangers. This great record established Weezer as a band who managed to be cool, by virtue of being genuinely uncool.

45
REBOUND
SEBADOH
DOMINO
OTHER SINGLE 1994: SKULL

Best listened to loud, 'Rebound' is a brilliant piece of rock/pop, played on hot-wired guitars and piston-pounding drums. Although it is a thrilling and wild ride, there is no sacrifice or compromise in terms of melodic structure. It was only really the lack of a strong image that prevented Sebadoh from becoming a bigger selling, more famous outfit; their intrinsic quality was abundant, and it was readily apparent to anybody with ears.

44
FASTER
MANIC STREET PREACHERS
EPIC
OTHER SINGLES 1994: SHE IS SUFFERING; REVOL

'Faster' was the first single taken from the Manic's magnum opus, *The Holy Bible*, and it was a very representative sample of the highly articulate, seething rage of that collection. Richey Edwards provided the lyric – a dense and wordy tristesse that deals with self-abuse – while James Dean Bradfield somehow manages to cram this avalanche of word and image into his vocal melody, as well as providing a guitar masterclass of controlled power and high-energy. The Manic Street Preachers had taken a giant leap forward with their sound; no longer ramshackle or lacking focus, 'Faster' was a jolt of pure electricity.

43
FIRE ON BABYLON
SINÉAD O'CONNOR
CHRYSALIS
OTHER SINGLES 1994: THANK YOU FOR HEARING ME; YOU MADE ME THE THIEF OF YOUR HEART

Written about the abuse that she and her siblings suffered at the hands of her mother – and in a wider context, the systematic abuse by famine that England inflicted upon the Irish people – 'Fire on Babylon' is sung with unconstrained passion over a hybrid reggae/trip-hop rhythm. O'Connor's voice ricochets around and in-between the beats, inescapably bringing to mind the sound of a furious angel.

42
LOST AND FOUND
DJ SHADOW
MO WAX
OTHER SINGLE 1994: WHAT DOES YOUR SOUL LOOK LIKE?

This single was a split between DJ Shadow and DJ Krush, whose superb track 'Kemuri' occupied one side of the record... but although 'Kemuri' was great, 'Lost and Found' managed to top it. Sampling U2's 'Sunday Bloody Sunday' to provide massively hard hit drums, the track is woven together utilising the unlikely sources of Fleetwood Mac and Robin Trower. This is an intense listening experience that draws the listener into a seductive world of sonic strangeness, peppered with snippets of dialogue courtesy of stand up comedian Murray Roman, including his unequivocally fabulous 'Speed Rap'.

41
SPEEDY MARIE
FRANK BLACK
4AD

After building his reputation with blood-curdling screaming during disturbing science-fiction based songs, Frank Black revealed his sweeter and softer side with 'Speedy Marie', a heartwarming, unambiguous love song dedicated to the woman with whom he was smitten. It is a cheery and luminescent tune, sung with manifest enthusiasm, and the clever Mr Black even spells out his sweetheart's name with the opening letters of a perfect fourteen-line sonnet, worthy of the bard himself.

40
EVERYTHING IS
NEUTRAL MILK HOTEL
CHER DOLL

Neutral Milk Hotel would later become a seminal band, but on this debut release, they were just a name that leader Jeff Mangum could shelter behind; up to this point, he had been engaged in making experimental sound collages, but 'Everything Is' was the tipping point that directly led to future triumphs. Here the sound is lo-fi, and the vocals are somewhat tentative and muffled – but the spark of sunny pop brilliance nevertheless shines through the playing, which is seemingly influenced by Velvet Underground riffs and glam rock, so the nascent band inadvertently end up sounding like impoverished cousins of Ultra Vivid Scene.

39
NAPPY HEADS
FUGEES
RUFFHOUSE
OTHER SINGLE 1994: VOCAB

This socially and politically aware hip-hop threesome gained their first glimpse of success with 'Nappy Heads', which combined futuristic, spacey beats that were chilled and fresh, along with earthy, reality-based raps, laced with humour and quick wit. Each unique member of the trio was strong; their individual personalities and talent shone through brightly… but in combination, these three Fugees were tremendously formidable.

38
SOMETIMES ALWAYS
THE JESUS AND MARY CHAIN
BLANCO Y NEGRO
OTHER SINGLE 1994: COME ON

The fifth album by The Jesus and Mary Chain, *Stoned & Dethroned*, yielded this stand-out single, written by William Reid. Having finished the song, he felt it sounded like one of the duets sung by Nancy Sinatra and Lee Hazlewood, and therefore a female vocalist (in the shape of Hope Sandoval of Mazzy Star) was recruited to duet with Jim Reid. The finished track unveils a country-tinged tale of recrimination and resolution in an on/off romance, all played with traditional JAMC edge, whilst the two vocalists prowl around each other, smitten but suspicious.

37
MERCHED YN NEUD GWALLT EU GILYDD
GORKY'S ZYGOTIC MYNCI
ANKST
OTHER SINGLE 1994:
PENTREF WRTH Y MÔR/
THE GAME OF EYES

Without sounding anything like them, Gorky's Zygotic Mynci always reminded me of The Incredible String Band… a kind of post-rock Incredible String Band. They seemed to share the same sense of joyous wonder and total lack of adherence to orthodox song structure. Accordingly, debut single 'Merched Yn Neud Gwallt Eu Gilydd' was a misshapen amalgam of folk, vaudeville, psychedelic rock and nursery rhyme. Sung half in Welsh and half in English, I had no clue what any of it meant, except that it was the kind of free-spirited, life-affirming noise that makes me smile and feel happy.

36
C.R.E.A.M.
WU TANG CLAN
LOUD
OTHER SINGLE 1994: CAN IT BE ALL SO SIMPLE

Opening with a looped piano and drum sample from 'As Long As I've Got You' – a 1967 track by The Charmels – a sombre soundscape is produced by RZA, the de facto leader of the Clan. Following this, only three more members of the group actually participate; Raekwon and Inspectah Deck each deliver a hard and fast verse concerning their upbringing and the role of street-level capitalism that shaped it, and Method Man contributes the bridge. Due to its depth and truth-telling, allied with the skill and fire of its performers, C.R.E.A.M. (an acronym of "Cash rules everything around me") would go a long way to establishing Wu Tang Clan as the foremost hip-hop crew on the planet, and they became a must hear act for music fans of all persuasions.

35
SAINTS
THE BREEDERS
4AD
OTHER SINGLE 1994: NO ALOHA

This single version of 'Saints' is different to the one on The Breeders album *The Last Splash*; it is rougher around the edges, sloppier, looser and more satisfyingly real and human as a result. The rhythm section of drummer Jim McPherson and bass player Josephine Wiggs work wonderfully well together, creating a mesmerising and undulating groove. Kelley Deal, relatively untutored on guitar, adds a raw edge, and her twin-sister Kim sings in a voice that somehow manages to be soft and tough at the same time, sounding like a sweet thirteen-year-old kid who has been smoking three packs of cigarettes a day.

34
NEW FRENCH GIRLFRIEND
THE AUTEURS
HUT
OTHER SINGLE 1994: CHINESE BAKERY

Luke Haines, who led The Auteurs, was the much needed antidote to vomit-inducing, preening rock stars who live inside a fame bubble. His songs were peopled by deeply-flawed, imperfect or even reprehensible characters; his world was not one of Wonderwalls… it was unheroic and vicious. 'New French Girlfriend' is, at points, extremely pretty, as gently strummed guitar combines with cello;

however, these passages cunningly lure the listener into a sonic sucker punch in which a weaponised guitar delivers slabs of noise that hit like a heavyweight knock-out punch, while Haines, sneering and snide, lisps his way through a lyric that is caustic and venomous in intent. Put simply, I adored The Auteurs.

33
BEER CAN
BECK
GEFFEN
OTHER SINGLE 1994: PAY NO MIND (SNOOZER)

Pitched somewhere betwixt De La Soul and mid-1960s Bob Dylan, it was a privilege to experience the flowering of Beck's own genius streak at this point in his career; he was eclectic, uninhibited, brash and bold. 'Beer Can' has a startling stream-of-consciousness approach – he sing/speaks his way through a dazzling array of imagery, at one point touching on his former job as a leaf-blower. The sound is multi-layered, and it rolls and tumbles along with samples from a Care Bears album, which are sprinkled like fairy-dust into every available crevice.

32
ABOUT A GIRL
NIRVANA
DGC

'Pennyroyal Tea' from *In Utero* was scheduled for single release, but cancelled following the death of Kurt Cobain, making this live unplugged version of a song originally released on *Bleach*, the first posthumous single. In truth, 'About a Girl' should have been a single first time around, but Cobain had worried that a song so poppy might be poorly received by Nirvana's grunge-fixated audience. Written after binge listening to The Beatles, this unplugged treatment of the song showcases its inherent melodic strength, as well as the surprising range of Cobain's singing voice, as he easily hits the high notes before continuing in his trademark purring rasp.

31
DO YOU REMEMBER THE FIRST TIME?
PULP
ISLAND

Pulp finally hit the top-forty with 'Do You Remember the First Time?', a song loosely based on Jarvis Cocker's recollection of losing his virginity, which formed part of a longer narrative about a sexually complicated relationship. Cocker croons and manages to convey his perplexity and wonderment fabulously well, as the band-written track whizzes and whirls with a suitably washed-out sound that fittingly reflects the ultimate mundanity of the much-anticipated act.

30
CUT YOUR HAIR
PAVEMENT
MATADOR

If some people only know one song by Pavement, it is most likely to be 'Cut Your Hair', which positively rips to shreds image conscious bands and record labels who obsess over details of personal appearance as they chase successful careers, without caring too much about the music that is supposedly of prime importance. Played at walking pace with sweet chipmunk-like backing vocals and a prominent, crashing guitar, Stephen Malkmus is acid-tongued as he sarcastically dissects his subject with snidely humorous and cutting lyrics; it's great fun in a yah-booish kind of way!

29
SLY
MASSIVE ATTACK
VIRGIN

'Sly', the first single taken from Massive Attack's second album *Protection*, featured new collaborators doing their bit in the pursuit of excellence and sonic diversity; Nicolette handles lead vocal duties, Craig Armstrong arranges and conducts the strings, and Vivien Goldman receives a writing credit. The lyric, at least in part, appears to be concerned with the concept of re-incarnation, while the overall sound is richly textured but still cool and relaxing. Simple percussion upfront in the mix is skipped over by the riveting singing voice of Nicolette, and the entire track has an otherworldly quality, making this an exhilarating and mysterious listen.

28
HEAVY VIBES
THE SENTINEL
BASEMENT

To release his music, Rupert Parkes most famous alias was Photek, but he did use others too, and here, as The Sentinel, he unleashed what could be termed a drum & bass classic, though in a multiplicity of ways, it really transcends any attempt at genre classification. 'Heavy Vibes' is atmospheric and has a touching, tender quality – a soulfulness that isn't easy to pull off when utilising frenetic beats such as the ones used here – yet as the pulsing synth lines build and build, the sampled human voices are used with enormous delicacy, and the speeding beats are never allowed to dominate this gorgeous track.

27
BLUEBEARD
COCTEAU TWINS
FONTANA

With snappy drums, dreamy guitars playing notes that seem to melt into the air, and the once-in-a-lifetime voice of Elizabeth Fraser as crystalline and magnificent as ever, this signalled that the knack for creating pop masterpieces in their own unique style had not been lost. The Cocteau Twins made my heart skip-a-beat in joyful abandon, and 'Bluebeard' was at one and the same time light and playful in tone, yet elegant and majestic in its execution.

26
SABOTAGE
BEASTIE BOYS
GRAND ROYAL
OTHER SINGLES 1994: GET IT TOGETHER; SURE SHOT

Beastie Boys had never tried to hide their punk rock roots, and on 'Sabotage' they return with a vengeance. Apparently, the song arose spontaneously when MCA began playing the distinctive bass-line in the studio; Ad-Rock then picked-up his guitar and Mike D took to the drum kit as the riff was pounded into shape. An exaggerated, half-serious lyric was then concocted – concerning studio producer Mario Caldato Jr and his alleged attempts to sabotage the session – the bass was given a fuzzy, distorted sound and turntable scratches were added. Finally, Ad-Rock led the rebellious, bratty vocal raps, and hey presto, it was done… an instant classic!

25
A HIT
SMOG
DRAG CITY

Dour, self-deprecating, very sarcastic… but also irreverent and extremely funny, 'A Hit' was apparently Bill Callahan's (aka Smog) response to a negative comment made by a recording studio owner concerning Callahan's hit-making potential – "It's not gonna be a hit, so why even bother with it?" was supposedly the quote, and this was used as the opening line of the song… though the real killer line in the third verse was "I'll never be a Bowie, I'll never be an Eno, I'll only ever be a Gary Numan" – ouch! Plodding and lo-fi, with deadpan vocals, this was never in a million years going to chart, and so it was very much self-fulfilling prophecy; however, it was also a stroke of conceptual genius worthy of Bowie or Eno in their prime creative years.

24
THE RED SHOES
KATE BUSH
EMI
OTHER SINGLE 1994: THE MAN I LOVE

Inspired by the classic film of the same title, 'The Red Shoes' is a song about a girl who puts on a pair of enchanted ballet slippers; they compel her to dance, without pause, until the magic spell is broken. This folk storytelling is given a complementary accompaniment of pipes and fiddles, which combine to create the sense of a pagan ritual being enacted… it is a devilishly potent reel that absolutely must be danced to, and Kate Bush voices the tale with a brilliantly nuanced performance that suggests vulnerability and a deep fear of the dark supernatural force that controls her.

23
INNER CITY LIFE
GOLDIE PRESENTS METALHEADZ
FFRR

With 'Inner City Life', Goldie arrived as a recording artist, and he took drum & bass/jungle into the heart of the mainstream by way of his wide-screen, technicolour approach to music-making. The soulful voice of singer Diane Charlemagne conjures up a range of emotions, painting a picture of a city under pressure, a city ready to blow up; she is given a backdrop of skittering explosive beats aligned to melancholy strings and a dark bass melody. The effect is eerie, a highly atmospheric combination of flesh, blood and machine that is emotionally affecting. This is music that reaches deep inside to touch the very soul of the listener.

22
VIOLENTLY HAPPY
BJÖRK
ONE LITTLE INDIAN

After a slow build-up, 'Violently Happy' morphs into a solid house music rhythm that is energetic and highly propulsive. Björk uses this as a launch-pad to display an unchecked, reckless emotion; she hurtles downhill on hard ice in a bobsleigh without brakes – her happiness is too extreme… surely there will be a crash at some point within the grooves of the record. Such is the boundless, feverish enthusiasm of this track, that one could be forgiven for expecting Björk to suddenly burst out of the speakers. Her performance here is truly breathtaking, like a blindfold high-wire act; 'Violently Happy' really is astoundingly good.

21
BEHIND BARS
SLICK RICK
DEF JAM

Gangsta rap mythology collides with grim reality here, as 'Behind Bars' was literally written, and rapped, from inside a jail cell, whilst Slick Rick was serving a five-year sentence for attempted murder. Since the recorded lyric came first, music was welded to the voice on the outside; this was done by Prince Paul, and then the track was re-mixed by Warren G. The end result is masterful, slow and gentle; it feels like a dream unfolding. This style is a perfect fit for Slick Rick's quick, but soft, microphone flow, as he displays vulnerability, describing the brutality of the system, the bullying and a failed attempted rape. 'Behind Bars' tells a harrowing story in three-minutes of consummate brilliance.

20
LITTLE STAR
STINA NORDENSTAM
TELEGRAM
OTHER SINGLE 1994: SOME-THING NICE

Frail, childlike vocals, impressionistic lyrics, Gregorian chant, soft jazz saxophone and dream-like atmospherics are just some of the disparate elements that combine to make 'Little Star' a unique kind of pop record… one that is so beguiling, it worms its way deep into the soul. This single alerted the world to the gifts possessed by Stina Nordenstam from Sweden. In 1996, the track was used as part of the soundtrack to the blockbuster movie *Romeo and Juliet* – and so it was that 'Little Star' charmed a world that had never before heard such a pure and beautiful sound.

19
ONE LOVE
NAS
COLUMBIA
OTHER SINGLES 1994: IT AIN'T HARD TO TELL; LIFE'S A BITCH; THE WORLD IS YOURS

Nas proved himself to be a ghetto storyteller of similar calibre to Iceberg Slim; his astonishing debut album, *Illmatic*, was a brilliant tapestry of word and beat, and one of its finest moments was the track 'One Love', which borrowed a title from Bob Marley and the main musical sample – a distinct piano part – from 'I Love Music' by Ahmad Jamal. Other than that, the credit belongs entirely to Nas; his lyric takes the form of a letter to a prison inmate in which a picture is painted of life in a downward spiral, fatherless children, tit-for-tat shootings and drug dealing. All these issues are discussed in a matter-of-fact style, albeit with recourse to a dizzying stream of rhymes that lack for nothing in clarity and immense lyrical dexterity.

18
ZOMBIE
THE CRANBERRIES
ISLAND
OTHER SINGLE 1994: ODE TO MY FAMILY

With 'Dreams' and 'Linger' – a pair of gorgeous, shimmering singles from their debut album *Everybody Else Is Doing It, So Why Can't We?* – The Cranberries, who hailed from Limerick, had already achieved deserved acclaim and chart success. Their second album, *No Need to Argue*, spawned 'Zombie', a track which upped the ante and changed the script. Prompted by the IRA bombing in Warrington which killed three-year old Jonathan Ball and twelve-year old Tim Parry, this song was overtly political and furious sounding. Deeply affected by this appalling act of terrorism, singer Dolores O'Riordan penned her response; it took a humanitarian approach, but the delivery was hard-hitting and aggressive, whilst still being tuneful enough to keep people listening. O'Riordan's voice is wracked with emotion and frighteningly intense, whilst around her the bass rumbles moodily, guitars are spiky and the drums are unmercifully beaten.

17
WHAT'S THE FREQUENCY KENNETH?
R.E.M.
WARNER BROTHERS
OTHER SINGLE 1994: BANG AND BLAME

The semi-acoustic, folk-tinged sound that had hitherto characterised the music of R.E.M. was promptly abandoned for 1994's album *Monster*, which was a full-on move towards a more orthodox, electric guitar-led rock sound. This back to basics manoeuvre was signalled by the single 'What's the Frequency Kenneth?', which exploded across the airwaves with wild abandon. It was, undoubtedly, the most straightforward single the band had issued in years… and it was outstanding; the guitar is brooding and dangerous, the drum patterns extraordinary, and Michael Stipe's singing performance of a hard-edged lyric is immaculate. Meanwhile, Mike Mills bass part prowls like a panther until… getting towards the end of the song… he suddenly slows down due to an attack of acute appendicitis. Incredibly, the unruffled band smoothly follow his tempo switch, and this mistake is willingly embraced and not corrected.

16
YOU DON'T LOVE ME (NO NO NO)
DAWN PENN
BIG BEAT

In 1967, Dawn Penn released a version of 'You Don't Love Me', a Willie Cobbs song that had been based upon Bo Diddley's 'She's Fine, She's Mine'. It had been cut at Studio 1 in Jamaica – with Coxsone Dodd producing – in the emerging rocksteady style, and it was a big local hit. Penn abandoned her singing career in the mid-1970s, but after a seventeen-year absence, she returned to re-cut 'You Don't Love Me' in an updated dancehall style with production team Steely and Clevie. With a chugging rhythm and a lyric that details a forlorn woman's lost love, the track is given an overarching hip-hop vibe, while Dawn Penn's voice is a superb vehicle for conveying deep emotional turmoil – and there is an aching saxophone solo which wonderfully mirrors her emotion. In summary, the tasteful and classy treatment afforded here to what is essentially a simple song, brilliantly reveals its evocative and haunting qualities.

15
GLORY BOX
PORTISHEAD
GO BEAT GO
OTHER SINGLES 1994: SOUR TIMES; NUMB

Portishead emerged into the public consciousness fully-formed and highly formidable; their debut album was one of era-defining excellence. Perhaps its most distinctive track was 'Glory Box', built upon snail-paced beats and an Issac Hayes sample. It was sleek and sensuous enough to imagine it as a (very!) alternative James Bond theme, and it could also be fairly described as elegant and highly refined. And yet, despite this sophistication, the track contains a gut-wrenching, turbulent guitar solo, and a vocal from Beth Gibbons that is authentically bluesy – without any off-putting Americanisms – as she delivers a lyric about deep sexual desire entangled in a web of gender stereotypes.

14
BOYS AND GIRLS
BLUR
FOOD
OTHER SINGLES 1994: PARK-LIFE; TO THE END; END OF THE CENTURY

Commenting on the rampant, anything goes sexual scene which enabled all sorts of couplings, 'Boys and Girls' was not in the least bit judgmental, but more an amused observation of this dizzying bacchanal. Accordingly, it is carnivalesque and trashy, a high-speed day-glow romp of repetitive lyrics and a bouncing, ping-pong ball riff. The beat is delivered via an ultra-simple drum program, the bass is pure euro disco, wheelspin guitar noises are produced and the vocal is one of bemusement and cor blimey Englishness. This put Blur into the top five of the hit parade for the very first time, though there would be plenty more to come from this talented young band.

13
A GIRL LIKE YOU
EDWYN COLLINS
SETANTA

Ex-Orange Juice singer Edwyn Collins composed 'A Girl Like You', and then recorded it with ex-Sex Pistol Paul Cook on drums, while Vic Godard provided backing vocals. The track was lovingly cloaked in Northern Soul clothing, but that was combined with a crisp, state-of-the-art production. Collins sings in a rich baritone and also plays exquisitely tasty guitar fills; it must have been immediately obvious that a fabulous record had been made. Still, it seemed so unlikely that Collins would ever have an actual hit that the song was apparently going to be offered to Iggy Pop. Fortuitously, before that could happen, the song took off across Europe, before eventually being picked-up in the UK, allowing Edwyn Collins to deservedly claim a top-three chart placing.

12
MY IRON LUNG
RADIOHEAD
PARLOPHONE

An iron lung is a life support system that effectively enchains the recipient of its benefits; obviously this is a heavy emotional burden to bear, and the user will often come to resent his or her reliance upon it. And so it was that 'My Iron Lung' became a perfect metaphor for the way in which Radiohead felt about 'Creep', their only hit up to that point. 'Creep' was a song they hated... and yet it sustained them; it was the song the public associated with Radiohead, and it was the song that their record label pressured them to replicate. As a consequence, 'My Iron Lung' was the sound of the band giving 'Creep' a middle-finger salute. But, unhappy with studio recordings of the song, a live version from a show at the London Astoria was used for this record; in place of a Beatles-like jangly opening, there is a melodic verse (albeit containing some very snarky lyrics) and then the band let rip in an act of sonic defiance. Jonny Greenwood and Ed O'Brien create a twin barrage of pitch-shifting, droning guitar noise that is visceral and highly exciting. Crucially, 'My Iron Lung' was an artistic triumph because it gave Radiohead an audience who would allow the group to push at the boundaries of their sound.

11
LET'S GET FUCKED UP
THE CRAMPS
CREATION
OTHER SINGLES 1994: ULTRA TWIST; HOW COME YOU DO ME?

Unequivocally hedonistic, the "live fast, die young" rock & roll lifestyle is celebrated here as an alternative to dying a slow death at the end of a boring life. 'Let's Get Fucked Up' is all about living life to the maximum, taking risks and not worrying about a tomorrow that might never come; it's about excess and having fun, it's about adopting a devil-may-care attitude and a come-what-may philosophy, all couched in simple, dumb language. The Cramps, by now, were well into middle-age, but seemingly as delinquent as ever; the music still stomps and throbs and we still hear Ivy's minimalistic approach to guitar playing as Lux grotesquely snarls, sneers, teases and leers into the microphone. Few things have ever sounded as good as The Cramps, and this is The Cramps at their primitive and raw best.

10

THE WILD ONES

SUEDE

NUDE

OTHER SINGLES 1994:

STAY TOGETHER; WE ARE THE PIGS

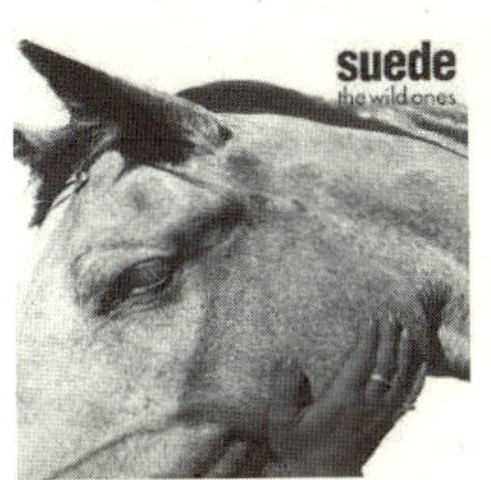

Sparse, and wearing its imperfection like a badge of honour, 'The Wild Ones' was something of a volte-face following the trashy glam excess and lusty cavorting that had been captured on previous Suede singles. This one showed a maturity and sensitivity that had hitherto been completely absent; it is a haunting, regretful ballad that combines strings with a brittle sounding guitar… and Brett Anderson sings in a low register that suggests he may well have been immersing himself in the music of Scott Walker. The overall impact of this great record was entirely at odds with the laddishness of the growing brit-pop pack – and it was all the more welcome for that very reason.

9

DELIA'S GONE

JOHNNY CASH

AMERICAN

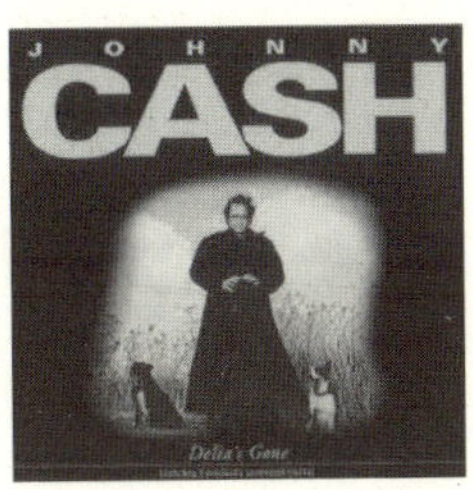

No longer wanted by any major record labels, Johnny Cash reluctantly signed to American Recordings which was run by producer Rick Rubin, commonly associated with the rap and metal genres; but Cash was offered full creative control, and Rubin very much honoured that promise. For the first time ever Cash recorded on his own, without unwanted studio musicians, and without any unnecessary sweetening to cheapen his work… and this transformed his career. 'Delia's Gone' is an early 20th-century talking blues that was written in the wake of the murder, in 1900, of a fourteen-year old girl named Delia Green, who was shot dead by a fifteen-year old boy named Mose Houston. The piece is narrated from the perspective of the killer, and over the sparsest of sparse acoustic guitar backings, the tale is told, detailing the chilling off-hand murder of the girl, and the subsequent regrets of the perpetrator as he languishes in a jail cell, now revealing his love for the victim whom he had hoped to marry. Johnny Cash, with his gnarled voice of experience, gravelly and unfathomably deep, brings huge sensitivity and dignity to the song; Cash was definitively back in business, having been re-cast in a thoroughly contemporary light.

8

7 SECONDS
YOUSSOU N'DOUR
AND NENEH CHERRY
COLUMBIA

'7 Seconds' gets its title and chorus refrain from the notion that for the first seven seconds of a child's life they are ignorant of, and immune to, all the problems of the world; the violence, the hatred, the oppression, starvation and fear. This is a beautiful sounding record but it does carry a somewhat sinister edge, burdened as it is by the performers' knowledge of what really awaits the innocent child – a knowledge that breeds anger and cynicism at the way in which our world works. The piece is grittily sung by N'Dour (in both French and the African language Wolof) yet the song is sweetened by the uplifting optimism expressed in the chorus, sung in the softer maternal tones of Neneh Cherry. The downtempo accompaniment is powered by a circular bass line and swirls of liquid synthesiser; this utterly beguiling record is a powerful statement concerning our common humanity… or lack thereof.

7

KASHMIR
PAGE & PLANT
ATLANTIC

'Kashmir' was a track on *Physical Graffiti*, Led Zeppelin's sprawling 1975 double album, and for many people, myself included, it was their greatest achievement and crowning glory. Here, Jimmy Page and Robert Plant reconvene with a hard-hitting band, alongside an orchestra of Moroccan and Egyptian musicians playing traditional instruments in traditional tunings, and this twelve-and-a-half minute re-recorded version is devastatingly brilliant – at least the equal of

Led Zeppelin's original. The groove remains intact, all the majestic grandeur is still present, the power and dynamics are still in place and Page & Plant still seemed to generate the old chemistry between them… and, if anything, had arguably improved as musician and singer. But this is not just a simple re-tread, but rather a fusion between two different musical traditions, between east and west; the orchestra are an equal and thrilling part of the reading, adding a flavour that had previously only been hinted at. A special hats-off must go to Michael Lee, whose drumming mixes power with grace and precision, in a quite virtuoso performance.

6

GRACE

JEFF BUCKLEY

COLUMBIA

I had seen Jeff Buckley perform as the singer in Gods and Monsters (Gary Lucas's band) at Tramps in Manhattan, as he set about building the reputation that earned him a major label record contract. Gary introduced me to Jeff, and I quickly discovered that as well as being extremely talented, Jeff was also highly likeable. One of the songs performed that night was 'Grace', which was a Buckley/Lucas co-write; it is a difficult song to analyse… a song of considered emotions, a song about the virtuous feelings brought about by true love, a song of fervour. Lucas plays a devilishly catchy riff with an almost east-European gypsy feel, and Buckley sings in a manner that few people have ever been able to equal. He whispers and then soars, seemingly without drawing breath, the aural equivalent of watching a bird riding the wind, swooping and rising and gliding majestically. Technically it is brilliant, but there is so much more to this than mere technique; there is a real emotional connection, a real understanding that this voice is coming from a place of deep, deep feeling inside a being made of flesh and blood, with all the myriad complications that this entails.

5
FADE INTO YOU
MAZZY STAR
CAPITOL

Narcotic and trance-like, 'Fade Into You' was a dark strand of dream pop, that instead of floating away in its undoubted ethereal loveliness, stays rooted to a deeper, earthier tradition of country blues. This is a heavy and intoxicating blend; the lyric, written by Hope Sandoval, is extreme and dangerously melancholic, and it is sung with a calm restraint that belies the underlying turbulence of the song. Composer and producer David Roback serves up a dry, sun-bleached and hypnotic acoustic soundscape, which allows musician and singer to sublimely fit together as a single, intuitive entity.

4
PONDEROSA
TRICKY
4TH & BROADWAY

All kinds of chemical excess and dependency were informing Tricky's music and lyrics; there was a total disconnect from any form of musical orthodoxy, being resolutely downbeat and yet still fresh and exciting. The drawled vocals and crawling tempos perfectly reflected the stoned, sluggish pace of his world. Here, over a head-nodding rhythm, Martina Topley-Bird takes the lead vocal; her uber-natural voice is soft and free from any professional gloss. Tricky shadows her with a low mumble, a kind of croaking undercurrent – "I drink 'til I'm drunk, and I smoke 'til I'm senseless", they croon. At mid-point, a tinkling piano is added; it sounds like a child's toy but it is just the perfect touch. "Beneath the weeping willow is a weeping wino", is the hook line of the song; after being heard just one time, it lodges forever in the brain… and that is a sure sign of undoubted pop brilliance.

3
PING PONG
STEREOLAB
DUOPHONIC

Light, nimble and breezy, and beautifully arranged with taste and delicacy, 'Ping Pong' feels like a space-age facsimile of groovy, sophisticated 1960s disco pop. But then there is the lyric… the deeply cynical lyric; concealed behind a vocal of sweet, summery purity, is a lament concerning the oppression of the masses, which sees them forced into economic servitude – with the attendant struggle to remain solvent – only for a bloody war to be concocted, whereupon they are now used as dispensable pawns in a game over which they have no control.

2
BLUES MUSIC
G LOVE AND SPECIAL SAUCE
OKEH
OTHER SINGLES 1994:
COLD BEVERAGE; BABYS GOT SAUCE

G Love and Special Sauce were a three-piece band from Philadelphia; they played, with endearing sloppiness, a music that incorporated rock, blues, soul and hip-hop. But none of this was known to me when I picked out a copy of 'Blues Music' from the racks at Yanks Records in Manchester; I bought it simply on the strength of the label that released it, reasoning that OKeh was a mark of quality that had never previously failed me, whenever I picked up soul and R&B records from the label's 1960s heyday. My instincts were rewarded with a record that I played over and over again – on very heavy rotation – being completely won over by its sound, that was located somewhere between 'Walk on the Wild Side' and 'For What it's Worth'. This is a slow-grooving track, with a snaking bass line and a half-sung, half-spoken vocal. It is a tribute to old-time blues music, with a bevy of name-checks given out to luminaries of the genre. Resolutely downtempo and as messy as a runny omelette, I truly loved this record.

1994

1

RED RIGHT HAND

NICK CAVE AND THE BAD SEEDS

MUTE

OTHER SINGLES 1994:

LOVERMAN; DO YOU LOVE ME?

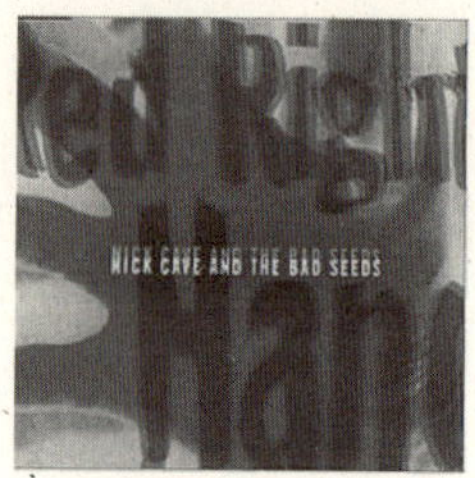

A lot of hard work went into the creation of 'Red Right Hand' – a title extracted from *Paradise Lost*, the epic poem concerned with divine vengeance, written by John Milton. To feel a proper connection to the lyric, Nick Cave filled up a notebook with descriptions of the town in which the song is set… he drew maps and sketched significant landmarks. As it turned out, the landscape he depicted was strongly reminiscent of Wangaratta, Cave's hometown. Only when the location was fixed and fully visualised was the lyric completed – a lyric that conjures up a striking, dark and dangerous figure, part deity, part devil, who strikes both awe and fear into the hearts of the people in the town. This presence is judge, jury and executioner; he bestrides the town, a grim and forbidding individual whose iron will is not to be challenged. The song is masterfully performed, unhurried, understated and carried forward by a repeated stab on the organ. Then there is a whistle of wind and an ominous bell rings loudly, signifying the coming of a harsh judgment; the organ swells, the bells chime, the song twists and weaves as the pace begins to pick up. We now find we are in the midst of an inescapable gothic horror with Nick Cave coldly narrating, without any hint of sentiment and without resorting to histrionics. The tale is told, with every single word ratcheting up the tension, icepick sharp and devastatingly deadly.

Above: I adopt a child at the Maradona bar in Barcelona with a striking resemblance to current United starlet Alejandro Garnach. Below: Rubbing shoulders with Opera superstar Jose Carreras. Both pics taken on a fabulous trip to the Catalan capital.

1995

EVENTS

The Great Hanshin earthquake in Japan kills over 5,500 people, with a further 300,000 displaced.

Twenty-one Bosnian Serb commanders are charged with genocide and crimes against humanity during the Balkan Wars.

The UKs oldest investment bank, Barings, collapses after securities broker Nick Leeson loses more than $1 billion by speculating on the Singapore stock exchange.

One hundred and sixty-eight people are murdered in the Oklahoma City bombing carried out by Timothy McVeigh and Terry Nichols.

Jacques Chirac becomes President of France.

The Srebrenica massacre sees thousands of Bosnian men and boys murdered, and mass rapes of women and girls by Bosnian Serbs under the command of General Ratko Mladic.

O.J. Simpson is found not guilty of murdering his wife Nicole Brown Simpson and Ronald Goldman.

The Indian city of Bombay reverts to its previous name, Mumbai.

Israeli P.M. Yitzhak Rabin is murdered at a peace rally in Tel Aviv.

The Dayton Agreement to end the Bosnian War is reached and signed in December.

Toy Story, the first full-length computer animated feature film, is released.

The first protease inhibitor to treat HIV/AIDS, *Saquinavir*, is approved; the annual death-rate falls dramatically.

The lowest ever UK temperature of -27.2°C is recorded.

Eric Cantona is banned for 8 months for a two-footed challenge on a Crystal Palace fan at Selhurst Park in January. Without him Manchester United lose the league on the final day of the season to Blackburn Rovers and the FA Cup Final 1-0 to Everton. That summer Alex Ferguson sells Mark Hughes, Andrei Kanchelskis and Paul Ince and a *Manchester Evening News* poll suggests a majority of fans want him sacked. United lose their first game of the season at Aston Villa and in September they are knocked out of Europe by Rotor Volgograd and the League Cup by York City. Cantona returns in October and scores from the penalty spot to earn a point against Liverpool but by the end of the calendar year Newcastle United are 4 points clear at the top of the table with 2 games in hand.

NOTABLE BIRTHS

Luke Shaw; Anthony Martial; Post Malone; Poppy (Moriah Rose Pereira)

NOTABLE DEATHS

Fred West; Peter Cook; Fred Perry; Donald Pleasence; Patricia Highsmith ; Vivian Stanshall; Eazy-E; Kenny Everett; Ginger Rogers ; Burl Ives ; Harold Wilson; Rory Gallagher; Lana Turner; Wolfman Jack ; Charlie Rich; Harold Larwood; Ida Lupino; Jerry Garcia; Mickey Mantle; Johnny Carey; Alec Douglas-Home; Don Cherry; Kingsley Amis; Louis Malle; Dean Martin; Richey Edwards.

NOTABLE FILMS

Dead Man Walking; *Heat* ; *The Usual Suspects*; *Kids* ; *Toy Story* ; *Braveheart*; *Shallow Grave*; *Get Shorty*; *Bad Boys* ; *12 Monkeys* ; *Leaving Las Vegas*

NOTABLE BOOKS

High Fidelity – Nick Hornby
Notes From a Small Island – Bill Bryson
The Horse Whisperer – Nicholas Evans
The Ghost Road (Regeneration #3) – Pat Barker
I Am Spock – Leonard Nimoy
Long Walk To Freedom – Nelson Mandela
The Unconsoled – Kazuo Ishiguro
Slowness – Milan Kundera
American Tabloid – James Ellroy

MY 1995

I was as settled as I'd ever been in this year; I'd struck a reasonably happy work-life balance, I had a decent income, a roof above my head and good friends. At the age of thirty-eight, my clubbing days had not yet ceased, but they had slowed down considerably, and I now knew when to call it quits and go home… although I still drank excessively, and my temper was sharp. One day, I came home from work early to discover a pair of would-be burglars in the process of breaking into my house; armed with a hammer, I attacked them. The consequences for their health and my liberty would have been seriously compromised if I'd managed to get a robust head blow in… but fortunately, I didn't. Also in this year, I lost a dear friend to HIV/Aids, but his family hid the true cause of death, because at the time, there was so much shame and stigma attached to that horrible disease. As always, I was obsessed by music, and my tastes remained extremely varied, although the modernity of releases on the Mo' Wax label truly captivated me, alongside tracks by Daft Punk and Tricky. Along with Mark Radcliffe, my friend Marc Riley was deejaying at the BBC, so on a few occasions I was invited into the studio to see the likes of John Cale and Peter Perrett record their sessions. I went to a lot of gigs with Marc too, as his +1 on the guest lists that came as a perk of the job. I was very grateful for his consideration and for my good fortune, but oddly, the most memorable gig I saw in 1995 was one that I actually bought a ticket for… and that was when Bob Dylan played a run of shows at the Apollo. He was raw and rocking with a punchy band in tow, and it was great to see such a titanic figure in a relatively small venue, especially as his attitude was spot on – he most assuredly did not go through the motions, but instead performed with intensity and enthusiasm.

100
RIDE
THE DANDY WARHOLS
TIM/KERR
OTHER SINGLE 1995: THE DANDY WARHOLS TV THEME SONG

From Portland, Oregon, The Dandy Warhols were the sweeter version of big brother band The Brian Jonestown Massacre; they had a pop sensitivity that was evident and irrepressible even though they did try to hide it. 'Ride' has a slurring, slow-motion monolithic riff as its centrepiece, and it is swamped in reverb, giving a neo-psychedelic feel, while the vocals are drawled at half-speed. Still, somehow or other, the melodic sensibilities win out and make 'Ride' a really cool little pop gem.

99
COLD TO THE TOUCH
BRIAN JONESTOWN MASSACRE
TANGIBLE

Acoustic guitars are nimbly picked as a thin lead guitar line worms its way between them, and the performance of the singer is heavily mannered and fey; the interplay is good… there is a lazy, stoned groove going on, kind of sloppy but loveable. To say this sounds like Altamont-era Rolling Stones is really to state the obvious – but if you're going to borrow or steal, why not borrow or steal from the best… and this does have undeniable charm.

98
A WHIM
DJ KRUSH
MO' WAX
OTHER SINGLE 1995: DIG THIS VIBE

Hideaki Ishi was a school drop-out who joined a gang and wound up as a Yakuza underling; thankfully he saw the light and embraced the possibilities that making music offered to him. He became DJ Krush and found redemption by following his creative muse. 'A Whim' was a split-single alongside DJ Shadow's track '89.9', but Krush's contribution definitely steals the show. It is a meditative piece of extraordinary scratching and mixing, atop hip-hop beats, jazzy horns and a crying harmonica which circle around a lone voice. There is much to love in the soulful and emotional simplicity of this track.

97
WHY WE FIGHT
TORTOISE
SOUL STATIC SOUNDS
OTHER SINGLE 1995: GAMERA/
CLIFF DWELLER SOCIETY

Chicago post-rock group Tortoise made music that was difficult to classify (and describe!); it was cerebral music but played with blood and guts, and that is pretty much what 'Why We Fight' amounts to. Whilst it is precise and complex, and the cross-rhythms fascinate and stimulate the places that less imaginative music doesn't reach, there is also a great deal of physicality displayed in the playing of each note and beat. This was certainly not dry, soulless and elitist fare; on the contrary, such refined appreciation of space and groove displayed an appreciable affinity with dub reggae and funk.

96
HEART OF THE PARTY
SEVERED HEADS
VOLITION
OTHER SINGLE 1995: DEAD OPEN EYES

'Heart of the Party' is an uptempo dance track – something of a banger in fact. It was seemingly perfect for the enormous rave scene in Sydney, Australia where the Severed Heads were based, but a closer listen soon reveals that singer Tom Ellard is delivering a warning about the excesses of the prevailing hedonism… not that his preaching is very convincing though, since he sounds for all the world like a dispassionate observer. So, as a cautionary tale, this is very weird indeed, as we hear Ellard icily deadpan – with no hint of sentimentality – "Who will tell my drunken friend that she will die and go to hell".

95
PULP FICTION
ALEX REECE
METALHEADZ

Jungle producer Alex Reece was part of the Metalheadz collective, centred around Goldie. Reece appreciated that all music needs evolution and progression, and with 'Pulp Fiction' he delivered a classic track that was a harbinger of change to come. He abandoned the intricate chopped beats and rave stabs that were staples of the sound, and he set a new agenda by moving on from the raw energy that was routinely associated with the jungle scene. 'Pulp Fiction' was sophisticated and futuristic; it travelled upon a minimal 2-step beat and a hypnotic bass line, with jazz trumpet also added to the mix. The net result was a record that was cool, clean, spacey and atmospheric… but as is so often the case, this earned Reece just as much scorn as acclaim, and to many, he became a prophet without honour in the jungle community. Such is the price of innovation – the fear of change all too often the mortal enemy of creativity.

94
THE WORLD'S A GIRL
ANITA LANE
MUTE

As Nick Cave's former partner, Anita Lane contributed to songs by both The Birthday Party and The Bad Seeds – the latter of which she was briefly a band member. However, she should not be seen as a mere adjunct to Cave's talent… Anita Lane had a lot to offer in her own right. 'The World's a Girl' sees her collaborate with Mick Harvey, and fellow Bad Seed Warren Ellis is also prominently featured on violin; it is a shuffling lamentation on the disappointment of a failed love affair, brought to an unsatisfactory conclusion by unfulfilled promises. Lane sings from a philosophical standpoint, her voice pleasant but impure, whilst the overarching sound echoes that of the Scarlet Rivera violin-led tracks on Bob Dylan's 1970s album *Desire*.

93
STREET STRUCK
BIG L
COLUMBIA
OTHER SINGLE 1995: MVP

Big L was from Harlem and he was just twenty-years old when 'Street Struck' was issued; it is a walking paced, squelching funk track that is atmospheric and smokey. Big L raps about the streets that he knows all too well – the hard, dangerous streets where young men were easily seduced into a life of gang membership, drug dealing, double crosses and lethal violence. He is unambiguous in his denouncement of this lifestyle; he cautions against it and advocates a positive, healthier approach to street life. The voice is simply mesmerising and the wordplay impressive; Big L was very much the real deal, but just four years later, he would be shot down and killed in a drive-by shooting.

92
ALPHA WAVE (PLASTIKMAN ACID HOUSE MIX)
SYSTEM 7
BUTTERFLY
OTHER SINGLE 1995: INTER-STATE

System 7 were formed by Steve Hillage and Miquette Giraudy, both ex-members of 1970s space-rock band Gong. They had been impressed by electronic dance music from its onset and formed System 7 as a techno/trance act and a vehicle with which to collaborate with a host of innovative and esteemed figures within the electronic dance underworld. Here, Richie Hawtin (aka Plastikman) is let loose to unleash all the power from his sonic arsenal and twisted mind, to build a pulsing, relentless, intense and rhythmic trip of a record, based on insistent repetition. 'Alpha Wave' is gripping; it has a nervous energy that few other records could even aspire to… this is acid techno deluxe.

91
CHILDREN
ROBERT MILES
DBX

Robert Miles was an Italian musician/DJ whose trance music was of the variety to be found in chill-out rooms. His father had returned home from the war in Bosnia and Herzegovina and told his son about the misery and death inflicted upon wholly innocent children; deeply affected, Robert sought to express his emotion in a piece of music. The track he created was dedicated to the youngsters his father had spoken of, and he named it 'Children'. It is an instrumental piece of melodic trance, built-up from an acoustic guitar lick that is integral to the track; but then a second "dream version" was released, this time including an instantaneously recognisable piano pattern combined with lush string sounds. This new interpretation seemed to really touch people emotionally; it swept from country to country and became the biggest selling record in the whole of Europe.

90
CHECKING IN, CHECKING OUT
HIGH LLAMAS
ALPACA PARK

Sean O'Hagan had been one half of Microdisney, and he had also been the keyboard player for Stereolab – but with The High Llamas, he had complete creative control. O'Hagan most definitely did not do rock music… crude guitars were not his thing. He tended toward classic pop, so The Beach Boys were an obvious point of reference, as were soundtrack writers such as John Barry and baroque popsters like The Left Banke. Accordingly, The High Llamas made music that was bright, melodic and intelligent – in short, music that was beautifully crafted and a pleasure to listen to. 'Checking In, Checking Out' ticked all of those boxes; its sound easily brings to mind great artists such as Steely Dan and The Beatles… it really is that fab.

89
HOLD ME, THRILL ME, KISS ME, KILL ME
U2
ISLAND

This massive slice of updated glam rock came from the soundtrack of the *Batman Forever* movie, and surely this is the record Marc Bolan was attempting to make during his overblown, overweight, cocaine-fuelled mid-1970s period of egomania and excess. Not that U2 were ever likely to fall into that trap; they are much too self-aware, as they ironically sing about rockstar hedonism without being immersed in its seductive embrace. This is lovingly constructed but pure pastiche; the snaking riff, the guitars cloaked in fuzz, the vocals swathed in phase, not to mention the hand claps, epic strings and camp theatricality which all conspire to make this single quite fantastic fun.

88
I WISH
SKEE-LO
SCOTTI BROTHERS
OTHER SINGLE 1995:
TOP OF THE STAIRS

'I Wish' is a self-deprecating pop/hip-hop track, somewhat against the prevailing trend; Skee-Lo displays vulnerability rather than bravado as he details the shortcomings that keep him from enjoying a happy love life. Samples from 'Spinnin'' – Bernard Wright's rubber-limbed funk track – provide most of the music, whilst shouting voices from Malcolm McLaren's 'Buffalo Gals' are incorporated as a reference to the Buffalo Springfield hit 'For What It's Worth'. Skee-Lo's rap is light-hearted and as friendly as an embrace; it is also a masterclass in rhythmic flow, due to his crystal-clear, natural and nuanced delivery.

87
FAT CATS, BIGGA FISH
THE COUP
WILD PITCH

Out of Oakland, California came this socially conscious hip-hop crew, strongly influenced by political thought of the communist variety. Pre-armed with an extensive vocabulary, sly wit and a rapid fire vocal technique, the musical element was added courtesy of a devastatingly funky horn, strings, flute and wah-wah guitar sample from 'The Rub' by George & Gwen McCrae, along with elements from Walt Disney's *Jungle Book*. The narrative here is a morality tale, told from the viewpoint of a low-level hustler whose methods of survival leave him with a low opinion of himself – until a stolen car, containing a tuxedo and a party invitation, sees him infiltrate the social elite. Amongst the high-rollers, the rich and the powerful, he listens; they are unguarded, and indiscreet as they reveal the magnitude of their own corruption and their utter contempt for whomsoever they step upon in their hungry pursuit of more, more, more. The hustler now realises that these people are no better than he is; they hustle in exactly the same way, just for much higher stakes…

86
KISSING THE SUN
THE YOUNG GODS
PLAY IT AGAIN SAM

Swiss band The Young Gods blended sampling technology with live drums and vocals, and 'Kissing the Sun' is loud, pounding and dramatic. It has a startlingly fearsome sound from opening note to end, and is somewhat akin to an imagined unholy alliance between Led Zeppelin and The Prodigy, as they perform a piece of Wagnerian bombast with trance-like interludes.

85
FRIENDS OF P
THE RENTALS
MAVERICK

The Rentals were founded by Matt Sharp, the bass player in Weezer; the initial idea was that the two bands were to run side-by-side, but by 1996, Sharp had left Weezer following the release of their second album. The Rentals were set-up to play in a style harking back to early 1980s new wave synth bands, but there was a deliberate air of innocence about their sound that never quite hid the depth and intelligence that was also a crucial part of the package. 'Friends of P' was the band's first single; it is fabulously catchy and Sharp sings in a near deadpan voice while female backing vocals add a classic pop element. The synths sound suitably vintage, and the whole thing bounces along just like an effervescing elephant.

84
THE ANGELS FELL
DILLINJA
METALHEADZ
OTHER SINGLES 1995: MUTHA*UCKA; TEAR DOWN (DA WHOLE PLACE)

This is eerie, melancholy and atmospheric. Real beauty is created by the heavenly synths that gracefully sweep across the surface, only to be undermined by the devilish, throbbing bass and the dislocated beats that are the other side of the coin, representing the brutal, unseen underbelly of the utopian dream. Dillinja plunders the *Blade Runner* soundtrack for samples and inspiration, and then twists the knife in hard, to the point where an already dystopian vision is further corrupted by chaos.

83
CRIMINOLOGY
RAEKWON FEATURING GHOSTFACE KILLAH
LOUD
OTHER SINGLE 1995: ICE CREAM

This opens with dialogue sampled from the gangster movie *Scarface*, before Wu-Tang Clan members Raekwon and Ghostface Killah trade dangerous storytelling verses of violent street-life; it is harsh, gritty and it depicts men at their worst. It could be argued that this track represents the glorification of a very negative lifestyle, but the simple truth is that the lyrics reflected a lived reality – this pair, children of the crack-pipe generation, had been surrounded by crime and violence since birth. Masterfully put together by Wu-Tang Clan main-man RZA, the hard beats and swirling soundtrack he provided for the rappers made this record a truly bruising epic.

82
PUSH THE FEELING ON
NIGHTCRAWLERS
4TH & BROADWAY

This is almost (but not quite) irritatingly repetitive; and it is undoubtedly cheesy… but somehow all the better for it. It is also simple, but refreshingly so, and there is not a single trace of pretentiousness in this fun, pure and brilliant dance track. Nightcrawlers were a Scottish act who originally released ‘Push the Feeling On’ in 1992, when it managed to become a number eighty-two hit. However, in 1995, American DJ Marc Kinchen gave it an extensive house style remix; now, the insistent rhythm simply refuses to give up, as layer upon layer continuously rises and falls, whilst the original vocal is chopped up and endlessly looped, reducing to a squiggle of nonsensical, wordless cuteness.

81
CLUBBED TO DEATH (KURAYAMINO VARIATION)
ROB DOUGAN
MO’ WAX

The Mo’ Wax label was releasing some brilliant music, and this neo-classical single from Australian DJ Mark Dougan was a high-quality example. It is an instrumental piece which combines strings and electronics with a prowling rhythm sampled from 'It's a New Day' by funk outfit Skull Snaps, and to add a touch of refinement, it also utilised a short excerpt from Edward Elgar's *Enigma Variations*. 'Clubbed to Death' mixes the warmth of the old world with ice-cold futurism; it made perfect sense for film directors to incorporate it into their movies, and these days 'Clubbed to Death' is best known because of its inclusion in *The Matrix* soundtrack.

80
ONO SOUL
THURSTON MOORE
DGC

For this single Thurston Moore takes a busman's holiday from his day job as head honcho and guitar terrorist of Sonic Youth. It is constructed around a great pop/punk riff, played in a skeletal and brittle sounding fashion. His voice is whispery and swathed in effects as he pays homage to Yoko Ono – described here as "The queen of noise" – and Patti Smith also gets an approving name-check in this ultra-cool, New York-ish piece of avant-garde art-rock.

79
GOVERNMENT
SILENT ECLIPSE
4TH & BROADWAY

Silent Eclipse were that rarest of rare phenomenon… a top-class UK hip-hop act and a British equivalent to NWA or Wu Tang Clan. Here, they savage John Major's Conservative government and leave them suitably battered and bloody from the onslaught.

78
CHINATOWN/
BONNIE AND CLYDE
LUNA
BEGGARS BANQUET
OTHER SINGLE 1995:
HEDGEHOG/
23 MINUTES IN BRUSSELS

'Chinatown' is the perfect cocktail of a track; guitars chime over a fluid melodic bass line and the sparsely-used drums, and Dean Wareham sings with childlike sweetness to produce an overarching sound that is just exquisite. But this is low-key stuff; it doesn't remotely scream out for attention, though it is a very rewarding listen. The double A-side is completed with a cover of Serge Gainsbourg's classic 'Bonnie and Clyde', carried along by a buzzsaw violin riff which creates a sound suggestive of the Velvet Underground being birthed in Paris rather than New York City. Duetting with Wareham on this French language marvel, was none other than Stereolab vocalist Laetitia Sadier, who gamely steps into the shoes vacated by Brigitte Bardot to add the icing on the proverbial cake with her superlative singing performance.

77
DYSTOPIAN DREAM GIRL
BUILT TO SPILL
UP
OTHER SINGLES 1995:
CAR/IN THE MORNING

Built to Spill were from Boise, Idaho; they were led by singer/guitar player Doug Martsch and characterised by the complexity of their song structures. On first listen, 'Dystopian Dream Girl' seems to be at odds with that characterisation; it seems to be disjointed and stumbling… but perseverance soon reveals the truth that these musicians are as tight as a nut. Absolutely nothing in the performance is accidental; this is convention-defying music, music that has its own internal rhythm that Martsch sings over in arresting style, with a lyric full of strange and potent imagery seen from the point of view of sensitive and emotional people who are slightly dislocated from orthodox thoughts and notions.

76
MOTOR AWAY
GUIDED BY VOICES
MATADOR
OTHER SINGLES 1995:
TIGERBOMB;
MY VALUABLE HUNTING
KNIFE

Robert Pollard both formed and fronted Guided by Voices, a band that originated in Dayton, Ohio. From their early 1980s inception, right up to the present day, they have been unbelievably prolific, releasing an incredible quantity of high-quality, uncompromising material. 'Motor Away' displays much of what is great about the band; it is a full-throttle, churning rocker with a big beating pop heart, and the somewhat lo-fi sound does not in any way diminish its spirit and life-affirming warmth.

75
TOM COURTENEY
YO LA TENGO
MATADOR
OTHER SINGLE 1995: CAMP
YO LA TENGO

'Tom Courteney' once again demonstrated Yo La Tengo's capacity for infusing their alt-rock sound with a glorious pop sensibility. Fuzzy guitars dominate proceedings, whilst a Beach Boys-style backing accompanies the main vocal. The lyric is cryptic but it triggers memories of British cinema and pop culture in the 1960s, name-checking Julie Christie, Eleanor Bron and Paul (as in McCartney). The single was accompanied by a funny and self-deprecating video in which Yo La Tengo are invited to open a show for the reformed Beatles; of course, that never happened, but they did have the honour of performing such an assignment for Johnny Cash.

74
MODULAR MIX
AIR
SOURCE LAB

Air were a pair of Parisian musicians who incorporated all the style and sophistication associated with that fair city into their debut single,

'Modular Mix'. This languid instrumental is a sort of funk that the mind can dance to; seemingly it came from outer space, such is its beautiful – almost too beautiful – slick and smooth perfection. Electronic music had rarely ever been this sensuous and seductive before.

73
STARLIGHT
MODEL 500
METROPLEX
OTHER SINGLE 1995: THE FLOW

This is simple, fragile and thoughtful techno from Juan Atkins, and the utilisation of space is reminiscent of the music made by King Tubby in 1970s Jamaica… Atkins seems to bounce sound around in slow motion. 'Starlight' is a stimulating listen because there is undeniably an unsettling edge to it, a hint of something monstrous in its DNA. This is very unsentimental music which unmistakably emanates from an environment that is troublingly harsh and unsafe.

72
BIB
MOUSE ON MARS
TOO PURE
OTHER SINGLE 1995: SATURDAY NIGHT WORLD-CUP FIEBER

Mouse on Mars were an act that did not rest on their laurels; they were quite unafraid of change and they never stood still. As a consequence, they utilised many different styles and there was a very healthy cross-pollination of different strands of music in their ever shifting oeuvre. Here, on 'Bib', they are clearly in playful mode; live drums are used in conjunction with electronics to create a dance track with some serious oomph, that also features squiggly sounds and angelic voices which emerge from deep within the mix.

71
DOLL PARTS
HOLE
DGC
OTHER SINGLES 1995: VIOLET; SOFTER SOFTEST

'Doll Parts' is a raggedy strummed ballad with a washed-out sound, evoking feelings of emptiness and a deep nagging pain. Courtney Love had written the song in 1991 about Kurt Cobain, with whom she had recently been intimate. She felt rejected and thought that her feelings of love were reciprocated because of what she perceived as his apparent lack of enthusiasm to commit to her. Love expresses her sorrow… but also a steely determination to change the situation: "I want to be the girl with the most cake" she declares, before stating that "Someday you will ache like I ache". She sings with a voice that is coloured by bruised defiance, deadly serious in her refusal to be a victim. The song simmers with power and a quiet intensity, as Hole display masterful restraint with their wonderful performance.

70
HE'S ON THE PHONE
SAINT ETIENNE FEATURING ETIENNE DAHO
HEAVENLY

Here we have a slice of poptastic euro-house that straddles the fine-line between cheesy and classy, and manages to emerge unscathed and smiling. Saint Etienne took a French language hit by Etienne Daho (called 'Weekend in Rome') and re-wrote it to feature Daho performing a spoken word section which delightfully complements the impeccable singing of Sarah Cracknell, who adopts the role of a nice, posh, academic girl attempting to escape from a relationship with a married man. With its hi-NRG disco stomp, 'He's on the Phone' resembled a collision between an end-of-the-pier comedy farce and an amyl nitrate fuelled bacchanal.

69
THE BUCKETHEADS
THE BOMB! (THESE SOUNDS FALL INTO MY MIND)
POSITIVA

This funkiest of funky retro grooves, replete with swinging horns, was given a house update by master-mixer Kenny "Dope" Gonzalez, and it proved to be irresistible. The original source material was a 1979 track by Chicago called 'Street Player'; this was cut into pieces by K-Dope who then added chunky beats and Latin seasonings until the track positively sizzled. The repeated phrase "Street sounds swirling through my mind" becomes an addictive mantra, and it was highly appropriate that this explosive record was called 'The Bomb!', because when it was dropped into a dance floor environment it caused a significant amount of mayhem.

68
HONEY WHITE
MORPHINE
RYKODISC

Morphine ploughed a distinctively lone furrow; their style was pretty much a unique combination in which alt-rock and jazz were equally and imaginatively utilised. 'Honey White' is based around a tenor sax riff that very appropriately brings to mind a swarm of bees; it rocks and buzzes as impressionistic words are added to the already highly potent brew. Morphine were just as powerful as any grunge band… and twice as smart as most of them; they really deserved to be much better known.

67
THE BREAK
URGE OVERKILL
GEFFEN
OTHER SINGLES 1995:
VIEW OF THE RAIN;
SOMEBODY ELSE'S BODY

The fifth album by Urge Overkill was *Exit the Dragon*, a dark and sprawling record, loosely conceptual about band life and the resultant temptations. Critically, it wasn't very well received, and nor did it sell in any great quantity. However, it did spawn three fabulous singles, one of which was 'The Break', a crunching Rolling Stones/Flaming Grooves soundalike. It is built from a lean and subtle killer riff, a sparkling drum performance, a radical, experimental guitar solo and a hoarse lead vocal from out on the edge… all of which are at the service of a soaring melodicism at the very heart of the song.

66
INTO THE BLUE
MOBY
MUTE
OTHER SINGLES 1995: EVERY-TIME YOU TOUCH ME; BRING BACK MY HAPPINESS

Having made considerable impact as a purveyor of impeccable dance tracks, here, Moby provides a total contrast – 'Into the Blue' is slow, meditative and tranquil. It was co-written with Mimi Goese, who also provides a graceful and melancholic vocal. Moby surrounds her voice with lustrous strings and a gently repeating piano phrase, while prominent beats anchor the comparatively feather-light sound as it soothes and refreshes the listener.

65
DOWNTOWN
NEIL YOUNG
REPRISE
OTHER SINGLE 1995: PEACE AND LOVE

In the early 1970s Neil Young built his reputation on the ability to write sweet and sensitive songs with very memorable tunes attached; however, there had always been another side to his musical personality… he had an equal passion for crash-bang-wallop rock & roll. 'Downtown' – cut with Pearl Jam acting as a backing band – falls into the latter category; it is loud, unsubtle and pretty goofy – just a celebration of rock & roll and the enjoyment of the simple pleasures it offers. Musically, it is little more than a giant circular riff that is batted around between the musicians; they sound as if they are having a ball, and that spirit of fun is transmitted through the grooves of the record. This is good time music that wears a wide, beaming smile.

64
DINOSAUR
KING CRIMSON
VIRGIN
OTHER SINGLE 1995: SEX SLEEP EAT DRINK DREAM

In their third decade of existence, this reconfiguration of King Crimson featured a "double trio" line-up of incredible musicians, and they released a quite stunning album called *Thrak*, from which 'Dinosaur' was chosen as a single. This fabulously fierce single packs in some momentous riffage, a Beatlesque melody and a quirky lyric sung by Adrian Belew who, alongside Robert Fripp, provides sharp-edged slices of angular guitar that cut cleanly through the dense rhythmic wall that surrounds them.

63
CIRCLES
ADAM F
SECTION 5
OTHER SINGLES 1995: LIGHTER STYLE; ENCHANTED

Adam F came from a musical family; his uncle was Rory Storm, a 1960s contemporary of The Beatles, and his father was 1970s glam popster Alvin Stardust. Young Adam was carving out for himself a rather more credible niche in the jungle/D&B scene, where he was at the forefront of innovation, and 'Circles' was a stand-out release. Whereas much of the jungle/D&B genre was purely rhythmic, without making any concession in terms of softening the hard, complex beats, 'Circles' was also hauntingly melodic, with a jazzy feel created via the inspired use of a sample from the 1976 Bob James track, 'Westchester Lady'.

62
NO GOVERNMENT
NICOLETTE
TALKIN' LOUD

After appearing as a featured vocalist on Massive Attack's album *Protection*, a resumption of Nicolette's solo career beckoned, heralded by this single. 'No Government' was originally featured on her 1992 debut album *Now is Early*; it is a slow, jazzy blues number with an afro-beat meets trip-hop sound. Lyrically, we hear a call for individual responsibility against the oppression of corrupt governments, while Nicolette's incredibly warm and soulful voice – and her crystal-clear delivery – adds a forthright quality to this unusual, but highly alluring record.

61
TIPP CITY
THE AMPS
4AD

After two years of incessant touring, The Breeders were worn out and needed to take a break; a hiatus was decided upon, but waiting around for the group to reconvene proved taxing for Kim Deal… she needed some action and therefore formed The Amps. This group was resolutely lo-fi in terms of song execution; they were raw and ragged around the edges, but this roughness was consciously retained, and not sandpapered out of existence. 'Tipp City' weighs-in at little more than two-minutes duration, but within that time-frame, we have a girl-group style introduction, superseded by a bone-rattling chug that resembles a washing machine in mortal combat with guitar, drums and Kim Deal's superbly elegant but wasted vocal. She sings a pretty incomprehensible lyric, but who cares… the whole thing just sounds so fabulous and groovy.

60
FAMINE/ALL APOLOGIES
SINÉAD O'CONNOR
CHRYSALIS

'Famine' displays not just Sinéad O'Connor's immense talent, but also her compassion and understanding of the way in which historical injustice can poison the soul of society unless the issue is confronted and addressed, thus allowing a healing process to follow. It is a wordy song concerning the so-called Irish Famine – which was in fact the systematic process of starvation and genocide instituted by the British Army – but not a single word is superfluous. The song is rapped rather than sung, and it uses the "All the lonely people" refrain from The Beatles 'Eleanor Rigby' as a recognisable emotional trigger. Sinéad really pushes at the boundaries of what a pop single can be… and she succeeds magnificently. As if that is not enough, flip the record over and you will find a genius reading of Kurt Cobain's 'All Apologies', sung lullaby soft as a heartfelt lament for the deceased Nirvana front man.

59
NATURAL ONE
THE FOLK IMPLOSION
LONDON

Lou Barlow could easily have rested on his laurels, because his tenure as part of Dinosaur Jr. and Sebadoh had already given him iconic status in the alt-rock pantheon. However, he declined the easy option and continued to push forward, so his work with The Folk Implosion moved into some strange new places… and 'Natural One' was a real revelation. It is a weird, trip-hop derivative with a narcotic feel; the bass is reptilian and the stingray guitars are menacing. Barlow sings ominously and without emotion, creating the distinct sense that the listener is being sucked into a ritualistic, shadow world that is heavily atmospheric and frightfully seductive.

58
I LIKE FUCKING
BIKINI KILL
KILL ROCK STARS
OTHER SINGLE 1995: THE ANTI-PLEASURE DISSERTATION

'I like Fucking' is a woman's view of the damage done by sexual repression – a repression that arises not just via the brainwashing of straight society that keeps women believing that "nice girls" must tolerate, rather than enjoy, sex… but also from the feminist dogma that excludes and censures sex with men. "I believe in the radical possibilities of pleasure", states Kathleen Hanna; the message is hard, as is the pumping, bass-heavy sound that Bikini Kill summon up to complement the vocal performance of Hanna, that moves from calm and subtly nuanced, into an untamed, free-spirited roaring of her convictions.

57
NEW GENERATION
SUEDE
NUDE

'New Generation' was the last single release to feature the guitar playing of the already departed Bernard Butler. It is yet another glam-rock anthem that simultaneously snakes and stomps as the guitar circles around Brett Anderson's rich tenor and the rhythm section contribute a very satisfying crunchiness.

56
HAMMERING THE CRAMPS
SPARKLEHORSE
SLOW RIVER
OTHER SINGLE 1995: SPIRIT DITCH

Sparklehorse came from Richmond, Virginia, and they were led by Mark Linkous, a multi-instrumentalist songwriter of considerable talent. He had been strongly influenced by Tom Waits, whose unconventional approach to making music offered a way around the hackneyed path of dull, mainstream guitar bands. 'Hammering the Cramps' sounds nothing like Waits, but it is imbued with his spirit; it places guitar high in the mix as an in-your-face challenge, capturing a refreshing spontaneity and devil-may-care attitude. The track seems simplistic – almost crude – as the band play an unchanging riff, inside which is buried the unheroic, fragile voice of Linkous, as he he offers up a lyric that is either coded (it may well allude to his heroin usage) or purely nonsensical. Either way, it is certainly intriguing, exciting and very, very effective.

55
HIGHER STATE OF CONSCIOUSNESS
JOSH WINK
MANIFESTO
OTHER SINGLES 1995:
DON'T LAUGH;
STAIRWAY TO HEADPHONES;
I'M READY

Josh Wink was an American DJ/ producer who released a stream of squelching, acid-drenched tracks that were not only classics of rave culture, but big sellers that took his music into the charts. 'Higher State of Consciousness' was an incredibly intense slice of euphoric, electronic madness, put together around a simple, unchanging beat. But the magic was revealed with the layering of sound, that just seems to rise, rise and rise again, as a distorted voice issues the proclamation "Moving to a higher state of consciousness". This was the sound of people getting truly high.

54
6AM JULLANDAR SHERE
CORNERSHOP
WIIIJA

Written by brothers Tjinder and Avtar Singh, and sung entirely in the Punjabi language, '6am Jullandar Shere' is mesmerising. Traditional Indian instrumentation and percussion is used to colour an unchanging riff, as the track becomes almost trance-like in the manner of The Velvet Underground classic 'Sister Ray'. I'm no linguist and so I have absolutely no idea what the song is about; fortunately, it matters little, because Singh the singer throws himself into it with evident relish, and his passion, along with the sound created, make this a fabulously memorable listening experience.

53
WHY I CRY
THE MAGNETIC FIELDS
MOTORWAY
OTHER SINGLE 1995: ALL THE UMBRELLAS IN LONDON

Sounding for all the world like some lost, minor key classic by The Kinks, 'Why I Cry' is a sad reminiscence of a lost love that still causes anguish. The arrangement is essentially kept to a drum beat and simple guitar strum, although shimmering electronics do sometimes intrude in the manner of painful thoughts. Stephin Merritt sings in a conceptually perfect mournful deadpan.

52
FAIRGROUND
SIMPLY RED
EAST WEST

With 'Fairground', Simply Red achieved a more ambitious sound than usual, one that fused Latin percussion – sampled from 'Give it Up' by The Good Men – with Mick Hucknall's innate melodicism and a genuinely touching lyric; a house-style piano part also added to the dance floor appeal. The track rolls and tumbles, its peaks a giddy rush on a roller-coaster ride of sound, and the impressive vocal from Hucknall, riding the full range of emotions offered up by his ruminations, is the cherry on top of this fabulous pop single.

51
HISTORY
VERVE
HUT
OTHER SINGLES 1995: THIS IS MUSIC; ON YOUR OWN

Here, for the first time ever, The Verve added strings to a recording; it must have been something of a eureka moment, as they enhance the group's music to an immeasurable degree – all the melancholy and emotional content of the song is greatly amplified. Wisely however, the strings work in conjunction with the orthodox instrumentation, rather than being dominant; the guitar playing set against the orchestration is quite extraordinary, as is Richard Ashcroft's raw and bruised voice as he delivers his bitter recriminations on a doomed relationship.

50
INITIALS BB
MICK HARVEY
MUTE

On hiatus from The Bad Seeds, the multi-talented Mick Harvey recorded *Intoxicated Man*, the first of four albums containing English language versions of the songs of Serge Gainsbourg. This spawned the single 'Initials BB', which Gainsbourg had written about his former lover Brigitte Bardot. The track incorporates moments from Dvořák's ninth symphony, while Harvey sings in an understated, matter-of-fact, conversational style over a crashingly dramatic piano opening, then superseded by grand, sweeping strings – a stark contrast which adds a sense of urgent importance to his solemn words.

49
SHIMMY SHIMMY YA
OL' DIRTY BASTARD
ELEKTRA
OTHER SINGLE 1995: BROOKLYN ZOO

ODB was the erratic wild card within the Wu Tang Clan; he had well documented problems with substance abuse, and spells of incarceration, but he was also humorous and self-deprecating, while his half-rap/half-singing style was completely original. 'Shimmy Shimmy Ya' has a brilliantly raw minimal beat – courtesy of Wu Tang alumnus RZA – and the fun-filled funkiness of the vocals is really smile inducing; this is just sing-a-long contagious.

48
WHERE WILL I BE
EMMYLOU HARRIS
THE GRAPEVINE

The voice of Emmylou Harris was a bewitching thing; she was a brilliant interpretive singer who could genuinely mine a song to reveal its arcane heart. However, it seemed that she was running out of steam a little bit… her records were becoming inessential. Fortunately, that changed when she teamed up with producer Daniel Lanois, who persuaded her to forego the acoustic backing that she traditionally incorporated on her records. Instead, he gave her subtle layers of atmospheric effects, creating an arresting soundscape sculpted to suit each song on the album *Wrecking Ball*, which re-defined and rejuvenated Harris's career. 'Where Will I Be' was written by Lanois; the lyric is a rumination on life as the narrator awaits death. It is a slow-burning lament that requires the singer to wear the song almost like a second skin. Harris is up to the task and inhabits it convincingly; she conveys both regret and fortitude with a voice of harsh experience that makes this a deeply moving record.

47
IN THE NAME OF THE FATHER
BLACK GRAPE
RADIOACTIVE
OTHER SINGLES 1995: REVEREND BLACK GRAPE; KELLY'S HEROES

After the Happy Mondays fell apart, Shaun Ryder soon put together Black Grape, taking along his old mucker Bez, and recruiting rapper Psycho along with a pair of Ruthless Rap Assassins, namely Kermit and Ged Lynch, and finally Paris Angels guitarist Wags, who illuminates 'In the Name of the Father' with a bright-as-a-button riff. The track is full of character, mixing up hip-hop, gospel and funk in a glorious genre-bending mash-up. The various voices combine in unholy alliance as the mildly blasphemous track celebrates individuality and absurdity over dull conformity.

46
POISON
THE PRODIGY
XL RECORDINGS

A strong hip-hop influence in the beats meant that 'Poison' wasn't as speedy and adrenalised as the usual Prodigy style; not that this was in any way a compromise, as Maxim Reality delivers the vocal with electrified intensity and obvious enthusiasm, and though the track may be more downtempo than usual, it still rumbles and pulses darkly, with a funkiness full of swaggering menace.

45
CALIFORNIA LOVE
2PAC FEATURING DR DRE & ROGER TROUTMAN
DEATH ROW
OTHER SINGLES 1995:
DEAR MAMA;
SO MANY TEARS;
TEMPTATIONS

After spending eight months in jail, 2Pac marked his return to freedom with the release of party anthem 'California Love', which made him a very hip virtual ambassador for the Golden State. Originally intended as an album track for Dr Dre, somebody presciently recognised the potential of the track as a stand-alone single. The bouncing uptempo groove, whirring synths, trademark vocoder chorus courtesy of Roger Troutman of funk legends Zapp, and, last but not least, 2Pac's inclination to celebrate a hedonistic scene in a quick-fire easy flow – very understandable in light of his recent incarceration – it all came together to become a huge commercial hit that transcended the ghettoisation of genre classification.

44
SPARKY'S DREAM
TEENAGE FANCLUB
CREATION
OTHER SINGLE 1995:
NEIL JUNG

With 'Sparky's Dream', Teenage Fanclub achieved power-pop nirvana… or anyway, as near as damn it. This is a frothing sugar-rush of sweet melody and chiming guitars; it sounds like a divine combination of The Byrds, Big Star and The Beatles with its jangling, harmonising and poptastic joyfulness.

43
TURN IT ON
FLAMING LIPS
WARNER BROTHERS

'Turn It On' is a single taken from the album *Transmissions From the Satellite Heart*; it is highly prescient in its depiction of a time when interactions between people would take place from their individual homes via computer screens. A wry Wayne Coyne enthuses about the coming of such technology, but he also hints at the feelings of isolation that may result from over-reliance on this resource. Around him, the track buzzes noisily; it leaves an impression of child-like glee in the way in which the song is performed. What the listener initially hears sounds like undisciplined and random noise… but of course, it is no such thing.

Every instrument has its place, and the tight but playful drumming masterclass by Steven Drozd ensures that this particular boat remains afloat and firmly anchored.

42
BELLYEYE
CARDIACS
ORG

Much maligned and critically unpopular, Cardiacs were so difficult to pigeon-hole that their music began to be classified as "pronk", combining, as it did, elements of progressive rock, psychedelia and art-punk. Sure enough, 'Bellyeye' is a positively kaleidoscopic blast of ideas, but it is nonetheless insanely catchy, despite all notions of tasteful restraint being completely abandoned. This is a huge-sounding epic with blasting horns, screeching guitars and keyboards that skitter through the frenzy whilst Tim Smith voices a bloodthirsty and leering lyric… it's just marvellous stuff!

41
FU-GEE-LA
FUGEES
RUFFHOUSE

Sure, the distinctive sound of 'Fu-gee-la' is laid-back and downbeat, but each of the three Fugees are nothing less than effervescent in their vocalising on this track. The rhymes employed in the lyric have a slightly stoned and surreal feel to them, overlaying the part reggae, part hip-hop, part pop backing track. The ingenious interpolation of Teena Marie's 'Ooo La La La' – sung by Lauryn Hill and providing the song's hook – is quite simply one of the most recognisable sounds of the decade.

40
LET IT FLOW
SPIRITUALIZED ELECTRIC MAINLINE
DEDICATED
OTHER SINGLE 1995:
LAY BACK IN THE SUN

It was an ingenious and effective move to add gospel singing to the already intoxicating space-rock that was the staple component of the Spiritualized experience. The soulful, reaching-for-heaven voice of the female singer set against the fragility of Jason Pierce's whisperings, creates a compelling juxtaposition. 'Let it Flow' dared to mix the sacred with the profane, and a wondrous alchemy took place which melded a religious element to the drug-assisted astral exploration that was central to the band's vision.

39
NO AWARENESS
DR OCTAGON
BULK RECORDINGS

Dr Octagon was a homicidal, extra-terrestrial gynaecologist from Jupiter, with yellow eyes and a highly active libido, who uses brutal, futuristic technology on his patients. He was born as an alter-ego for Kool Keith, the Ultramagnetic MCs maverick. Tracks were recorded with KutMasta Kurt, which were heard by producer Dan the Automator, who then got involved along with turntablist Qbert. The sound they created was amazing, somewhat akin to being sucked into a psychedelic horror story with trip-hop beats attached. Keith's lyric – and delivery – was a revelation; he employed a surrealist approach to both. In summary, this is a humorous, grotesque and absurdist trip through a science-fiction landscape… 'No Awareness' was like nothing I'd ever heard before, and it was incredibly exciting.

38
I HATE ROCK 'N' ROLL
THE JESUS AND MARY CHAIN
BLANCO Y NEGRO

A stand-alone single from the JAMC, returning them to the concept of noise for the sake of noise; with anti-authoritarian belligerence, they bite at the record company hands that feed them and strain against the leash. 'I Hate Rock 'n' Roll' is loud, rude, badly behaved and bristling with petulant bratty aggression – never before had such ungrateful, disobedient unreasonableness been transformed into such brilliant rock and roll.

37
GOLD
PRINCE
NPG
OTHER SINGLES 1995:
PURPLE MEDLEY; EYE HATE U

The music of Prince had lost the capacity to surprise, but that was not because there had been any notable decline in quality, and 'Gold' was a grand demonstration of this great artist's enduring talent. Prince himself compared the track to his 1980s landmark 'Purple Rain', and indeed, it did not suffer by comparison. This is a sweeping, soaring power ballad, with a rousing, irresistible chorus and a guitar solo that breathes fire. In addition, Prince sings exquisitely, combining tenderness and power, creating a record that is the sound of a master craftsman operating at pretty close to his highest level.

36
ALRIGHT
SUPERGRASS
PARLOPHONE
OTHER SINGLES 1995: MAN-SIZE ROOSTER; LOSE IT; LENNY

'Alright' bounded out of jukeboxes and transistor radios, full of cheerful cheekiness and charm; totally irrepressible and bashed out over a bouncing piano riff like Chas & Dave on whizz, it was as catchy and sunny as Cliff Richard's 'Summer Holiday' or 'Y Viva España' by Sylvia. 'Alright' painted an indelible picture of teenage culture – the drinking of alcopops, getting snogged and waking up with love-bites on the neck – and the fact that Supergrass were indeed authentically young (and clearly enjoying themselves to the max) made this even more likeable.

35
INSOMNIA
FAITHLESS
CHEEKY
OTHER SINGLE 1995: SALVA MEA

'Insomnia' was a club record that seems to be addressing the exhausting side-effects of club culture; being up night after night, chasing the buzz, until the body-clock is wrecked and sleep just won't come. It is a frenetic dance track that twists and shifts, from urgent and edgy to melancholic and delightfully melodic. The fabulously evocative sound structure is enhanced by a brilliantly conceived and executed spoken word/slow rap vocal from Maxi Jazz, whose world-weary delivery and choice phrasing resonates with anyone who has ever suffered with the twilight-life disorientation of the insomniac.

34
NEEDLE IN THE HAY
ELLIOTT SMITH
KILL ROCK STARS

'Needle in the Hay' is a song about the spirit-sapping waste of heroin addiction, a grizzly tale told in beautifully transparent metaphorical style by Elliott Smith, who accompanies himself on acoustic guitar, playing an endless walking phrase. He sings with weary resignation, fully aware of his grim situation, but also with the restraint of a man who knows only too well that the little energy he does have must be very carefully managed. The softness of Smith's voice seems to draw the listener ever closer toward him in order to properly hear what he has to say. This is such a powerful record that despite its quietness, there is still a huge emotional impact – a fact recognised by film director Wes Anderson who used the song for a crucial scene in his hit movie *The Royal Tenenbaums*.

33
THIS IS THE CALL
FOO FIGHTERS
ROSWELL
OTHER SINGLES 1995:
I'LL STICK AROUND;
FOR ALL THE COWS

At this point, Foo Fighters were a one-man band consisting solely of ex-Nirvana drummer Dave Grohl, and 'This is the Call' was the excellent debut single release. Grohl was obviously carrying a lot of cultural baggage and he was just going to have to live with the inevitable Nirvana comparisons… but this he handled impeccably. He was clearly moving on, but at the same time, he was not going to run and hide from his past either. Consequently, 'This is the Call' sounded quite a lot like Nirvana, but crucially the angst and intensity were stripped away, as was the often cynical world view, meaning that Foo Fighters were just as loud as Grohl's former band, but they were lighter. There was positivity in evidence and an unashamed pop edge that very much displayed a Buzzcocks influence. In time, Grohl would put together a full band, and as the years passed, he became a stadium filling superstar. Somewhere along the way, I began to lose interest, finding the music to be increasingly dull and bombastic – but that can never diminish what a great debut single 'This is the Call' self-evidently was.

32
LIFE IS SWEET
CHÉMICAL BROTHERS
JUNIOR BOY'S OWN
OTHER SINGLE 1995: LEAVE HOME

Ed Simons and Tom Rowlands met at Manchester University and they began deejaying using the name The Dust Brothers which they filched from the producers of The Beastie Boys, presuming that this wouldn't really matter since they would never be famous… but as their own star began to rise, the threat of litigation led to a name change, and they became The Chemical Brothers. This track, taken from their debut album *Exit Planet Dust*, is a collaboration with singer Tim Burgess of The Charlatans, and it well and truly bridges the gap between dance and indie rock culture as it offers up a banging slice of big beat, ferocious bass line, a swirling storm of effects and a well-judged, restrained and somewhat counter-intuitive, bittersweet vocal.

31
TWIGGY TWIGGY
PIZZICATO FIVE
MATADOR
OTHER SINGLE 1995: HAPPY SAD

Pizzicato Five formed in Japan as far back as 1979, but they only truly discovered their forte after hearing De La Soul's album *3 Feet High and Rising*, after which they embraced sampling techniques in order to embellish their sound. This kick started the Shibuya-kei scene, based upon a cut-and-paste aesthetic that pillaged kitschy western pop culture from the 1960s and re-packaged it in a bright and shiny, deliberately inauthentic form. 'Twiggy Twiggy' was released in 1991 as a track on the album *This Year's Girl*; it is dizzying, groovy pop that nodded towards a swinging 1960s of mini-skirts, models and discotheques. As jaded western ears searched for something fresh, Pizzicato Five struck a deal with the hip and respected Matador label, who gave the aural helium of 'Twiggy Twiggy' a belated and limited single release.

30
WHERE THE WILD ROSES GROW
NICK CAVE AND THE BAD SEEDS AND KYLIE MINOGUE
MUTE

Explaining that he had been quietly obsessed with fellow antipodean Kylie Minogue for a good number of years, and that he had long wanted to write a song for her, Nick Cave finally unveiled his new singing partner – a Nancy Sinatra to his own Lee Hazlewood. Cave had included their duet on his album *Murder Ballads*, but the track practically begged to be a single and duly became a deserved hit. The song was written to play out as a dialogue between a darkly disturbed killer and his unsuspecting victim, and the two voices work sublimely together to create a highly tense and brooding atmosphere. Cave's voice is as deep and stern as ever, whilst Minogue sounds tremulous and fragile. As the tragedy unfolds, the singers are accompanied by a mournful combination of violins, piano, gently strummed guitar and bells over a minimalistic drum beat, deftly evoking a sun-dappled clearing, a rippling stream and fields of gently swaying grass… an idyllic scene that will soon be violated by a brutal and bloody murder.

29
FREAK LIKE ME
ADINA HOWARD
EASTWEST

Sampling Sly and the Family Stone and Bootsy's Rubber Band – besides using hip-hop beats to underpin its smooth and slinky R&B soundscape – Adina Howard's debut single was stamped with a most excellent pedigree. Sultry and steamily sensual, 'Freak Like Me' was very seductively sung by Howard, and the high-end production enhanced rather than swamped the superiority of the song. Tru Faith & Dub Conspiracy would later score a substantial hit covering the track in a garage style, and Sugababes would hit the jackpot with a brilliant, huge-selling version that combined 'Freak Like Me' with Gary Numan's 'Are Friends Electric?'. However, it was thanks to Adina Howard that the world was first turned on to the sheer class and quality of this fabulous song.

28
LOVE SONGS ON THE RADIO
MOJAVE 3
4AD

A sad, sad song, slide guitar and an angelic voice are pretty much everything on offer here, on a record full of melancholy and heartbreak. Neil Halstead, who plays guitar, and Rachel Goswell, who sings, had both been members of shoegaze band Slowdive, who morphed into Mojave 3. As Halstead's songs became quieter and more folk-influenced, the sound of the band changed direction too; it became a dreamy, drifting kind of country-tinged blues in which mournful whispers are picked up in the wind. 'Love Songs on the Radio' mines a deep well full of mystery and despair; superficially it is comparable to the music of Mazzy Star and the torch songs performed by Julie Cruise on the *Twin Peaks* soundtrack, and yet there is easily enough individuality here to make this track stand apart as something special and unique.

27
RANGE LIFE
PAVEMENT
BIG CAT
OTHER SINGLES 1995:
FATHER TO A SISTER OF THOUGHT;
RATTLED BY THE RUSH

Controversy rained down on Pavement thanks to a verse in 'Range Life' which is clearly –

despite protestations to contrary by writer Stephen Malkmus – mocking alt-rock superstars Smashing Pumpkins and Stone Temple Pilots, dismissing them as irrelevant. Incensed, Pumpkins band leader Billy Corgan went so far as to have Pavement removed from the bill of the Lollapalooza tour. Anyway, leaving controversy aside, 'Range Life' is partly a wistful evocation of a hassle-free, blissful, slacker life-style, and partly a realisation that such a life-style is, in truth, impossible to maintain. The song meanders pleasantly in an understated style, decorated with delicate musical flourishes… a touch of pedal steel here, a skittering on the piano there, such that the music never drags. This is the melodious equivalent of a lazy, but very enjoyable stroll in the afternoon sunshine.

26
SURVIVAL OF THE FITTEST
MOBB DEEP
LOUD
OTHER SINGLES 1995: TEMPERATURES RISING; SHOOK ONES (PART 2)

'Survival of the Fittest' by Mobb Deep was one of the high-points of 1990s New York hip-hop. It is a chilling track, utterly persuasive in its depiction of a dog-eat-dog environment in which pity is a weakness and compassion too rare a luxury to be shared with anybody else. The lyrics are hard as bullets; nothing is superfluous and the rhymes are delivered with a deadly and razor-sharp cadence. Behind the rap is a gritty, ominous and suffocating sound, built-up by producer Havoc via a sample of 'Skylark', a jazz track by Barry Harris and Al Cohn, and this is further supplemented by rock-hard beats (courtesy of Q-Tip) that sound like nails being driven into a coffin lid.

25
THE DIAMOND SEA
SONIC YOUTH
GEFFEN

'The Diamond Sea' first appeared as a nineteen-minutes long epic on Sonic Youth's *Washing Machine* album, but it was edited down to five minutes and twenty-six seconds and released as a single – which perversely also contained another version of the same song, that clocked in at just shy of twenty-six minutes! Despite being so truncated, the song worked extremely well as a single. Being somewhat slimline and slight, the track ambles along leisurely with a relaxed vocal from Thurston Moore, but as it progressively builds in intensity and volume, the three-guitar line-up of Sonic Youth begin to really let rip as the guitars coil around each other, meshing and entwining, becoming one gigantic wave that eventually crashes, breaks and gradually drifts away.

24
HALAH
MAZZY STAR
CAPITOL

There is lingering pain being articulated here; a broken

relationship has left issues unresolved, words unsaid… but whilst the door of potential reunion remains slightly ajar, there is a lack of finality to the situation which becomes a conduit of destructive emotion. David Roback serves up quite a briskly-paced track as a canvas upon which Hope Sandoval paints her tale of woe, and she sounds suitably sultry, solitary and bereft. If you can imagine Patsy Cline singing through a psychedelic fog, you won't be a million miles away from the sound achieved here by Mazzy Star.

23
THE UNIVERSAL
BLUR
FOOD
OTHER SINGLE 1995:
COUNTRY HOUSE

Blur had travelled fast and far; they were now the second most popular pop group in the UK – the rather charmless Oasis were numero uno – and bearing that in mind, 'The Universal' was quite a bold choice as a single. Sure, it was beautiful, unnervingly beautiful, all *too* beautiful in fact; it was a fabulous construction of antiseptic, ultra-clean sound, with the atmosphere of a stark and chilly dentist's surgery. However, this perfectly suits its futuristic theme… one of loneliness and disconnection from others, the attempt to hold onto fading memories of community in a time before progress had alienated people and removed tender-heartedness and emotion from our society.

22
LIQUID SWORDS
GZA
GEFFEN
OTHER SINGLE 1995:
COLD WORLD

Opening to the sound of dialogue taken from the film *Shogun Assassin*, the scene is set for GZA to step up to the microphone and ride the supremely good rhythms provided by fellow Wu Tang Clan member RZA. Utilising a repeated and insanely hypnotic organ stab, GZA bobs and weaves his way across the track, displaying amazing vocal dexterity; always unhurried, his words flow effortlessly with entertaining and street-smart philosophical poetry.

21
IT'S OH SO QUIET
BJORK
ONE LITTLE INDIAN
OTHER SINGLES 1995:
ISOBEL; ARMY OF ME

Originally written in German in the 1940s, an English language translation was recorded in 1951 by American singer and comedic actress, Betty Hutton. For decades, the song was largely forgotten, but then 'It's Oh So Quiet' was picked up by Björk and it received an incredibly dramatic reading that she begins in little more than a childlike whisper, beckoning the listener to move in closer, at which point the song erupts with the sound of a swing-era style big-band playing at full tilt, as Björk squawks and gleefully exercises her lungs to full capacity. Thereafter, the song alternates between gentle and abrasive passages, constantly catching the listener off-guard. In a nutshell, this is an audacious and unsettling record that is as exciting and fun-filled as the most thrilling fairground ride imaginable.

20
HUMAN NATURE
MADONNA
MAVERICK
OTHER SINGLES 1995: BED-TIME STORY; YOU'LL SEE

Following her album *Erotica*, and the coffee-table photography book *Sex*, the moral watchdogs had snapped and snarled at Madonna; "she's gone too far", they claimed – but although they stopped short of stating that a woman's place was in the kitchen, their vitriol was far more offensive than Madonna's taboo challenging songs and image could ever be. With 'Human Nature', the singer bared her teeth and bit back; with the repeated refrain of "Express yourself, don't repress yourself", the song carried a message of positive female empowerment as well as explicitly answering her critics. Unrepentant, she declares "I'm not sorry", as she uses a kind of lean-machined R&B vibe to convey her message. 'Human Nature' also has a futuristic sheen which is highly appropriate, as such backward-looking and regressive attitudes were attacked head-on.

19
CRUSH WITH EYELINER
R.E.M.
WARNER BROTHERS
OTHER SINGLES 1995: STRANGE CURRENCIES; TONGUE

Central to this song is a nagging, echoing guitar riff, while the ambiguous and compelling lyrics are intriguingly open to interpretation. Thurston Moore of Sonic Youth is also present here (supplying backing vocals) as R.E.M. repay a debt of gratitude for the influence his band has had on them. Musically speaking though, the biggest inspiration for this song was the New York Dolls because 'Crush with Eyeliner' aims to replicate the sleaze and swagger that was an inherent part of the Dolls DNA, and Peter Buck's guitar solo on this track uncannily emulates the sound of Johnny Thunders in all his glory. 'Crush with Eyeliner' is the sound of R.E.M. stripped of their folk influences and showing that they could mix rock with art and still achieve quite outstanding results.

18
AFRO-LEFT
LEFTFIELD FEATURING DJUM DJUM
HARD HANDS
OTHER SINGLE 1995: ORIGINAL

Pounding tribal rhythms, combined with the electronic progressive house that was Leftfield's signature sound, made for an exciting mash-up. Another exotic element was the vocal by Neil Cole (aka Djum Djum) in what was purportedly an unspecified African language – later revealed to be a brilliant ethnic forgery as it was simply gibberish. Also thrown in for good measure was an unusual and highly distinctive twanging rhythm, played on a single-stringed African instrument called the berimbau. 'Afro-Left' was a thrilling hybrid of the ancient and the modern, coming together to create something vibrant, stimulating and special.

17
HURT
NINE INCH NAILS
INTERSCOPE

'Hurt' was written by Nine Inch Nails leader, Trent Reznor, as a chilling confessional that deals with depression, self harm and drug addiction. Although it is certainly bleak and full of self-loathing, this is nevertheless a remarkable song and a magnificent recording, sung with utter conviction and soundtracked by a cold, grinding, funeral-paced machine music that perfectly matches the sombre sentiments of the lyric. Further down the line, Johnny Cash would offer his own interpretation of the song; thanks to his exquisite phrasing, without even changing a single word, he transformed the meaning of the song to suit his own needs, handling it from the perspective of an old man who has survived travails, and is looking back at his failings and simultaneously reflecting upon the love that sustained him. Cash received well-deserved plaudits for his rendition of 'Hurt', but that should not diminish in any way the greatness of the Nine Inch Nails original.

16
SO REAL
JEFF BUCKLEY
COLUMBIA
OTHER SINGLES 1995: LAST GOODBYE; ETERNAL LIFE

Having completed a large portion of the sessions for his album *Grace*, Jeff Buckley recruited guitar player Michael Tighe, who brought with him the ravishingly beautiful main riff of what became 'So Real'. The song begins with an elegant acoustic guitar part, before kicking fully into gear and crackling with spontaneous energy as Buckley sings mesmerically. The lyric is simple but deep, conjuring up the image of a haunting past relationship where emotions remain so strong that there is never any escape from the feelings that remain so very, very real.

15
MISSING
EVERYTHING BUT THE GIRL
BLANCO Y NEGRO

'Missing' was written by Ben Watt and Tracey Thorn as a lovelorn ballad in a folk/jazz style; it was pleasant enough and elevated to a degree by Thorn's mournful vocal. Issued as a single in 1994, it did okay, but no more than that… it was, in fact, fairly unexceptional. However, in October 1995, re-mixed by Todd Terry, it was once again issued as a single. This time, now presented in a pumping house style, all the emotion contained in the original version was somehow magically amplified, with the longing in the songs lyric being much better expressed over the harder dance beats. The mixing of the two styles was utterly convincing and cohesive, and this dance version was a huge improvement on the relaxed, and overly polite original. New life had been breathed not only into the track itself, but also into the career of Everything But The Girl.

14
THE HEARTS FILTHY LESSON
DAVID BOWIE
BMG
OTHER SINGLE 1995:
STRANGERS WHEN WE MEET

Reuniting with Berlin-era collaborator Brian Eno, suggested that David Bowie was preparing to push the more artistic side of his creativity to the fore; after fifteen-years of trying to please others, he would once again please himself. 'The Hearts Filthy Lesson' preceded the album *Outside*, and it set the tone for a period in which Bowie challenged both himself and his audience. This is a grinding slice of industrial funk, with an incoherent, fractured lyric, like a montage of scattered thoughts. There is a dystopian, futuristic feel, but everything seems incomprehensible and wired. Mike Garson tinkles the ivories in classic *Aladdin Sane*-style, but this can hardly be considered even remotely retrograde in the midst of this very forward-looking jumble of enthusiastic noise and lofty conceptualisation.

13
WATERFALLS
TLC
ARISTA
OTHER SINGLES 1995: RED LIGHT SPECIAL; DIGGIN' ON YOU

TLC were a three-piece girl group from Atlanta, Georgia who performed in a hybrid rap/R&B style. Teamed with fellow Atlanta residents, production team Organized Noize, they created this transcendental groover. Socially conscious, it deals with illegal drugs, violence and the HIV/AIDS epidemic. Although no punches were pulled, the delivery didn't sound preachy or self-righteous, and musically there were similarities to the classic mellow funkiness of Sly and the Family Stone at their peak. This slinky record, with its memorable chorus hook – owing a debt to the Paul McCartney song of the same name – was pretty darned close to pop perfection.

12
DOWN BY THE WATER
PJ HARVEY
ISLAND
OTHER SINGLES 1995: C'MON BILLY; SEND HIS LOVE TO ME

Simple, dark, haunting, intriguing and more than a little bit unsettling, it could only be PJ Harvey; here she is playing a creepy blues number in a most unorthodox manner. Her riveting voice is accompanied by humming, moaning, synthesised organ and orchestral trills, while her lyrics – an update on the traditional 'Salty Dog Blues' – tell the tale of a woman who drowns her daughter… naturally enough, this conveys a strong feeling of deranged menace, and the track as a whole is totally gripping from first note to last.

11
GANGSTER'S PARADISE
COOLIO FEATURING L.V.
TOMMY BOY
OTHER SINGLE 1995: TOO HOT

Amidst the deluge of hits scored by Stevie Wonder in the 1970s, there was one that got away – 'Pastime Paradise' from the album *Songs in the Key of Life*; somehow or other, it was surprisingly overlooked when it came to singles being selected. However, Coolio saw the potential to do something with the song, and piece by piece he built-up the outstanding symphonic rap track that became 'Gangsta's Paradise'. The strings from Stevie's original are retained, but the chorus – sung by L.V. accompanied by ghost-like choristers – is an interpolation. The verses are performed by Coolio, who uses religious imagery to set the scene as he tells the tale of a twenty-three-year-old who has taken another man's life, and doubts that he will reach age of twenty-four himself. Staring into the abyss, he realises that his actions must have consequences, and he is full of fear and regret. Coolio raps out the tale most convincingly. This sweet-sounding music, with a tough and uncompromising lyric, yielded a combination that proved to be pure pop dynamite.

10
BIRTHDAY CAKE
CIBO MATTO
EL DIABLO
OTHER SINGLE 1995:
KNOW YOUR CHICKEN

Cibo Matto were Yuka Honda and Miho Hatori – a pair of Japanese women based in New York – and 'Birthday Cake' was their first single. It is a weird and wild song about… baking a birthday cake! In fact, the lyrics go way beyond surrealism, into the realm of silliness and absurdity, and they are shouted, full throttle with fiendish glee, as a racket of bumping and grinding noise soundtracks this brilliantly glorious piece of dada-infused punk rock.

9
FANFARE
ERIC MATTHEWS
SUB POP

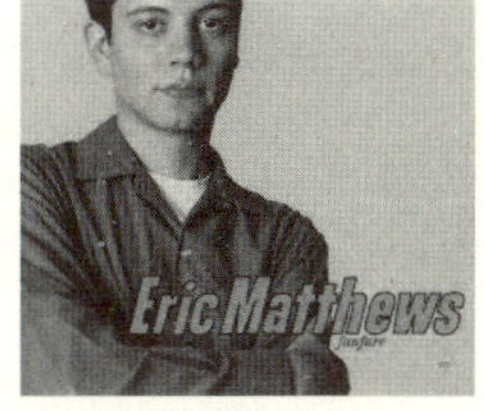

Eric Matthews had been one half of a sophisticated pop band called Cardinal, and his role as multi-instrumentalist and arranger prepared him for his first solo venture, an orchestral pop masterpiece of an album entitled *It's Heavy in Here*. The opening track of the album was 'Fanfare', which is grand, luxurious and breathtaking, a perfect melding of ambitious orchestration with a rock band base. Jason Falkner – once of Jellyfish – is on hand to play a tasteful and perfectly judged guitar solo, whilst Matthews provides an understated vocal for a rather portentous lyric. Pop hadn't sounded as epic as this since the days of The Left Banke and Kaleidoscope; this was stirring music and it really warmed the cockles of my heart.

8

I GOT ERECTION

TURBONEGER

HIT ME

OTHER SINGLES 1995:

BAD MONGO; DENIM DEMON

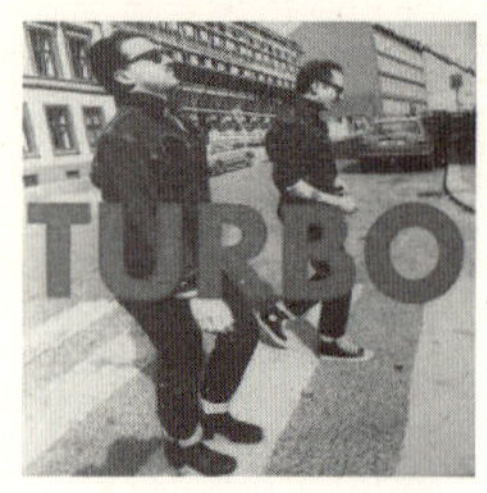

Turboneger was a none too subtle alias used by Norwegian band Turbonegro; in fact, nothing about them was particularly subtle, except for their sense of humour. They developed a hybrid punk/speed metal style – think Alice Cooper or the New York Dolls, but played by Slayer – and they christened it deathpunk. As for their look, they presented a supremely cool but over-the-top homoeroticism of moustaches, denim and leather. 'I Got Erection' was loud, fast, concise and blatantly crude and rude… in short, absolutely fantastic.

7

HELL IS ROUND THE CORNER

TRICKY

4TH & BROADWAY

OTHER SINGLES 1995:

OVERCOME ; BLACK STEEL

An elegant sample from 'Ike's Rap' by Isaac Hayes is the springboard with which Tricky propels this amazingly rich and fertile trawl through the corners of his mind. The lyrics, explosive as dropped bombs, are presented as part of a complex web that draws us inexorably inwards, to reveal the myriad nightmare visions behind the ghostly whisperings that Tricky uses to communicate. Martina, his accomplice and foil, sings a lustrous, slow blues as counterpoint to the deadly murmur, and the effect is just devastatingly brilliant.

6

BORN SLIPPY

UNDERWORLD

JUNIOR BOYS OWN

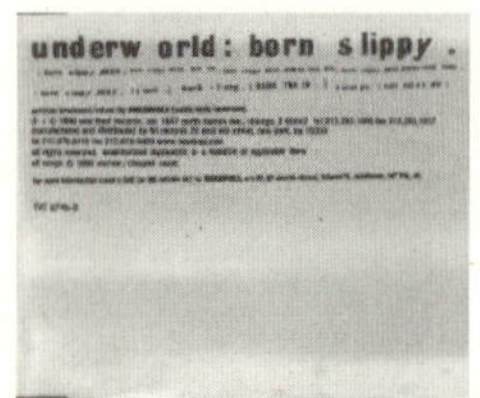

'Born Slippy' is a fabulously propulsive, beat-driven slice of techno that is like the amphetamine rush of cheap speed – it ticks along so you're just about feeling the sensation… and then boom!; it turns into a frenzy of wild excitement. But, although an excellent track, the B-side is where the real magic happens; here we have lurking a piece entitled 'Born Slippy Nuxx'. Despite a similarity in the title, it is completely unrelated to the other side, and this is quite simply one of the defining musical pieces of the 1990s. Used by Danny Boyle for the *Trainspotting* soundtrack, it has a haunting quality, as well as Karl Hyde vocalising a fragmented lyric inspired by a drunken night in Soho, as he tries to join together a series of unconnected images. Recorded in one take, and responding to the beats, Hyde momentarily gets stuck – "Lager, lager, lager, lager" he repeats, stalling for time, not realising that he is inadvertently birthing an iconic phrase that a whole generation will come to seize upon as a liberating, hedonistic chant.

5

PROTECTION

MASSIVE ATTACK

WITH TRACEY THORN

VIRGIN

OTHER SINGLE 1995: KARMACOMA

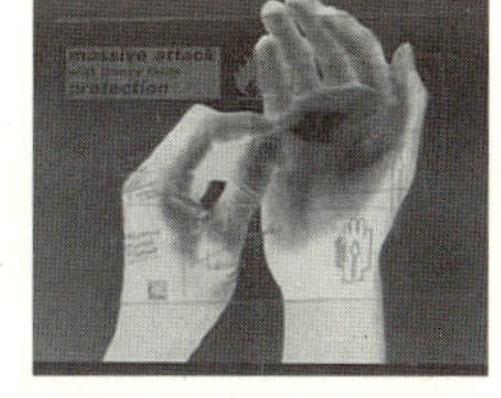

Tracey Thorn of Everything But the Girl is the featured vocalist on this uplifting, highly atmospheric scorcher from Massive Attack; it was an inspired pairing. Her vocals are honeyed, but they contain steeliness at the core; she sounds convincing and resolute as she states her intention to offer herself as a shield to a lover who needs protection. Thorn is provided with a slow and very striking groove to work with; it is built around a drum sample and a distinctive recurring wah-wah guitar figure taken from 'The Payback' by James Brown. By this time, Massive Attack were proving themselves to be a group of enduring high quality.

4

FAKE PLASTIC TREES

RADIOHEAD

PARLOPHONE

OTHER SINGLES 1995:

JUST; HIGH AND DRY

Here, we have parallels drawn between decorative 'Fake Plastic Trees' and the life being led by the narrator, who is in a state of crisis as the realisation dawns that all the constructs which hold his world together are unreal and phoney, and consequently, he himself is a fake. This is a cynical song seen from the point of view of a very jaundiced eye, but it is also meditative and dreamy, as well as being an astute verbalisation of the way in which thoughts are mulled-over in a half-awake state. The piece is slowly played; it ebbs, flows and alternates between quiet passages – where a ghostly organ underpins Thom Yorke's aching vocal – and huge orchestral swells which carry a heavy weight of emotion. The track sounds absolutely nothing like anybody else; Radiohead had reached the point where their music was altogether unmistakable and unique.

3

MIS-SHAPES/

SORTED FOR E'S AND WIZZ

PULP

ISLAND

OTHER SINGLES 1995:

COMMON PEOPLE; DISCO 2000

By now, Pulp were a big deal… proper pop stars in fact. But this did not prevent them from issuing subversive singles such as this two-headed beauty that casts a distrustful eye upon their environment, both geographical and cultural. 'Mis-Shapes' is quite an uptempo number which sees Jarvis Cocker sickened of witnessing nights out in Sheffield where flocks of identically dressed and coiffured beer monsters would intimidate and bully anyone with the temerity to look different from them. The song imagines these persecuted lone and nerdy misfits – the mis-shapes – banding together in an alliance of the weak, and then turning upon and defeating their tormentors. The fact that the beer monster bullies being mocked and castigated were now a large part of Pulp's audience, was an irony not lost on the band. The second song, 'Sorted for E's and Wizz', swipes at the prevalence of drug taking in rave culture; it opines that chemically-enhanced enjoyment is ultimately a hollow experience. Cocker sets about stating his case via a hilariously savage lyric that denounces the herd mentality that promotes a "drugs are good" attitude. Appropriately, the musical soundtrack is queazy, wobbly and washed out, making me think of the sound a fairground ride might make when the generator malfunctions and it slowly breaks down and grinds to a desultory halt.

2

YES

MCALMONT AND BUTLER

HUT

David McAlmont and Bernard Butler were a pair of supremely talented individuals brought together on the rebound following acrimonious splits from their previous bands (McAlmont from Thieves and Butler from Suede). 'Yes' was the first song they wrote together and it was also their first release. Butler, in control of the sound, builds-up a grand, elaborate, sweeping and ornate backing track, upon which the flamboyant McAlmont unleashes his incredible voice, a powerful, soaring and awe-inspiring instrument. Clearly the stars were aligned, the blue touch paper was lit, and the controlled explosion produced by this alliance of talent was of epic proportions. The fact that the song contains just a single repeated verse is of no consequence; neither does it matter that the lyric is a bitter and barely disguised attack on the duo's former band mates... but what does count is that this is ambitious, majestic, pop of rare quality – an uncompromising, soulful and exquisite jewel.

1

DA FUNK

DAFT PUNK

SOMA QUALITY RECORDINGS

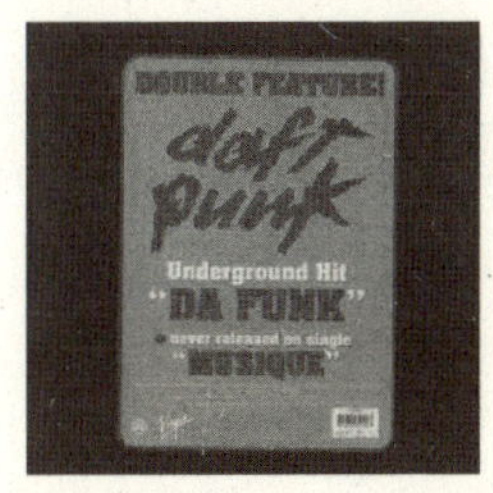

When it was first released, 'Da Funk' knocked me sideways; it was the best record I'd heard in years. To say I was obsessed by it, would be an understatement; I was in love with it would be a more accurate description. After a week spent working, my Friday evening ritual was to pump out 'Da Funk' on my stereo, three or four times on repeat... it filled me with joy, put me in a great mood and readied me for a big night out. Although classified as an acid-house track – and to be fair, the squelching synth rhythms and thumping drum beats certainly fit the bill – there was much more to it than that. To start with, 'Da Funk' is (predictably!) wildly funky; it also wiggles and wriggles with a prominently insistent and inescapable guitar part. Besides this, it grooves too, so even though the internal dynamics are in constant rotation, the gear changes are silky smooth, and we, the listeners, enjoy a very fine ride indeed as we delight in such a fantastic and mind-blowing trip.

With Denis & Lois in New York,

1996

EVENTS

The IRA bomb on Corporation Street in Manchester city centre. Fortunately there are no fatalaties.

Michael Jackson and Lisa Marie Presley divorce.

Chechen rebels engage in fierce conflict with Russian troops.

The mass murder of sixteen infants and a teacher is committed by Thomas Hamilton in Dunblane, Scotland; the murderer then commits suicide.

In Burundi, the massacre of over four hundred and fifty Hutu people is committed by Tutsi militia.

The Israeli government launches 'Operation Grapes of Wrath', a series of major attacks on Lebanon.

The *MV Bukoba* sinks in Lake Victoria in Tanzania; nearly one thousand people are killed.

Dolly the Sheep, the first mammal to be cloned from an adult cell, is born in Midlothian, Scotland.

Prince Charles and Diana Spencer are divorced.

Fox News Channel is launched.

Bill Clinton defeats Republican candidate Bob Dole and is re-elected President of the USA.

Eric Cantona almost single-handedly leads a youthful Manchester United team to the league and cup double, overhauling Newcastle United in a thrilling title race before scoring the winner himself in a 1-0 FA Cup final win over Liverpool. Cantona is named PFA and FWA Player of the Year just 12 months after the press and public attempted to hound him from the country. United complete the treble when Manchester City are relegated on the final day of the season.

The European Championships are held in England, where the home team reach the semi-finals before losing on penalties to eventual champions Germany

NOTABLE BIRTHS

Lewis Capaldi; Tom Holland; Lorde

NOTABLE DEATHS

François Mitterrand; Gerry Mulligan ; Gene Kelly; Boris Tchaikovsky; Bob Paisley; George Burns ; Jeffrey Lee Pierce ; Bernard Edwards; Johnny Guitar Watson ; Timothy Leary; Jon Pertwee; Ella Fitzgerald; Veronica Guerin ; Albert 'Cubby' Broccoli; David Tudor; Tupac Shakur; Spiro Agnew; Nicu Ceaușescu; René Lacoste; Beryl Reid ; Eva Cassidy; Tiny Tim ; Tommy Lawton; Faron Young ; Willie Rushton; Jack Nance

NOTABLE FILMS

Sleepers; *Mars Attacks*; *Romeo and Juliet*; *From Dusk till Dawn*; *Sling Blade*; *I Shot Andy Warhol*; *When We Were Kings*; *The Cable Guy*; *Secrets and Lies*; *Scream*; *The English Patient*; *Mission Impossible*; *Fargo*; *Trainspotting*; *Dead Man.*

NOTABLE BOOKS

Frank McCourt – *Angela's Ashes*

George R.R. Martin – *A Game of Thrones*

Chuck Palahniuk – *Fight Club*

Alex Garland – *The Beach*

Stephen King – *The Green Mile*

James Ellroy – *My Dark Places*

Edna O'Brien – *Down By The River*

MY 1996

Generally speaking, my disposition tends toward the downbeat; I am prone to bouts of soul-searching and melancholia but in 1996 my life seemed to be on an even keel; it truly seemed as though there was barely a cloud on the horizon. Overall, work was going pretty well… apart from one blip when I was reluctantly persuaded that the acquisition of an HGV driving license would be an asset; I therefore undertook a course of lessons, only to fail the driving test for exceeding the speed limit; secretly I was relieved. I wasn't comfortable driving large vehicles, because I was only too aware of my tendency to lose concentration – the world was a much safer place without me being behind the wheel of a ten-tonne truck. My leisure time was well spent with friends, and attendance at gigs remained a regular part of my life.

The biggest event of the year was probably Oasis playing at Maine Road – genuine excitement seemed to surround the show. Dennis & Lois, my friends from New York, flew-in to be in attendance; I didn't go because I was completely immune to the group's purported charms… to my ears they sounded dull and regressive. Among the performers I did see and enjoy were Super Furry Animals, Spiritualized and, amazingly, a rejuvenated Arthur Lee, playing the classic songs from his days with the Los Angeles band Love… he was incredible. I went to the Haçienda a couple of times, on the first occasion to see Martin Rev of Suicide; he performed somewhere in the bowels of the building in a space that I'd previously not been aware of – the audience was small, but among them was Rob Gretton. We exchanged pleasantries, but sadly it would be the last time I'd ever see him as he died far, far too soon just three years later. On the main stage I saw Tricky, with his back toward the audience, cloaked in darkness, creating a heavy and suffocating atmosphere; it was a magnificent performance. These were my last visits to the iconic club that had figured so prominently in my life; the following year it would cease to exist.

The Sex Pistols were revisited as well, in two different ways. Firstly, I appeared on a North West Arts TV documentary (presented by Mark Radcliffe) with the likes of Malcolm McLaren, Tony Wilson and Glen Matlock, discussing the group's impact in filmed interviews… which was fun. Secondly, the Pistols re-formed for the appropriately named *Filthy Lucre* Tour. I was given a fistful of tickets, which I distributed among friends, and so it was that in a builder's transit van a dozen of us headed off to Finsbury Park for an all-day spectacular. Oh dear! I was abused and spat at by a gaggle of identi-punks for having the temerity to be attired in a suit… "Imposter!" they cried, "You're not a punk!" Well, I guess they were right, because I most certainly was not whatever it was they believed punk to be. As for the Sex Pistols, they were highly proficient and put on a nice show, but apart from the novelty value, it was a meaningless and pointless pantomime. In the context of the 1970s they had been vital and necessary; now they were very much a part of the establishment, a museum piece… in punk-speak, they were boring. A much more significant negative was the IRA bomb that detonated in Manchester city centre; eight miles away at home in Denton, I heard the explosion as the heart of the city was torn apart.

I was in a happy place in 1996!

100
FRACTAL FLOW
SILVER APPLES
ENRAPTURED

Silver Apples were an experimental electronic band formed way back in 1967 when they were way ahead of the curve. Their second album, released in 1969, featured a cover photograph of the duo – Simeon and percussionist Danny Taylor – in the cockpit of a Pan Am airplane. This led to a legal battle that stopped the group's career dead in its tracks; seemingly, they disappeared into thin air, although over the years their reputation began to grow. Out of the blue, in 1996, came this single, 'Fractal Flow', featuring Simeon with new partner Xian Hawkins. Their reputation and legacy remained secure, because this is an elegant and melodically strong piece of eccentric electronic pop, that hums and drones in the same style as the group's 1960s output. Ironically, in the 1990s this sounded absolutely contemporary; the rest of the world had finally caught up with Silver Apples.

99
UNIVERSAL FREQUENCIES
HIS NAME IS ALIVE
4AD

His Name is Alive, a band from Livonia in Michigan, are impossible to categorise because their sound is constantly evolving. On this single they present a kind of dreamy, cosmic Beach Boys vibe, but undercut with a dread sense of foreboding. Beautifully sung and produced with great attention to detail, 'Universal Frequencies' plays like the ominous ghost of 'Good Vibrations'.

98
SON OF MOOK
RED SNAPPER
WARP

The track opens with harsh, hissing electronics, followed by a resonant stand-up bass. Then live drums play a lean and arresting beat, as hard and fat horns enter the fray and begin to snake into all four corners of the piece. Finally, even more electronic noise fills any remaining gaps, and we wonder is it jazz?… is it experimental dance?… is it this or is it that? In the end, we conclude that it is simply Red Snapper, and it's a flame-thrower of a record that scorches wherever it is aimed.

97
WAIL
JON SPENCER
BLUES EXPLOSION
MUTE
OTHER SINGLE 1996:: 2 KIND-SA LOVE

This is muscular and absolutely ferocious; all the levels are shoved well into the red and every single aspect of the performance is extreme and pushed to the limit. The end result is that 'Wail' sounds as if a young and lean Elvis Presley is lead singer of The Butthole Surfers while they are jamming wildly on an abstract blues number.

96
SCOOBY SNACKS
FUN LOVIN' CRIMINALS
SILVER SPOTLIGHT
OTHER SINGLES 1996:: THE GRAVE AND THE CONSTANT; THE FUN LOVIN' CRIMINAL

Featuring dialogue sampled from both *Pulp Fiction* and *Reservoir Dogs* (earning film director Quentin Tarantino a writing credit) 'Scooby Snacks' put New York band Fun Lovin' Criminals into the hit parade. The song is a staccato blues shuffle, played leanly and minimally. The rapped verses describe a bank robbery in exaggerated cartoon-style, but inserted between these is a sublime chorus that is as catchy as measles, stating that the bank robbers are "Running around all whacked off of Scooby Snacks" – a street-slang term for the prescription drug *Diazepam*. Although too tongue-in-cheek to be taken at all seriously, 'Scooby Snacks' was, nonetheless, a cool and catchy piece of swaggering musical theatre.

95
RIVERBOAT SONG
OCEAN COLOUR SCENE
MCA
OTHER SINGLES 1996:: THE DAY WE CAUGHT THE TRAIN; THE CIRCLE; YOU'VE GOT IT BAD

Mod-revival bands tend to bore me; I find the narrow parameters they impose upon their sound in order to chase an unattainable authenticity leaves their music sounding predictable and tired. Ocean Colour Scene were just as retro as the rest of the Paul Weller-fixated pack, yet here they manage to combine their Flamingo Club flavours with a healthy dollop of Led Zeppelin (by pilfering the riff from the hard-rock behemoth's 'Four Sticks') and hit upon a sound that was arresting, attention-grabbing, urgent and quite exciting.

94
NUDE AS THE NEWS
CAT POWER
MATADOR
OTHER SINGLE 1996:: UNDERCOVER

'Nude as the News' is a self-lacerating, scab-picking song about an abortion that Chan Marshall – aka Cat Power – had undergone when twenty-years of age. Played on a scratchy and persistent guitar, the performance prickles and churns, though the harshness of the sound is yet surpassed by the intensity in Marshall's strong and clear voice. Her words are ambiguous, but each syllable seems to quiver, imbued as they are with naked emotional turmoil. This is an extremely powerful listening experience that in many ways echoes depression-era folk/blues with its spooky combination of ugliness and beauty.

93
I WANNA BE THERE
MODEL 500
R&S

Remixed by drum and bass producer Wax Doctor, this peerless slice of

Detroit techno from Juan Atkins – the originating maestro of the scene – opened the minds and ears of a younger generation who populated underground British clubs. It is minimal, powerful and brilliantly paced, with beats that are programmed to perfection supporting deep synth lines, deep bass lines and a deep male voice repeating the phrase "I Wanna be There". In terms of quality and taste, this is absolutely impeccable stuff; 'I Wanna be There' set the standard for others to aspire to.

92
VIRTUAL INSANITY
JAMIROQUAI
SONY
OTHER SINGLES 1996::
COSMIC GIRL;
DO U KNOW WHERE YOU'RE COMING FROM?

Jay Kay – the self-styled "cat in the hat" and leader of London hipster funksters Jamiroquai – had developed some pretty outlandish concepts; he wanted to weld spacey head-music to the dance-floor. Some people laughed and mocked, but the idea was not much different to that previously employed by the likes of Sun Ra and George Clinton; they too had faced ridicule, but in the end had the last laugh. With 'Virtual Insanity', Jamiroquai wrapped up the big idea inside an irresistible dance groove, and in doing so, they created a truly memorable single. Inspired by a trip to Japan, Kay wrote about overpopulation, ecological collapse and the negative impact on human interaction brought about by technological advancement. Although describing a futuristic dystopian nightmare, the piano-led disco stylings and the warmth of the performance meant that the general public lapped it all up; the record was effortlessly cool, whilst still asking very pertinent questions… and in that sense it was truly subversive.

91
PLANETARY SIT IN
JULIAN COPE
ECHO
OTHER SINGLE 1996::
I COME FROM ANOTHER PLANET BABY

'Planetary Sit In', taken from his album *Interpreter*, sees Julian Cope displaying his penchant for delivering extremely pretty, sunshine-dappled pop with psychedelic overtones. It has a beautifully sung lyric of cosmic strangeness that manages to sound very jolly. No matter how far out Julian travelled – and he was undoubtedly a fairly regular astral wanderer – he never seemed to lose his knack for making lovely, but odd, pop records… and 'Planetary Sit In' is a real cracker.

90
SPINAL SCRATCH
THOMAS BANGALTER
ROULE

Outside his main gig as being one half of Daft Punk, Thomas Bangalter was busy making his own music, or else collaborating with other musicians. In 1996, he briefly had a band called

Da Mongoloids, along with Armand Van Helden and Junior Sanchez, and later, another collaboration would yield the international hit 'Music Sounds Better With You' under the name of Stardust. Here though, with the Buzzcocks punning 'Spinal Scratch', the ingenious Parisian created a unique sounding and tremendously funky banger, in which cut-up samples of George Benson's 'The World is a Ghetto' are looped and scratched over a harder-than-iron beat. Of course, it sounds quite a bit like a Daft Punk track, but it is wilder and crazier, almost as if Daft Punk were performing a high-wire act at the circus.

89
RETURN OF THE MACK
MARK MORRISON
WEA

During this period British singer Mark Morrison was living a violent and turbulent life, and he had to serve several prison sentences... but 'Return of the Mack showed the world his creative side. It is a superb slice of attitudinal 1980s-style R&B, in which Morrison adopts the character of a jilted lover who ups his game in order to metaphorically rub the nose of his ex into the dirt. Several samples are used to produce this rubber limbed, slippin' and slidin' track, but most prominent is the beat from Tom Tom Club's immortal 'Genius of Love'. A swaggering Jamaican-style vocal from Morrison tops off the track, which went on to become a chart topper in the UK, and a number two on the USA billboard chart.

88
DREAM KITCHEN
MARK STEWART
MUTE

Simon Mundey is the man at the controls on this occasion, rather than Adrian Sherwood, and the result is a less brutal outing than was customary for Mark Stewart... but there is still no concession to orthodoxy, and no attempt to make a more palatable record that might just infiltrate the mainstream. Instead, what is served up is a gigantic, juddering, cavernous dub, with some very disturbing sounds bubbling up beneath the surface. Several voices are heard – including that of the unmistakable reggae maestro Bim Sherman – while the subject matter of this monumental and wondrous song is consumerism and the acquisition of unnecessary possessions.

87
DIRTY SOUTH
GOODIE MOB
LAFACE
OTHER SINGLE 1996::
SOUL FOOD

This features Big Boi, guesting from fellow Georgia act Outkast, and over a lazy, almost sleepy, beat, the crew take turns at the mic countering the ignorance and prejudice they encounter due to their supposedly uncool geographic location. At times they actually drawl in exaggerated southern-style as they ask "What you niggas know about the dirty

South?", echoing Lynyrd Skynyrd's early 1970s 'Sweet Home Alabama' in its defiance of deep-seated and entrenched attitudes.

86
FASTLOVE
GEORGE MICHAEL
VIRGIN
OTHER SINGLES 1996::
JESUS TO A CHILD;
SPINNING THE WHEEL

Although 'Fastlove' is a dance track, and its subject matter is an advocation of non-committal sexual liaison over and above painful and complicated relationships, it is not carefree or particularly hedonistic. Instead, it is imbued with wistfulness and a sense that behind the thrill-seeking of a succession of one-night stands there is an emotional emptiness. Brilliantly constructed, this has a slinky bump-and-grind kind of groove, and George Michael croons so seductively; there is a tangible animal magnetism in his teasing, prowling and sophistication. This was a very bold single, because its theme of sexual excess during an era of abstinence flew against the prevailing trend, as did its slick and sumptuous sound amidst the brashness of britpop guitars and the aggression of gangsta rap.

85
NIERIKA
DEAD CAN DANCE
4AD
OTHER SINGLE 1996::
THE SNAKE AND THE MOON

Here we have electronics and tribal rhythms, combined with strong male and female voices singing in a foreign tongue. The rhythm is unceasing and the voices hypnotic, positioning this track a long, long way from conventional pop music... but it is highly rewarding nevertheless. 'Nierika' is a refreshing, cleansing and head-expanding record that definitely deserves attention.

84
TAHITIAN MOON
PORNO FOR PYROS
WARNER BROTHERS
OTHER SINGLES 1996::
100 WAYS;
DOGS RULE THE NIGHT

A pulverising bass, fuzzy guitars and savagely beaten drums produce here an untamed and dangerous noise; abruptly it halts, giving way to a gentle acoustic strum, over which Perry Farrell sings with great delicacy about being on a capsizing boat that forces him to swim to the shore, not knowing if he has strength enough to make it there... according to Farrell, this was based upon a real-life incident. The song moves backwards and forwards between hard and soft styles, between darkness and light, between hope and despair; perhaps it is all about finding beauty through endurance? Whatever, this is a fascinating record that sounds damned good.

83
NEVER GET AHEAD
BOBBY CONN
TRUCKSTOP

Bobby Conn is a pop classicist, and here he lovingly delivers a musical homage to the bubblegum-era Motown sound of The Jackson 5. The track actually manages to match 'I Want You Back' for sheer effervescence, although Conn's use of violin as lead instrument displays his individualistic streak. So, too, does the lyric – sung in an outrageous falsetto – in which Conn totally subverts the template, entwining sexual metaphor and opposition to authority; "You're never gonna get ahead, giving head to the man", he choruses… and we can only shake our heads and wholeheartedly agree.

82
YOU'RE GORGEOUS
BABY BIRD
ECHO
OTHER SINGLE 1996:: GOODNIGHT

Stephen Jones was a prolific songwriter who issued his solo recordings under the name Baby Bird. In order to tour, he formed a band called Babybird, and the group's second single was 'You're Gorgeous'. This tells the tale of a seedy photo-shoot, during which the manipulation and exploitative intentions of the photographer lead the model to misinterpret his signals, resulting in a twisted and tragi-comic sexual farce. Blessed with a fabulously catchy chorus, the track was an immediate earworm. Jones's fruity baritone is most excellent as he narrates this ever-so-slightly unsettling song.

81
AIN'T GOIN' TO GOA
ALABAMA 3
ONE LITTLE INDIAN

Formed after a chance meeting during a rave in Peckham, Alabama 3 released this sarcastic, funny and very pertinent debut single that also happened to be riotously good. The group were routinely dismissed as a novelty act due to the aliases – replete with colourful personas – that the group members adopted and, as if to give further ammunition to their detractors, they refused to conform to the vogue of making music purely in a single style; country, blues, gospel and acid house were all miraculously fused together in an unholy alliance. 'Ain't Goin' to Goa' is an outstanding demonstration of the certain fact that this unlikely bunch could make some seriously great music.

80
IF I RULED THE WORLD (IMAGINE THAT)
NAS FEATURING LAURYN HILL
OTHER SINGLE 1996:: SWEET DREAMS

If the title gives the impression that this track might be a saccharine sweet utopian vision rather than something more rooted in reality, then that impression would be wrong; the musings here are most definitely based on actuality. Cocaine without any garbage additive is on the wish list, as is – in the midst of the AIDS/HIV crisis – unprotected sex. The combination of the crisp and very much to-the-point raps that Nas spits out, and the silky soulfulness of Lauryn Hill's character-filled voice, is not just effective… it is quite outstanding.

79
I DIG YOU
BOSS HOG
GEFFEN
OTHER SINGLE 1996::
WINN COMA

Boss Hog, featuring Jon Spencer and his wife Cristina Martinez, were an occasionally functioning band who ran parallel with The Jon Spencer Blues Explosion. Their track, 'I Dig You', seems to crawl like a reptile on a cliff face; it is agile and lithe, defying both gravity and the urge to kick-up into a higher gear, as it remains resolutely low-key. The husband and wife team also sing in an exaggeratedly kooky fashion, declaring their mutual love by exchanging a series of sweet nothings – "I dig your barbecued lips" being just one such expression of endearment.

78
8 STEPS TO PERFECTION
COMPANY FLOW
OFFICIAL RECORDINGS
OTHER SINGLE 1996::
INFOKILL/POPULATION CONTROL

From Brooklyn, New York, Company Flow were an underground hip-hop act who pushed the genre forward towards a higher artistic plane via their refreshingly progressive attitude. '8 Steps to Perfection' has a ghostly and futuristic sound; a kind of slow jam with hard beats. Here, the rappers are breathing fire; they are smooth, smart and passionate, and there are no tired clichés to litter and tarnish their conceptual and abstract use of language.

77
TRASH
SUEDE
NUDE
OTHER SINGLE 1996::
BEAUTIFUL ONES

Gone was the wonderful weirdness that Bernard Butler had brought to Suede's music, filling it, as he did, with his guitar abstractions; his replacement, Richard Oakes, had a more traditional writing and playing style. This made Suede a more straightforward sounding band, but at the same time it ushered in a period of huge commercial success; indeed, 'Trash' became the group's biggest-selling single. The less cluttered sound of the track seemed to propel Brett Anderson to even loftier artistic heights; his lyric is a witty, self-referencing gem that places Suede in amongst the lowlife, painting them as pop outsiders. The overall sound is suitably glam, camp and dramatic whilst Anderson – positively relishing the space in which he has to sing – croons rather deliciously.

76
MILK
GARBAGE
MUSHROOM
OTHER SINGLE 1996::
STUPID GIRL

I hadn't really liked Garbage very much; their glossy, hard-rock bombast, mixed with pop hooks, just turned me off. However, that changed with the release of this single version of 'Milk'; the song had previously featured on the group's debut album, but this was an entirely new recording featuring input and vocals from Tricky, and he added a degree of tension and edginess which had hitherto been completely absent. His rasped utterances, muttered from the gutter, were juxtaposed with the crystalline, heavenly singing of Shirley Manson, and this elevated the track far above the mundane. It was just the platform that Manson required to unleash the song's desperately emotional chorus… and unleash it she did, to quite stunning effect.

75
SHE CRIES YOUR NAME
BETH ORTON
HEAVENLY

Beth Orton married her love of 1960s English folk-rock (e.g. Pentangle and Fairport Convention) to contemporary electronic sounds, and in so doing became a standard bearer for a style labelled as folktronica. She collaborated extensively with William Orbit, and he was the co-writer of 'She Cries Your Name'; it is an intoxicating single. The disparate elements blend together seamlessly; there is an eerie quality evident in Orton's plaintive vocal, while the plucked guitar and sympathetic orchestration evoke an overwhelming sense of emptiness. The track chimed deeply with ravers, who, in the aftermath of a night of euphoria, would seek some calm, clean come-down music to chill-out too; it is true that 'She Cries Your Name' does fit that bill perfectly, but its charms are not exclusively the preserve of sun-blasted hedonists – the appeal is quite rightly widespread.

74
SECRET LIAISON
SOURCE DIRECT
GOOD LOOKING
OTHER SINGLES 1996::
THE CRANE; STONEKILLER

The so-called "Amen Break" is a drum break sample taken from a 1969 track called 'Amen, Brother' by soul band The Winstons; it is the most sampled track in history, with over 5,000 recorded usages. The sample features on countless hip-hop and drum-and-bass tracks (some of which are already featured in this book) but on 'Secret Liaison', Source Direct use it superbly well to give the piece its insistent groove.

However, there is much more going on than just that one single element; there is fine utilisation of space, jazzy piano flourishes and dreamy washes of synthetic strings. Although still teenagers when this single was released, Source Direct crafted a beautiful piece of music here; it is both tasteful and mature, without in any way sacrificing the raw edge that made it such a drum-and-bass staple.

73
LOVEFOOL
THE CARDIGANS
MERCURY
OTHER SINGLE 1996:: BEEN IT

'Lovefool' is a pop masterclass; everything about the track is shiny and exciting. Nina Persson sings a somewhat depressing lyric about willingly putting up with mistreatment from a boyfriend with whom she is besotted. Despite this apparently unpromising subject matter, she sings the tale brightly and cheerily, amidst a hook-laden accompaniment that is uber-catchy and just a trifle kitsch.

72
EL SCORCHO
WEEZER
DGC
OTHER SINGLE 1996::
THE GOOD LIFE

'El Scorcho' was the song chosen to promote *Pinkerton*, the second Weezer album; unfortunately, it flopped. Radio programmers – in their infinite wisdom – simply didn't find it suitable to air; consequently *Pinkerton* also suffered from a corresponding lack of sales. The sad irony is that 'El Scorcho' is a fabulous single, with its bold and slinky come-ons that lead into enormous sing-along choruses. The fun lyrics are either very obscure or completely nonsensical – though they do manage to reference Public Enemy, Green Day, Black Sabbath and Half Japanese – and along with the unruly party vibe of the track, this thoroughly deserves a great big thumbs up.

71
CLONES
THE ROOTS
DGC
OTHER SINGLES 1996::
THE HYPNOTIC;
CONCERTO OF THE
DESPERADO; WHAT THEY DO

The Roots, from Philadelphia, differed from many of their hip-hop peers by employing live musicians to create their jazz-tinged sound. They had the required lyrical chops too, and as 'Clones' amply demonstrates, they delivered their intelligent and thought-provoking rhymes with genuine intensity and great dexterity, pointing an accusatory finger at the plethora of phoney gangsta rappers who are interested only in earning dollars, rather than challenging the negative stereotype that they perpetuate. 'Clones' is a fine example of The Roots high-class individualism.

70
UNDER CANVAS UNDER WRAPS
THE DELGADOS
CHEMIKAL UNDERGROUND
OTHER SINGLES 1996:: CINECENTRE; SUCROSE

Named after the Tour de France cycling champion Pedro Delgado, this Glaswegian four-piece started their own record label rather than signing to somebody else's, and 'Under Canvas Under Wraps' was an early single. Musically it is sharp and angular; the guitars buzz and the drums are clattered. At the heart of the cacophony is a sweet pop melody, forcefully sung by Emma Pollock, with the distorted voice of Alun Woodward providing a counterpoint for her to bounce off and around.

69
COTTON WOOL
LAMB
FONTANA
OTHER SINGLES 1996:: GOD BLESS; GOLD

The Mancunian duo of musician Andy Barlow and vocalist Lou Rhodes emerged in this year as Lamb, and they caught the zeitgeist perfectly. Led by the double bass playing of Paddy Steer, 'Cotton Wool' combined a trip-hop sensibility with elements of drum-and-bass, jazz and experimental noise. This foundation was overlain by the very English, almost folk-singer style, of Rhodes, and it is this mélange that makes the single such an arresting and multi-faceted listen. All the pieces fit together perfectly around the song's emotional core, where considerable depth and some degree of darkness can be found.

68
THE CHISELERS
THE FALL
JET

The Fall had tumbled into a mid-decade slump; for a few years their work was at best lacklustre and at worst completely boring… but happily, 'The Chiselers' was a welcome return to form. It features an outrageously glam guitar riff, Mark E. Smith with a bee-in-his-bonnet, seemingly chewing on a wasp, helium backing vocals from Julia Nagle, and a bratty, 1960s bubblegum turn at the microphone from Brix Smith that leads to a false ending and reprise, led by the still grouchy Mr Smith. 'The Chiselers' is nuts in a good way; fabulously exciting, it sounds like nothing else on earth… except for The Fall.

67
THE OPERA HOUSE
OLIVIA TREMOR CONTROL
THE BLUE ROSE RECORD COMPANY
OTHER SINGLE 1996:: THE GIANT DAY

The mere mention of this band's name makes my heart flutter; I was obsessed with The Olivia Tremor Control and their sprawling, neo-psychedelic album *Music from the Unrealised Film Script: Dusk at Cubist Castle*. They hailed from Athens, Georgia, and were part of the musical collective known as *Elephant 6*, which banded together Neutral Milk Hotel, Apples in Stereo, Elf Power and others. 'The Opera House' has a sound which is located somewhere between *Revolver*-era Beatles and The Butthole Surfers – in other words, it is both sonically adventurous and highly melodic. The lyric concerns growing up and learning life lessons via the dramas that are played out onstage at 'The Opera House'.

66
MICHAEL GERALD'S PARTY MACHINE PRESENTS KILLDOZER AND ALICE DO-NUT
TOUCH AND GO

Two of the American underground's most extreme alt-rock acts combine for this three track single. Track one sees Alice Donut tackle The Bee Gees' 1967 track 'Every Christian Lion Hearted Man Will Show You'; they substitute muscle in place of the original's whimsy and it's a great reading of a great song. Track two sees Killdozer plough through Procol Harum's 'Conquistador'; in its original form, this was a big favourite of mine, but I nonetheless love the brutal treatment it receives here. Track three sees the two bands combine as Kill Donut to perform the *Hair* medley 'Aquarius/Let the Sunshine In', which they rampage through with irreverent glee – all in all, superb stuff!

65
BLUE FLOWERS
DR. OCTAGON
MO WAX
OTHER SINGLE 1996:: 3000

Dr. Octagon, the sinister, space-travelling alter-ego of Kool Keith, returned from the outer reaches of the cosmos with 'Blue Flowers', a track which combines the wicked beats and soundscapes created by producer Dan the Automator, with the menacing, out-of-left-field vocals of the clearly insane Dr. Octagon, to produce the simple but brilliant pop-hook of the song's title. Completely out on his own, Kool Keith was leading hip-hop into hitherto neglected areas; in time, others would follow his example, adding experimentation and risk-taking to a genre that was in danger of hitting the wall.

64
SOMETHING CHANGED
PULP
ISLAND

'Something Changed' was a song that had been written and rehearsed a full decade earlier; but now Jarvis Cocker dredged it up, gave it a polish, changed a few words… and hey presto!… another mini-classic. The lyric is concerned with the degree that chance plays in our lives – the random way in which we meet someone who becomes important to us. This is quite a simple, understated song with very few flourishes; acoustic guitar and synth-strings dominate the sound, then a short guitar solo is added, and that's it… complete and quite wonderful. A perfect example of the principle that very often less is definitely more.

63
1979
SMASHING PUMPKINS
HUT
OTHER SINGLES 1996::
ZERO; THIRTY THREE;
TONIGHT TONIGHT

Marrying traditional rock instrumentation to studio-derived effects, '1979' saw Smashing Pumpkins moving away from their roots and becoming a more experimental outfit. It is appropriate that this single announced the change of approach, since it is a coming-of-age tale, and was given the title '1979' by Billy Corgan because that was the year in which he turned twelve-years old and began the move into adolescence. The lyric is shot through with arresting imagery and the smooth, rolling sound of the track is very easy to become immersed in; there is an almost narcotic quality that is seductive and hypnotising.

62
STAKES IS HIGH
DE LA SOUL
TOMMY BOY
OTHER SINGLE 1996::
ITZSOWEEZEE

Seeking a harder sound than previously found on De La Soul records, the group teamed-up with producer Jay Dee (aka J Dilla) and this turned out to be a genius move. Jay Dee sets them up with a sound that is edgy and full of drama, as De La Soul unambiguously attack the state of hip-hop at that moment in time. The commercialisation of the genre is commented on, and the negative effect it has on impressionable listeners through the glorification of gangster lifestyles is resolutely criticised. 'Stakes is High' is performed with intensity and panache, and this track really threw down the gauntlet. Sure, it upset some of the biggest players in hip-hop, but, as is often stated, "the truth hurts".

61
MANHOO
CARDIACS
THE ALPHABET BUSINESS CONCERN
OTHER SINGLE 1996:: ODD EVEN

'Manhoo' was a limited release of only one thousand copies, and also the first of four proposed single releases – although only the follow-up, 'Odd Even', was ever issued. 'Manhoo' begins with the sound of children singing, but when the track kicks-off properly there is a warped and weird kind of psychedelic sound that is not at all whimsical, but rather impassioned and extreme. There is an exciting punkish energy generated as the children continue to sing, accompanying Tim Smith whose performance is downright intense and compelling… as indeed is this amazing single.

60
PAROLES
MIKE INK
WARP

Wolfgang Voigt is the artist here, operating under the pseudonym "Mike Ink", one of over thirty he has adopted over the course of a highly productive musical career. 'Paroles' is a sensational slice of freaky, funky, techno that bleeps, squiggles and explodes. It is hard but playful, using human voices in an inspired way; they are indistinct to the point where they become another musical element. This superb dance track is a total joy to experience.

59
BECOMING MORE LIKE ALFIE
THE DIVINE COMEDY
SETANTA
OTHER SINGLES 1996::
SOMETHING FOR
THE WEEKEND;
THE FROG PRINCESS

The Divine Comedy are a band from Northern Ireland, whose only constant is singer/writer Neil Hannon; his work is full of wit, verve and musical panache. 'Becoming More Like Alfie' displays all of these attributes – it is a breezy number with more than a hint of Burt Bacharach in its use of bossa nova style horns. Hannon, singing with cheery clarity, tells the tale of a man hurt in love, feeling that he has been too refined, too sensitive and, as a consequence, too vulnerable. Therefore, he takes inspiration from the *Alfie* character – portrayed on film by Michael Caine – he resolves to toughen-up, to become a little coarser and more self-assured in the style of this celluloid character, thinking that his life will surely improve through the shape-shifting device of simply 'Becoming More Like Alfie'.

58
DINNER WITH DELORES
PRINCE
WARNER BROTHERS
OTHER SINGLES 1996:: BET-CHA BY GOLLY WOW; GIRL 6

Although 'Dinner With Delores' wasn't one of the great classics that pepper Prince's back-catalogue, it was still a gorgeous example of his awesome talent. Featherweight in sound, this features an attractive, chiming guitar pattern as Prince croons a fairly inconsequential lyric, hinting at oral sex, before unleashing a deliciously-toned guitar solo... then he simply announces that the song is over. So, despite being rather slight – and one suspects that it didn't really require much effort from Prince as far as composition or recording was concerned – his innate craftsmanship and ear for melody combined to make this a highly worthwhile and desirable piece that simply oozes charm.

57
DJED
TORTOISE
THRILL JOCKEY
OTHER SINGLES 1996::
GALAPAGOS 1;
THE TAUT AND THE TAME

'Djed' finds Tortoise sounding a bit Neu-ish as they adapt Klaus Dinger's motorik rhythm to their own purposes. The track is a long and winding road; it never sits still, always holding the attention of the listener as various instruments seamlessly interchange and take turns in becoming prominent. The mood goes from cheerful to sinister, from light to dark, and a long xylophone section is introduced which then gives way to distorted and dissonant electronic sound. This truly is a journey in sound – 'Djed' is just sheer brilliance.

56
GIRL/BOY
APHEX TWIN
WARP

'Girl/Boy' by sonic adventurer Richard D. James – wearing his Aphex Twin hat – is a single of two extremes – the neo-classical (with prominent cello) representing femininity, and the pistol-quick, hard and heavy beats representative of masculinity. Combined, they become a third, very beautiful and more complex entity, proving that simple conceptual thinking, executed with precision and superb technique, is an unmistakeable hallmark of true artistry.

55
CAR SONG
ELASTICA
GEFFEN

Released as a single only in Australia and the USA, 'Car Song' is about sex in an automobile. Most appropriately, a push-and-pull, piston-pumping sound is incorporated, and astonishing *Roaring Twenties*-style backing vocals add to the giddy excitement. Meanwhile, Justine Frischmann sings with cool self-assurance on this fabulous single, that succeeds in combining sauciness with artfulness.

54
THAT WAS MY VEIL
JOHN PARISH AND POLLY JEAN HARVEY
ISLAND

Polly Jean Harvey had a collaborative relationship with John Parish that stretched back to her stint in his band Automatic Dlamini, before the formation of her own PJ Harvey ensemble. Seeking to stretch herself as a lyricist, she instigated a partnership with Parish where she would write the words to his music, and in this fashion they made an excellent album together, *Dance Hall at Louse Point*, from which 'That Was My Veil' was extracted. It is a slow and sparse song that is already inflected with aching sadness, but Mick Harvey from the Bad Seeds provides a spooky organ solo, further adding to the doom-laden gothic atmosphere in this song of dark despair.

53
ON AND ON
ERYKAH BADU
UNIVERSAL

Erykah Badu announced her arrival with the confident and quite stupendous new soul of 'On and On'. Unhurried and stripped down, there is an African flavouring in the sound and rhythm – particularly in the minimalistic percussion that anchors the track. Despite the relative lack of adornment, the music still cooks with a languorous groove, a fat, rolling bass, subdued keyboards with a jazzy tint and Badu's wonderfully controlled voice that drew comparison with the likes of Billie Holiday and Ella Fitzgerald.

52
THIS HERE GIRAFFE
FLAMING LIPS
WARNER BROTHERS
OTHER SINGLE 1996::
BRAINVILLE

The Flaming Lips were enormous fun; for sure, the debt of influence owed to The Butthole Surfers was gigantic, but The Flaming Lips – as evidenced by 'This Here Giraffe' – were lovable, and they never strayed towards the darkness that their counterparts often revelled in. Even so, the use of dissonance and experimental sound meant that mainstream audiences often found them too difficult to embrace. By way of example, the bass line here is incredibly unorthodox, though quite brilliant, and hey… are those pan-pipes floating into the mix? It all sounds pretty weird and wonderful, but at the heart of the song is just a deep love of pop music. They utilise a classic pop format, choc-full of hooks, and Wayne Coyne's ever so cheerful vocal is the cherry on top of this already very sweet cake.

51
SUPER BON BON
SOUL COUGHING
SLASH

Soul Coughing were all regulars at *The Knitting Factory*, a venue in New York which leaned very much towards experimental music making. The frontman of the band, Mike Doughty, was the doorman – famed for his improvised comedic raps – whilst the other band members all played in various groups who appeared at the club. Soul Coughing became a wildly improvisational assembly whose idiosyncratic approach earned them a large audience in the USA; Doughty himself described the sound of the band as "deep slacker jazz". As for 'Super Bon Bon', this rests securely on the drums and an irresistible double bass riff; electronics crackle beneath the groove, and eccentric stream of consciousness lyrics are delivered in a fractured rap-style by Doughty. Like it or loathe it, 'Super Bon Bon' is one of those "once heard, never forgotten" kind of tracks.

50
SETTING SUN
CHEMICAL BROTHERS
VIRGIN

Even the presence of irritating Britpopper Noel Gallagher cannot ruin this single. It is built upon a no-holds barred, floor-shaking barrage of beats and wailing sirens, with heavy psychedelic back-tracked sounds swirling like dervishes throughout. The immense potency is palpable as the piece soars ever higher. Unsurprisingly, Gallagher tries to pretend that he is John Lennon as he serves-up a lyrical offering owing much to 'Tomorrow Never Knows'; this is worked into the track on waves of phase and echo, producing music that can only be described as a mind-blowing, epic trip.

49
PATIO SONG
GORKY'S ZYGOTIC MYNCI
FONTANA

The nearest Gorky's ever came to a bona-fide hit single was with 'Patio Song', which reached number forty-one on the hit parade. It's a lovely record in which the band's excessively crazy instincts were reined-in and replaced by charming tunefulness and a simple, sweet lyric that gently celebrates love and the joy of life itself. At the mid-point, the song moves up a gear as brass is added, and the lyric is sung in the Welsh language. Put succinctly, this is a record that is guaranteed to lift the mood.

48
POEMS
NEARLY GOD
ISLAND

'Poems' came from Tricky's second album, which was credited to Nearly God because his record label wouldn't permit two albums by him to be released in the same year. 'Poems' was written in collaboration with ex-Specials/Fun Boy Three singer Terry Hall, who, along with Martina Topley-Bird and Tricky himself, provides the vocals, with each taking a turn at the microphone and adding a different flavour to the bleak, zonked-out sonic landscape they inhabit. This is a dark and strange record, that seems to convey deep disappointment about the nature of relationships… but it is, nonetheless, extremely hypnotic and compelling.

47
YOU'RE NOT ALONE
OLIVE
RCA
OTHER SINGLE 1996:: MIRACLE

Tim Kellett, a one-time member of both Durutti Column and Simply Red, joined forces with Robin Taylor-Firth of electronic act Nightmares On Wax, and along with vocalist Ruth-Ann Boyle, they formed Olive. The sound of 'You're Not Alone' is dominated by skittering percussion and a devastating keyboard riff. Sung with great conviction by Boyle, the track is a winning combination of dance beats and pop smarts. This high-quality record was just a minor hit before a deluge of re-mixes and different versions propelled it to number one on the chart, bestowing thereafter iconic status amongst clubbers of the era.

46
THE MAN WHO LOVED BEER
LAMBCHOP
CITY SLANG
OTHER SINGLE 1996:: HANK

From Nashville, Lambchop function as a large and fluid collection of musicians who, with writer/singer/ leader Kurt Wagner at the centre, play a constantly evolving strand of alt-country music. 'The Man Who Loved Beer', taken from the group's album *How I Quit Smoking*, was lyrically an adaptation of the poem 'The Man Who Was Tired of Life'. Steel guitars and strings provide a sombre backing, along with the rhythm of a single hand-drum, as Wagner voices the graceful lamentation with a fatalistic air of resignation that is precisely what the song requires.

45
THE ACCIDENTALS
BROADCAST
WURLITZER JUKEBOX
OTHER SINGLES 1996:: THE BOOK LOVERS; LIVING ROOM

Broadcast hailed from Birmingham, though on the evidence of their other-worldly music, I was surprised that they hadn't simply fetched-up as visitors from some parallel universe. 'The Accidentals' was their first release, and it has a spectral, haunting quality that feels almost sacred. It is built-up from a sample taken from Joseph Losey's 1967 film *The Accident*, which had a screenplay written by Harold Pinter; this would be the first piece of an enticing paper-trail left by the group, that pointed towards a catalogue of esoteric delights. 'The Accidentals' is also a masterclass of minimalism with its economic but enthralling sound, and the sparse eight lines of lyric from which Trish Keenan – without any hint of over-dramatisation – extracts maximum impact.

44
SUMMER CANNIBALS
PATTI SMITH
ARISTA

Patti Smith had taken an eight-year sabbatical from music whilst she raised her children, but during this period she had endured the deaths of her husband Fred 'Sonic' Smith, brother Todd Smith, her close friend Robert Mapplethorpe and Richard Sohl, the keyboard player from The Patti Smith Group. On the plus side, by this point in her career, she had the status of living legend… but such a stature can easily prove to be a poisoned chalice that consigns the recipient to the category of museum piece. Naturally, her return was much heralded and highly anticipated, and thankfully Patti was not diminished by the weight of expectation; she remained fully vital and did not disappoint in any way. Her album *Gone Again* was a triumph;

in many respects it was clearly an homage to the ghosts who now inhabited her thoughts and dreams. 'Summer Cannibals' was lifted from the album; it is a re-working of an unreleased 1970s song written by Fred 'Sonic' Smith. Here it is given a taut, lean treatment; it rocks in a most idiosyncratic fashion. Unsurprisingly, the piece is poetic and the imagery of the chorus is vivid and visceral – but what really makes this track special is Smith's extraordinary and unique voice, which is brimful of passion, dignity and defiance... during her hiatus it had become even more impressive than previously, and this was a very, very welcome return.

43
WOMAN
NENEH CHERRY
HUT
OTHER SINGLE 1996::
KOOTCHI

'Woman' sees Neneh Cherry revisit James Brown's 1960s soul hit, 'It's a Man's, Man's, Man's World', and re-write it from a female perspective. She turns the song into an ode to feminine toughness and endurance, as well as a tribute to the love brought into the world through motherhood. Cherry infuses the song with her own soul-power, such that it never for a second feels like a parody of James Brown; it is something quite different... the other side of the coin. This great record is shot-through with the independent spirit of its singer and lyricist, and she performs the song with palpable pride in not only her own strength, but that of other women too.

42
LITTLE TROUBLE GIRL
SONIC YOUTH
DGC

Here we have Kim Gordon harmonising perfectly with Kim Deal of The Breeders/Pixies; the sound has strong echoes of that gifted to The Shangri-Las by iconic producer Shadow Morton. It is the ideal accompaniment for this tale of a girl brought up to be a "good girl" – a kind of flawless American princess who will love "nice things" and be happy and compliant. The problem is that this 'Little Trouble Girl' has a mind of her own; she meets a boy and becomes pregnant, shattering her parents' illusions in the process. The song is carried off with great aplomb; it incorporates a delicious degree of subtlety that makes it something of an anomaly in Sonic Youth's largely high-powered back-catalogue... something of an overlooked gem too.

41
PEARL'S GIRL
UNDERWORLD
JUNIOR BOY'S OWN
OTHER SINGLES 1996:: ROW-LA; BORN SLIPPY NUXX

Titled after the name of a racetrack greyhound, 'Pearl's Girl' was, most appropriately, a slice of quick-paced techno. This time the mesmerising beats and rhythms contained a stream-of-consciousness lyric from Karl Hyde which concerns a night spent clubbing on Hamburg's Reeperbahn, and later, in a heightened state of consciousness, sitting on the docks watching the boats on the river illuminated by bonfires, with the sound of Al Green still playing inside the mind.

40
ATLIENS
OUTKAST
ARISTA
OTHER SINGLES 1996::
ELEVATORS (ME & YOU);
JAZZY BELLE

'ATLiens' was the title track of the second Outkast album; at this point, Big Boi and Andre 3000 were both just twenty-years old, but their music had taken a giant leap in quality and maturity, reflecting the rapid growing-up the pair had gone through since their emergence two-years before. Here the rhymes are deadly serious, but they are laced with humour and delivered not with a scowl but with a smile. Southern pride is their chosen topic as they strike back at the taste-makers from both the east and west coasts who had failed to show much in the way of respect for these Outkasts. The group's sense of disconnection from the centre of the hip-hop community is eloquently displayed, as is their desire to celebrate their roots in Atlanta, Georgia. Here, flesh and blood musicians were used for recording, and there were pointedly no samples; Outkast were steering their sound away from orthodoxy and towards something uniquely creative.

39
DON'T BE MEAN
THE RAINCOATS
ROUGH TRADE

Kurt Cobain's enthusiasm for the music of The Raincoats brought about a new interest in the group; in 1994, after a ten-year hiatus, they re-convened, played a show and recorded a John Peel radio session. Then, in 1996, a full re-union saw them record and release the album *Looking in the Shadows* and the single 'Don't Be Mean'. It was wonderful to have them back, and most gratifying to hear that the sound was as playfully naive as ever – the juxtaposition between the sweet and the abrasive remained solidly in place. Here, on 'Don't Be Mean', Gina Birch regales us with a paranoid parable of love, and then… the thrilling sound of new recruit Ann Wood's violin cuts into the song; I swear that on first hearing, the hairs on the back of my neck stood upright and goosebumps appeared on my flesh.

38
SECRET HEART
RON SEXSMITH
INTERSCOPE

Ron Sexsmith is a master craftsman of song, whose melodic flair rivals that of Paul McCartney. Perhaps his most well-known song is 'Secret Heart', and his understated performance here is superb. He sings each line with empathy and understanding, and we can well believe that he has intimate knowledge of the vagaries of unrequited love. 'Secret Heart' is the kind of song that Roy Orbison would have been proud to sing in his imperious pomp, and it would not have sounded remotely out of place amongst his classic 1960s singles.

37
FLOWERS IN DECEMBER
MAZZY STAR
CAPITOL
OTHER SINGLE 1996:: I'VE BEEN LET DOWN

Round about this time, a subtle change occurred in Mazzy Star's sound; the heavy reverb on the guitar disappeared. Fortunately, all of the beauty still remained, and here we have gorgeous melodies picked out on acoustic guitar by David Roback, a sliver of violin adding delicate shades and a single drum beat providing all the necessary rhythm. Harmonica is also utilised to great effect, bookending the song, and, as always, Hope Sandoval sings exquisitely, unburdening herself of the woe created by the lack of understanding in a relationship which ends up causing its inevitable destruction.

36
THE MAN DON'T GIVE A FUCK
SUPER FURRY ANIMALS
CREATION
OTHER SINGLES 1996:: SOMETHING 4 THE WEEKEND; IF YOU DON'T WANT ME TO DESTROY YOU; GOD SHOW ME MAGIC; HOMETOWN UNICORN

Sampling the line "They don't give a fuck about anybody else" from Steely Dan's classic track 'Showbiz Kids', repeating it more than fifty times, and then releasing the track as a single, may have seemed something of a perverse move… but the fact that Super Furry Animals chose to do just that struck a mighty blow against ridiculously outmoded censorship issues. The song itself is a non-specific protest anthem aimed at anybody who wields authority to the detriment of others. It employs the quiet then loud formula wonderfully well, going from softly sung verses to absolutely explosive choruses, with the added bonus of a wild and seemingly endless outro.

35
STANDING OUTSIDE A BROKEN PHONE BOOTH WITH MONEY IN MY HAND
PRIMITIVE RADIO GODS
COLUMBIA
OTHER SINGLE 1996: MOTHERFUCKER

A slow, squirming bass line and metronomic hip-hop beats mostly carry this song (apart from a slightly discordant piano break and a coda of funeral bells and crashing waves) while the contrasting blues and hip-hop styles are fused together wonderfully well to create something pretty unique. The chorus consists of a sample taken from 'How Blue Can You Get?' – a 1964 track by BB King, who sings "I've been downhearted baby, ever since the day we met" – and the verses flesh out the feelings of disconnection between a couple who only ever make each other unhappy. This was Primitive Radio Gods debut release and it earned them great success in the USA; disappointingly, it was not something they could ever come close to replicating.

34
E-BOW THE LETTER
R.E.M.
WARNER BROTHERS
OTHER SINGLE 1996:
BITTERSWEET ME

At this point, R.E.M. were the biggest selling band on planet Earth; however, they greatly valued their own integrity and autonomy, and they had the confidence to trust their own instincts. This explains why the lead single from their much anticipated album *New Adventures in Hi-Fi*, was the dirge-like, spoken word folk of 'E-Bow the Letter', featuring returning heroine Patti Smith on backing vocals. To casual fans and radio programmers, this must have seemed plain weird and unlikable, but to those who had followed the band from its early years – or those who liked their rock stars to take risks and challenge perceptions – it was utterly compelling, atmospheric and eerily moving.

33
STREET SPIRIT (FADE OUT)
RADIOHEAD
PARLOPHONE
OTHER SINGLE 1996:
THE BENDS

Radiohead stood in direct opposition to the hedonism and laddishness of the Britpop bands, and 'Street Spirit' conveys a deep unease about materialism and acquisitional excess. They were not providing Tony Blair with credibility enhancing photo opportunities, nor were they cavorting like prize-winning bumpkins across the glossy pages of *Loaded* magazine. Their music was thoughtful, thought-provoking and built to last. Here, the featured guitar arpeggio played by Ed O'Brien, and the torment conveyed in Thom Yorke's voice, paint a bleak picture of an impending collapse.

32
BROKE
MODEST MOUSE
SUB POP
OTHER SINGLES 1996:
A LIFE OF ARCTIC SOUNDS
INTERSTATE 8

Broken promises, broken hearts and broken relationships are the cheery subject of this song. Washington band Modest Mouse play a fractured kind of slacker rock; it is concise and full of self-recrimination – which turns into anger – as the song rattles along like a vintage car, before finally grinding to a halt.

31
WOKE UP STICKY
PETER PERRETT IN THE ONE
DEMON

In 1994, Peter Perrett ended a fourteen-year sabbatical by releasing an EP called *Cultured Palate* with a new band called The One. Emboldened by its reception, he now added his name as a prefix to the band name, and then released 'Woke Up Sticky'. Although heavily cloaked in ambiguity – so it could potentially be read as a sex song – this is almost certainly a paean to hard drug usage, a device that he had previously employed when writing near-hit 'Another Girl Another Planet' as leader of The Only Ones. Another carry-over from the past is Perrett's use of almost poetic verse remaining as a constant; this new song was fascinating and chock-full of wonderful prose. The band too are certainly no musical slouches, and the playing of Jay Price on guitar is comparable with that of John Perry in The Only Ones. It was great to have Peter Perrett back and making music once again, but predictably, his unfortunate habits and unreliability meant that this soon proved to be a false dawn.

30
STEM
DJ SHADOW
MO WAX
OTHER SINGLE 1996:
MIDNIGHT IN A PERFECT
WORLD

Drums that sound like ricocheting machine gun fire are combined here with sumptuous strings, creating a gripping and pulse-quickening tension with the use of these contrasting elements. DJ Shadow is a master of sound manipulation and 'Stem' perfectly displays his musicality and skill in taking seemingly disparate musical elements and forging them into remarkable new shapes and forms.

29
HYPERBALLAD
BJÖRK
ONE LITTLE INDIAN
OTHER SINGLE 1996:
POSSIBLY MAYBE

On 'Hyperballad', Björk collaborates with producer Nellee Hooper; they use a shuffling rhythm and electronic squalls that eventually give way to a full-on house beat. As a pure instrumental, this would still be a fascinating musical piece, but with the addition of Björk's lyric, it becomes incredible. She sings a story which describes her waking and standing upon a cliff top; she hurls whatever possessions are at hand over the edge and into the abyss, and she also imagines throwing herself over to certain death, musing on what sound her body might make as it impacts with the rocks below. These destructive ideas somehow seem to exorcise her darkest thoughts, and now, purged of them, she returns to her sleeping lover feeling happier and renewed.

28
LIFE IN MONO
MONO
ECHO

Mono were a duo consisting of singer Siobhan de Maré and musician Martin Virgo, and 'Life in Mono' was their debut single. This is a very classy torch-song, sung with great tenderness and fragility. The trip-hop beats make it dance friendly, and the harpsichord accompaniment (sampled from John Barry's soundtrack to *The Ipcress File*) lends the song an exotic retro-sheen.

27
DON'T LET GO
EN VOGUE
EASTWEST

Songwriter credits and production duties were shared around by a whole host of people in the making of this magisterial and bluesy R&B offering from female foursome En Vogue; the old adage of too many cooks spoiling the broth just did not apply. 'Don't Let Go' is a strong and perfectly arranged song that is sung with such a degree of sassy attitude that it turned out to be hard-edged and distinctive enough to stand-out from the sea of mediocrity that this genre of music had generally become.

26
SINGLE-BILINGUAL
PET SHOP BOYS
PARLOPHONE
OTHER SINGLES 1996:
BEFORE
SE A VIDA É
(THAT'S THE WAY LIFE IS)

The life of a travelling executive is the subject of this thumping, big-beat Pet Shop Boys track; aeroplane travel, hotels, restaurant food, discotheques and sex are all part of the lyrical tapestry as Neil Tennant delivers a first-person narrative with all of his usual sophisticated panache. The clipped delivery is almost mechanical as he lives out a routine that has become second nature… a repetitive and joyless programme that is enabled by a generous, unchecked expense account.

25
INDO SILVER CLUB PARTS 1&2
DAFT PUNK
SOMA

Following the success of their previous single 'Da Funk', and perhaps fearful of being over-hyped, Daft Punk concealed themselves by releasing 'Indo Silver Club' as a twelve-inch single with the artist being uncredited. It features two separate treatments of the same instrumental track; part one is hard, Detroit-style techno, whilst part two is a Chicago house-styled piece. Both of these are fantastic dance tracks, and while the origins and influences are obvious, they are given the Daft Punk treatment, and it is that unmistakable stamp which ultimately defines them.

24
TAKE ME BABY
JIMI TENOR
T&B VINYL
OTHER SINGLES 1996:
CAN'T STAY WITH YOU BABY
OUTTA SPACE

Finnish whiz kid Jimi Tenor first gained significant attention with this track, released by T&B (a label formed by DJs Twitch & Brainstorm, who were resident at Edinburgh techno club *Pure*). It is a groovy, house-style track with retro / modern 1960s flourishes; a brass section and Hammond organ solo are both incorporated. Tenor sings in a monotone voice above the artful, repetitive electronic rhythm; this is quirky and attention-grabbing funky fun… and it is also very catchy.

23
NAKED EYE
LUSCIOUS JACKSON
GRAND ROYAL

'Luscious Jackson', a female rap-rock trio, were the first act recruited by The Beastie Boys for their new record label, and 'Naked Eye', a stand-out song, was a deserved hit. It is based around a seductively hooky sung chorus, while the verses – dealing with wide-open, naked emotion – are rapped. This is a slinky sounding record, and the girls are sassy, smooth and totally in control.

22
FREED FROM DESIRE
GALA
BIG LIFE

'Freed from Desire' is a classic of Euro-dance; the opening synth riff is a stroke of sheer genius… once heard, it lives inside the head forever. The piano riffs sparkle and the lyrics are positive – and even if you miss them, there is an inescapable "Na, na, na, na, na" section. Oh, and if the above is not enough, it is also sung with fire and strength; in short, it is totally uplifting. The author and singer is Gala Rizzatto, a Brooklyn-based Italian who was inspired by her boyfriend (to whom the song was dedicated); he was a member of the National Ballet of Senegal, and Gala noted the ability of the Senegalese community to remain happy and positive, even whilst living in squalor, whereas much more affluent people, living in chic neighbourhoods, seemed only to embrace misery.

21
RUSTY CAGE
JOHNNY CASH
AMERICAN RECORDINGS

Unchained was the second album that Johnny Cash made with Rick Rubin at the controls, and these recordings revitalised the artist and made him relevant to a younger audience. Part of the appeal was listening to Cash take songs that were well-known to this new audience, and then completely reshaping them with his own inimitable style. The single chosen from *Unchained* was 'Rusty

Cage', written by Chris Cornell. It had been a huge hit for Cornell's band Soundgarden, who played a grunge / metal hybrid. But Cash imbues the song with all his worldly wisdom; it is performed in a brisk, country style that leads to a dramatic and hard-hitting breakdown. Cash infuses the song with his own personality, and hence it is gritty and tough, but also soulful and sensitive; his version was southern gothic storytelling in song.

20
HENRY LEE
NICK CAVE AND THE BAD SEEDS AND PJ HARVEY
MUTE

'Henry Lee' was another single lifted from Cave's *Murder Ballads* album; it is a variant of a 19th-century Scottish folk song called 'Young Hunting', and it had been covered by hundreds of artists (including Bob Dylan) before the Bad Seeds got around to delivering this chilling interpretation. PJ Harvey is cast as the vengeful woman scorned; she trades lines with Cave as the grisly tale unfolds, and she proves to be the perfect foil. Her voice, lighter than his, encircles and winds around Cave's gravelled tones, and they both play their respective roles fantastically well. This mutual understanding of the macabre nature of the material makes this such a compelling listen.

19
LUCKY
LEWIS TAYLOR
ISLAND
OTHER SINGLE 1996:
WHOEVER

Lewis Taylor grew up with an equal love of soul music and the progressive end of rock music. He toured as a guitarist in The Edgar Broughton Band, and following that he adopted the pseudonym Sheriff Jack, releasing albums of the psychedelic variety in 1986 and 1987. A decade later, he had finally managed to meld his twin loves, and emerged with a self-titled album and the single 'Lucky'. Guitar-based, but with a distinctly soulful sound, Taylor sings in a voice that is reminiscent of Marvin Gaye; in addition, there is a touch of Brian Wilson in the arrangement, and something comparable to Jeff Buckley in the evident sense of release that his music brings about. 'Lucky' begins a bit like Joe Meek's 'Telstar', before morphing into something altogether more funky; it swells, throbs, echoes and grooves. Taylor sings of a twisted, unrequited love, and he is sufficiently confident to deliver a highly nuanced performance in which the quality of his singing is exceptional. Piano and layered voices rise, bringing to mind Marvin Gaye's 'Let's Get it On', while a restrained, but still scorching guitar break erupts, which could easily be mistaken for one of Prince's finest efforts. I realise I have used many admiring comparisons in this review, but not a single one of them is trite; Lewis Taylor had an incandescent talent, and 'Lucky' is a brilliant record… no more and no less.

18
FLUORESCENCES
STEREOLAB
DUOPHONIC
OTHER SINGLE 1996:
CYBELE'S REVERIE

Stereolab employ the interesting device of stacking the two highly distinctive voices of Laetitia Sadier and Mary Hansen on top of each other; they do not harmonise at all. Instead, they create a kind of push-and-pull effect that draws attention to what they are actually singing about – and here we have a lyric concerned with the sensory perception of external stimuli. Musically, the sound is dense; there are backing vocals, flutes, vibraphones and much, much more, creating a giddy, dizzying kind of upbeat lounge music.

17
DESIGN FOR LIFE
MANIC STREET PREACHERS
SONY
OTHER SINGLES 1996:
KEVIN CARTER
EVERYTHING MUST GO
AUSTRALIA

'Design For Life' was the first song written by The Manics following the disappearance of band figurehead, Richey Edwards; Nicky Wire described it as "A bolt of light from a severely dark place", and it propelled the band into the national consciousness and beyond the preserve of NME readers. The song is stirring and thought-provoking, with lyrics describing the way in which advertising slogans are used to dumb-down the proletariat and keep them compliant to the whims of the ruling classes. It is a call-to-arms of a kind where books are the weapons, and education is the tool of enlightenment and freedom. Mike Hedges was selected as producer on the strength of his string-laden work on McAlmont & Butler's hit record 'Yes'; this turned out to be an inspired choice because 'Design for Life' sounds sumptuously grand, without ever being bellicose – it seems to float as light as a feather before building towards the anthemic chorus and then remaining at full-power and maximum intensity to the very end of this magnificent track.

16
READY OR NOT
FUGEES
RUFFHOUSE
OTHER SINGLES 1996:
NO WOMAN NO CRY
KILLING ME SOFTLY

To my ears, 'Ready or Not' is the finest track in The Fugees oeuvre; it has a completely spooky and out-there backing track, featuring breaking waves and whirring helicopter blades. A simple, single snare drum provides the rhythm, and the rest is just a magical melding of voices. Lauryn Hill provides sweet soulfulness with a sung introduction, and then a slick change sees unhurried raps from Pras, Wyclef Jean and Hill which add perceptive depth to the piece. The song originated from a similarly titled soul hit for The Delfonics, but only the chorus survives since The Fugees multi-faceted approach means the re-booted song now contains elements of pop, soul, reggae and hip-hop, with avant-garde sonics thrown in for good measure.

15
LIGHT AIRCRAFT ON FIRE
THE AUTEURS
HUT
OTHER SINGLE 1996:
KIDS ISSUE

One never quite knows what Luke Haines is raging about, and 'Light Aircraft on Fire' is, lyrically, seriously on the obscure side. Fortunately, I long ago concluded that this really does not matter at all. It is sufficient that he does rage, that he does vent his fury, unleashes his bile and issues forth his invective, because it is thrilling, and his bitterness acts as a much needed counterweight to the scales that are loaded-up with crates of records advocating mindless hedonism, made by talentless half-wits dressed and moulded to look like whatever pop stars are supposed to look like. Haines voice is a flame-thrower, a sort of musical scorched-earth policy, and so 'Light Aircraft on Fire' *may* be a metaphor for a dying relationship… or it *might* be a comment on the desperation of a record industry that can see the writing on the wall… or it could even be about a light aircraft – I don't know and I don't care… but I do know that it sends chills up and down my spine.

14
FAILURE
SWANS
ARTS & COMMERCE
OTHER SINGLE 1996:
DIE TUR IST ZU

'Failure' is a snail-paced account of the huge disappointment felt by the songs narrator; the weight of accumulated failure has become an unbearable burden. Michael Gira voices the track in a baritone that drips with resentment felt towards the "many bastards (who) succeed". Obviously, nobody wishes to feel the way he feels, but to some degree or another, many of us can empathise with the narrator's bitterness and his desire to give an uncaring world the proverbial middle finger. Church-like atmospherics accompany Gira's unholy sermon; it is a nice touch because, in many ways, the song can be read as an anti-religious funeral of man's hopes and dreams.

13
BEWILDERED
BIM SHERMAN
MANTRA
OTHER SINGLE 1996:
SOLID AS A ROCK

The honey-voiced reggae veteran Bim Sherman had been associated with Adrian Sherwood's On-U Sound label for a number of years – featuring on the collaborative series of *Singers & Players* LPs – but in 1996, his own album *Miracle* was released, with Sherwood in the producer's chair. Restraint was very much the order of the day; rather than the expected wild dub experimentation, a magical, mellow and deeply spiritual album was created that defied all genre classifications, as it melded together dub, reggae, electronica and eastern rhythms (courtesy of tabla master Talvin Singh). Practically every track from the album could easily have been a great single, but 'Bewildered' was duly chosen, and the fact that it was recycled from the singer's back catalogue mattered not one jot. This re-interpretation is magnificent; over mesmerising eastern strings and tastefully minimal guitar (played by Skip McDonald) a gentle rhythm is tapped out on tabla, soothing and exotic. The voice of the maestro is then added, as Sherman summons from deep within his soul a vocal performance that is jaw-droppingly beautiful and absolutely awe-inspiring.

12
KNOW YOUR CHICKEN
CIBO MATTO
BLANCO Y NEGRO
OTHER SINGLES 1996:
SUGAR WATER; SUPER RELAX

Cibo Matto incorporated hip-hop beats and muted jazz horns as musical accompaniment for 'Know Your Chicken', an offbeat tale concerning the purchase of a pair of chickens from a Brooklyn street vendor, one coloured blue and the other magenta. The blue one runs away, but the magenta one sticks around as a pet until the arrival of a lover who cooks it and serves it for dinner. Time passes and twins are born to the couple… one coloured blue and the other magenta. This bizarre and slightly macabre fable is sweetly sung with much enthusiasm; it is a record that could be easily dismissed as silly and juvenile, but somehow or other, such a judgment is transcended by the vibrancy of performance and the catchy hooks that abundantly litter the song.

11
PRINCE OF THE RODEO
TURBONEGRO
HIT ME
OTHER SINGLES 1996:
PROMOSEXUAL
SUFFRAGETTE CITY

Turbonegro, the sleazy, scandalous and Scandinavian gonzo leather boys, returned with new lead guitarist Euroboy firing off high-power glam riffs and blistering solos across an electrical storm of an album called *Apocalypse Dudes*. But preceding this was the 'Prince of the Rodeo' single, which, amazingly, was even more energised and over-the-top than the album; it was like Alice Cooper on steroids and The Ramones on speed. The track is a relentless barrage of thunderous drums and bass, dizzying guitar and a screamed lyric that aims to offend any puritan who might have the good fortune to encounter it, depicting, as it does, macho cowboy rodeo riders who are undermined with smutty, homoerotic innuendo. The whole experience is a hedonistic, decadent, thrill-seeker of a record; it is in-your-face, unapologetic, infectious and catchy as hell.

10

HALLO SPACEBOY

DAVID BOWIE

FEATURING PET SHOP BOYS

BMG

OTHER SINGLE 1996: TELLING LIES

In its original form, 'Hallo Spaceboy' had appeared on David Bowie's album *Outside*. Written by Bowie and Brian Eno, it was a fine track – very hard and heavy, with a strong Nine Inch Nails vibe… Bowie himself compared it to "Jim Morrison meets industrial". Also noteworthy was the lyrical influence of sound poet Brion Gysin; his reported final words, "Moondust will cover me", were altered to become "Moondust is killing me" – this phrase supplied one of the song's main hooks. However, for the single version, Pet Shop Boys were recruited as re-mixers, and they radically reconstructed the track; it became much lighter, and backing vocals were added as the sound veered towards a hi-NRG disco feel. There was also an additional verse (sung by Neil Tennant) which was constructed from snippets of Bowie's evergreen 'Space Oddity' – this returned the Major Tom character back into Bowie's work for a third and final outing.

9

IT FELL OFF THE BACK OF A LORRY

DENIM

ECHO

Denim was the chosen pseudonym of ex-Felt frontman and leader, Lawrence Hayward – or, as he preferred it, simply Lawrence. 'It Fell Off the Back of a Lorry' was a genuine pop classic that if recorded by Blur, or perhaps Supergrass, would have been a nailed-on number one hit record… but in the hands of Denim, it very unfortunately sank pretty much without trace. The track is a bounce along concoction of whirring synth, glam guitar, pub-style sing-along piano and a thumping drum beat. Lawrence sings what is essentially a two-line lyric in the role of a chancer who is caught bang-to-rights in possession of stolen goods; he pleads his innocence to the arresting officer, while female backing vocalists and even small children add their voices to his cause. This record really is very, very good… but in commercial terms, it was all to no avail.

8

CHRISTIANSANDS

TRICKY

ISLAND

OTHER SINGLES 1996:

TRICKY KID; MAKES ME WANNA DIE;

SMOKING BEAGLES (COLLABORATION WITH SUB SUB)

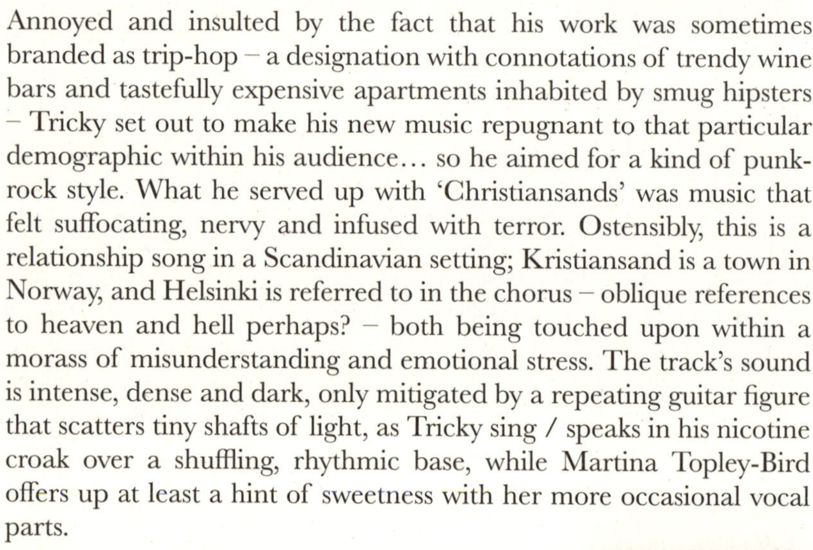

Annoyed and insulted by the fact that his work was sometimes branded as trip-hop – a designation with connotations of trendy wine bars and tastefully expensive apartments inhabited by smug hipsters – Tricky set out to make his new music repugnant to that particular demographic within his audience… so he aimed for a kind of punk-rock style. What he served up with 'Christiansands' was music that felt suffocating, nervy and infused with terror. Ostensibly, this is a relationship song in a Scandinavian setting; Kristiansand is a town in Norway, and Helsinki is referred to in the chorus – oblique references to heaven and hell perhaps? – both being touched upon within a morass of misunderstanding and emotional stress. The track's sound is intense, dense and dark, only mitigated by a repeating guitar figure that scatters tiny shafts of light, as Tricky sing / speaks in his nicotine croak over a shuffling, rhythmic base, while Martina Topley-Bird offers up at least a hint of sweetness with her more occasional vocal parts.

7

DEVIL'S HAIRCUT

BECK

DGC

OTHER SINGLE 1996:

WHERE IT'S AT

Beck teamed up with production team The Dust Brothers, most famous for their work in revolutionising the sound of The Beastie Boys. Their hip-hop focussed style gave Beck a whole new spectrum of colour to work with, of which he made full and successful use throughout *Odelay*, the resultant album – and 'Devil's Haircut' was one of the standout tracks. It is an irresistible mix of breakbeats, pop and Beck's abstract but poetic punk-rock lyrics. The main riff, played on guitar by Beck, was appropriated from 'I Can Only Give You Everything', a 1960s rock staple popularised by Them, MC5, and The Troggs. Drumbeats were sampled from Pretty Purdie's 'Soul Drums' for the chorus, and Them's version of James Brown's 'Out of Sight' on the verses. A grooving bass line and some typically eccentric flourishes from The Dust Brothers completed the track, and the result was a record which will live long in the memory.

6

FIRESTARTER

THE PRODIGY

XL

OTHER SINGLE 1996: BREATHE

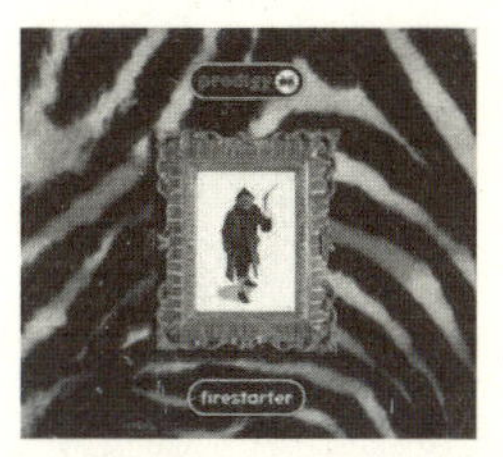

This is heavy, heavy, and thrice heavy techno, that snarls and bares its teeth; an enormous big-beat raver with a monstrous synth riff, and Keith Flint's unhinged and incendiary vocal. Upon release, this record grabbed us by the throat, shivered our timbers and left us as gibbering wrecks; it had "hit" written all over it, and accordingly it shot to number one on the hit-parade, putting the wind up the repressive guardians who seek to control our quotidian existence. Only 'God Save the Queen' by The Sex Pistols and 'All Shook Up' by Elvis Presley had ever previously been perceived as being this threatening to the natural order and morality of society. Despite this, even little children in the street found the song irresistible; they adopted curious poses, twisted their bodies, contorted their features and yelled "I'm a fire-starter, a twisted fire-starter, hey hey hey!". What a fabulous, insurrectionary and unforgettable piece of work.

5

THE ROCKING CHAIR

ANDREA PARKER

MO WAX

OTHER SINGLE 1996:

MELODIOUS THUNK

Andrea Parker's background as a trained cellist is fairly evident when listening to 'The Rocking Chair', which is a melodramatic melding of electronics, percussion that resonates like a heartbeat, a blank, unemotional voice and a grandiose string arrangement. The lyric offers no clue as to what is affecting the narrator, but a sense of imminent danger is conveyed, and as the strings swoop and the tension rises, we could be in the midst of some operatic re-telling of Hitchcock's *Psycho*. Andrea Parker's reputation had been built on her ability to produce dance tracks that doubled-up as head music; here, on the resolutely downtempo 'The Rocking Chair', the dance elements are forsaken for a nightmarish voyage into the imagination, via deep and dark musical exploration.

4

PEPPER

BUTTHOLE SURFERS

CAPITOL

OTHER SINGLE 1996:

JINGLE OF A DOG COLLAR

'Pepper' gave The Butthole Surfers a hit of sorts; a complete fluke for sure, but still, it got significant daytime radio play, and in a perverse act – perhaps aimed at pissing-off the purists who were ready to shout that the band had sold out – they appeared on *The David Letterman Show*… resulting in their core audience deserting the group. So, it could be said that 'Pepper' was the song that killed The Buttholes, but to these ears, it just sounds fantastic. Guitarist Paul Leary had conjured-up the riff during sessions for the album *Electriclarryland*, and the band added a programmed hip-hop style beat, parts played backwards, hints of sitar and spoken verses with sung choruses. This led to speculation that the band were either ripping-off or lampooning Beck, whose 1994 hit 'Loser' had employed the same basic structure. The Buttholes denied this, and stated that their real influence was interest in the music of Tricky, Massive Attack and Soul II Soul. As for the selling-out charge, the lyrical content of 'Pepper' was hardly likely to have been written as a cynical ploy to garner a hit; penned by Gibby Haynes, it is a recollection of ten real people he had known as a youth in Texas – including a "Football player rapist" and a racist named Bobby – all of them heading, in one way or another, to unsurprising death and destruction.

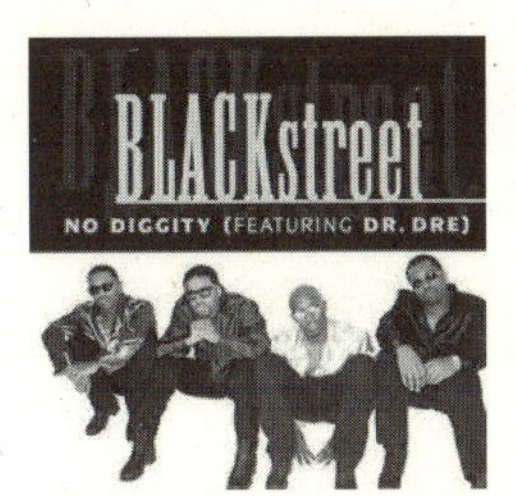

3
NO DIGGITY
BLACKSTREET
FEATURING DR. DRE
INTERSCOPE

Teddy Riley (the founding father of the New Jack Swing genre, in which hip-hop and R&B are fused together with gospel-influenced vocals) had a song, and Dr. Dre had a beat that he had originally offered to Tupac, before Dre ceased his relationship with both the rapper and the Death Row record label in highly acrimonious fashion. So, Riley and Dre combined resources to come up with 'No Diggity', but only after having extracted a key sample from 'Grandma's Hands' – a Bill Withers song – the repeated use of which gave the track a musical hook that was pure dynamite. But there were problems as far as recording was concerned… Riley had a group called Guy who flatly refused to do the track; his second group, Blackstreet, had major reservations too. The difficulty was that a song about men's blatant sexual desire for women (dubbed "playettes") who may or may not oblige them depending upon the man's affluence, did seem to teeter very much on the edge of poor taste – the inference in the lyric that the women portrayed were equally strong, high-spirited and complicit in the mating game, could easily be lost. In the end, it fell to Riley to sing the opening lines himself, so that if the track received flack, he would be directly in the firing line. After Riley, Dre followed, and then the rest of the group lent their soulful voices to this irresistible track, before female rapper Queen Pen spat out a fierce rap, in which she flaunts her expensive tastes, possessions and self-confidence, in a fine and brazenly independent style.

2

NOVOCAINE FOR THE SOUL

EELS

DREAMWORKS

OTHER SINGLES 1996: SUSAN'S HOUSE

RAGS TO RAGS;

YOUR LUCKY DAY IN HELL

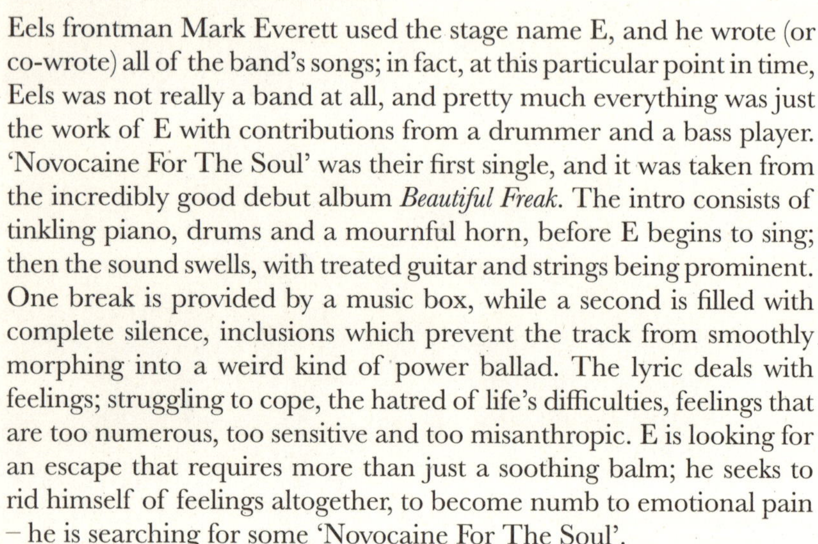

Eels frontman Mark Everett used the stage name E, and he wrote (or co-wrote) all of the band's songs; in fact, at this particular point in time, Eels was not really a band at all, and pretty much everything was just the work of E with contributions from a drummer and a bass player. 'Novocaine For The Soul' was their first single, and it was taken from the incredibly good debut album *Beautiful Freak*. The intro consists of tinkling piano, drums and a mournful horn, before E begins to sing; then the sound swells, with treated guitar and strings being prominent. One break is provided by a music box, while a second is filled with complete silence, inclusions which prevent the track from smoothly morphing into a weird kind of power ballad. The lyric deals with feelings; struggling to cope, the hatred of life's difficulties, feelings that are too numerous, too sensitive and too misanthropic. E is looking for an escape that requires more than just a soothing balm; he seeks to rid himself of feelings altogether, to become numb to emotional pain – he is searching for some 'Novocaine For The Soul'.

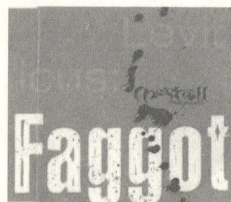

1

LEVITICUS: FAGGOT

MESHELL NDEGÉOCELLO

MAVERICK

OTHER SINGLES 1996:

WHO IS HE AND WHAT IS HE TO YOU?

NEVER MISS THE WATER

Meshell Ndegéocello fused funk, soul, jazz, rock, reggae and poetry into a deep, slowly grooving masterwork that occupies a category all of its own. 'Leviticus: Faggot' has a freaky / funky sound, reminiscent of psychedelic-era Temptations tracks, as produced by Norman Whitfield, and the subject matter concerns a boy in a deeply religious family, who initially is perceived to be soft. His father attempts, but fails, to toughen him up, and it soon becomes obvious that he is gay. In the eyes of his parents, the boy is sin incarnate, and when their prayers to change him inevitably fail, they throw him out onto the streets on his sixteenth birthday. Ndegéocello handles the delicate topic perfectly; that is to say, she tackles it head-on and unapologetically. Her use of the word "faggot" is clearly designed to make ears prick-up and listen… and then, hopefully, to make those with bigoted attitudes question themselves and examine their own prejudices. Managing to align this challenging material – with its message advocating tolerance and acceptance – to a track that works fantastically well beneath the mirror-ball on the dance-floor, was, quite simply, a stroke of musical genius.

My steady job didn't last that long but I loved it

1997

EVENTS

Yasser Arafat returns to Hebron, after an absence of thirty years, following the Israeli handover of the last controlled West Bank city.

Comet Hale-Bopp makes its closest approach to Earth.

The DVD format is launched during the Academy Awards in Los Angeles.

Heaven's Gate cultists commit mass suicide in their compound in San Diego.

The first space burial takes place as a Pegasus Rocket carries the remains of twenty-four people into orbit.

Tony Blair, the leader of the (New) Labour Party, becomes Prime Minister of the UK ending 18 years of Tory rule.

The Confederation Bridge opens in Canada; it is the world's longest bridge.

The UK hands sovereignty of Hong Kong to The People's Republic of China.

The Pathfinder space probe lands on the surface of Mars.

The remains of Che Guevara, executed in Bolivia in 1967, are returned to Cuba for burial.

Fashion designer Gianni Versace is assassinated in Miami Beach.

The F.W. Woolworth Company, a staple of the British high street, closes after one hundred and seventeen years of trading.

Diana Spencer, the Princess of Wales, and her lover Dodi Fayed, are killed, along with driver Henri Paul, in a car crash in Paris.

Scotland votes in favour of devolution; the Scottish Parliament is formed two years later.

Wales votes in favour of devolution and the National Assembly for Wales is formed.

Al-Qaeda carries out a terrorist attack in Mostar, Bosnia and Herzegovina.

In Japan, nearly seven hundred children suffer epileptic attacks during the screening of a Pokemon episode.

Days after winning the league title for the fourth time in five seasons, Eric Cantona unexpectedly announces his retirement from football. Chelsea win the FA Cup, Manchester City are relegated to the third tier of English football.

BIRTHS

Bobby Cheng; Maisie Williams; Donny van de Beek; Lautaro Martínez; Max Verstappen; Marcus Rashford.

DEATHS

Townes Van Zandt; Colonel Tom Parker; Brian Connolly; Tony Williams; The Notorious B.I.G.; Terry Nation; LaVern Baker; Fred Zinnemann; Willem de Kooning; Laura Nyro; Allen Ginsberg; Laurie Lee; Jeff Buckley; Ronnie Lane; Betty Shabazz; Jacques Cousteau; Robert Mitchum; James Stewart; William S. Burroughs; Ben Hogan; Fela Kuti; Luther Allison; Mother Teresa; Burgess Meredith; Jimmy Witherspoon; Roy Lichtenstein; Glen Buxton; John Denver; Samuel Fuller; Michael Hutchence; Kathy Acker; Stephane Grappelli; Billy Bremner; Jimmy Rogers; Nicolette Larson; Diana Spencer.

FILMS

Con Air; *Live Flesh;* *Grosse Pointe Blank*; *The Fifth Element*; *Donnie Brasco*; *Insomnia*; *Cop Land;* *Good Will Hunting*; *Gummo;* *Lost Highway*; *Jackie Brown;* *L.A. Confidential*; *Titanic;* *Boogie Nights.*

BOOKS

J.K. Rowling – *Harry Potter and the Philosopher's Stone*

Arthur Golden – *Memoirs of a Geisha*

Arundhati Roy – *The God of Small Things*

Annie Proulx – *Brokeback Mountain*

Don DeLillo – *Underworld*

Ryu Murakami – *In the Miso Soup*
Peter Carey – *Jack Maggs*
Charles Frazier – *Cold Mountain*

MY 1997

I would attain the age of forty during this year, and it seemed, even to me, that I had reached a level of contentment that I had previously struggled to find. Comparing this most recent decade with the one that preceded it, I realised that my twenties were full of chaos, turbulence and unhappiness; convinced that all of that was behind me and consigned to the past, I was very much relieved. Work-wise, I was still overseeing the running of what had grown to become seven busy and profitable fruit and vegetable concessions within a supermarket chain. Domestically, I set about brightening-up my home, and I had it painted in bold blues and yellows. I was popular, having many friends and many more friendly acquaintances, and although I was in a somewhat tumultuous relationship, even there, the good outweighed the bad. I had also developed a taste for nice clothes; not for me the fashionable designer sportswear and jeans look… I was brash and flash in an array of (cheaply bought!) high-end finery – a cream rubber suit and leopard print shirt for example. As a look, I guess it was very much like early Roxy Music, but it certainly turned a few heads, and in general, I was loving life. Work kept me relatively fit, but I also played five-a-side football twice a week; it was highly competitive with a group of good players, amongst whom I comfortably held my own.

As ever, I followed Manchester United at home and abroad; a game against Monaco was the perfect excuse for a five-day debauch along the French Riviera. I threw a fortieth birthday party on the train station platform at Stalybridge, where a splendid buffet bar provided fine ales and spirits. Hundreds of people showed up, and a hand-drawn greetings card from Frank Sidebottom was a nice surprise. Frank's series of lectures at Timperley Labour Club had been magical events, and I attended several other great club nights; as ever, music soundtracked my every move, though for some reason, I went to fewer gigs during this year. One memorable gig I did attend was a performance by Massive Attack at the Apollo; on every level it was brilliant – stunning and thought-provoking both aurally and visually. Less so was David Bowie, who was appearing at the relatively intimate Manchester Academy; I went along in eager anticipation, but was left disappointed because guitarist Reeves Gabrels seemed intent on dominating the show. He spoiled song after classic song with horrible and tasteless squalls of guitar noise that filled every available nook and cranny; the concept of "less being more" had presumably escaped him – shell-shocked, I retreated to a place of safety… the bar.

As understated as ever, I celebrate my 40th at Stalybridge train station

100
NANCY BOY
PLACEBO
HUT

Placebo were a rock band from London with an androgynous image and a style that incorporated elements of glam, punk, industrial and metal. 'Nancy Boy' was the fourth single released from their debut album, and it was the one that established the trio as hit makers because it crashed into the UK top five, despite – or aided by? – the lyric (written by singer Brian Molko) containing themes of drug use, gender fluidity and bisexuality. This is brazen, loud, melodramatic and the chorus hook is most appealing. Molko sings in a thin, high-pitched and decidedly un-macho voice; at the time he was aged twenty-five, but he sounded like a bratty and petulant teenager – across the nation, black-clad teenagers embraced him as one of their own.

99
VIC ACID
SQUAREPUSHER
WARP

Tom Jenkinson, a fan of both Frank Zappa and Jaco Pastorius, took these unlikely influences into his work as Squarepusher. With 'Vic Acid', he created a mischievous slice of drum and bass by using the omnipotent 'Amen' breakbeat in a highly creative way; the beat loops endlessly and sounds like chattering teeth, as space dust pops and explodes on the tongue and the bass track hula hoops around it most energetically. This is a dizzying, high-speed ride of a record that can be neatly summed up with just two words… great stuff.

98
I AM A TREE
GUIDED BY VOICES
MATADOR
OTHER SINGLES 1997: BULL-DOG SKIN; WISH IN ONE HAND

The prolific and prodigiously talented Guided by Voices served up several gems during this year, but 'I Am a Tree' was definitely the pick of the bunch. On this occasion, it was not penned by Robert Pollard, but instead by guitarist Doug Gillard. The song takes a hugely imaginative and metaphorical look at life and love, and although certainly tinged with sadness, it is nevertheless played and sung in a celebratory way. In general, the Guided by Voices ethos to music-making was always passionate and spirited, and these two adjectives clearly apply to 'I Am a Tree', making what was already a quite wonderful song sound even better.

97
STEREO
PAVEMENT
DOMINO
OTHER SINGLE 1997: SHADY LANE

'Stereo' is by no means a traditional kind of song; it consists of a beat and meandering bass line, over which Stephen Malkmus sing/speaks a stream-of-consciousness lyric dropping cultural references, including a couple of lines pondering whether Geddy Lee (the incredibly high-voiced singer in Rush) has a normal speaking voice. A couple of "Hi ho Silvers" later, we gallop from Lone Ranger imagery into a high-octane chorus in which Malkmus screams that he is "on the stereo". Admittedly, this is an odd, but very endearing sound.

96
FLASHBACK
LAURENT GARNIER
F COMMUNICATIONS
OTHER SINGLE 1997: CRISPY BACON

When this track is playing, there is a hint of magic in the air; Laurent Garnier locates the groove in a rumbling synth riff, and it just seems to grow and grow and grow. This single idea is stretched to the limit… but it is a brilliant idea! With the aid of a vocoder, Garnier makes a series of announcements and exhortations, in particular his view that "acid (house) was a state of mind"… and indeed it was. The sparseness and atmospheric echoing groove certainly harks back to the birth of house music in Chicago a decade previously, but whatever the era or genre, this was a superb single.

95
BARREL OF A GUN
DEPECHE MODE
MUTE
OTHER SINGLES 1997: IT'S NO GOOD; HOME; USELESS

By this point, Depeche Mode had been around for a while, and the never ending treadmill of album-tour, album-tour, had seen them wisely opt to take an extended break. After a four-year hiatus they needed to return with a strong single, something that would be a statement of intent… and with 'Barrel of a Gun' – a song about depravity that necessitated a dark and devilish performance – they did exactly that. Produced by Tim Simenon of Bomb the Bass, hard hip-hop style beats were married to the traditional mix of electronics and guitars. The sound growled and snapped, viscerally conveying an element of danger. Heroin-addicted singer Dave Gahan found much to connect within Martin Gore's insightful lyric, and he sang with world-weary resignation. Overall, although the track is undeniably intense and uncompromising, the spark of pop genius remained, and so the record did not repel their core audience; on the contrary, it was, and still is, held in fond embrace.

94
DOIN' TIME
SUBLIME
GASOLINE ALLEY
OTHER SINGLE 1997: WRONG TIME

'Doin' Time' is sung from the standpoint of a man who feels so trapped by his love for a cheating girlfriend, that the relationship feels like incarceration. The song is given a very contemporary trip-hop beat with a smooth vocal that glides effortlessly through the track. A heavily-sampled bossa nova version of jazz standard 'Summertime' (played by flautist Herbie Mann) helps give the piece a cool, Caribbean flavour, further accentuated by some lovely reggae stylings. The end result was a totally chilled, wonderfully tuneful and low-key downtempo delight.

94
MONKEY WRENCH
FOO FIGHTERS
CAPITOL
OTHER SINGLE 1997:
EVERMORE

On 'Monkey Wrench', Dave Grohl references his own broken, long-term relationship, lambasting himself for his failings and concluding that rather than sticking around to cause more pain, he should, for the sake of the other person, walk away and cease to be a problem. As Grohl exercises his demons with a no-holds barred vocal, the musicians attack the song with a hard-pounding, jackhammer riff, played with both precision and power in equal measure. So far, so good – but the real magic of the track is to be found in the two melodic choruses, the first containing a repeated cry of "One in ten", and the second with the refrain "Don't wanna be your monkey wrench".

93
EVEN AFTER ALL
FINLEY QUAYE
EPIC
OTHER SINGLES 1997:
SUNDAY SHINING;
IT'S GREAT WHEN WE'RE TOGETHER

Finley Quaye was the younger brother of former Elton John guitarist Caleb Quaye, and, it was claimed, a half-uncle to Tricky. He made his recording debut as the voice of 'Finley's Rainbow', a 1995 single by A Guy Called Gerald. His own music, as heard on 'Even After All', contained a strong flavouring of the sweetest strand of reggae music, mixed together with trip-hop beats. On top of this easy-on-the-ear sound that seems to float around the aether, Quaye sings a fractured and idiosyncratic lyric in a very distinctive style, incorporating eccentric phrasing in which his gentle voice rolls and stretches the vowels, producing an effect that could be described as playful, blissed, probably stoned… but extremely cool.

92
SHE'S A STAR
JAMES
FONTANA
OTHER SINGLES 1997:
TOMORROW;
WALTZING ALONG

By this point, guitarist Larry Gott had quit James in order to design furniture; the band owed two hundred and fifty thousand pounds in unpaid tax and things were looking fairly bleak. James desperately needed a big record to pull them out of the mire, and they achieved it with the album *Whiplash*, a record which saw them retreating from the experimental bent of their most recent work, into the safe, middle-ground of electric pop-rock. 'She's a Star' was the lead single from the album and it begins with the same piano motif that made the Bessie Banks/Moody Blues hit 'Go Now' so memorable, before a pleasingly Hawaiian-sounding, manipulated guitar is introduced. Tim Booth then sings eloquently about the magical inner-power of the female population – sliding into falsetto at various points – and though the track is a little plodding in parts, the chorus redeems the situation, with its simple repetition of the titular phrase creating a soaring, joyous exhalation and an inescapably glorious sound.

91
WIDE OPEN SPACE
MANSUN
PARLOPHONE
OTHER SINGLES 1997:
SHE MAKES MY NOSE BLEED;
TAXLOSS;
CLOSED FOR BUSINESS

Mansun were a band from Chester, who first formed in 1995 as barely competent musicians; however, what they may have lacked as far as musicianship is concerned, they more than made up for with strong songs and inventiveness. 'Wide Open Space' was written by the band's frontman Paul Draper, its title gifted to him thanks to a TV program he was watching. A hypnotic piano riff anchors this tuneful song, which rises to enormous crescendos featuring multiple layers of background vocals. An unfashionably epic guitar solo is included, but it is in no way superfluous or gratuitous, and as a whole, everything just seems to gel. Mansun had a hit that boosted their career, and 'Wide Open Space' – via a Paul Oakenfold re-mix – went on to became a huge club success too.

90
GREENBACKS
MF DOOM
FONDLE 'EM
OTHER SINGLE 1997: DEAD BENT

'Greenbacks' was our introduction to the masked rapper with the superhero alias of MF Doom; it was an independent release and his second single. The raw vitality and talent of its creator is immediately obvious; the wordplay is tough but exemplary and the track is very imaginatively constructed. In terms of content, a slice of musical street theatre is played out that is both poetic and verging on the satirical; it is a parable of sorts, which concludes with the message that money is no substitute for love – a notion that is well worth constant reiteration.

89
BEFORE TODAY
EVERYTHING BUT THE GIRL
VIRGIN

'Before Today' was the fourth and

final single taken from the *Walking Wounded* album, on which Everything But the Girl, encouraged by the Todd Terry remix of 'Missing' that had so revitalised their career, embraced electronic instrumentation and dance beats, rather than the acoustic-driven sound that had first established them. 'Before Today' is a blissful synthesis of emotion – via Tracey Thorn's anguished vocal – and the cold indifference of the machined beats and manipulated sounds. It is a song of pain that just happens to be sublime in its execution. Everything But the Girl had finally mastered the art of making adult oriented music that was dignified, while still retaining an uncompromising edge.

88
MY WORLD
THE O.C.
FFRR
OTHER SINGLES 1997: FAR FROM YOURS; CAN'T GO WRONG

Here, producer DJ Premier provides a masterful beat (with a Morricone type spaghetti-western vibe) while The O.C. displays his lyrical gift with an impressive, naturalistic flow as he expounds his thoughts on what he considers to be the "copy-catting" of so many rap acts. "I'm bored with it", he states emphatically, and then proceeds to throw down the gauntlet, leading by example on a quest to re-introduce class and originality into a genre that was undergoing very severe growing pains.

87
DISCOTHEQUE
U2
ISLAND
OTHER SINGLES 1997: STARING AT THE SUN; LAST NIGHT ON EARTH; MOFO; IF GOD WILL SEND HIS ANGELS; PLEASE

At the time much was made of U2's seismic change in style and sound; some sections of the press lauded this, while others dismissed it as bandwagon-jumping into the lucrative dance scene. In truth, U2 hadn't really changed that much at all; 'Discotheque' is still based upon one of The Edge's tasty guitar riffs, and although the vocal is positioned a bit further back in the mix than was usual, it is still unmistakably Bono at the microphone. All that had really happened was the band becoming confident enough to allow a certain playfulness to exist within their music; they were now sufficiently self-assured to experiment with sound, and here they do that very well indeed. 'Discotheque' sounds like furious and funky fun.

86
SINK TO THE BOTTOM
FOUNTAINS OF WAYNE
ATLANTIC
OTHER SINGLES 1997: BARBARA H; SURVIVAL CAR

'Fountains of Wayne' were a New York band who cribbed their name from a lawn ornament store. The punky power-pop of debut single 'Radiation Vibe' had been rather nice, but to my ears, 'Sink to the Bottom' was even nicer. It is simple, straightforward pop, played over a chugging, plinky-plonky synthesiser riff that erupts with a soda syphon of a chorus. The song is so romantic and open-hearted that even a cynic such as I sometimes feels the need for a little taste of such sweetness.

85
BROWN PAPER BAG
RONI SIZE & REPRAZENT
TALKIN' LOUD
OTHER SINGLES 1997:
HEROES; SHARE THE FALL

New Forms, the somewhat over-hyped Mercury Prize winning album that spawned this single, was so bloated by its two-hour twenty-minute duration, that it failed to adequately hold the listener's attention; however, taken in bite-sized chunks, the music did have much to offer. 'Brown Paper Bag' is blissful, vaguely jazzy and extremely cool; the vocals are intriguing, the beats are perfect and the incorporation of wild sounds provides constant aural stimulation.

84
WHAT DO YOU WANT ME TO SAY?
THE DISMEMBERMENT PLAN
DESOTO
OTHER SINGLE 1997:
THE ICE OF BOSTON

This features a phenomenal bass line that seems to tiptoe through the verses, while the chorus is dominated by big guitars. "What Do You Want Me To Say?" is the bewildered cry of a shattered soul who is struggling to come to terms with the sorry state of his relationship; apparently Travis Morrison was in the midst of recording a vocal for the song when he received a phone call from a girlfriend who summarily announced that she was dumping him. This moment of life imitating art goes a long way in helping to explain the pained frenzy of Morrison's performance.

83
GÓRECKI
LAMB
FONTANA

By using a sample from Górecki's *Third Symphony* (the *Symphony of Sorrowful Songs*) and then applying a dance beat with a love-lorn lyric expressing undying devotion, Lamb had hit upon something very special… something that is passionate and rhythmic like the act of love itself. Add in Lou Rhodes's clean and crystalline vocal – which pierces like an arrow tip to the heart – and this superb song is elevated to an even higher level.

82
NOT IF YOU WERE THE LAST JUNKIE ON EARTH
THE DANDY WARHOLS
CAPITOL
OTHER SINGLE 1997:
EVERY DAY SHOULD BE A HOLIDAY

Dedicated to friends and arch-rivals The Brian Jonestown Massacre, in truth the song was more likely aimed at the girlfriend of the Dandy's frontman Courtney Taylor-Taylor who, according to him, had picked up a heroin habit whilst he was away on tour. The song is performed in cheery garage-rock style, with plenty of bounce and buoyancy and a somewhat retro-feel. There are also glorious helium-filled vocal harmonies and, given the subject matter of the song, an incongruously bright delivery of the song from Taylor-Taylor, who pointedly sings the choruses of "Heroin is so passé" with a good deal of glee and relish.

81
TOXYGENE
THE ORB
ISLAND
OTHER SINGLE 1997: ASYLUM

Commissioned to create a re-mixed version of Jean Michel Jarre's 'Oxygene 8', The Orb completely re-assembled the track to the point where very little of the original remained; Jarre reputedly threw a hissy-fit and refused to release the track. Undaunted, The Orb re-titled it 'Toxygene' and issued it themselves, earning the biggest hit of their career. The piece begins with a music hall song leading into a lengthy ambient introduction that concludes with the sound of a speeding car and a voice saying "Now wait a minute". After that, we are off on a merry electronic jig that contains traces of dub, and we hear what can only be described as the aural equivalent of riding a high-speed fairground carousel.

80
FLY LIFE
BASEMENT JAXX
MULTIPLY

'Fly Life' was the first hit for Basement Jaxx, and they became chart regulars in its wake; it was first issued in 1996 as part of an EP, before this new mix – with added vocals from Glamma Kid – was released as a single. Blending house music with ragga, this was idiosyncratic and fresh. 'Fly Life' is highly energetic and uplifting, and frankly it was so lovable that I just wanted to give the record a great big hug! Others happily soaked up the good vibes that it gave off and took the overarching celebratory feel to be an irresistible invitation to dance.

79
THE HITS HURT
THE PASTELS
DOMINO
OTHER SINGLE 1997:
UNFAIR KIND OF FAME

Somewhat lo-fi, slightly wonky, a bit of a dirge and tunelessly sung… but it is also charming, clever, unapologetic and independently spirited. This group were free-thinkers who were unafraid to experiment with random noises to come up with a sound that was fantastically liberating. 'The Hits Hurt' is, like all singles by The Pastels, a thing of rare beauty to be cherished by the discerning listener.

78
JÓGA
BJÖRK
ONE LITTLE INDIAN
OTHER SINGLE 1997:
BACHELORETTE

Here we encounter lush, classically-styled strings underpinned with electronic beats. Accompanying this swooping and swirling sonic landscape, Björk, in her amazingly impressive naturalistic yelp, sings an ode to her native home, Iceland, and also to her best friend, mixing-up the emotional and geographical with an additional reference to a state of emergency. To be honest, 'Jóga' is a little bit bewildering… but who cares, it is also quite stunning.

77
LIKE DYLAN IN THE MOVIES
BELLE AND SEBASTIAN
JEEPSTER

Faux middle-of-the-road folk-rock stylings with baroque adornment… what on Earth was going on? It was dubbed either jangle pop, twee pop or chamber pop – take your pick – and the key band of the genre (in fact, at the time, the most name-dropped band in the UK) was Belle and Sebastian. Here, singer Stuart Murdoch concocts a lyric which references *Don't Look Back*, D.A. Pennebaker's documentary film of Bob Dylan's 1965 British tour. His delivery is fey, but the words are concerned with rising paranoia whilst undertaking a dark walk home, with the fear of being attacked and violated seeming not to be irrational at all… in fact, it almost looks like an inevitability. A rough and ready electric guitar solo is also served-up, which somehow fits perfectly. All-in-all, this is very beguiling indeed; at first, I was definitely sceptical, but ultimately glad that I was finally won over.

76
THE PERFECT DRUG
NINE INCH NAILS
INTERSCOPE

Commissioned to deliver a song for the David Lynch film *Lost Highway* – with a one-week deadline – Nine Inch Nails went into the studio and experimented. The result was a surprise to everyone, not least singer Trent Reznor who has publicly voiced his dissatisfaction with the track. No doubt for him this is just too lightweight, too catchy and too damned poppy; however, we are all free to form our own opinions and enjoy what Reznor views as a misstep. The track incorporates a drum & bass rhythm, along with guitar and vocals, in which a woman is complimented for being comparable to 'The Perfect Drug' because of her ability to deliver thrills and surprises. Ok, for Nine Inch Nails this was something of an anomaly, but I for one liked it.

75
TRIUMPH
WU-TANG CLAN FEATURING CAPPADONNA
LOUD
OTHER SINGLE 1997:
IT'S YOURZ

'Triumph' was a veritable tour de

force from Wu-Tang Clan, and it is the only single to feature all eight group members, as well as future member Cappadonna. The track is introduced by Ol' Dirty Bastard, and then, one-by-one, the crew display their spellbinding word-craft and rapping ability; it is a riveting listen and one that benefits from multiple repeat plays. No choruses are required here – this is just end-to-end brilliant street poetry.

74
TOO FAR
KYLIE MINOGUE
DECONSTRUCTION
OTHER SINGLES 1997: SOME KIND OF BLISS; DID IT AGAIN

Firmly slamming the lid on her past life as a kind of walking, talking Barbie Doll whose records were pure saccharine, Kylie Minogue recorded the album *Impossible Princess* on which she experimented, and in the process empowered and liberated herself. The music was now darker and tougher, incorporating various dance styles as well as rock music (via collaboration with The Manic Street Preachers). 'Too Far' was self-written and she co-produced with Brothers in Rhythm; it features drum & bass beats during the song's epic intro, and later Minogue herself plays some trance-style piano accompanied by a string arrangement. Although this is, for sure, an uptempo dancer, Kylie also expressed her feelings in a lyric which speaks to the frustration and sense of claustrophobia of her earlier career. Tellingly – and regrettably – 'Too Far' failed to chart; evidently Minogue's audience were not yet ready to embrace change.

73
IRON MAN
STEREOLAB
DUOPHONIC
OTHER SINGLE 1997: MISS MODULAR

Fired up by an explosive drum pattern, this wordless track finds Stereolab experimenting playfully and clearly having a ball in the studio; it sounds like the main theme of an imaginary movie – John Barry meets the Radiophonic Workshop perhaps? In any case, this was a stand-alone single, and one that can fairly be described as a distinct oddity… but a very cool one nonetheless.

72
NEW PATHS TO HELICON, PT 1
MOGWAI
WURLITZER JUKEBOX
OTHER SINGLE 1997: CLUB BEETROOT, PT 4

This record begins so quietly that it is practically inaudible, but then, out of the aether, a guitar appears, cloaked in echo and reverb, playing a descending melody. The sound shifts as a bass riff enters, followed by more guitar, and then, a full minute and a half into the track, a slow drum beat is introduced. A minute later, the song pauses for a split second before the payload is delivered and the song explodes in a frenzy of noise that continues until the guitars and drums finally cease, and the softly played bass riff and opening guitar melody bring proceedings to a very satisfying close. This single was my pleasant introduction to the very more-ish sound of Mogwai.

71
HAIL MARY
MAKAVELI (2PAC FEATURING OUTLAWZ)
DEATH ROW
OTHER SINGLES 1997:
I WONDER IF HEAVEN GOT A GHETTO;
WANTED DEAD OR ALIVE

A slow haunting beat with chimes and pipes seems to place us inside a Shaolin Temple… but alas, an ill-wind is blowing through it. Released six-months after Tupac was murdered (using his stage-name Makaveli) 'Hail Mary' reputedly took less than an hour to complete – fifteen-minutes to write the lyric and around thirty-minutes for Hurt-M-Badd to construct the beat – but such haste did not impact negatively on the track in any way, shape or form. Tupac repeatedly uses religious imagery to speaks out about the negative light in which he is viewed, and he inveighs against the violence that surrounds him. This was the sound of a man getting his house in order and preparing to grow and flourish artistically; tragically, it was not to be.

70
AIN'T THAT ENOUGH
TEENAGE FANCLUB
CREATION
OTHER SINGLES 1997: START AGAIN; I DON'T WANT TO CONTROL YOU

Teenage Fanclub had a catalogue bursting at the seams with great tunes, and 'Ain't That Enough' is run very close as my top choice for 1997 by their two other releases that year; in the end though, Gerard Love's composition wins out because it is such a bright, sunshine-dappled and uplifting song of all encompassing love. There is a pastoral feel such that one can almost smell damp grass, while the guitars jangle, a glockenspiel chimes and the vocal harmonies, reminiscent of The Byrds in their 1960s prime, are quite simply superb.

69
SUN HITS THE SKY
SUPERGRASS
PARLOPHONE
OTHER SINGLES: RICHARD III; LATE IN THE DAY; CHEAP-SKATE

By now, Supergrass had added melodic complexity and heavily textured sound to the speedy rush of their early records. They had also somewhat slowed the tempo without losing the sense of joyous abandon in their music. 'Sun Hits the Sky' had plenty going on, but it still glides along effortlessly until some Pete Townshend-style guitar chords introduce an utterly brilliant power-pop chorus. We are also treated to an organ solo of great subtlety before the track concludes with bass and conga getting involved in a funky jam. Throw-in some vaguely psychedelic sounding lyrics, along with the band's wonderful chemistry, and 'Sun Hits the Sky' couldn't fail to win over even the hardest of hearts.

68
KICK IN THE DOOR
THE NOTORIOUS B.I.G.
BAD BOY
OTHER SINGLES 1997:
LAST DAY; HYPNOTIZE;
MO MONEY MO PROBLEMS;
SKY'S THE LIMIT; NASTY BOY

Christopher Wallace (aka The Notorious B.I.G. and Biggie Smalls) was murdered in March of this year, sixteen days before his second album, *Life After Death*, was released. In order to meet the inevitable posthumous demand for product, a slew of singles was issued, amongst which was 'Kick in the Door', which opens with a skit of a phone call into a radio show, followed by excellent use of a sample from 'I Put a Spell on You' by Screaming Jay Hawkins, which takes us into the track proper. Biggie then raps in his unique style, proclaiming himself to be the rap king of New York, whilst taking aim at others that he feels do not measure up to him; none of the chiding is blatant, but Nas, Jeru the Damaja, Raekwon, Ghostface Killah and even his own producer DJ Premier are all verbally jabbed and jibed. As was common in hip-hop, the track has a cartoonish sense of menace – humorous but uncomfortably dark. Subsequently, following the slaying of Biggie and Tupac Shakur, the jokes didn't seem quite so funny.

67
NETHERWORLD
LSG
HOOJ TUNES
OTHER SINGLE 1997:
HIDDEN SUN OF VENUS

LSG is an alias used by German electronic music wizard Oliver Lieb, and whilst his track 'Netherworld' is uptempo dance music that functions perfectly on a dance-floor, it works equally well as music for the mind. Beginning with a clanging, industrial beat that gives way to smoky, deep-trance, there are little touches and tweaks that keep the mind occupied, but they never interfere with the overall flow of the track. This is definitely one to kick any sleeping endorphins into top gear, in order to induce those much desired feelings of euphoria.

66
SUMMER SMASH
DENIM
EMIDISC

It was finally going to happen for Lawrence; at last he was going to get into the charts. It seemed so inevitable because 'Summer Smash' – a song about having a hit record – was so bright, sunny, cheerful and catchy. The chorus of "Summer Smash, da da da da da" was a slice of simplistic genius; it bounces along and it made us smile – oh yes, this was bound to be a hit. But then... Diana, Princess of Wales, died in a car crash in Paris; the mood of the country was sombre, and the BBC, desirous not to offend anybody, took the decision that this unfortunately titled ditty should be exiled from the airwaves. His chance was well and truly gone; poor Lawrence was thwarted by a cruel twist of fate.

65
TOGETHER AGAIN
JANET JACKSON
VIRGIN
OTHER SINGLE 1997:
GOT 'TIL IT'S GONE

Janet Jackson wrote 'Together Again' in commemoration of a personal friend who had died of AIDS, along with all the other victims and their loved ones worldwide. Originally, it was a ballad, but when re-arranged as a more uptempo disco track, the joyous melody was enhanced and the song seemed to become celebratory and life-affirming, reminding us to live our lives as best we can while we have the opportunity to do so. Almost by necessity, this has a big, bold sound, matched by a diva-ish vocal performance from Jackson that is somewhat reminiscent of Diana Ross.

64
PRISONER OF THE PAST
PREFAB SPROUT
KITCHENWARE
OTHER SINGLE 1997:
ELECTRIC GUITARS

Here the drummed introduction – an unashamed homage to 'Be My Baby' by The Ronettes – is followed by a lush arrangement of strings and horns, playing a beautiful, yet simple melody of a kind that only the most gifted of writers are capable of creating. The lyrics to 'Prisoner of the Past' detail the addled and vengeful thoughts of a male stalker who imagines that, in the after-life, he will forever be able to haunt the woman who spurns him, so in death, she shall never escape him. Classy, intelligent pop had always been the forte of Prefab Sprout, and 'Prisoner of the Past' is no exception in that regard.

63
AUTUMN SWEATER
YO LA TENGO
MATADOR
OTHER SINGLES 1997:
SUGARCUBE; LITTLE HONDA

This song is blessed with a subtle lyric describing a meeting between the narrator, who feels insecure and emotionally naked, and his much more self-assured ex-lover, who wears as her metaphorical armour an 'Autumn Sweater'. Taken from the album *I Can Hear the Heart Beating as One*, which found Yo La Tengo at their artistic peak, this was a key track; it has a unique, funky groove, courtesy of conga drums and a deadly bass line, while an organ is employed to provide the melody. In addition, the vocal of Ira Kaplan is perfectly judged, sounding as it does just like a quiet conversation.

62
LA FEMME D'ARGENT
AIR
SOURCE

Available as a single only on a very limited twelve-inch edition, 'La Femme D'Argent' was the sumptuous opening track from Air's debut album *Moon Safari*. This is a record to be savoured, being gloriously chilled-out and relaxing, but never, ever bland. Air somehow extracted incredibly warm tones from their range of electronic tools, on what is, in effect, an amazing club tune for people who don't want to dance. 'Femme D'Argent' is rich with highly-refined flavours in which the listener can truly luxuriate.

61
WHAT DO YOU WANT FROM ME?
MONACO
POLYDOR
OTHER SINGLE 1997:
SWEET LIPS

With New Order in the midst of a prolonged sabbatical, Peter Hook combined with David Potts to form Monaco, who released just one album, *Music for Pleasure*, and from that source came this sunny little nugget. The lyric concerns the breakdown of the relationship between Hooky and Caroline Aherne, but it was certainly not given a maudlin treatment. In fact, it inevitably sounds very similar to New Order – but with a much more smiley face – and it bounces along nicely thanks to Hook's unmistakable and characteristically excellent bass line. The "Sha-la la la la-la la" refrains build towards a splendid chorus that is the icing on the cake of this fabulously shiny pop single.

60
MOANER
UNDERWORLD
JUNIOR BOYS OWN
OTHER SINGLE 1997: JUANITA

'Moaner' made its first appearance on the movie soundtrack to *Batman & Robin*. In Germany, it was issued as a single and became so popular that the sale of imported records was sufficient to make a dent on the UK chart. This is extremely uptempo and exciting, having the feel of an out-of-control heartbeat racing toward explosion. It is techno *in excelsis*, building and building, on and on as the beats get ever harder; finally, the intensity levels drop – though the tempo does not – as Karl Hyde's stream-of-consciousness lyrics begin, filled with dark imagery. When the energy level of the music begins to rise once again, his delivery becomes ever more frenzied until it is both breathless and breathtaking… if one word has to suffice, I guess it would be wow!

59
NAXALITE
ASIAN DUB FOUNDATION
FFRR

'Naxalite' is a term used to refer to Indian groups who operate close to the border with Bangladesh; they wage a violent struggle against oppression and exploitation as they strive to create a classless society. This track, by Asian Dub Foundation, is a salute to the fighting spirit of the Naxalites, and although it mainly uses Indian instruments, there are elements of dub technique borrowed from Jamaican reggae, and it has a rocking rhythm in similar style to The Clash. In short, this amounts to a melting pot of different cultural influences, with only shared ideals to connect them, but in the cry for justice, it sure makes a mighty sound.

58
BIG STAR
THE JAYHAWKS
AMERICAN RECORDINGS
OTHER SINGLE 1997:
THINK ABOUT IT

Following the loss of Mark Olson, one of their principal songwriters, The Jayhawks responded by releasing an ambitious and sprawling album entitled *The Sound of Lies*, from which came this sparkling slice of country-flecked power-pop from the pen of Gary Louris. 'Big Star' is a wry look at the success and fame that had eluded The Jayhawks; the lyrics imagine how utterly brilliant and fabulous it would be to achieve stardom – but they are of the sly and subtle leg-pulling variety. The truth, as Louris knew very well, was that his band had achieved a level at which their longevity was guaranteed, whereas the pressure of being a big star had seen many of his peers catastrophically crash and burn.

57
TWO MASKS
SOURCE DIRECT
SCIENCE
OTHER SINGLES 1997: CAPITAL D; CALL & RESPONSE; DARK METAL

This is drum and bass of the highest order, well thought-out and choc-full of differing flavours that disconcertingly shift in tone from one character to another, in a heartbeat. It feels a bit like being endlessly pursued around a maze, conjuring-up images of an unhinged, axe-wielding Jack Nicholson in *The Shining*.

56
GABRIEL
ROY DAVIES JR. AND PEVEN EVERETT
XL

Written by Davis Jr. and Everett, with Everett on vocal and trumpet, 'Gabriel' is a superb example of garage-house that became an unlikely UK chart hit. It is a majestic slow burner in which the sparse instrumentation allows the soulful voice plenty of room to pull on emotional levers while the thunderous bass gets the job of moving the body. The inclusion of trumpet fanfares is a masterstroke; it lends the already imperious track an even greater degree of gravitas.

55
SAVE TONIGHT
EAGLE-EYE CHERRY
POLYDOR

Son of Don Cherry (and half-brother of Neneh), Eagle-Eye was born and raised in Sweden, and he developed his own individual style as demonstrated on his debut single, 'Save Tonight', which was a worldwide hit. The track is bright with a crisp beat that underpins acoustic guitars and an underlying layer of electronics, while Cherry's voice is smokey and appealing. The lyrics themselves are simple, but they eloquently express the regret of an enforced parting from a lover.

54
HIGH NOON
DJ SHADOW
MO' WAX
OTHER SINGLES1997:
Q-BERT MIX LIVE!

'High Noon' was DJ Shadow's response to the popularity of UK big beat; it is constructed from the reverberating drums played by Curtis Knight on the Jimi Hendrix track 'Flashing'. Yet more samples are interwoven to give depth to the track, and the crowning glory is a wild, psych-guitar riff extracted from Giant Crab's 'The Answer Is No'. The whole piece is expertly put together and the result is a thumping, cinematic dance monster.

53
MURDERERS, THE HOPE OF WOMEN
MOMUS
CREATION

Nick Currie, aka Momus, is such a literate artist, that it comes as little surprise to find that he takes the title of 'Murderers, the Hope of Women' from a fairly obscure expressionist play written in 1909 by German painter Oskar Kokoschka. The cultured and highly refined Momus presents to us acoustic chamber pop with a vicious streak running right through the middle; lyrically, the excellent psychodrama outlines a theory that marriage is a prison, and for the female can even amount to a kind of slow murder. Momus portrays a killer who marries Sweet Fanny Adams and then smothers her inside his own concept of domestic bliss, until the woman reaches the end of her tether and takes her own life.

52
16 DAYS
WHISKEYTOWN
OUTPOST RECORDINGS

Whiskeytown were making a gallant attempt to make country music more popular; their fiddles and pedal steel sound was beefed-up with drums and electric guitars. Actually, their music was strongly reminiscent of The Flying Burrito Brothers, with uber-talented singer/songwriter Ryan Adams in the role of Gram Parsons. Here, on '16 Days', he duets with violinist Caitlin Cary in a rootsy, high-spirited romp; it is hugely catchy and sung in very fine style with great enthusiasm.

51
NOT IF YOU WERE THE LAST DANDY ON EARTH
BRIAN JONESTOWN MASSACRE
THE COMMITTEE TO KEEP MUSIC EVIL
OTHER SINGLE 1997: GIVE IT BACK

Responding in double-quick time to perceived criticism from The Dandy Warhols, whose 'Not If You Were the Last Junkie on Earth' was interpreted as a chiding of Brian Jonestown Massacre leader Anton Newcombe, he wrote 'Not If You Were the Last Dandy on Earth' as a cruel parody and a sharp rebuke. Despite carrying this hostile baggage, a fine record was produced, sounding not unlike an amphetamine-fuelled Rolling Stones, with mocking "ba, ba, ba" backing vocals delivered in sarcastic style. Newcombe takes direct aim at what he saw as The Dandy's lack of originality, and their indebtedness to The Brian Jonestown Massacre.

50
DEADWEIGHT
BECK
GEFFEN
OTHER SINGLES 1997: THE NEW POLLUTION; SISSYNECK; JACK-ASS

Moving away from the style of *Odelay*, which had established him as a major star, Beck began to experiment with more exotic South American flavours; consequently inside the lively and funky rhythm of 'Deadweight', there is a tasty added ingredient which lends a decidedly Brazilian flavour to proceedings. 'Deadweight' is also a melodic delight, as Beck sings a down-on-his-luck tale of gambling and losing in Las Vegas. First appearing on the soundtrack to the film *A Life Less Ordinary*, 'Deadweight' can be viewed as a harbinger of change in Beck's career – a further mutiny against any attempt to limit his musical horizons.

49
THE SAINT
ORBITAL
INTERNAL

Following huge success with 'Satan Live', an album-sized single, Orbital released another crowd-pleasing hit with 'The Saint', taken from the soundtrack of the big-screen update of the 1960s TV series. This is a superb rendition of the classic theme, with kettle drums adding boldness to the evocative tune that was originally composed by author Leslie Charteris, as a simple whistled melody.

48
THE RAIN (SUPA DUPA FLY)
MISSY ELLIOTT
ELEKTRA
OTHER SINGLE 1997: SOCK IT 2 ME

In this period, Missy Elliott featured on numerous collaborations, but 'The Rain' was the first single to carry her name as the featured artist. Producer Timbaland provides a reverberating beat and a sample of Ann Peebles singing 'I Can't Stand the Rain', which creates the hook for the chorus, around which Missy Elliott raps with an ultra-confident swagger. The melding of old and new is seamless, and the overall effect is one of existing in a dream state where time is constantly shifting back and forth.

47
EX-CON
SMOG
DRAG CITY

Assisted in the role of producer and primary musical accomplice by alt-rock high-priest Jim O'Rourke, Bill Callahan (aka Smog) serves up this wonderfully bizarre hybrid of new wave and country rock in which Callahan melds his undemonstrative voice and mordant wit to a merry combination of bubbling synthesiser and snare drum, as a tale of dislocation and self-deprecating thought unfolds.

46
NOTHING LASTS FOREVER
ECHO AND THE BUNNYMEN
LONDON
OTHER SINGLES 1997:
DON'T LET IT GET YOU
DOWN; I WANT TO BE THERE

Reformed after a nine-year break, with 'Nothing Lasts Forever', Echo and the Bunnymen returned with an excellent single; even the presence of Liam Gallagher on backing vocals couldn't detract from this big-hearted, sensitively treated and beautifully introspective ballad, where the strings – and Will Sergeant's tasteful guitar sonics – act as a perfect foil for Ian McCullough's subdued, but still emotional vocals.

45
UP JUMPS DA BOOGIE
MAGOO & TIMBALAND
BLACKGROUND

Opening to the sweet sound of R&B singer Aaliyah, before Timbaland and Magoo trade rapped verses, we then have the arrival of another stellar guest – in the form of Missy Elliott – who proceeds to take her turn at the microphone. The track is slinky and funky, with a distinct party vibe, and the mix of synth, guitar and electronic beats is intoxicatingly moreish.

44
FAITHFUL
FANTOM
SOURCE

'Faithful' was a one-off studio collaboration between Gregory Darsa, Julien Jabre and Luna Skopelja under the name Fantom, and it is an outstandingly groovy example of French house music. Using samples from 'At Midnight' and 'Moscow Diskow' by disco act T-Connection and French new wave act Telex respectively, a sound is created that makes me picture a cartoon steam train bouncing down the railway track, stopping to pick up more passengers as the music veers off into very strange jazz/funk terrain, and then setting-off on its crazy journey once again. This is a fabulous record that should have been better known; I'm convinced that it would have been a dance-floor bomb.

43
ENVANE
AUTECHRE
WARP
OTHER SINGLE 1997: CHIASTIC SLIDE

What constituted a single was getting harder to define; 'Envane' was available as a four-track EP with a running time of over thirty-five minutes. It was also available as two twelve-inch singles (sold separately) where each track was the re-interpretation of a central theme. The most immediate of these was 'Goz Quarter', which employs both vocal and scratching samples from the track 'No Awareness' by Dr Octagon. This bears comparison to certain pieces of classical music in the way that it shifts from a melancholic opening to more outré territory, constantly teasing the listener by hinting at a crescendo that never arrives. Nevertheless, this journey through sound dimensions is highly satisfying; on first hearing it seems quite simple, but further listening reveals that the complex polyrhythms are busy entwining themselves around the mind.

42
INSINUATION
FOLK IMPLOSION
COMMUNION LABEL
OTHER SINGLES 1997: KINGDOM OF LIES; POLE POSITION

Lou Barlow of Sebadoh formed The Folk Implosion with John Davis, as a partnership of equals. This extra-curricular outfit did not carry the weight of expectation under which Sebadoh laboured, and consequently they often sounded a fresher and more naturalistic outfit. 'Insinuation' was taken from the album *Dare to be Surprised* and it opens with sparse but funky drum and bass, before guitar and strings are introduced, along with easy-on-the-ear harmony vocals. The sound as a whole is highly satisfying; it is a demonstration of near perfect rock/pop that somehow contrives to share stylistic similarities with both Simon & Garfunkel and Depeche Mode.

41
FORTIFIED LIVE
REFLECTION ETERNAL
RAWKUS

Reflection Eternal were a rap outfit from Brooklyn, formed by Talib Kweli. For this debut single, both Mos Def and Mr. Man guest in the role of featured artists, and the *boom bap* beat contains samples from 'Tom Drunk' by U-Roy & Hopeton Lewis and a pair of Patrice Rushen tracks, 'Let There Be Funk' and 'Sojourn'. The rhymes themselves just tell it as it is, line after line, which is fascinating, entertaining and illuminating. Each rapper seems to be well and truly on fire, and they ride the scratchy lo-fi rhythm with effortless grace, making this single something of a hip-hop symphony.

40
UNIVERSAL MAGNETIC
MOS DEF
RAWKUS

The debut single from Mos Def was the audacious and precocious 'Universal Magnetic'; using nothing more than a simple snare drum beat, Mos Def spends the first minute of the record rapping out his introduction, until a swinging rhythm sees him really begin to flow. His lines here are light-hearted jests which tumble rhythmically from his lips; amongst others, he compares himself to Melle Mel, Tenor Saw and Richard Pryor. It is all a good deal of fun, and 'Universal Magnetic' is a fantastic party jam.

39
TRUTH IN ADVERTISING
NEGATIVLAND
EERIE MATERIALS

'Truth in Advertising' is a sound collage which satirises an advertising industry that is unwilling to deal with probing enquiries, preferring instead to simply repeat their message. This is thought-provoking and uncomfortable listening, as we smile through gritted teeth, realising that pretty much each and every one of us influenced to some degree by cynical and persuasive advertising.

38
MISS AMERICA
DAVID BYRNE
WARNER BROTHERS
OTHER SINGLE 1997:
DANCE ON VASELINE

'Miss America' is a song written from the point of view of an immigrant who buys into the image of America as being a great big, sexy place; he wishes to experience this for himself, but instead, he finds a total lack of inclusiveness – for him, the American dream is unattainable… his social-status will prevent him from ever feeling that he really belongs. It is a wickedly humorous song, with vulgarity and profanity liberally sprinkled throughout, adding emphasis to the song's meaning. Played in full-on Latin-style, and sung sardonically by David Byrne, who, twenty-years after his breakthrough as the driving force of Talking Heads, was proving that his artistic prowess remained unimpaired by the passage of time.

37
HELP THE AGED
PULP
ISLAND

'Help the Aged' is a self-deprecating ballad in which lyricist Jarvis Cocker – at the grand old age of thirty-four – feels that the ageing process is changing him. Cocker was dead-set on the song being released as a single, whereas guitarist Russell Senior disliked it so much that he actively lobbied against it… in the end, Cocker won the argument and Senior promptly left the band. Although the song had been written with a certain flippancy, upon completion, that element completely disappeared; with an arrangement that begins in a hush but ends in a stupendous roar, Cocker's delivery gives his compassionate words a poignancy that he had never originally intended.

36
HOLY RIVER
PRINCE
NEW POWER GENERATION

Prince remained a consummate musical practitioner of very high-quality, and the release of 'Holy River' further emphasised that fact. The legal wrangling which had seen him drop his name in favour of a symbol – as well as scrawling the word "slave" across his cheek – had confused and alienated a large part of his audience who subsequently dropped him and stopped listening… but with 'Holy River' they missed out on an absolute gem. This is a gentle, mid-paced ballad that neither has, nor requires, a catchy chorus but, propelled by a fluid bass line, it seems to fly on gossamer wings. Lyrically, the song is concerned with spiritual enlightenment and the contentment that Prince was feeling following his marriage to Mayte Garcia. There are little unobtrusive flourishes – such as a short harpsichord section – to decorate the aural tapestry, and the track concludes with a trademark, liquid guitar solo.

35
REMEMBER ME
BLUE BOY
JIVE
OTHER SINGLE 1997:
SANDMAN

DJ Alexis Blackmore released his music under the pseudonym Blue Boy, and with 'Remember Me' he achieved an artistic and commercial high point. The track was constructed via samples taken from both a studio and a live recording of 'Woman of the Ghetto' by soul music veteran Marlena Shaw. Combining a deceptively simple, but highly effective bounding rhythm, along with Shaw's vocals, Blackmore created an atmospheric dance floor monster with memorable hooks aplenty.

34
SOMEWHERE
PET SHOP BOYS
PARLOPHONE
OTHER SINGLE:
RED LETTER DAY

Following the brilliant subtlety of 'Red Letter Day', the Pet Shop Boys pendulum swung to its opposite extreme with this glittering, melodramatic and way over-the-top disco/hi-NRG reading of Bernstein and Sondheim's classic show-tune from *West Side Story*. Here it is painted a bright shade of pink and fully appropriated on behalf of the queer community. Purists may scoff and despair, but I find this ultra-camp rendition of 'Somewhere' – also incorporating 'I Feel Pretty', another *West Side Story* standard – to be strangely moving, as well as glorious fun.

33
PLASTIC WORLD
KOOL KEITH
FUNKY ASS

Fresh from his *Dr. Octagon* project, Kool Keith teamed up with KutMasta Kurt for the album *Sex Style* and its attendant single 'Plastic World'. Over a wild and spine-tingling soundtrack with an unrelenting beat, Keith distances himself from all the factions that existed in hip-hop; the bogus gangsta rappers, the copycats and the commercially-minded variety who mix their sounds with R&B, they are all skilfully ridiculed and taken to task in a masterful put-down of anyone with less than pure artistic reasons for ever committing music to record.

32
DEMONS
SUPER FURRY ANIMALS
CREATION
OTHER SINGLES 1997:
THE INTERNATIONAL LANGUAGE OF SCREAMING;
PLAY IT COOL;
HERMANN LOVES PAULINE

'Demons' was the fourth single release taken from the Super Furry Animals second album, *Radiator*; all of them were modest, but significant hits which managed to put complex harmony, inventiveness, humour, style and a very distinct edginess into the charts. 'Demons' is a superb single that alternates between quiet reflection and rousing choruses. The lyrical content is utterly surreal and very imaginative, while the musical element, broadly speaking, is hybrid psychedelic folk-rock… but within that blurry envelope, there is still space enough for the appearance of a Tijuana-style brass band!

31
ELECTRICITY
SPIRITUALIZED
DEDICATED
OTHER SINGLE 1997: I THINK I'M IN LOVE

In 1997, all of the various strands, ideas and potential that Spiritualized possessed, somehow came together and coalesced; their album *Ladies and Gentlemen We are Floating in Space* was a masterpiece, and without doubt one of the decade's finest albums. The lead single taken from it was 'Electricity', which opens with Doors-like keyboards that are followed by an absolutely monumental kick; the sound becomes immense and we hear a hot-wired version of the blues, with a harmonica part that positively bleeds. With throttle set to full, the track soars ever higher, reminiscent of the cosmic boogie of prime-time Hawkwind… but at the controls here is Jason Pierce, and he is in complete command as the track spirals relentlessly upwards to the end.

30
HEAPS OF SHEEPS
ROBERT WYATT
HANNIBAL

'Heaps of Sheeps' saw Robert Wyatt finally re-discover a sense of playfulness not heard since the early 1970s; it also re-introduced him to an old associate from that era in the form of Brian Eno. Together they create a wonderfully bright sounding record, with a fabulous synthesiser sound on top of a rollicking rhythm – and very silly backing vocals – over which we hear Wyatt's inimitable voice. He regales us with a tall-tale concerned with the counting of sheep in an attempt to fall asleep; one by one, the sheep jump over a gate as they should do… but then, suddenly, they refuse to budge. A huge pile-up of animals thus ensues, creating what can only be described as… er… 'Heaps of Sheeps'.

29
KING WASP
ADD N TO X
SATELLITE
OTHER SINGLES 1997: ASTHMA; THE BLACK REGENT

Add N to X were an electronic band from London, with a penchant for songs of an adult nature. 'King Wasp' incorporates a looped sample of blues classic 'I'm a King Bee' by Slim Harpo, plus squelching and squealing electronic noise, an approximation of the "glitter beat" and vocals that are treated so as to be indecipherable, but instead become effective as another musical element. The upshot of it all is a sexy, mechanical grind, perfect for soundtracking the work of a dominatrix… or, I guess, equally good for doing the ironing at home.

28
OUTTA SPACE
JIMI TENOR
WARP
OTHER SINGLE 1997: SUGAR-DADDY

This is space-age lounge music with a funky vibe, that grooves along as an instrumental for most of the song's duration, before Jimi Tenor throws in a vocal reminiscent of Funkadelic in their P-Funk pomp. Tenor was mining a unique musical seam, and nuggets like 'Outta Space' are precious gems for sure.

27
KOWALSKI
PRIMAL SCREAM
CREATION
OTHER SINGLES 1997:
STAR; BURNING WHEEL

Primal Scream re-emerged with new bass player Mani (from The Stone Roses) and they made this fabulous sounding record that borrowed a bass line from Funkadelic, and sampled the immaculate drum track from 'Halleluhwah' by Can. The song was named after the central character in cult film *Vanishing Point*, and selected snatches of dialogue from the film are peppered throughout the track – which has an appropriately apocalyptic feel – while Bobby Gillespie whispers a lyric that amounts to little more than a synopsis of the film. Nevertheless, 'Kowalski' is an excellent example of the fact that you don't necessarily need a great song in order to make a great record.

26
GOING OUT OF MY HEAD
FATBOY SLIM
SKINT

Norman Cook, formerly of The Housemartins and Beats International, had adopted the name Fatboy Slim and re-invented himself as an excellent DJ/producer. He made a string of big beat dance anthems, and 'Going Out of my Head' was the one that set the tone. Cook borrowed The Who's 'I Can't Explain' guitar riff – from the version by Yvonne Elliman – and the mighty drums of John Bonham from Led Zeppelin's funk influenced track 'The Crunge', and he created an exciting and artful mix, with the insistent guitar riff bouncing along on top of the beats. The vocal consists of a single repeated line from the 'I Can't Explain' track, and this provides the title for this irrepressible and irresistible piece.

25
THIS IS A LIE
THE CURE
FICTION

The parent album, *Wild Mood Swings*, was critically derided, but 'This is a Lie' – which came as a promo single, rather than being commercially available – is a somewhat hidden and undervalued gem from the extensive Cure songbook. It is a mid-paced, string-laden lamentation on the pain and confusion that life throws our way; the choices we make that we later realise may be wrong and detrimental to our hopes of happiness. This is a song about feeling trapped, and Robert Smith provides a suitably sensitive, yet emotionally raw vocal performance, that is a highly convincing expression of deep hurt.

24
FREE
ULTRA NATÉ
STRICTLY RHYTHM

This song was seized upon by the gay community because of its upfront message of empowerment for the persecuted and downtrodden. 'Free' is a genuinely anthemic garage house record that is powered along by piano and a bright, repeated guitar phrase that serves as a very memorable hook. Although the track is a rousingly powerful piece of music, there is also a melancholic element to make it authentically soulful. Ultra Naté's performance is top-notch too; she summons-up an unbelievable energy that is unleashed into a magnificent vocal track, full of true passion and pride.

23
THE HUNCHBACK OF SAN FRANCISCO
PERRY BLAKE
POLYDOR

Irishman Perry Blake's debut single was 'The Hunchback of San Francisco', a beguiling piece of lyrical contemplation, with an accompaniment that is partly elaborate chamber pop, and partly downtempo electronica. Blake tells his tale with softly delivered poetic phrases – which only add to the general air of sadness and despair – as they conjure up images of a down-at-heel and lonely man trying to cope in a pitiless emotional environment. Unobtrusively melodic, this was a marvellous single; in my mind, I imagined Perry Blake to be a kind of post-modern version of Nick Drake.

22
WOKE UP THIS MORNING
ALABAMA 3
ONE LITTLE INDIAN
OTHER SINGLE 1997: SPEED OF THE SOUND OF LONELINESS

Before *The Sopranos* TV series began airing with 'Woke Up This Morning' as its theme tune, this single should already have been a hit record… but for some reason, it was not; perhaps it didn't get the requisite radio support due to its subject matter, which concerned the real-life case of a woman named Sara Thornton, who murdered her husband after suffering sustained spousal abuse over a twenty-year period. In any case, it is a song that is much more about female empowerment than it is the glamourisation of gangsters. Played as an upper mid-tempo blues/gospel number, harmonica and synthesiser licks are incorporated which meld the old-style forms to a more modern interpretation, helping to make 'Woke Up This Morning' the startlingly good and highly distinctive record that it is.

21
OUTTASITE (OUTTA MIND)
WILCO
REPRISE
OTHER SINGLE 1997:
MONDAY

Following the demise of Uncle Tupelo, it initially seemed that of the co-leaders' new bands, it would be Jay Farrar's Son Volt who would make the greater impression… but then came Wilco's second album, *Being There*, which was a delight from start to finish. Sprawling over two discs, its pivotal song, 'Outtasite (Outta Mind)', was included in two different versions as well as being issued as a single. It finds the band abandoning much of their country-flavoured sound to play instead a brand of classic rock, comparable to Big Star or The Flamin' Groovies. Although 'Outtasite' is a song about losing out in love, it is played with jubilation; rising upward from the opening bars, it soars and swoops magnificently, as the guitars ring out and Jeff Tweedy sings with the self-assured swagger of a man certain that he is fronting a great band who are playing a great song.

20
HOW THE WEST WAS WON AND WHERE IT GOT US
R.E.M.
WARNER BROTHERS
OTHER SINGLE 1997:
ELECTROLITE

A repeated piano motif forms the basis of what proved to be the final single by the original R.E.M. line-up, as drummer Bill Berry departed the band during this year. The simple rhythm deployed here is quite mesmerising, and the musicians adroitly play around it with consummate good taste. Michael Stipe provides a strong vocal, clearly enunciating each enigmatic phrase, in a lyric that appears to be concerned with decline, deception and ultimately failure.

19
STAR FRUITS SURF RIDER
CORNELIUS
MATADOR

Keigo Oyamada had been a member of Japanese pop duo Flipper's Guitar. Following their demise, he chose Cornelius as a pseudonym, in tribute to the character of the same name in the film *Planet of the Apes*. He developed a quirky, experimental style, and his third album, *Fantasma*, was picked up for international release, from which 'Star Fruits Surf Rider' was the lead single. Over a tic-toc rhythm, all manner of dissonance occurs – though it is juxtaposed with a very sweet melody – while Cornelius sings softly in Japanese, followed by big, bright choruses in the English language. This is a record that twists and turns relentlessly, but each and every wriggle manages to bring a very pleasant surprise.

18
SPARKS FROM THE MOTHERSHIP
DAWN OF THE REPLICANTS
EASTWEST
OTHER SINGLES 1997: ALL THE CHEYENNE CABOODLE; VIOLENT SUNDAYS; RHINO RAYS

Dawn of the Replicants were a Scottish band who made highly inventive, guitar-based music that was full of vim and vigour. The lead song from this five-track EP was 'Lisa Box' and it was one of the band's early signature songs. Employing a stop-start approach, this fizzes and crackles with whizzing synthesiser, as little musical touches appear and disappear in a heartbeat, and although generally upbeat, a sinister sounding vocal describes the unpleasantness surrounding the wedding of 'Lisa Box'.

17
TUBTHUMPING
CHUMBAWAMBA
EMI

'Tubthumping' is one of those songs with such hard-hitting immediacy, that the impact remains memorable no matter how much time has elapsed; its melding of dance/punk/swing, the hip-hop style beats and enormously high energy levels – not to mention the way in which British drinking culture is captured in a non-patronising fashion – are all factors in making this song so persuasively enchanting. But, it is the raucous, communally chanted chorus that cements the song in our collective consciousness. Lest it be forgotten, in the words of guitarist Boff Whalley, 'Tubthumping' was written about "the resilience of ordinary people"... and it is this that gives the song its big-hearted compassion.

16
DRINKING IN L.A.
BRAN VAN 3000
AUDIOGRAM

Bran Van 3000 were a Canadian electronica collective founded by James Di Salvio and E.P. Bergen. 'Drinking in L.A.' was their first single, and it was inspired by an incident in which Di Salvio awoke, face down, on a lawn in Hollywood, following a rather heavy session on the sauce. The song admirably captures the superficiality of the hedonistic Hollywood lifestyle, parodying it to perfection with a kitschy combination of lounge and hip-hop. The verses are rendered as a slow rap, while the accompaniment is provided by dreamy, billowing harmonies interspersed with casually tossed insults and eerie sound effects, transporting the disconcerted listener into the midst of a weary bacchanal. 'Drinking in L.A.' is both a peek into the lives of others, and a genius record too.

15
DEAD MAN WALKING
DAVID BOWIE
BMG
OTHER SINGLES 1997:
LITTLE WONDER;
SEVEN YEARS IN TIBET;
I'M AFRAID OF AMERICANS

At this time, the rejuvenated David Bowie was in the process of cross-fertilising guitar-based rock with brutalist techno; *Earthling*, his album of the period, proved to be a very divisive piece of work, though in fact it has aged rather well. The album has a plethora of great songs, but perhaps the best of all is 'Dead Man Walking' with a title and sentiment that maybe gives a clue as to how Bowie was beginning to view his waning commercial status. Big hits that had once come easy, now proved to be elusive. Sure enough, 'Dead Man Walking' didn't manage to crack the top thirty of the UK chart, but it was a fabulous record nevertheless. The song features prominent drum and bass beneath swirling verses that break into a memorable chorus featuring Bowie – his voice as magnificent as it had ever been – supported by the voice of bassist Gail Ann Dorsey, singing over a guitar riff re-worked from Bowie's 1970 song 'The Supermen'. Incidentally, said riff had originally been gifted to the young and struggling pre-fame David Bowie by his contemporary – and equally struggling – the pre-Yardbirds and Led Zeppelin, Jimmy Page.

14
GBI (GERMAN BOLD ITALIC)
TOWA TEI
COALITION
OTHER SINGLES 1997: HAPPY; PRIVATE EYES

Towa Tei is a Japanese keyboard playing turntablist who first found fame as part of post-disco sensations Deee-Lite; this musical maverick then forged a solo career that yielded much fine and idiosyncratic music. 'GBI' features the voice of Kylie Minogue over eccentric and playful beats; she sings from the perspective of a typeface. If this is some sort of obscure metaphorical device, I have to admit that it is completely lost on me… but so what. The effect of this stylised musical surrealism is pretty bizarre, but the record is joyously creative fun.

13
ALL MINE
PORTISHEAD
GO DISCS
OTHER SINGLE 1997: OVER

Punchy horns, heavily reverbed heavy beats, wah-wah guitar and the extraordinary voice of Beth Gibbons channeling her inner Shirley Bassey, make this a torch-song with all the dynamic impact of a James Bond theme… and yet, 'All Mine', for all its retro leanings, is given an unmistakably modernist sheen. Portishead's innate ability to stun and surprise was all present and correct.

12
COME TO DADDY
APHEX TWIN
WARP

According to Aphex Twin himself, this was made as a drunken time-wasting exercise, but somehow 'Come to Daddy' took on a life of its own and captured the attention of the public with its (way!) over-the-top theatrics; this aural *Hammer Horror* portrayed evil whilst wearing a knowing smirk. It has been suggested that this track was meant as a parody of 'Firestarter' by The Prodigy, and to me this theory does indeed make a lot of sense. However, it must also be pointed out that in spite of the joke element of the piece, it is actually a wicked slice of techno, propelled ever onward by a blurred flurry of beats, and when experienced in conjunction with the brilliant and hilarious video that accompanied the single, this became an absolute must hear, must see delight.

11
SONG 2
BLUR
FOOD
OTHER SINGLES 1997: BEETLEBUM; ON YOUR OWN; M.O.R.

'Song 2' was first recorded as a demo by Damon Albarn; it was slow and played acoustically, but crucially, it did feature the song's distinctive "Woo-hoo" chorus in a whistled form. Perceptively, Graham Coxon suggested that the song should be played loud as well as being sped up.

This was done, but during recording, Coxon played a deliberately crude guitar part; the band found this funny since it was a kind of sonic repudiation of the way in which they were perceived. As a joke, the record company was asked to release it as a single, with the presumption that they would deem it to be far too extreme, but curiously, the label were more than happy to oblige, and Blur had a huge hit on their hands. 'Song 2' was also the second track on their contemporaneous album, with a playing time of two minutes and two seconds; most appropriately, the single reached number two on the charts.

10

THE DRUGS DON'T WORK

THE VERVE

HUT

OTHER SINGLES 1997:

BITTERSWEET SYMPHONY; LUCKY MAN

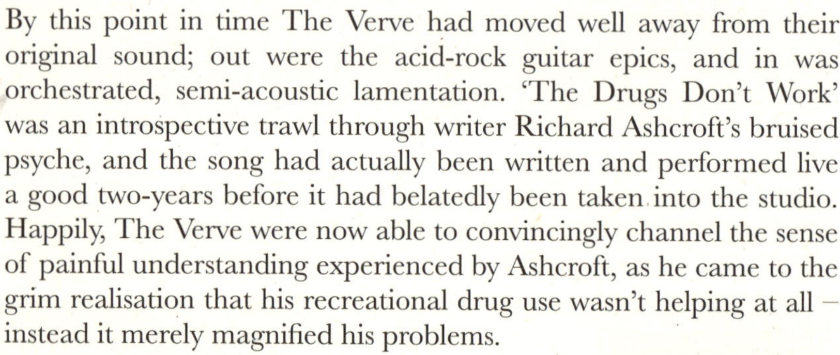

By this point in time The Verve had moved well away from their original sound; out were the acid-rock guitar epics, and in was orchestrated, semi-acoustic lamentation. 'The Drugs Don't Work' was an introspective trawl through writer Richard Ashcroft's bruised psyche, and the song had actually been written and performed live a good two-years before it had belatedly been taken into the studio. Happily, The Verve were now able to convincingly channel the sense of painful understanding experienced by Ashcroft, as he came to the grim realisation that his recreational drug use wasn't helping at all – instead it merely magnified his problems.

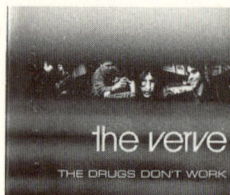

9

BLOCK ROCKIN' BEATS

CHEMICAL BROTHERS

FREESTYLE DUST

OTHER SINGLES 1997:

WHERE DO I BEGIN;

ELEKTROBANK; THE PRIVATE PSYCHEDELIC REEL

This is the kind of single that takes you by the throat, shakes you about and then slams you against the wall. Essentially it is an artfully mixed collection of samples, including enormous drum beats – from Bernard "Pretty" Purdie – which are aligned to a bass riff pilfered from 'Coup' by 23 Skidoo, topped-off by a vocal sample of an aggressive sounding Schoolly D, who proclaims "Back with another of those Block Rockin' Beats". This record whistles, squeals and bangs hard... very hard indeed.

8

TAKE A RUN AT THE SUN

DINOSAUR JR.

BLANCO Y NEGRO

Grace of My Heart was a film set in the Brill Building – New York's songwriting factory – and from the soundtrack came 'Take a Run at the Sun', which is a very un-Dinosaur Jr. sounding song. It came about when J Mascis decided to accept the challenge of providing music that these fictional songwriters could conceivably have composed at various stages of the ever-changing 1960s. Accordingly, 'Take a Run at the Sun' is a beautiful and wonderfully loving soundalike of *Pet Sounds*-era Beach Boys, replete with theremin effects and delightfully dreamy harmonies.

7

BITTERSWEET

LEWIS TAYLOR

ISLAND

This effortlessly cool track begins with a repeated piano note and just a hint of flute, synth and fuzzy guitar that soon give way to a sparse arrangement of drum and piano, along with the emotionally expressive baritone voice of Lewis Taylor. Then, more voices and an incredibly busy but tasteful bass line are added; interweaving with skill and precision, they build and build towards a climactic exultation. Every nuanced element here seems natural and unforced as the song flows along in a gracefully upward arc. In an interview, Aaliyah described 'Bittersweet' as the "perfect song", and she pretty much hit the bull's eye with that remark.

6

MAKES ME WANNA DIE

TRICKY

4TH & BROADWAY

With subdued beats and a mournful piano, we have here an intriguing song that is sung with beautiful hesitation by Martina Topley-Bird, performing the role of Tricky's distorted mirror image – she angelic and he demonic; Tricky himself remains a shady and barely audible background presence, whispering into Martina's ear as she sings. The song has a hypnotic quality, unchanging in mood… a kind of solemn, devotional mantra. It appears to be a song about the obsessive love of somebody or something, but who or what is not revealed; it remains a tantalisingly hidden secret that we are not privy to. But what we do know for certain is that this record is a pre-millennial blues classic.

5

AROUND THE WORLD

DAFT PUNK

VIRGIN

OTHER SINGLE 1997: BURNIN'

'Around the World' was taken from the album *Homework*, thus named due to the fact that Daft Punk recorded at home, quickly, cheaply and following impulse rather than becoming overly analytical. 'Around the World' exemplifies this working method; as it bursts through the speakers, this music feels alive with a wonderfully fresh sense of spontaneity. That it is also a sublime example of the makers' extraordinary musical gifts is also readily apparent. The track is elasticated disco magic, built around a bass line that seems to scream out the word "dance!" A sprinkling of keyboards adds a honey-sweet flavour to the unchanging beat , while the vocal contribution consists of the single phrase 'Around the World', repeated one hundred and forty-four times. Believe it or not, this is unbelievably catchy – heavenly joy somehow captured on vinyl.

4

INTO MY ARMS

NICK CAVE AND THE BAD SEEDS

MUTE

OTHER SINGLE 1997:

(ARE YOU) THE ONE I'VE BEEN WAITING FOR?

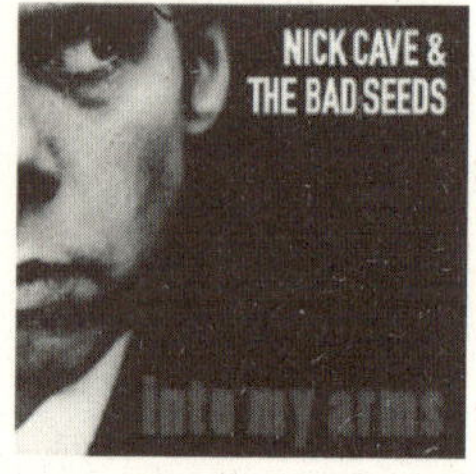

After the break-up of two hugely important relationships, Nick Cave was inspired to write this song of thwarted love, employing religious allegory to demonstrate the depth of his feeling. To further emphasise the sincerity of his words, he denies himself the cloak of musical artifice, stripping back the sound until all that remains is a simple piano melody, underpinned with minimal bass guitar. The song sounds like an appeal for forgiveness from a solitary man, with Cave's voice foregrounded. Eschewing his customary fire and brimstone approach, he sings humbly, with no props to fall back upon; just the simple, unadorned truth and his declarations of love… a plea from the soul for comfort and compassion, and an end to the suffering brought about by his deep desire.

3

PARANOID ANDROID

RADIOHEAD

PARLOPHONE

OTHER SINGLES 1997:

KARMA POLICE; LUCKY

For Radiohead, 'Paranoid Android' represented a great leap forward in their quest to escape the constraints of a formulaic style of song construction. They sought inspiration in The Beatles track 'Happiness is a Warm Gun', and structurally 'Paranoid Android' follows that example, being a fusion of three diverse sections edited together to create a six-and-a-half minute long piece that, for the most part, sprawls and shuffles along in a languorous, melodic mix of acoustic and electronic instrumentation. Tempo changes occur without ever being jarring, and the song changes pace and flows along in the manner of a car journey in mid-morning traffic. The lyric was triggered by an unpleasant experience in an L.A. bar, surrounded by a gaggle of hostile cocaine-fuelled yuppie types, and perhaps this explains why Thom Yorke sings like a depressed man who is perplexed by the realisation of his own simmering anger. All that remains is for a brief, furiously played and highly unorthodox guitar solo to bring this ambitious epic to a triumphant close.

2
RISINGSON
MASSIVE ATTACK
VIRGIN

Here we have Massive Attack stripped back to their core trio of 3D, Daddy G and Mushroom, with no guest vocalists to bring some light and sweetness to their deep, dark, dubby sound and introspective, often paranoic raps. The incorporation of a punk/new-wave influence is now evident as they serve up a monolithic, reverb-drenched, moody and atmospheric sound with an ominously prowling bass. The track is claustrophobic and full of deep, dark dread; it seems to relentlessly creep-up on the listener with nightmarish intent, before stopping dead in its tracks… only for a rat-tat-tat of the drums to set it lurching forward once more, redolent of Boris Karloff in *The Mummy*. This is a no-chorus song, without any obvious meaning, and yet it is absolutely compelling, with several individual lyrical phrases so potent that they stick like pins into the psyche. Although a chill wind definitely runs through 'Risingson', it is clear that there were no cobwebs in the work of these never complacent Bristolians.

1
BRIMFUL OF ASHA
CORNERSHOP
WIIIJA
OTHER SINGLE 1997:
GOOD SHIPS; WE'RE IN YR CORNER

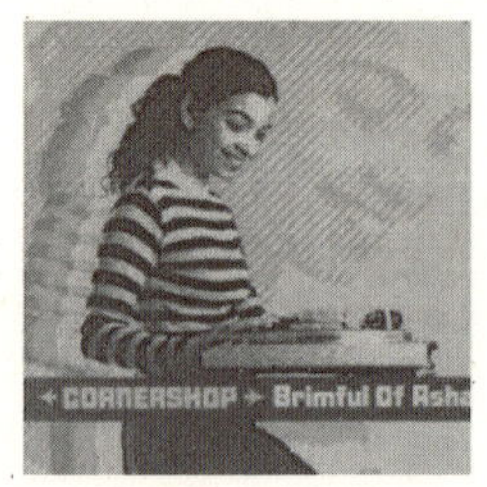

The absolutely pivotal music and dance scenes embedded within Bollywood films had left quite an impression upon Tjinder Singh, the singer and composer of Cornershop's 'Brimful of Asha'. Ostensibly, the song pays tribute to Asha Bhosle, the singer of over twelve thousand songs used for film scenes, but the fact that the word "asha" also means "hope" in Hindi, was utilised by Singh to widen the lyrical scope of the song to discuss the poverty, corruption and struggle that is an everyday fact of life for too many Indians. The song's narrator listens to Asha Bhosle records to provide hope and respite during hard and sorrowful times, so the chorus of "Everybody needs a bosom for a pillow, mine's on the forty-five" sums up the sentiment, which evokes the comfort provided by an optimistic record transmitting a sense of buoyancy and assurance, allowing the listener to feel less troubled, and thus able to find some sleep. The music here is essentially a simple Velvet Underground-style chugging riff, and it serves as the perfect accompaniment to Singh's upbeat vocal. This is an exciting and sunny record that is full of memorable hooks, and there are unlikely name checks for Marc Bolan, Jacques Dutronc and Trojan Records, illustrating the fact that the language of music is truly universal. Initially, Cornershop only scored a lowly number sixty hit with this beautiful record, but thankfully help was at hand; Norman Cook (aka Fatboy Slim) was so enamoured with the record that for no fee, he re-mixed the track, speeding it up and altering the pitch. Deservedly, it now took off; it was irresistible and all over the airwaves – thus, in 1998, Cornershop achieved a number one hit record. They didn't seem particularly pleased; a *Top of the Pops* appearance saw them looking positively glum-faced. I hope that with the passing of time, they can look back upon their magnificent achievement with much more affection..

1998

EVENTS

Around ten thousand people are killed in Afghanistan, due to earthquakes in the Takhar region.

A massacre in Likoshane starts the Kosovo war.

NASA announces that probes have shown the moon has enough water in polar craters to support a human colony.

The Good Friday Agreement is signed by the Irish and British governments, and all the major political parties in Northern Ireland, with the exception of the DUP; the hostilities that have plagued the province are officially ended.

Riots in Indonesia targeting Chinese Indonesians, kill approximately one thousand people.

France beat Brazil in Paris to win the World Cup.

More than two thousand die in an earthquake in Papua New Guinea.

The Second Congo War begins; it will continue until 2003 leaving over 5.4 million people dead.

In China, the Yangtze River floods; more than twelve thousand people are killed.

Osama bin Laden instigates terrorist attacks on United States embassies in Tanzania and Kenya; two hundred and twenty four people are killed, and four thousand five hundred injured.

Google Inc. is founded in California.

General Augusto Pinochet, the barbaric Chilean dictator, is arrested and charged with human rights violations whilst visiting the UK for medical treatment; his friend, Margaret Thatcher, is furious.

Hurricane Mitch makes landfall in central America, killing approximately eleven thousand people.

Russia and the USA commence the joint construction of the International Space Station.

President Bill Clinton is impeached for lying under oath when questioned about his affair with White House intern Monica Lewinsky.

Manchester United begin what will become a triumphant season, whilst Manchester City compete two divisions below them. As a sentimental gesture, Alex Ferguson loans (and then sells) the talented Terry Cooke to the Blues, and he goes on to spark their eventual promotion.

NOTABLE BIRTHS

Lisandro Martinez; Kylian Mbappé; Declan McKenna; Trent Alexander-Arnold

NOTABLE DEATHS

Sonny Bono; Michael Tippett; Carl Perkins; Carl Wilson; Enoch Powell; J.T. Walsh; Judge Dread; Cozy Powell; Wendy O. Williams; Tammy Wynette; Pol Pot; Linda McCartney; James Earl Ray; Carlos Castaneda; Eldridge Cleaver; Justin Fashanu; Frank Sinatra; Roy Rogers; Jackie Blanchflower; Akira Kurosawa; George Wallace; Gene Autry; Ted Hughes; Jean Marais; Stokely Carmichael; Roland Alphonso

NOTABLE FILMS

The Thin Red Line; The Big Lebowski; *Rushmore*; *Life is Beautiful*; *Saving Private Ryan*; *The Truman show*; *Antz*; *A Simple Plan*

NOTABLE BOOKS

Harry Potter and the Chamber of Secrets – J K Rowling
About a Boy – Nick Hornby
The Hours – Michael Cunningham
Inversions – Iain M. Banks
England, England – Julian Barnes
A Beautiful Mind – Sylvia Nasar
Blues Legacies and Black Feminism – Angela Y. Davis

MY 1998

It is often the case that calm comes before a storm, and so it was that my period of tranquility was nearing an end. The job I'd been working at for the previous twelve years became insecure; a new broom with new ideas was installed by the supermarket chain from whom we leased space, tasked with overseeing the endeavours of those to whom space was leased. Our ideological approach was now incompatible with the new working model being instituted, and so our position became untenable. Following a harsh exchange of words with this new broom, my employer took the decision to cease trading, which was something of a blow for him given that he was walking away from a profitable business. The landlords offered me the chance to take over, but my loyalty lay with the man who had been a good employer to me; I did not want to be seen to profit from his misfortune. In addition, because of my contribution to the success we had enjoyed, I had been offered a large sum of severance pay, in the event that our endeavour came to an end in precisely these sort of circumstances; I reasoned that, with such a sum of money, I could open a shop myself. But disappointingly, when push came to shove, the amount of money I received was only half of what I had been promised – it was still a relatively large sum, but the shortfall certainly compromised my options as I searched for shop premises.

Then, during the same period of time, my mother became ill; a small sore beneath one eye appeared that was dreadfully painful. I took her to a clinic, where her condition was deemed to be serious, and she was admitted to hospital with what was diagnosed as a very rare case of Erysipelas, a bacterial infection with parasitic flesh eating properties. Soon, half of my mother's body was an open sore, which was horrible and terrifying. She was in a living hell and spoke to me of wanting to die. I visited her every day as she lay in her hospital bed, and one evening my brother said to me that he thought she wouldn't be able to last for much longer. Obviously, I shared his thoughts, but the effect of them being verbalised reduced me to emotional rubble – I broke down and sobbed uncontrollably. Amidst all of this turmoil, I diligently searched for shop premises to open my very own fruit and vegetable business, and finally found a suitable – and just about affordable – shop to let in Hazel Grove, Stockport. That same evening, I visited my mother and told her my news… "I'm naming it after my dad" I said, "it's going to be called Mr. Ed's". For the first time in a long while, she smiled; she had missed my dad so much since his death. "Let's get you out of here to see it", I continued, adding that "I'm ordering the sign tomorrow". Although in the grand scheme of things, this was only a tiny little thing, I saw how much it gave my mum the motivation to continue, and before the shop opened, my mother was finally released from the hospital where she had been for five long months.

It was decided that I should move into her house in order to help her, whilst simultaneously selling my own home for an injection of much needed funds. An ambulance brought my mum home, and the neighbours came out onto the street to welcome her back. Following her illness, she was terribly weak and physically impaired, but she sat in her favourite armchair, home at last. Less than one hour later, I saw her face drop unnaturally – it was unmistakably a stroke, so immediately back to the hospital she went. Thankfully, she did recover from this awful setback, and, a few weeks later, I opened my shop. Shortly afterwards, mum was well enough to be driven over for a tour of the new premises; the joy that the outing gave to her lifted my own depleted spirits, and with hope and optimism I set about the task of running the shop. It was not an easy job; I rose at three o'clock in the morning to go to the market and buy produce. I then unloaded, set-up the shop, and was generally never home before six o'clock in the evening – in other words, I was working a fifteen-hour day, six days per week, with all the paperwork on top. On the plus side, I was making a small profit; "It will get better", I told myself…

Of the gigs I saw this year the best were: Spiritualized at Manchester Uni; Mercury Rev at Manchester Uni; Pulp/Eels at Manchester Apollo and Massive Attack at Manchester Apollo.

I have to say that 1998 provided a wealth of great singles. To select the 100 tracks I will discuss, I whittled down my long-list of over four hundred releases, to a short-list of two hundred, from which, the choices I eventually made, required many hours of angst-filled deliberation!

100
BEAT GOES ON
THE ALL SEEING I
EARTH

The All Seeing I were a group from Sheffield who provided yet more substance to the Steel City's reputation for spawning exceptional and experimental electronic music. This first single was a cover of the Sonny Bono written hit-record for Sonny & Cher. Here, the groove is stretched out, accentuating certain sounds, and a simple, steady beat is added. Also included is a sampled vocal taken from Buddy Rich's version of the song, and it all goes together to create a fabulously cool track that drew the attention of Britney Spears's management team, who then asked The All Seeing I to produce yet another version of the song, which subsequently appeared on her debut album.

99
MASQUERADE
THE FALL
ARTFUL

The first Fall single in two years – and the first in two decades without Craig Scanlon – found the group, if not quite at the top of their game, still interesting and relevant. Co-composer Julia Nagle plays keyboards that sound uncannily like a *Space Invaders* game, while the rest of the band simply chug along as Mark E. Smith, his voice showing clear signs of wear and tear, makes obscurely gnomic utterances that may or may not allude to the group's desperate financial situation. A child's voice then interjects, offering a modicum of clarity, before the song comes to a close. Ok, this was not of the calibre of former triumphs, but it was yet another single by The Fall that reinforced their proud status of standing defiantly in opposition to any and all prevailing trends.

98
COLOURED CITY
LAURENT GARNIER
F COMMUNICATIONS

Finely machined techno and a human voice are simply put together, and the combination is totally arresting. This adrenalised music is perfect underneath a mirror ball, but just as good blasting through headphones whilst walking betwixt monolithic tower blocks in the stark urban landscape of the city streets.

97
RUDE BOY ROCK
LIONROCK
TIME BOMB RECORDNGS
FURTHER NOTEWORTHY SINGLE 1998: SCATTER AND SWING

In sampling 'Nimrod', a 1965 ska single by The Skatalites, British act Lionrock set about adapting it for a late twentieth-century audience.

Electronic adornments add to the sonic palate, and the swinging, horn-based track is welded to a big, bold beat. This track is audacious, brash and brimful of sparkling effervescence; it has an uplifting sound that was guaranteed to put smiles on faces and get the party started with a bang.

96
GIMME SOME MORE
BUSTA RHYMES
ELEKTRA
OTHER SINGLE 1998:
TEAR DA ROOF OFF

Regular sidekick DJ Scratch produces this track, and he mixes his beats with a violin sample taken from the classic Alfred Hitchcock film *Psycho*. It is a brilliant piece of music, but Busta Rhymes is certainly up to the task of matching it with an explosively rapped vocal. His breathless, high-speed rhyming flow is incredible, not just in terms of rapidity, but also in the clarity of the rhymes, with not a single word blurred. On this great track, Rhymes rides the rhythms with ease, and with a very evident sense of humour.

95
GO DEEP
JANET JACKSON
VIRGIN
OTHER SINGLES 1998:
YOU; EVERY TIME;
LUV ME, LUV ME; PIECE OF
MY HEART; I GET LONELY

Janet Jackson's 1997 album *The Velvet Rope*, was written, produced and conceived by Jackson herself, along with Jimmy Jam and Terry Lewis; it pushed R&B into places it had never been before and became the benchmark for others to follow. A raft of hit singles came from it, including 'Go Deep', a risqué number that moves from dance-floor to bedroom, with the singer always wielding the power and exercising control. The track has a positively rude and funky feel, through which Jackson's seductive and silken purr dances entrancingly in and out.

94
FREE SATPAL RAM
ASIAN DUB FOUNDATION
PHASE 4

Satpal Ram visited an Indian restaurant in Birmingham one night in 1986 with two friends; six white men attacked them, and Ram was glassed in the face with a broken bottle. Forced to fight back, he stabbed his assailant who was then taken to hospital, but the man refused treatment and later died of his injury. Subsequently, Satpal Ram was convicted of murder by an all-white jury, who could not understand his defence because he spoke Bengali and no interpreter was provided to translate; in short, he became yet another victim of the racism inherent in the British justice system. By issuing this angry and potent single which details the facts of the case, Asian Dub Foundation bravely took it upon themselves to campaign for justice and call for the release of Satpal Ram.

93

FURIOUS ANGELS
ROB DOUGAN
CHEEKY

Australian Rob Dougan was a re-mixer who professed not to like re-mixes; he was also associated with the dance scene… but his music wasn't really danceable. His true passion seemed to be orchestral scores – but even these he would twist into new shapes by introducing elements of blues, trip-hop and electronica. 'Furious Angels' is a dark, atmospheric mix of electronics, strings and beats, with Dougan providing a spooked vocal performance with deep and ominous lyrics. This is startlingly good, extremely powerful music that has a compellingly apocalyptic feel.

92
EURODISCO
BIS
WIIIJA

For those who tend to take both music and themselves far too seriously, Bis were the spawn of the devil; their crime was to make records that were purely for fun, just because they were bright, cheerful and absolutely loved pop music. For 'Eurodisco', the group adopt a tuneful and energetic electro-pop dance groove that is chipper and chirpy, choc-full of oohs and aahs, and has even more than the requisite quantity of bounce to the ounce – and in my view, there is nothing whatsoever wrong with that.

91
I'M LONELY
HOLLIS P. MONROE
JIVE

This deep house classic had been around for a couple of years before the *Jive* label gave it a major release. The track comes replete with a hip-shaking, snaking bass groove, gospel-style church organ and minimal electronics, and even before Monroe begins to sing, the listener is fully engaged. But when he does appear, his voice is high in the mix, and it feels like he is delivering the emotional lyric to you and you alone. Everything is so very real and raw, and yet somehow tasteful and artistic at the same time. 'I'm Lonely' has a sound highly reminiscent of the great records released by Jamie Principle on *Trax Records* in the original heyday of house music; in other words, it is a gem.

90
SAD CUNT
THE CREATURES
SIOUX
OTHER SINGLE 1998:
ERAZER CUT; 2ND FLOOR

Alongside their day-job as part of Siouxsie and the Banshees, the pair of singer Siouxsie and drummer Budgie indulged the more quixotic elements of their artistry with The Creatures. Here, we find them experimenting with what the limits of a pop single can be as they employ a potent mix of African-influenced percussion, harsh electronica and acoustic guitar, alongside Siouxsie's voice – as recognisable as ever, but somehow improved with age… less strident, more nuanced – ending up with something akin to dubby, electric country blues. 'Sad Cunt' is a fabulous song with an insistent vocal hook, and shorn of its provocative title, it may very well have been a hit. However, The Creatures had morphed into something that existed well outside of the mainstream, and compromise was simply not an option.

89
TOO FAR
KYLIE MINOGUE
BMG
DECONSTRUCTION
OTHER SINGLE 1998:
BREATHE

Further demonstrating the extent to which she had taken creative control over her own work, 'Too Far' was composed entirely by Kylie Minogue, who also co-produced the track with Brothers in Rhythm. Over drum & bass beats and a recurring piano motif, Kylie speaks the introduction to the song in rapid-fire style, and the vocals then continue in this hurried manner as if she is desperate for her words to be heard; she sings about the chaos and confusion in her life which leave her feeling a strong sense of claustrophobia. The whole piece is brilliantly conceived and superbly executed, with its raw edges and huge emotional charge.

88
TRAVELLIN' MAN
DJ HONDA
RELATIVITY

A sample from 'Whatever's Fair' by Jerry Butler is used here to provide a smooth, 1970s soul-flavouring for 'Travelling' Man', which features Mos Def on vocals. This is a rich and warm sounding record, and Mos Def is talented enough to deliver an effortlessly mesmerising rap as he quotes from John Denver's 'Leaving on a Jet Plane', perfectly capturing the emotional wrench of leaving people and places behind when the urge to undertake a journey of self-discovery is just too strong to resist.

87
CAN'T LET GO
LUCINDA WILLIAMS
MERCURY
OTHER SINGLE 1998:
RIGHT IN TIME

Lucinda Williams was highly respected; her talent was undoubted, but it took until her fifth album, *Car Wheels on a Gravel Road*, for her to create a truly commanding piece of work that would fully showcase her gifts – and it justly became a commercial success and critical sensation. 'Can't Let Go' was taken from the album, and it conjures up the atmosphere of the honky-tonk joints in the American south with uncanny accuracy. The song was written by Randy Weeks, who had been asked by Williams if he was agreeable to her recording it, after she heard him perform it live. In her hands, 'Can't Let Go' became a barnstorming *chugga-chugga* mover, a rhythmic to-and-fro toe-tapper that even people who claim not to like country music find irresistible. Williams sings the bittersweet lyric of clinging on to a failing love affair with the resigned air of a woman who knows that she's only postponing the inevitable… but like a veteran rodeo rider, she's not letting go until she finally gets thrown.

86
CEMENT MIXER
CLINIC
ALADDIN'S CAVE OF GOLF
OTHER SINGLE 1998:
MONKEY ON YOUR BACK

Nodding towards Laurie Anderson's 'O Superman' with the "Ah, ah, ah, ah" opening, we then crash artfully into a Dadaist collision of cryptic verse and thrilling, visceral noise. Clinic immediately won my heart with 'Cement Mixer' and I couldn't wait to see them. When that happy moment arrived, and they appeared on stage in surgical scrubs and masks, producing their wondrous *Cadbury's Smash* men version of rock and roll, I, for one, was truly hooked for life.

85
PLEASE HEAR MR. FLIGHT CONTROL
THE MUSIC TAPES
ELEPHANT 6

The Music Tapes was a vehicle for Julian Koster – a member of the Elephant 6 collective – to create and release his own music. Also a member of Neutral Milk Hotel, Koster blended his narrative lyrics with a *musique concrète* style, often created on self-invented instruments. 'Please Hear Mr. Flight Control' begins as a fairly straightforward and somewhat twee acoustic strum, before taking-off – in extremely lo-fi fashion – with a vertically skyward trajectory. This totally beguiling record is gleefully childlike in its enthusiastic approximation of flying.

84
STAY
BERNARD BUTLER
CREATION
OTHER SINGLES 1998: NOT ALONE; A CHANGE OF HEART

The eagerly anticipated debut solo single by Bernard Butler clearly demonstrated two things; firstly, it showcased the grandiosity that set Suede apart during his tenure as guitarist and musical creator. With 'Stay', he takes a lilting acoustic ballad and builds it up into a relentless and dynamic wall of sound… it is an absolutely glorious piece of music. But secondly, it proved that however astounding a musician he was, he was not a convincing vocalist. Suede had often been compared to Ziggy-era David Bowie, and like Mick Ronson before him, Butler seemed somehow unsuited to the demands of a solo career. Suede had undeniably suffered from the loss of Bernard Butler; their songs, which had once skipped, now just seemed to plod along. But equally, Butler's music missed the subversion and theatricality that Brett Anderson had brought to the party. 'Stay' was excellent – perhaps Butler's best ever solo track – but if it had been recorded with Anderson, it may well have been immortal.

83
THIRTYSIXTWENTYFIVE
FOUR TET
OUTPUT
OTHER SINGLE 1998:
MISNOMER

Kieran Hebden, one-third of post-rock outfit Fridge, chose Four Tet as the moniker for his solo project, and this debut single took its title from the length of the track… thirty-six minutes and twenty-five seconds. It is an instrumental piece that is highly suitable for insomniacs; a musical journey that fuses trip-hop beats, atmospheric brain food and cool, cerebral jazz.

82
THE MILITIA
GANG STARR
NOO TRYBE

DJ Premier serves up a deliciously head-banging beat, and his Gang Starr partner Guru is joined for rapped cameos by the utterly ferocious Freddie Foxxx (aka Bumpy Knuckles) and original Gang Starr member Big Shug. Taking turns at the microphone, they illuminate us with their quick-witted insights while celebrating their union in very fine style.

81
AVA ADORE
SMASHING PUMPKINS
HUT
OTHER SINGLE 1998: PERFECT

Smashing Pumpkins were becoming increasingly experimental, and here, with the incorporation of a looped drum track that chugs along like a locomotive, they have the perfect springboard for ricocheting guitar and a dramatic vocal from Billy Corgan. So, without sacrificing any of their art-rock leanings, the addition of electronics within their arsenal – along with a swoon-worthy chorus – made 'Ava Adore' a really fabulous pop record.

80
BLACK ICE
GOODIE MOB FEATURING OUTKAST
LAFACE
OTHER SINGLES 1998:
THEY DON'T DANCE NO MO';
WATCH FOR THE HOOK

Goodie Mob member Big Gipp was working alone on the writing of 'Black Ice'; close by, OutKast were working on a new album… and so it came to pass that they were recruited to add verses to Gipp's existing work. What they created together is a mellow, Southern-fried rap workout that has something of a psychedelic edge to it, as Big Gipp begins to outline a tale concerned with succumbing to pharmaceutical temptation. The simmering heat begins to rise further as Big Boi handles a verse, but then

André 3000 takes a turn at the mic and leaves the track in smoke and flames as he deliriously quotes from William Shakespeare's *Julius Caesar* in a descriptive rap masterclass.

79
WHO DO YOU LOVE
MOJAVE 3
4AD
OTHER SINGLE 1998:
SOME KINDA ANGEL

Magically managing to locate the "Wild mercury sound" – as Bob Dylan so memorably described the sonics of his masterpiece *Blonde on Blonde* – Mojave 3 use it to further enrich 'Who do You Love'; so what was already a fine song is graced with the added lustre of a haunting organ part and punctuating guitars. The track just begs for an elegantly nuanced vocal… and happily it receives just that, along with the strains of a Tijuana-style trumpet. In summary, this is a great record of elegance and very good taste.

78
EL PRESIDENT
DRUGSTORE
ROADRUNNER

Drugstore were a London-based band whose sound straddled both britpop and dream pop; they were led by Brazilian singer/songwriter Isabel Monteiro and they toured as a support act for Radiohead. Thom Yorke was somewhat taken with them, and so agreed to duet on 'El President', a song in tribute to Salvador Allende, the democratically-elected Marxist President of Chile, who was undemocratically ousted in a coup by the Chilean military, covertly backed by the CIA. Allende was reported to have committed suicide… but it is much more likely that he was summarily executed on the same day as the coup. A mournful cello and acoustic guitar begin the record, preparing the way for the emotional, sorrowful and angry voices of Monteiro and Yorke to plainly state the facts, describing soldiers hurtling in on helicopters and leaving the President dead.

77
SUNSHINE + GASOLINE
GODSPEED YOU!
BLACK EMPEROR
aMAZEzine!

Canadians Godspeed You! Black Emperor had released only one album before this single emerged, so their ascent into becoming one of the most potent and important post-rock outfits had really only just begun; nevertheless, even at this early stage of development, everything is firmly in place. A voice recording of an ex-carnival worker talking about circus freaks – and the freaks in mainstream society – is unsettling and discomforting; how do we feel about its use here? Immediately we are put on the spot… what can we conclude from this content? We are forced to confront the issue of censorship and to question any deep-rooted prejudice that we may have. And while we ponder these questions, a tidal wave of sound washes over us; it is a majestic, mysterious and unfaltering sound, full of depth and restrained power… a sound as mighty as the roar of a turbulent ocean.

76
ADRENALINE
THE ROOTS
MCA

Because of their use of live instruments, The Roots from Philadelphia had a very different sound to most hip-hop acts; throw into the mix the eclecticism, and they became a unique proposition indeed. 'Adrenaline' is a really stripped-back affair, featuring a stabbed piano and a hard beat; the track is jolting, percussive and gritty. Lyrically, we hear Malik B, Dice Raw and Beanie Sigel running riot, blasting all and sundry within their field of vision, before joining forces for the truly adrenalised choruses.

75
HELD
SMOG
DRAG CITY
OTHER SINGLE 1998: EX CON

When I discovered Smog, it was love at first hearing… and since then, I have never once been disappointed with a Smog record. 'Held' is based upon a stomping riff, over which a synthesiser buzzes away, whilst the deep voice of Bill Callahan sings droll but poetically downbeat lyrics. This devastatingly simple track is essentially an update on the Delta blues, but carried-off with such wonderful panache that the only sane conclusion is that Bill Callahan is possessed by a rare touch of genius.

74
LITTLE BLACK ROCKS IN THE SUN
ADD N TO (X)
MUTE

An ominous vocoder announcement introduces 'Little Black Rocks in the Sun', which then begins in restrained fashion with a mesmerising drum pattern dominating the sound. There is an aural fog of synthesiser drone with bleeps and squalls of electronic noise suggestive of deep-space. Then the vocoder announcer returns again as the track twists, warps and changes shape; the beat completely alters and furious machine noises are emitted while the pitch shifts upwards. When the beat eventually ceases, the droning machines continue to emit frightful sounds that wrap around each other until… silence; the plugs are pulled and the trip is over. Wow, what a record!

73
HAND IN YOUR HEAD
MONEY MARK
MO' WAX
OTHER SINGLE 1998:
MAYBE I'M DEAD

Mark Ramos Nishita – aka Money Mark – was principally renowned as a keyboard-playing studio collaborator of The Beastie Boys; in 1995 he had released a solo album of organ workouts, but now he upped his game, and his second album, *Push The Button*, was a much more pop-flavoured and funky affair. 'Hand in Your Head' was the lead single; it has a bright, sunny sound with jazzy keyboard inflections, while Money Mark sings in a pleasant and relaxed style, and there is a very appealing strut amidst its slinky, finger-snapping grooves.

72
END TO END BURNERS
COMPANY FLOW
RAWKUS

Company Flow was a New York hip-hop trio; their sound was unorthodox and 'End to End Burners' is a mind-blowing mixture of abstract art, tough beats and lyrics that are sprayed like graffiti onto a canvas of subway trains and tenement blocks. This is hip-hop of extreme intensity, pushing at the limits of the genre to find new pathways to explore.

71
NEVER ENDING
MATH EQUATION
MODEST MOUSE
UP

'Never Ending Math Equation' seems to be saying something about the universe and time, and concluding that we, as individuals, get lost within cycles of endless repetition, *and* in the general vastness of infinity. To me, it says "Don't take everything so seriously (especially myself); just get on with living as best you can". This philosophical discourse takes place over a tic-toc rhythm and an elliptical guitar riff. This is a quietly ambitious song – quirky for sure, but extremely cool regardless.

70
THE POISONED WELL
QUASI
MATADOR

Quasi were a band from Portland, Oregon, consisting of ex-spouses Janet Weiss on drums (formerly of Sleater-Kinney) and Sam Coomes, a multi-instrumentalist who had been in the band Heatmiser alongside Elliott Smith, who is actually the subject of 'The Poisoned Well'. This is a mid-paced, piano-led ballad that is beautifully enhanced by a delightful George Harrison-style lead guitar, whilst Coomes sings, in a disarming manner, the sad, bittersweet and poignant lyrics… "We went through Hell, just to get to Hell" being one such example.

69
JE PENSE À TOI
AMADOU & MARIAM
POLYDOR

Amadou and Mariam are a couple from Bamako in Mali. Both blind from a young age, they met at the Mali Institute for the Young Blind and bonded over a shared passion for music. They initially made a name for themselves by playing sparse, Malian blues, but over a period of time, their music became more expansive. From 1996 onwards, they based themselves in Paris, and the re-location saw them achieve a French radio hit with 'Je Pense à Toi' – which translates as 'I Think of You'. It is a gently lilting song that features hand drums, violin and majestically played guitar, all entwining beautifully, and with Amadou's keening vocal to the fore, as Mariam harmonises, this is absolutely exquisite music.

68
CRACKING UP
THE JESUS AND MARY CHAIN
CREATION
OTHER SINGLE 1998:
I LOVE ROCK 'N' ROLL

Back on Creation Records, where it had all begun for them, brothers Jim and William Reid were barely on speaking terms, but nonetheless 'Cracking Up' is a fully cohesive slice of avant-garde rock and roll. Underpinned by a sinister sounding guitar riff that is given plenty of space inside a minimalist framework that includes simple bass, drums and just a smidgen of piano, this echoes like an empty urban subway in the darkness. A beautifully considered vocal, further enhancing outsider credentials, is then the icing on the cake of yet another Jesus and Mary Chain classic.

67
HARD KNOCK LIFE (Ghetto Anthem)
JAY-Z
DEF JAM
OTHER SINGLES 1998: CAN I GET A…; MONEY, CASH, HOES; WISHING ON A STAR

For rap artistes aiming for big hits and mainstream acceptance, it had become *de rigueur* to sample a recognisable 1970s or 1980s pop hit… but Jay-Z added a bit of a twist to the practice by plundering a Broadway show-tune – namely 'It's the Hard Knock Life' from *Annie* – and this attention-grabbing ploy earned him his biggest hit up to that point in time. The sweet saccharine of the childrens' sampled voices are an ironic counter-point to the tough, regimented beat and the harshness expressed in Jay-Z's lyricism.

66
ONLY WHEN I LOSE MYSELF
DEPECHE MODE
MUTE

'Only When I Lose Myself' is a wistful song that is favoured with a cinematic, trip-hop treatment, somewhat similar to releases by Andrea Parker and Rob Dougan. Along with producer Tim Simenon, Depeche Mode create a sweeping and majestic soundscape, while singer Dave Gahan sensitively narrates a lyric concerning painful self-examination and inner realisation.

65
HIDEAWAY
THE OLIVIA TREMOR CONTROL
FLYDADDY

Black Foliage, the second album by The Olivia Tremor Control, was every bit as bold, ambitious and sometimes downright overwhelming as had been their preceding album, *Dusk at Cubist Castle*; despite this, it still managed to yield this near-perfect pop single – two and a half minutes of Beach Boys-style bliss that contains a barrage of different instruments, perfectly melded to create an awe-inspiring and uplifting wall of sound. Considering how many contrasting elements are interwoven into the song, 'Hideaway' is remarkably cohesive, and it is topped-off with a concise lyric which advocates truthfulness as a way of coping with hurt and distress.

64
APRIL FOOLS
RUFUS WAINWRIGHT
DREAMWORKS

'April Fools' was the debut single by Rufus Wainwright – the son of Loudon Wainwright lll and Kate McGarrigle, and brother to Martha Wainwright. So, we obviously have here an exceptionally musically talented family… but Rufus is very much the glittering star of the Wainwright tribe, and this single serves as a fine introduction to his œuvre. It is a love ballad rendered from the point of view of an outsider looking in at the ludicrous oddities of the mating game. Led by pounding piano and surrounded by pretty chocolate-box ornamentation, Rufus unveils a musical style in which the influence of cabaret show-tunes is highly prominent. As for his vocal contribution, again we find an artist significantly at odds with prevailing trends; he sings with an impudent, frothy charm, and I have to concede that I did become ever so slightly obsessed with Rufus Wainwright; he was a great performer, and his subsequent recordings have figured hugely in my listening pleasure throughout the years.

63
COME ON
NEW POWER GENERATION
NPG

Written, sung and produced by Prince, this New Power Generation single also featured Chaka Khan on backing vocals. It is a slinky, slow and funky jam that is uplifted by the writer's mastery of the pop form, and from start to finish it is well supplied with ornate flourishes and unobtrusive, yet irresistible hooks. As a statement single, this did not scream genius in the manner of 'Kiss' or 'When Doves Cry', but if you get close enough, this is a record that can warmly caress you whilst whispering seductively in your ear.

62
NICKI LIGHTHOUSE
OF MONTREAL
100 GUITAR MANIA

'Nicki Lighthouse' wanders around town doing harmless things in her own unique way; but the boring people say she is the strangest person there has ever been and they just don't like her. Fortunately, the song's narrator is a big fan and is unafraid to say so. This is a super charming record, performed in lovely lo-fi fashion by members of the Elephant 6 collective – calling themselves Of Montreal – who emerged from Athens, Georgia.

61
REVOLUTION 909
DAFT PUNK
VIRGIN

'Revolution 909' was the fifth and final single extracted from *Homework*, Daft Punk's debut album, and it is a rebuke to the French government for attempting to suppress – through a mixture of ignorance and fear – the burgeoning rave scene. Opening with the sound of police sirens and a megaphone announcement telling people to go home, what follows is a pounding, repetitive dance vamp that rises, falls and rises again. Although probably released only as a holding operation before new material was available, this nevertheless has the Daft Punk signature sound of quality attached, meaning that it is still a thumpingly good record.

60
BANANA CHIPS
SHONEN KNIFE
UNIVERSAL

Japanese all-female punk rock trio Shonen Knife unashamedly borrowed the style of The Ramones – a reality that they have never tried to disguise; in fact, they do occasionally play gigs as the *Osaka Ramones*. The release of 'Banana Chips' revealed a magical melding of speedy riffing and an absurdist, but absolutely captivating lyric, served up in a sub-three-minute timing. This energetic anthem to fried banana is simply sizzlingly hot.

59
INTERGALACTIC
BEASTIE BOYS
GRAND ROYAL
OTHER SINGLES 1998:
BODY MOVIN';
THE NEGOTIATION
LIMERICK FILE

'Intergalactic' gave Beastie Boys their only ever UK top-five hit record, and it contains strong elements of the electronic sounds that were so popular at the start of their career. As usual, they shout out their very funny and satirical raps, though it should be stressed that it was never the case that Beastie Boys were a novelty act; on the contrary, their beats hit hard and their rapping is crisp and very much on-point. Personally, I often consider them to be the missing link between Public Enemy and Frank Zappa…

58
JUST DON'T GIVE A FUCK
EMINEM
AFTERMATH

1998 was the year when Eminem first made waves with both his debut single, 'Just Don't Give a Fuck', and the *Slim Shady* EP from which it was taken. The song samples 'I Don't Give a Fuck' by Tupac, and it is the first introduction to the Slim Shady character which Eminem created as an *alter ego*, thus allowing him to say the unsayable. During the second verse, Eminem dismisses fellow white rappers Vanilla Ice, Everlast and Miilkbone as his inferiors – of course, he was perfectly correct with this assessment. His lyrics are vicious, but funny, and his flow is relaxed and natural; at one point he states "This is the sneak preview", and indeed 'Just Don't Give a Fuck' does act as such, being the launch pad for an incredible talent that would be fully unleashed over the course of the next few years.

57
IF ONLY
QUEENS OF THE STONE AGE
LOOSE GROOVE
OTHER SINGLE 1998: BEAVER

Debuting this year with what remains (perhaps?) their finest single, were Queens of the Stone Age, who evolved out of stoner rock band Kyuss. Led by singer, guitarist and songwriter Josh Homme, the group came roaring out of the blocks with 'If Only', which borrows Ron Asheton's monster riff from the Stooges 'I Wanna be Your Dog', but they add to it a hypnotic, grooving sensibility, and a lyric concerned with the highs and lows that come from drug usage.

56
A PERFECT DAY ELISE
PJ HARVEY
ISLAND

Drums and stunning bass are heavily to the fore on 'A Perfect Day Elise', on which Polly Harvey uses her striking voice to great story-telling effect as she articulates a tale about the titular figure of Elise who is murdered by drowning because she spurns the unwanted advances of Joe – who goes on to take his own life with a gun. This is a more obviously produced record than we had previously heard from Harvey, with strings and sound effects employed to enhance the fatalism of the song; she was clearly expanding her musical horizon and moving forward as an artist of immense depth and talent.

55
OUTSIDE
GEORGE MICHAEL
EPIC

In April 1998 George Michael was arrested in Beverly Hills – whilst cruising for sex in a public toilet – by a plain-clothes police officer masquerading as a consensual participant in the act. Michael was convicted of this misdemeanour in what amounted to a very public attempt at shaming him. His response came via this single which celebrates *al fresco* sex and directly references his arrest, aiming to remove some of the scandalous stigma attached to homosexuality in general, and his own in particular. It is also a marvellous record in its own right, without any of the luggage being attached; jubilant in tone, this is a funky, disco celebration, awash with strings that hark back to the Philly-sound of the 1970s, plus some very contemporary electronic bleeps as well. Throw in George Michael's always sumptuous singing voice – and a tongue-in-cheek video that parodies the whole affair with cheeky élan – and the result is a fabulous piece of art that speaks volumes about sexual repression and casts a very favourable light on the media vilified singer.

54
ALL MY GHOSTS
FRANK BLACK
& THE CATHOLICS
PLAY IT AGAIN SAM
OTHER SINGLES 1998:
I GOTTA MOVE
DOG GONE

The album from which 'All My Ghosts' was lifted took all of two days to record; its raw and immediate sound unnerved the record label and an eighteen-month long dispute ensued, before the record was finally released. But 'All My Ghosts' really benefits from the warts-'n'-all approach to recording; it is imperfectly crunching garage rock that has incredible presence, and, as a consequence, is fabulously refreshing. The guitars are stunning, the drums thump like heavyweight boxers, the harmony vocals are rather lovely and the lead vocal by Frank Black is intensely emotional and wired.

53
ONE MORE HOUR
SLEATER-KINNEY
KILL ROCK STARS
OTHER SINGLE 1998:
L LITTLE BABIES

Sleater-Kinney founders Carrie Brownstein and Corin Tucker had been in a private romantic relationship that had eventually broken down. Without permission, they were outed in a controversial article printed by *Spin Magazine*; deeply upset by this invasion of privacy, they set about writing and recording *Dig Me Out* – their third album – from which 'One More Hour' was taken. It is an emotionally-charged commentary on their break-up, featuring incredible vocal interplay between the pair, as a clearly hurt Tucker cries out "I needed it", whilst a more stable-voiced Brownstein offers consolation. Fired-up by a crackerjack drum performance from new band member Janet Weiss, as well as the all-guitar/no-bass attack of Tucker and Brownstein, this is as visceral a slice of alternative music as one could ever wish for.

52
AQUARIUS
BOARDS OF CANADA
SKAM

'Aquarius' begins with a slap-bass sample taken from the song of the same name on the soundtrack of the film *Hair*, and then vocal samples from episodes of *Sesame Street* are added; if you think that sounds a bit peculiar, then you are correct. The track seems to hang in the sky like a kite, only grounded by an unchanging beat, until the final few bars of the song when it becomes more strident. This is subtle psychedelic music, suggestive of a child's tea party taking place in outer space; in 1960s jargon, I guess we could say it is totally outasight!

51
1982
MISS KITTIN & THE HACKER
LOW SPIRIT RECORDINGS

French duo Caroline Hervé and Michel Amato were re-christened as Miss Kittin and The Hacker, and '1982' was their debut single. It is an early example of electroclash, a mash-up of techno and trash glam that was both decadent and fun, and it captures the aesthetic perfectly. The track is built upon a basic, but highly effective, synth riff and there is a simple name-checking lyric that salutes the likes of Depeche Mode, Soft Cell and Kraftwerk, while simultaneously lampooning the whole synth-pop scene that spawned them. This is a highly self-aware, but curiously loving track; a great listen and perfect beneath the mirror ball as well.

50
MONKEY DEAD
SUNHOUSE
INDEPENDIENTE
OTHER SINGLE 1998: ANIMAL

Sunhouse were a band from the Midlands led by songwriter Gavin Clarke; he had befriended film-maker Shane Meadows whilst the pair worked in dead-end jobs at the Alton Towers amusement park. Fast-forward a few years and Meadows contacted Clarke to ask him to provide songs for the soundtrack of his film *Small Time*. This gave Clarke the incentive which led to the formation of Sunhouse, whose music found a home in my heart on very first hearing. 'Monkey Dead' is an acoustic guitar and organ shuffle, topped by a wearily introspective vocal that is exceptionally profound due to its great articulation and sincerity.

49
MULDER AND SCULLY
CATATONIA
BLANCO Y NEGRO
OTHER SINGLES 1998:
ROAD RAGE; GAME ON;
STRANGE GLUE

The X-Files was an enormously popular TV series and the principal characters in the show were FBI agents Mulder and Scully; so, the fact that this song bore their name and used them as archetypes to represent everyone who is involved in a strange relationship, was bound to attract attention. But there is much more to this song than just the name-dropping; it rocks without forsaking melody, it has absolutely killer pop-hooks and the proudly unaffected Welshness of Cerys Matthews marvellous singing voice is yet another plus.

48
LIAR
ROYAL TRUX
DOMINO
OTHER SINGLE 1998:
I'M READY

The four-track EP that spawned 'Liar' found Royal Trux at their imperious best; never before had they sounded so focused and exhilarating. 'Liar' is dirty and scuzzy outsider rock & roll and it dares to do things that other groups wouldn't even have thought about. Parts of it sound like they are playing inside a tumble-dryer, whereas other sections are blessed with vivid clarity, in which the guitars are toothpick sharp and the vocals are spat out as inflammatory remarks aimed at ruffling feathers or inciting an altercation.

47
I WISH YOU WERE A GIRL
12 RODS
V2

12 Rods were a band from Ohio who had relocated to Minneapolis, and there they had built-up a reputation for playing a sharp, angular style of new wave-ish rock. On 'I Wish You Were a Girl', that approach was discarded in favour of a more even, gentle sound for a song which speaks about the painful yearning felt by an ostensibly heterosexual man who falls in love with another man and struggles to make sense of his feelings.

46
FREE FALL
CORNELIUS
MATADOR

'Free Fall' finds Cornelius experimenting with a guitar-rock format, and so we hear guitar and drums kicking up a veritable storm whilst Cornelius contributes a highly melodic vocal. Then, an epic guitar solo interrupts the flow before the hard riffs and soft vocals re-appear, only to wind down again into nothingness. This song displays the artist's willingness to take risks with his music and an equally keen unwillingness to be easily pigeonholed and classified; it isn't his greatest track by any means, but it is still very good and very interesting.

45
PEOPLE ARE STRANGE
STINA NORDENSTAM
EASTWEST

Here, the Swedish singer with the incredibly gentle and fragile voice, covers the Robbie Krieger/ Jim Morrison song first recorded by The Doors. In contrast to the bold, declamatory original, Stina Nordenstam delivers a quiet and mediative version, where she is accompanied by plucked acoustic instruments and subtle electronics. This is a riveting and spooky performance of the song, in which she inhabits the role of a seemingly strange person who is looking outwards at a hostile and forbidding environment.

44
IMPROVISE
JURASSIC 5
PAN
OTHER SINGLES 1998:
CONCRETE SCHOOLYARD;
JAYOU

Jurassic 5 were blessed with not one, but two members who could provide them with outrageously good sonics; DJ Nu-Mark and extraordinary turntablist Cut Chemist sourced 1970s funk samples and used them to create an ear-catching beat with a bass-line that is just begging to be rapped over. Not to be outdone, the four MCs move the microphone between themselves like wildfire – each and every vocalist is sharp and quick-witted and they project positivity rather than stale cliches. In the hands of Jurassic 5, hip-hop was art.

43
I DON'T BELIEVE YOU
THE MAGNETIC FIELDS
MERGE

Steven Merritt, the songwriting leader of The Magnetic Fields, certainly knew the value of having a good tune to hang his ever-so-clever lyrics upon, and that is precisely the case with 'I Don't Believe You', on which tremendously melodic synth-pop provides the seductive ear-candy that coaxes listeners into engaging with a song about the insecurity caused by a deceitful lover. Delightful lyrical couplets, each having a bitter sting in the tail, carry a message of admonishment from the narrator who has clearly been pushed too far.

42
SUNDAY
SONIC YOUTH
GEFFEN

'Sunday' is probably better known for the supporting video – filmed by Harmony Korine and featuring Macaulay Culkin and Rachel Miner – but the song itself is criminally under-appreciated because it is a subtle and low-key gem. It opens with a pretty, repeating guitar phrase that gives way to a gently rocking chugga-chugga rhythm borrowed from 'Skeleton' by Helium. The Sonic Youth trademark distortion and noise only pops-up briefly, which allows Thurston Moore to softly croon a bittersweet lamentation on the state of a relationship that is slowly coming apart.

41
NEEDIN' U
DAVID MORALES PRESENTS THE FACE
MANIFESTO

New York DJ and producer David Morales had been a regular at Paradise Garage where legendary DJ Larry Levan had played and re-mixed 'My First Mistake' by The Chi-Lites and 'Let Me Down Easy' by Rare Pleasure. His great familiarity with these tracks paid dividends when Morales took samples from each in order to create 'Needin' U', on which a hypnotic piano and drum groove forms the basis of a track that takes a few sonic detours into arm-waving euphoria, before returning to the irresistible groove. This house music classic is the epitome of dance floor magic.

40
PLOCK
PLONE
WARP

Plone were a duo from Birmingham who attracted an audience by playing live gigs in support of local groups such as Pram and Broadcast. In 1997, Plone released their debut single, 'Press a Key', which led to them signing a deal with Warp Records and releasing 'Plock', which to date is their only other single release. 'Plock' (what a great word!) is a highly inventive record with an arresting sound created via use of vintage analogue keyboards and guitar effect units. A ghostly melancholia seems to infuse the record, not lessened by a vocoderised vocal that sounds like the musings of a solitary man being lost in the vastness of space. Beguiling and beautiful, 'Plock' is a left-field pop delight.

39
RABBIT IN YOUR HEADLIGHTS
UNKLE
MO WAX

Unkle was a musical project launched by Mo' Wax founder James Lavelle, comprising of himself and DJ Shadow. Lavelle wanted to create some song-based tracks as opposed to instrumental trip-hop recordings. To this end, a plethora of guest vocalists including Richard Ashcroft, Alice Temple, Badly Drawn Boy and Mike D became involved, resulting in an album called *Psyence Fiction*. Unfortunately, this was something of a let-down; it meandered, and often the singers didn't fit well with DJ Shadow's music – somehow there was a strangely evident incompatibility. The one exception to this rule was 'Rabbit in Your Headlights'; this had originally been intended as a collaboration with Radiohead, but Thom Yorke had been wanting to do something outside the group format and eventually his insistence prevailed. In the event, his performance was magnificent and the track as a whole was absolutely cohesive; Yorke's voice and DJ Shadow's piano-led atmospherics were just meant for each other. The result was a dazzling piece of indefinable music of enduring high-quality.

38
CHILD PSYCHOLOGY
BLACK BOX RECORDER
CHRYSALIS
OTHER SINGLE 1998: ENGLAND MADE ME

The intriguingly named Black Box Recorder were a group consisting of ex-Auteurs personage Luke Haines, along with vocalist Sarah Nixey and John Moore, who was a former member of Jesus and Mary Chain. They debuted with 'Child Psychology' which instantly alienated radio programmers due to its beautifully sung – but lyrically brutal – chorus of "Life is unfair, kill yourself or get over it". The verses are spoken by Nixey in an unemotional, deadpan manner, and they concern incidents from an unhappy childhood; being expelled from school; refusing to speak and an artificial Christmas tree that played 'Silent Night' being three such examples. Black Box Recorder were revealed to be thought-provoking provocateurs with a smooth-as-satin sound that owed a debt to nobody else; in other words, fantastic!

37
CHILDREN AT PLAY
MAX TUNDRA
WARP

Max Tundra is the stage name of Ben Jacobs and 'Children at Play' was his first release; it is twelve minutes of madcap joy beginning with a childlike, tropical-sounding melody, before travelling through a landscape of drum & bass, jazz, funk and wildly playful electronic madness. There is a strong feeling of innocence in this track and it makes me smile. Somehow, it sounds like freedom... or maybe a little bit like Stockhausen's music would sound after an evening of binge-watching Laurel & Hardy.

36
ICE HOCKEY HAIR
SUPER FURRY ANIMALS
CREATION

'Ice Hockey Hair' was the title track of a four-track EP containing songs which were deemed to be unsuitable album material. Here we have a song about the perceived *naffness* of a mullet hairstyle – amusingly described as 'Ice Hockey Hair' – and it is a fabulous piece of pop that seems to combine the sounds of techno with the sweetness of ELO, The Beach Boys and 10cc. This is a heady and highly-potent pot-pourri of a record.

35
FANTASTIC CAT
TAKAKO MINEKAWA
MARCH
OTHER SINGLE 1998: KLAXON

Takako Minekawa was an electronic musician from Japan; her records were melodic and eccentric – none more so than 'Fantastic Cat' which is an ultra-charming, absurdist track with a ping-ponging synth rhythm and a lyric of dadaist simplicity sung in a cheerfully naive style. This is one of those pieces that melts away cynicism and disillusion; it is pure pleasure and once heard, is never forgotten.

34
LOTUS
R.E.M.
WARNER BROTHERS
OTHER SINGLE 1998:
DAYSLEEPER

'Lotus' is the sound of the new re-configuration of R.E.M., following the retirement of drummer Bill Berry; it is more keyboard-led than previously, and perhaps a little bit moodier... but overall it doesn't stray too far from the band's signature sound. Although sparingly used, Peter Buck's guitar lines are as elegant as ever, and Michael Stipe uses his voice almost percussively to deliver – with startling intensity – a somewhat surrealistic lyric.

33
HUNTER
BJÖRK
ONE LITTLE INDIAN
OTHER SINGLE 1998: ALARM CALL

Military beats, futuristic techno soundscapes, hints of Icelandic folk music and ice-edged strings… the disparate sounds found within this track are stunningly beautiful, and Björk allows the listener to appreciate them fully by singing with a curious mixture of strength and restraint. The inspiration for the song came to her when she realised that she now had the responsibility of providing for a group of people by dint of releasing music that the public might actually purchase; in a sense, they were dependent upon her and she had, in effect, become the hunter-gatherer of the tribe.

32
DOO WOP (THAT THING)
LAURYN HILL
RUFFHOUSE
OTHER SINGLE 1998:
EX-FACTOR

Tunefully dissecting gender politics, 'Doo Wop (That Thing)' was the much-anticipated record with which Lauryn Hill launched her solo career following the break-up of The Fugees. A tinkling piano underpins the song, which also features 1960s-style soul horns, doo-wop harmonies and raps that examine the gender gap from both male and female perspectives.

31
QUEUE
SEAN LENNON
GRAND ROYAL
OTHER SINGLES 1998:
HOME;
HALF HORSE HALF MUSICIAN

Being the son of John and Yoko must have been an inescapable and gigantic burden to carry into one's solo career… but Sean Lennon didn't allow himself to be diminished by the pressure, and he was even confident enough in his own individuality to have Zac Starkey – son of Ringo – on the drums. For support, he leaned on his girlfriend Yuka Honda of the band Cibo Matto, with whom Sean had played bass guitar. Together, they cooked-up a bright and sunny sound with a positive and uplifting lyric, but melodically 'Queue' is… dare one say it, McCartney-esque! Sean's voice is undeniably similar to his father's – albeit a tad sweeter perhaps – and the overall sound here is not at all retro-leaning. Despite all the baggage, this is a fabulous record.

30
CANDLEFIRE
DAWN OF THE REPLICANTS
EASTWEST
OTHER SINGLES 1998:
HOGWASH FARM;
SKULLCRUSHER;
BORN IN BASKETS

Being in a band signed to a major label, but not attracting significant sales, is not a pleasant situation to be in… but that is where Dawn of the Replicants found themselves.

'Candlefire' is a marvellous record containing a stunning guitar riff, hooks galore and an outstanding melodic structure; it reached number fifty-one on the hit-parade – and that was as good as it got for Dawn of the Replicants…

29
RUFF RYDERS' ANTHEM
DMX
DEF JAM
OTHER SINGLES 1998:
GET AT ME DOG;
STOP BEING GREEDY; SLIPPIN'

DMX was pretty much everywhere in 1998; he collaborated with the likes of Jay Z and LL Cool J, as well as masterminding his own solo endeavours. 'Ruff Ryders' Anthem' comes from DMX's debut album *It's Dark and Hell is Hot*, and it turned out to be one of his most crucial cuts, despite the fact that he took a lot of persuading to even record it. DMX dismissed the adrenalised beat created by producer Swizz Beatz as sounding too much like a rock and roll track, but in truth the beat has a military cadence and once backing vocals were added – and DMX was coaxed into performing a highly energetic rapped vocal – a hip-hop classic was the result.

28
LET'S SHAKE HANDS
THE WHITE STRIPES
ITALY
OTHER SINGLE 1998:
LAFAYETTE BLUES

My friend Russ Taylor of *Crocodile Records* was a garage-rock aficionado, and he tipped me off about The White Stripes at an early stage of their development; "They're gonna be massive" he enthused. At the time, I couldn't quite imagine that – but I did think they sounded great. This debut single doesn't just bark… it has teeth and it bites. Although cheaply recorded in their living-room, it still explodes from the speakers with a flurry of drums, razor-sharp shards of guitar noise and an impassioned vocal; this is spectacular stuff. R.I.P. Russ, and a multitude of thanks.

27
…BABY ONE MORE TIME
BRITNEY SPEARS
JIVE

The first that the world ever heard of Britney Spears was on this debut single, and it immediately catapulted her to mega-stardom. A clutch of record companies had already turned down the opportunity to sign Britney on the grounds that she had no audience appeal(!) but Jive took the plunge and sent her off to Sweden to work with writer/producer Max Martin. He gave her '…Baby One More Time' to perform after it had previously been rejected by Backstreet Boys, TLC and English boy-band 5ive, and the sixteen-year old Spears immediately nailed the song which was clearly relatable for any teenager. She had listened to Soft Cell's version of 'Tainted Love' for inspiration, and consequently delivered a vocal that transitioned deftly from cutesy to husky. The sadomasochistic connotations in the title saw the words "Hit me" deleted, and so it was that '...Baby One More Time' hit the air-waves (no pun intended) and became a fully-deserved, worldwide smash-hit.

26
COME SEE THE DUCK
DEERHOOF
BANANO

This is raucous, mad-cap and way out of left-field stuff from American alt-rockers Deerhoof. For those looking for quantity over quality, the brevity of the song might be off-putting – it plays for a mere one-minute and seven-seconds – but on this record, every second counts, as we hear a barrage of joyous noise and quirky, cartoonish vocals.

25

CELEBRITY SKIN
HOLE
GEFFEN

Whereas previously Hole had sounded like scruffy and dangerous rock & roll outsiders, this first record in two-years was streamlined and had the word mainstream running all the way through it; but funnily enough, this air-brushed smoothness seemed to suit them. Billy Corgan was included in the songwriting credits, and his panache and know-how is very evident as the song veers between hard, jagged guitar riffing and pretty, delicate interludes. Courtney Love bases the theme of the song on *The Wasteland* by T.S. Eliot, and also includes phrases from Shakespeare and Dante Gabriel Rossetti, as she delivers a robust, and highly-authoritative vocal.

24
COME TOGETHER
SPIRITUALIZED
DEDICATED
OTHER SINGLE 1998: I THINK I'M IN LOVE

This single comes from the extraordinary catalogue of delights that is *Ladies and Gentlemen We Are Floating in Space* – the Spiritualized *magnum opus*. 'Come Together' has a huge pulsing sound, a mighty horn riff, a gospel choir and a wailing harmonica, all of which provide the backdrop for a lyric about an unhealthy reliance on narcotics in order to keep pain at bay. Jason Pierce sings with a chilling intensity, as if he is exorcising demons of the skin-crawling variety; this is a really great record.

23
IF YOU TOLERATE THIS YOUR CHILDREN WILL BE NEXT
MANIC STREET PREACHERS
EPIC
OTHER SINGLE 1998: THE EVERLASTING

The title for this track was borrowed from the tag-line of a Spanish Civil War propaganda poster depicting a child murdered by General Franco's fascists; but more generally, the song was inspired by Welsh volunteers who joined the International Brigades to resist Franco's forces. The chosen subject matter is also an indication of the esteem in which The Manics held

The Clash, since that latter group had already covered similar themes in their song 'Spanish Bombs'. But here, proceeding at a stately pace atop a rock-steady beat, The Manic Street Preachers paint a vivid picture of conflicting emotion in a lyric which quotes from those who were in the midst of the fight, with verses that lead into an anthemic, string-propelled chorus. This thought-provoking and melancholic piece brilliantly displays The Manics mix of mature social-comment and epic pop mastery.

22
GENEVIEVE (THE PILOT OF YOUR THIGHS)
PERRY BLAKE
POLYDOR

With a sound pitched somewhere betwixt that of Scott Walker and Nick Drake, this promises to be something special, and Perry Blake delivers with an enigmatic song arranged for strings and hauntingly discrete electronics. Without resort to vocal histrionics, Blake conjures up a sense of unease… or perhaps decay… as cellos rhythmically saw-away, imparting a sense of despairing grandeur. The lyric is relatively sparse and unthreatening, and yet the way in which each syllable is meticulously delivered suggests that some dark secret, something shameful or some hideous malignancy is at the very heart of this eerie delight.

21
TROPICALIA
BECK
GEFFEN

As ethnic forgeries go, 'Tropicalia' is great. Here, Beck employs a Brazilian samba-style, so the music is light, breezy and evocative of a festival vibe – we can practically see people dancing to the bossa nova beat and hear the "Cha cha cha's". However, this is just a cunning front which allows Beck to smuggle in a lyric concerned with the tourist industry and the poverty and misery that is hidden behind the façade of bright colours and wide-smiling vendors. Although not the brutal, smash-in-the-face perspective delivered by the Sex Pistols on 'Holidays in the Sun', this is a much more nuanced take on very similar themes.

20
WHIPPIN' PICCADILLY
GOMEZ
HUT
OTHER SINGLES 1998:
COULDN'T GET MYSELF ARRESTED; 78 STONE WOBBLE

Gomez were a young band based in Southport who quickly garnered critical praise for their melodicism and rootsy style. Having won the Mercury Prize for *Bring It On* (their debut LP) it was the third single taken from the album that gave them a hit… and it is not hard to see why, because 'Whippin' Piccadilly' is very easy to love. It has a rolling groove which features bottleneck blues guitar and lo-fi electronics, and it is a narrative song that tells the tale of a group excursion to Manchester in order to see Beck – who is described as being "dressed in a suit and looking like a lunatic" – performing at the Academy. Much enjoyment and revelry is hinted at in a song which captures perfectly the high-spirits and camaraderie of youth stumbling towards adulthood; it is a charming snapshot of good times spent together.

19
LITTLE HONDA
YO LA TENGO
MATADOR

On their album *I Can Hear The Heart Beating As One*, Yo La Tengo took a giant leap forward; it was a consistent and cohesive collection of excellent tracks. Among its delights was this Beach Boys song, written by Brian Wilson and Mike Love back in 1964. Yo La Tengo offer up a superb re-interpretation of what had initially been fairly lightweight fare; the amplifiers are cranked-up high, and fuzzy guitars are loudly played over a simple drum beat. The vocal is off-hand and so nonchalantly cool that this could almost have been a Jesus and Mary Chain record…

18
THE ROCKAFELLER SKANK
FATBOY SLIM
SKINT
OTHER SINGLE 1998:
GANGSTER TRIPPIN

This is a bold, no-holds barred, big-beat juggernaut that had the simple aim of knocking us off our feet. A whole collage of samples are barely contained within 'The Rockafeller Skank'; it is almost bursting at the seams with different flavours. To begin with we have the hip-hop derived vocal that repeats throughout the track – "Check it out now, the funk soul brother" – this was taken from 'Vinyl Dogs Vibe' by Vinyl Dogs, voiced by Lord Finesse. Also included is a taste of Northern soul – courtesy of 'Sliced Tomatoes' by The Just Brothers – some twangy, surf-style guitar, via tracks by John Barry and Duane Eddy, plus some rock & roll drumming taken from 'I Fought the Law' by The Bobby Fuller Four. In summary, this is a dizzying blend of components that is given a dramatic arrangement by Fatboy Slim, who managed to create a highly potent slice of energetic dance floor dynamite with obvious pop appeal to boot.

17
NOT DARK YET
BOB DYLAN
COLUMBIA
OTHER SINGLE 1998:
LOVE SICK

Bob Dylan hadn't released an album of self-composed songs for seven long years; many people presumed that the muse had simply deserted him… after all, he hadn't released a consistently great album since *Blood on the Tracks*, more than twenty-years previously. So it was that there must have been very few people who would have predicted the near-miracle return to his finest form that was the album *Time Out Of Mind*. Personally, for me, the highlight of the record was this single, 'Not Dark Yet'; it is a beautifully written, revelatory song in which the narrator confronts his own mortality. Dylan sings with a weary and unsentimental acceptance of the dying of the light, yet he is full of fortitude and dignity. As an artist in the autumn of his years, Dylan was once again imparting his worldly wisdom with a breathtaking and unflinching clarity.

16
MUSIC SOUNDS BETTER WITH YOU
STARDUST
VIRGIN

Thomas Bangalter of Daft Punk formed Stardust alongside DJ Alan Braxe and vocalist Benjamin Diamond. Simply using a looped sample of the guitar riff from Chaka Khan's song 'Fate', and then adding synthesised bass and drums – along with piano and a minimalist lyric – the track turned out to be utterly infectious, drawing on the funk tradition, and yet somehow seeming eerily futuristic. The trio had created a sublime piece of dance-pop, with a propulsive, disco bass line and a vocal hook to make it unforgettable. Having achieved near perfection with the first track they had ever recorded, Stardust then amicably disbanded, apparently believing that such an action created a sense of magic and mystery!

15
THE CERTAINTY OF CHANCE
THE DIVINE COMEDY
SETANTA
OTHER SINGLE 1998:
GENERATION SEX

At the same time that guitar bands – as exemplified by Oasis – were all about dumbing down and plodding, and whilst "lad culture" – as exemplified in *Loaded* magazine – thrived on offending anyone with even a single iota of sensitivity, Neil Hannon was having none of it; his songs for The Divine Comedy became ever more ambitious and grand. 'The Certainty of Chance' is a wry look at a poor soul whose life is drifting by as he or she awaits the day when their dreams will come true. The song is orchestrated with great finesse, allowing plenty of space for little delicate touches to exist, and Hannon croons in a rich baritone. The effect on the lucky listener is stunning; here is a pop music that reaches for the stars.

14
ROSA PARKS
OUTKAST
LAFACE

Although titled as a tribute to civil rights campaigner Rosa Parks, the result was a lawsuit, on Parks behalf, claiming misrepresentation. Whatever the rights and wrongs of the case may have been, the fact that this single was a brilliant piece of music is indisputable. Without sacrificing so much as a scintilla of their integrity, Outkast were now displaying their innate pop sensibilities, and 'Rosa Parks' has more bounce to the ounce than seems possible. Their effervescence could barely be contained, and Outkast were rapidly becoming an unstoppable force who were re-writing the rule book. As a final note, they even nod to their southern, country roots by including a very non hip-hop harmonica solo... and even this works brilliantly.

13
NO SURPRISES
RADIOHEAD
PARLOPHONE

The breathtakingly beautiful introduction to 'No Surprises' really grabs me and sends a shiver of anticipation running down my spine... and when Thom Yorke's vocal comes in, his voice, completely devoid of machismo, grabs me even more. He sings about the subjugation of the bruised and unhappy workers, who shout their anti-government slogans, but ultimately carry on as they are, settling in the end for pretty houses with pretty gardens. This is thoughtful and thought-provoking stuff that has a dream-like quality in terms of sound, but a dream-shattering lyrical quality. Put simply, this is a consummate Radiohead song, and it haunts me to this day.

12
HOLLAND, 1945
NEUTRAL MILK HOTEL
ORANGE TWIN

The leading lights of the *Elephant 6* collective were undoubtedly Neutral Milk Hotel, led by Jeff Mangum. This – only their second single – comes from *In the Aeroplane Over the Sea*, their second album, and it is one of the band's loudest and most uptempo tracks. Fuzzy noise is a feature of all the instruments, and the guitars in particular are overdriven and distorted. This propulsive track positively rattles as it proceeds on its way, while Mangum handles the vocal in an authentic, natural and intuitive way, with his voice actually wobbling in parts of the song. The lyric is perplexing; although there are clear allusions to the death of Anne Frank, who, along with her sister Margot, died of typhus in the Bergen-Belsen concentration camp, there are also other, less clear, references that seem to allude to the death of other people in different places and time-zones. Curiously, a mariachi-style trumpet joins the musical accompaniment in the build-up to the finale of this fascinating track.

11
MY FAVOURITE GAME
THE CARDIGANS
POLYDOR

This opens with a nagging guitar hook that repeats at various points throughout the song, but when Nina Persson's vocal enters the fray, the track really accelerates on a hard-driving drum beat and a fat, fuzz bass. Whilst the verses are crammed full of words, the chorus is sparse, to the point and effective; Persson sings from the point of view of someone in a failing relationship, realising that all her efforts to make it work are ultimately doomed because the lover she was trying to steer in a safe direction is hopelessly out of control. Persson's performance is fantastic – her voice is strong but the resignation is palpable as she moves away from the wreckage of a failed romance. The Cardigans had already shown that they could produce cute and clever pop records, but 'My Favourite Game' was something completely different; a powerhouse performance and a triumph.

10

GET IT ON

TURBONEGRO

SYMPATHY FOR THE RECORD INDUSTRY

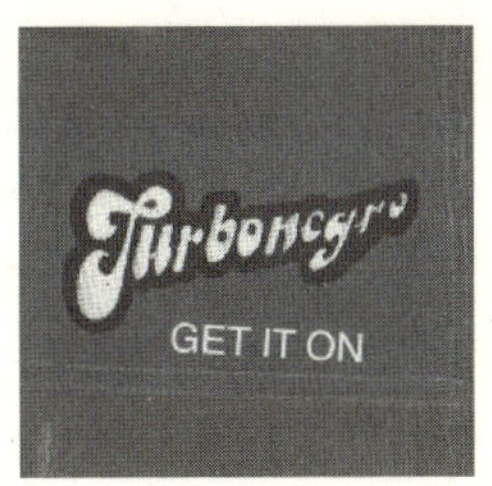

This was released as a seven-inch picture disc single (backed by the fabulous 'Don't Say Motherfucker Motherfucker') and it begins with an assault of thunderous drums that sound like rampaging elephants, before Euroboy throws-in some devastatingly cool guitar riffs; if you like your rock and roll to be the kick-ass variety, then this is as good as it gets. Tribute is paid to Alice Cooper via the "I like it, love it" refrain (lifted from 'I'm Eighteen') and despite being weakened by his heroin addiction, a frenzied Hank Von Helvete fully matches the intensity of the musicians with a throat-shredding vocal. The fact that Turbonegro often played with tongues placed firmly in their collective cheek, didn't seem to diminish their music in any way – they were never, ever a joke band. For the huge excitement that they generated, we are forever in their debt, and I for one salute them… hail the Apocalypse Dudes!

9

CHANGES

2PAC

DEATH ROW

OTHER SINGLE 1998: DO FOR LOVE

'Changes' was the third posthumously released 2Pac single – actually a re-made, re-modelled and re-mixed version of a track he had first recorded back in 1992. It features a hard-hitting, consciousness-raising rap on the issue of racism in American society; "The war on drugs" (actually double-speak for "The war on poor black people") gets a mention, as does police harassment and endless cycles of endemic poverty. But what is of the utmost importance is the reference to reconciliation between black and white people; 2Pac clearly recognises and advocates the need for a change in attitude. Elsewhere, the murder of Black Panther founder Huey P. Newton is called out, and the song ends prophetically with 2Pac mimicking the rat-a-tat sound of gunfire as he imagines himself being shot and killed. Also notable is the clever employment of a sample from Bruce Hornsby and the Range's smash-hit "The Way it Is', because it perfectly accords in both a thematic sense, and as a way of widening the appeal of 2Pac's song. Articulate and persuasive – as well as being highly talented – a force for good in the world was lost when 2Pac was slain.

8

THIS IS HARDCORE

PULP

ISLAND

OTHER SINGLES 1998:

PARTY HARD; A LITTLE SOUL

This title track from the sixth Pulp album looks at show-business fame, and in particular the way in which people are used by the industry until their lustre fades, and then, with all the life sucked out of them, they are discarded and replaced by younger, newer and more malleable types from the unceasing production line. What happens to these people, Jarvis Cocker wonders… and when will it be his turn to face the guillotine? Aiming for a creepy and profoundly uneasy-listening sound, a sample of 'Bolero on the Moon Rocks' by the Peter Thomas Sound Orchestra is jigsawed throughout the track to help achieve this unusual end. Little that had gone before in pop music had ever sounded as deliberately queasy as this lounge-music from hell, and with Cocker's perceptive, bitter lyric aimed at shattering the glass in the narcissists' mirror, whilst simultaneously debunking the myth of glamour that is peddled by star-makers, 'This is Hardcore' was undoubtedly one of the finest tracks of the decade.

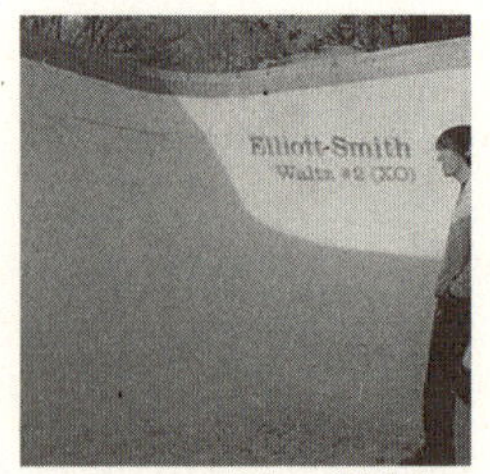

7

WALTZ #2 (XO)

ELLIOTT SMITH

DREAMWORKS

Elliott Smith's moment of undoubted genius came with 'Waltz #2 (XO)', a song in which he looks back at growing up in Cedar Hill, Texas, with Bunny – his mother – and Charlie, his always judgemental and constantly critical step-father. The song is played as a saloon-bar piano ballad, and the setting is a karaoke bar in which the atmosphere is strained… tending towards anger. Bunny steps-up and sings 'Cathy's Clown' – her expression blank as she performs, staring off into space. Next up is Charlie, and stung by her perceived rebuke, he retaliates by offering up a rendition of 'You're No Good'. In the final verse, Smith examines his own feelings; wading through the emotional undercurrent of the evening, he imagines a Charlie-free world and also ponders his disappointment with his mother, before concluding with "XO, Mom" (meaning hugs and kisses). This is a song of incredible depth that Smith manages to pull-off with an awesome lightness of touch.

6

INERTIA CREEPS

MASSIVE ATTACK

VIRGIN

OTHER SINGLES 1998:

TEARDROP; ANGEL

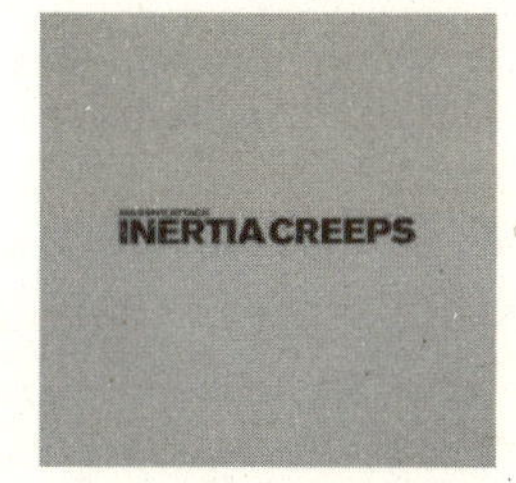

With no featured guests on 'Inertia Creeps', the core trio of Massive Attack produce an eerie, atmospheric piece with a strong Turkish flavour intrinsic to its exotic sounds and rhythm. There is a nifty sample taken from 'ROckWrok' – a fairly obscure, early Ultravox single – and the lyrics, by Robert Del Naja, describe a spent relationship that struggles on nevertheless, only existing by dint of the lies and deceit that both parties inflict upon each other and themselves. Del Naja delivers the lyric in a whisper, while fuzz-guitar and electronic sounds fill up the spaces, creating a somewhat claustrophobic effect. Massive Attack's earlier singles, 'Teardrop' and 'Angel', had both seen big chart action, but there was no such interest forthcoming for 'Inertia Creeps'; but this is no reflection on the quality of the single, because it is stunning.

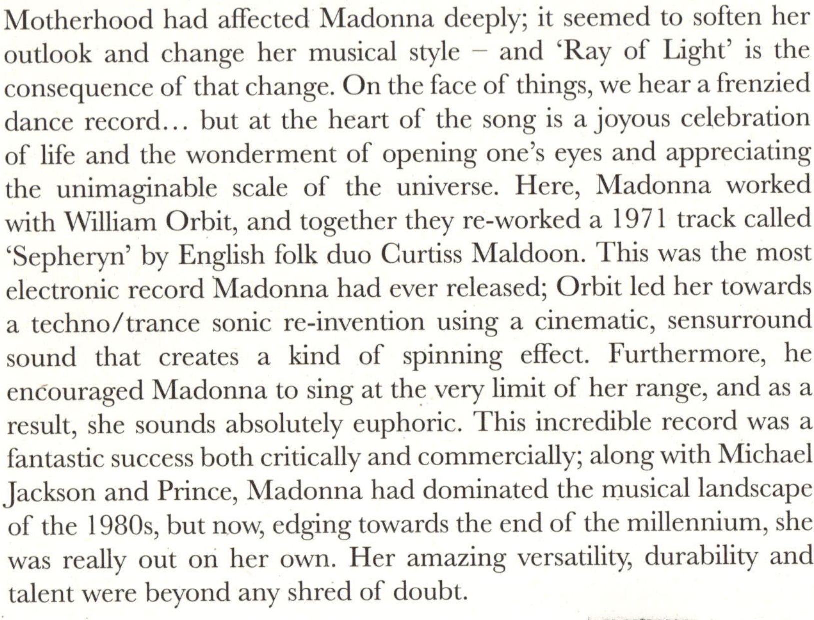

5

RAY OF LIGHT

MADONNA

MAVERICK

OTHER SINGLES 1998: FROZEN;

THE POWER OF GOODBYE;

DROWNED WORLD/SUBSTITUTE FOR LOVE

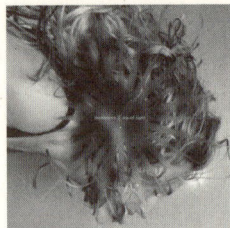

Motherhood had affected Madonna deeply; it seemed to soften her outlook and change her musical style – and 'Ray of Light' is the consequence of that change. On the face of things, we hear a frenzied dance record… but at the heart of the song is a joyous celebration of life and the wonderment of opening one's eyes and appreciating the unimaginable scale of the universe. Here, Madonna worked with William Orbit, and together they re-worked a 1971 track called 'Sepheryn' by English folk duo Curtiss Maldoon. This was the most electronic record Madonna had ever released; Orbit led her towards a techno/trance sonic re-invention using a cinematic, sensurround sound that creates a kind of spinning effect. Furthermore, he encouraged Madonna to sing at the very limit of her range, and as a result, she sounds absolutely euphoric. This incredible record was a fantastic success both critically and commercially; along with Michael Jackson and Prince, Madonna had dominated the musical landscape of the 1980s, but now, edging towards the end of the millennium, she was really out on her own. Her amazing versatility, durability and talent were beyond any shred of doubt.

4

A.M. 180

GRANDADDY

WILL

OTHER SINGLES 1998:

SUMMER HERE KIDS;
EVERYTHING BEAUTIFUL IS FAR AWAY;
LAUGHING STOCK

Grandaddy would go on to become my favourite group of the era, and 'A.M. 180' was my gateway into their music… a music that felt warm, humane and weirdly futuristic (in a lo-fi sort of way). They came from Modesto in California, a place with beautiful, agricultural land, but also high levels of pollution, and this dichotomy always informed their musical style. The group were led by ex-professional skateboarder Jason Lytle; he was the sole songwriter and therefore responsible for their very appealing unorthodoxy. 'A.M.180' opens with a simple, but wonderful keyboard hook, before the guitars and drums crash into the song and Lytle gently sings about the romance of just being with somebody you love, without really doing much at all. Then the guitars fall silent, leaving just voice and drums to continue, before the keyboard hook returns to launch the song into unrestrained joyfulness. When I first heard this magical song, I tingled with delight – and it still has exactly the same effect when I hear it now.

3

SEXY BOY

AIR

CAROLINE

OTHER SINGLES 1998:

CALIFORNIE;

KELLY WATCH THE STARS; ALL I NEED

Air, a duo from Versailles, broke into the mainstream with 'Sexy Boy', a single full of wit and charm. Their marriage of electronics with fuzzy guitar creates a highly sensuous sound, further enhanced by what one initially presumes to be a breathy female vocal – however, in reality it was ingeniously created by Nicolas Godin and Jean-Benoît Dunckel manipulating their own voices with a pitch modulator. The verses are soft and dreamy, whereas the pounding choruses are quite the opposite – and it is they that contain the song's killer hook. Thoroughly addictive and absorbing, 'Sexy Boy' is a chic and fun combination; as an approximation, it sounds something like a collaboration between Daft Punk, German electronic pioneers Cluster and Jane Birkin revisiting her work with Serge Gainsbourg.

2

HONEY

MOBY

MUTE

OTHER SINGLE 1998: RUN ON

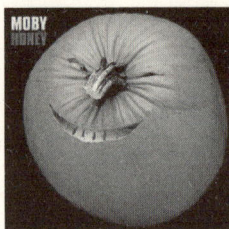

Listening to a box-set of folk/blues recordings called *Sounds Of The South* (compiled by noted musical archivist Alan Lomax) inspiration struck Moby pretty forcibly, and it took his music off at a tangent. He borrowed four lines from a 1960 track called 'Sometimes' by blues singer Bessie Jones, and used them as building-blocks to create 'Honey'. Around the repeated vocal sample – which is accentuated by backing vocalists on the word "Sometimes" – a rhythmic tour-de-force is constructed in which piano is used percussively, drums and synchronised hand-claps add a gospel feel, guitar licks provide some colour and a techno edge is present too. It all adds up to a mesmerising piece of music that respects and acknowledges the past, whilst at the same time being absolutely contemporary sounding. The track was included on the soon to be released album *Play*, where this working methodology provided the template for tracks that helped to propel the album to previously unimaginable commercial heights… and this bestowed upon Moby himself the poisoned chalice of true international stardom.

1

GODDESS ON A HIWAY

MERCURY REV

V2

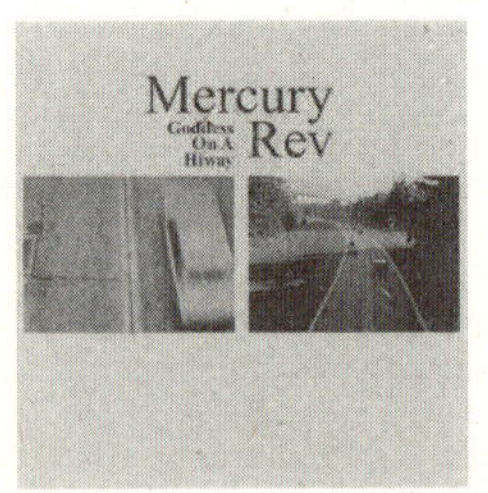

The career path of Mercury Rev had seemingly reached a dead-end, and there appeared to be no future for them beyond recording a final album as some kind of middle-finger to an uncaring world; that album would be *Deserter's Songs*, and somewhat surprisingly – to put it mildly – it completely and utterly transformed the group's fortunes. The first single taken from the album was the devastatingly good 'Goddess on a Hiway', a song which had been written nearly a decade earlier by frontman Jonathan Donahue while he was still a member of

The Flaming Lips. The theme of the piece is departure… preparing to leave a person or a place behind. The words are uncomplicated but very eloquent, and they are imbued with a heart-rending fragility. On the musical side, with assistance from producer and ex-band member Dave Fridmann, the group move away from their previous neo-psychedelic sound towards something more epic in scale, in which strings, horns and woodwind all feature. This sonic shift is quite remarkable, and there is a distinctly old-school feel readily apparent; if previously the group's musical palette had consisted of bright, day-glow colours, now we hear the aural equivalent of sepia-tinged, muted browns and greys. So, 'Goddess on a Hiway' is not just a wonderful song with a soaring refrain, but also a sound excursion into places unvisited for many a year. This transportive music conjures-up an unlived past, full of half-forgotten fragments of memory, and it succeeds in nourishing both mind and soul.

Following United in the 90s was brilliant as they swept (almost) all before them at home and in Europe. 1999 was the pinnacle as Fergie finally won the European Cup - (top) Derek and I are in San Marino and (below) a typical Euro away in that fabulous season. "Football, Bloody Hell!" as the great man said.

1999

EVENTS

The Euro Currency is established by the European Central Bank.

Bertrand Piccard and Brian Jones became the first people to circumnavigate the globe by hot-air balloon.

NATO launches air-strikes against Yugoslavia – their first ever assault on a sovereign state.

The Columbine High School massacre takes place, when teenage pupils Eric Harris and Dylan Klebold shoot to death twelve fellow students and one teacher before killing themselves.

TV presenter Jill Dando is shot dead on the doorstep of her house in Fulham, London.

Napster, a music downloading service, is created.

The Jiji earthquake kills 2,415 people in Taiwan.

Boris Yeltsin resigns as President of the Russian Federation, leaving Vladimir Putin as his replacement.

Manchester United become the first English club to win the treble of Premier League title, FA Cup and – in dramatic fashion in Barcelona – the Champions League.

BIRTHS

Diogo Dalot ;Kai Havertz ;Mason Mount

DEATHS

Iris Murdoch; Dusty Springfield;Stanley Kubrick;Joe DiMaggio; Dennis Viollet; Yehudi Menuhin; Ernie Wise; Alf Ramsey; Anthony Newley; Skip Spence; Roger Troutman; Oliver Reed; Dirk Bogarde; Shel Silverstein; Screaming Lord Sutch; Dennis Brown; Victor Mature; Moondog; Hoyt Axton; Doug Sahm; Quentin Crisp; Curtis Mayfield; Charlie Byrd;Joseph Heller; Grover Washington Jr.

BOOKS

Harry Potter and the Prisoner of Azkaban – J.K. Rowling
Disgrace – J.M. Coetzee
Amsterdam – Ian McEwan
Be Cool – Elmore Leonard
Devil's Valley – André Brink
The Long Firm – Jake Arnott
Mr Wroe's Virgins – Jane Rogers
The Tesseract – Alex Garland

FILMS

Fight Club; The Matrix; Star Wars: Episode 1 – The Phantom Menace; Eyes Wide Shut; Boys Don't Cry; The Blair Witch Project; The Virgin Suicides; Being John Malkovich; *Notting Hill*; *The Talented Mr. Ripley*; *American Beauty*;

MY 1999 (and beyond…)

The regular fifteen-hour days I was working left me with very little time or energy for anything else. I arrived home and sat-down with my mother, whose determination to overcome her handicaps was truly inspiring; we would eat and then I inevitably nodded-off, before eventually staggering up to bed. However, I did give myself time-off on Saturdays to go and watch Manchester United play and I was rewarded with some outstanding football that culminated in a treble-winning season. I'd not had either the time or money to go to any European away games during this year, but the final of the Champions League was a must-do. I booked to travel with the unofficial U.F. Tours – as I had always done previously – but because they were considered undesirable by the club, United managed to scupper their plans to buy-up thousands of tickets in Barcelona and then sell them on as a flight-inclusive package; having pre-sold these packages, U.F. Tours found themselves in deep trouble and they declared themselves bankrupt on the morning of our flight. Not surprisingly, pandemonium ensued at the airport, and it seemed initially that we would not be able to travel; however, the prospect of thousands of extremely irate football supporters rampaging around the terminal saw procedures overlooked and the flight gates opened;

so, off we went, and with a match ticket in my pocket I was in good spirits… until we arrived at our hotels, only to find that they were either double- or treble-booked, with no possibility of a refund forthcoming. In the event, we found somewhere else to stay and duly paid for our rooms once again. One of our party, an old friend of mine called Dessie Burns, had his wallet pick-pocketed on the metro; we had a whip-round to make-up his loss, but back on the metro he was pick-pocketed again! As a consequence, we had a second whip-round and this time asked him to be a bit more careful. The match itself was dull and disappointing, until the final few moments when it became incredibly dramatic and ultimately triumphant. There was much merry-making and we caroused throughout the night… but the very next day, on the flight home, Dessie had a heart-attack; it was a very sobering experience and it placed the jubilation of the last few days into its proper perspective.

On the musical front, despite the financial and leisure time restrictions, I was able to get to some gigs, usually thanks to the influence of Marc Riley which often afforded guest-list access. We saw Mercury Rev, Grandaddy, Spiritualized, Clinic and The Super Furry Animals among others, all of whom made me feel happy. By contrast, I was much less happy one night when I became the victim of a bar assault; as I protected myself from one assailant, another one smashed a bottle into my face. I fell unconscious to the ground, whereupon my assailants (and others) kicked me and stamped on my head. Taken to the hospital, I was left with a severe eye injury, a broken nose and a damaged ear – in other words, I was a mess. The police did make arrests, and the case duly went to Crown Court, but to my deep dismay, it quickly became apparent that there had been unforgivable negligence in building-up a case; key witnesses had not been interviewed simply because they lived in another part of the country. Ultimately, the people who had seriously injured me simply accepted binding-over orders – essentially they were slapped on the wrist and told not to misbehave again. I guess I was more disappointed than angry, but I was hugely depressed by the whole experience… a depression which was compounded by the fact that for several weeks I was unable to work and having to pay other people to do my job; a luxury I could not afford. The whole sorry affair cost me thousands of pounds, which was a huge setback as I struggled to establish my business.

As we counted down towards the year 2000, the world seemed

to be going millennium crazy; all kinds of improbable theories and predictions were aired and speculated upon, but of course, not one of these cataclysmic happenings occurred and, for most of us, the event was just a damp squib… we woke up in the year 2000 to a day that was much the same as the previous day.

On the other hand, much would happen in the ensuing years. On the world stage, the attack on the twin-towers of the World Trade Center and the subsequent invasions of Afghanistan and Iraq would make the whole world feel less safe. Vladimir Putin would come to dominate the Russian political landscape, while the USA would elect, in turn, first a black President, immediately followed by a sexist, racist bigot who made half of the country – and most of the rest of the world – cringe with embarrassment. Here in the UK the New Labour experiment would crash and burn, discredited by Tony Blair's willingness to wage an illegal war. In 2010, the newly elected Cameron and Osborne Tory government gave us austerity, causing misery for millions, and then they took a hugely reckless gamble with the prosperity and security of the nation by holding a referendum on whether or not to leave the European Union. Tragically the xenophobes, led by Nigel Farage and proven liar Boris Johnson, won the day, leaving us all, once again, as the proverbial sick man of Europe. Then, a world-wide pandemic occurred, causing millions of deaths and a prolonged sense of isolation, as lockdowns were imposed by a government who ignored the laws they were inflicting upon the rest of us. Throughout all this turbulence, I regretfully came to the conclusion that, at heart, I was not an entrepreneurial type of person, and so I closed my business – with a definite feeling of relief, even though I was heavily in debt. I resolved to work hard to pay my way out of the economic black hole I was in, and when I eventually achieved that goal, there was at least some sense of personal satisfaction.

In the early 2000s, I had returned to my musical calling, and since that time I have prioritised this area of my life more than any other, playing hundreds of gigs and releasing a veritable avalanche of music, often through German Shepherd Records, an independent label I set-up in conjunction with Bob Osborne. The passage of time has inevitably seen family and some of my closest friends pass on; they will remain forever with me in my heart. Meanwhile, my own health, which had been generally good, took a severe turn for the worse in my mid-50s. Over a short period of time, I underwent open-heart surgery, struggled with pneumonia and had more major surgery following a diagnosis of lung cancer. Somehow I survived it all and counted my blessings; my cup remains at least half-full. Along the way, I even managed to find love, and during the aforementioned lockdowns, I challenged myself to write a book… and if you are reading this, I thank you. This is the last issue of three volumes of writing on music from 1970 up until 2000; it ends here because the single, as a format, practically ceased to exist at some point in the early 2000s, as more and more music was accessed by downloading and streaming. I guess it is also true to say that, as I advanced in age and new music emerged, I no longer felt in the swing of things – as George Harrison so wisely opined back when I was just twelve-years old, "All things must pass". I have very much enjoyed the musical journey, and all the friendships that I've been rewarded with along the way, and looking back at it all has been such a delight… truly I have been blessed.

100
MICROPHONE MATHEMATICS
QUASIMOTO
STONES THROW
OTHER SINGLE 1999: HITTIN' HOOKS

One fine day, ace producer and beatmaster Madlib decided to rap to his own beats… but the problem was that he didn't like the sound of his own voice; hence, he manipulated it to create a high-pitched version that sounded like a comic book character. Next, he invented an animated alter-ego called Lord Quas, and so it was that Quasimoto was bizarrely conceived as an equal partnership made up of the real Madlib and Madlib in the guise of Lord Quas. 'Microphone Mathematics' works as a very listenable piece of alt-hip-hop, and equally well as a playful satire on the conformity of content and style in the gangsta rap genre.

99
REMOTE CONTROL/THREE MCS AND ONE DJ
BEASTIE BOYS
GRAND ROYALE
OTHER SINGLES 1999:
ALIVE

At this time, The Beastie Boys were enjoying a creative high-point and their records were highly appealing. This double A-side features a big rock riff on 'Remote Control', whilst the title of 'Three MCs and One DJ' accurately describes the minimalist approach to the track, on which Mix Master Mike creates a scratching groove that allows the three Beasties to display their lyrical chops to the maximum.

98
THE FREE DESIGN
STEREOLAB
DUOPHONIC

With percussively played piano, occasional horn fanfares, grooving organ and a gurgling rhythm – all topped-off with a clean, pure and unaffected vocal from Lætitia Sadier, once more Stereolab demonstrated their unerring knack for creating head music that was actually fun to listen to.

97
REVENGE OF THE BLACK REGENT
ADD N TO (X)
MUTE
OTHER SINGLE 1999:
METAL FINGERS IN MY BODY

The Black Regent had first arrived in 1997 on the debut single by Add N to (X), and he makes a re-appearance here. Heralded by a hyper-distorted synth-bass march, the music alternately soars to heavenly heights, or else it twists and becomes grotesquely corrupted – though the overall balance of the sound is dark and sinister. Nor is any light-relief offered by a whispered female voice which transforms into a kind of grand, neo-operatic supplication to some hidden, devilish entity.

96
LET'S START A FAMILY (BLACKS)
BONNIE PRINCE BILLIE
SUB POP

Despite Will Oldham's voice being somewhat sweetened by a female harmony vocal – and the inclusion of a chipper "Doo-doo-doo" chorus – 'Let's Start a Family' has a very ominous, backwoods feel that is further amplified by a ceaseless and menacingly simple rhythm. The lyric does no more than hint at some attritional malady, but it is more than enough to set the mind to wondering what the hell is going on…

95
GET A MOVE ON!
MR. SCRUFF
NINJA TUNE
OTHER SINGLE 1999: HONEYDEW

Mr. Scruff is the stage-name of Stockport resident Andrew Carthy, one-time Kwik Save shelf-stacker and wildly eclectic tea-loving DJ. 'Get a Move On!' was taken from his breakthrough second album, *Keep it Unreal*; it incorporates samples from 'Bird's Lament' by Moondog, and consequently there is a wonderfully grooving jazz feel to the track. In addition, the simple vocal taken from 'Hypin' Woman Blues' by T-Bone Walker is hugely effective. Essentially, Mr Scruff was working in a comparable style and using similar musical tools to the much more celebrated Moby, and he was equally successful in melding the sounds of past and present into a beautifully blended brew.

94
VIVID
ELECTRONIC
PARLOPHONE
OTHER SINGLE 1999: LATE AT NIGHT

Whereas the first incarnation of Electronic sounded as if Bernard Sumner was very much at the creative helm, things had now changed, and 'Vivid' is most certainly steered by Johnny Marr's more rootsy tastes, further reinforced by the inclusion of Jimi Goodwin from Doves on bass and Black Grape drummer Ged Lynch – definitely more prosaic collaborators than previous guests Karl Bartos and Pet Shop Boys. The song features a crying harmonica from Marr and the band create an atmospheric groove, and although Sumner's lyrics are very much of "The cat sat on the mat" rhyming variety, he throws himself into them with genuine gusto which serves the song rather well.

93
OUR COASTAL HYMN
LES SAVY FAV
DESOTO

Here, employing clever lyrical metaphor, New York art-rock outfit Les Savy Fav examine life's disappointments and the temptation to wish them to come to an abrupt end. For such a downbeat subject, the song is given a raucous, upbeat treatment that switches between loud and quiet passages, and it is never,

ever dull. Singer Tim Harrington doesn't really do finesse, but instead he serves up a feast of highly intense emoting in an extremely no-holds barred fashion.

92
TONY BLAIR
CHUMBAWAMBA
NO LABEL

This track – issued as a mail-order only Christmas present for Chumbawamba fans – masquerades as a sweet, retro pop song in which a girl falls for a boy who has deceived her with his perfidious approach to the truth; of course, in reality, it is an expression of the deep disappointment felt by a growing number of the population in the lack of idealism and integrity within the New Labour government. After the elation following the rout of the Conservative Party at the 1997 general election had started to subside, the truth began to dawn that New Labour were not really much better than the Tories… and Prime Minister Tony Blair was simply Margaret Thatcher in pants.

91
STOP THE ROCK
APOLLO 440
STEALTH SONIC
OTHER SINGLE 1999:
HEART GO BOOM

Apollo 440 were fronted by singer Ian Hoxley, who, under the nom-de-plume of Mary Byker, had once led grebo band Gaye Bykers on Acid. The single 'Stop the Rock' is a knowing reclamation of those roots, being based, as it is, on 'Caroline' by Status Quo. Using Quo's mighty riff as a springboard, we are launched into an electro/dance celebration, with nods toward both Madonna and The Beach Boys woven into the track's frenetically-paced fairground rhythm.

90
WE ON FIRE
HOT BOYS
CASH MONEY

Hot Boys were a New Orleans hip-hop outfit, one of whom was future superstar Lil Wayne. Their sound was generally fresh and effervescent, but 'We on Fire' (taken from the album *Guerilla Warfare*) is particularly raw and energetic, and it just doesn't let up. Each line is delivered as a question, to which the answers are not easily digestible dinner-table fodder for Middle America.

89
BARBER'S ADAGIO FOR STRINGS (REMIX)
WILLIAM ORBIT
WEA

Taking one of the most recognisable pieces of classical music known to humankind and transforming it into a dance track was a pretty bold move by William Orbit… and many would have presumed that such ambition was doomed to failure. But Orbit, with a deep understanding of the dynamics of the piece, trusted his instincts and the successful transformation into a pulsating synth-driven slice of trance music is testament to his outstanding ability – and indeed his willingness to challenge himself and his audience to embrace music from well outside the narrow sphere of reference available to most of the rave generation.

88
YOU MAKE ME FEEL
ARCHIVE
INDEPENDIENTE
OTHER SINGLES 1999:
CLOUD IN THE SKY;
TAKE MY HEAD;
THE WAY YOU LOVE ME

In 1996 I had purchased the first couple of singles released by Archive; I loved their sound and they fascinated me… but ultimately I concluded they were really rather slight songs that just happened to have been on the receiving end of a fabulous production job. Now, with an adjusted line-up in place, the group returned and they sounded just as as sleek and chiselled as previously – but this time there was something extra… an emotional underbelly that seemed to be on the very edge of eruption. 'You Make Me Feel' bears comparison with the epic scale of Portishead's work; there is a dynamic range that can switch from prettiness to aggression in a heartbeat, while the pristine female vocal carries more than just a hint of flesh and blood vulnerability.

87
HERE IT COMES
DOVES
CASINO
OTHER SINGLES 1999:
SEA EP; CEDAR EP

Doves literally rose from the ashes of Sub Sub, after that band's rehearsal room in Ancoats burned down, along with their equipment. The post-disco sound of the earlier group was quickly abandoned as Doves threw themselves into a new beginning with music that leant much more towards alt-rock. 'Here it Comes' immediately locates a mellow groove and doesn't let go of it throughout the entirety of the track, which is pleasantly redolent of a lazy, sunny day spent idly letting the imagination run riot. The wistful vocals are delivered over a hard-hitting drum beat and organ swirls, until a piano breakdown gives way to horns, which in turn are succeeded by the return of a piano, playing out the final notes of an understated, but very impressive piece of music.

86
FOR REAL
TRICKY
ISLAND

Having found himself backed himself into a stylistic corner, Tricky made an effort to enhance and expand his sound by working with American producers (DJ Muggs and Dame Grease) on his album *Juxtapose*. In truth, the album was not a complete success, but 'For Real', extracted from it, did prove to be a very strong single; it is a relatively stripped-back affair and somewhat more conventional sounding than Tricky's earlier work, but with his voice prominently positioned over acoustic guitar and beats, there is a thrilling immediacy. Lyrically too, the track is very strong, as Tricky – with audible contempt – examines his position within the bubble of the recording business.

85
A2G
BLACKALICIOUS
QUANNUM PROJECTS
OTHER SINGLE 1999:
DECEPTION

Blackalicious were a hip-hop duo from Sacramento in California – consisting of rapper Gift of Gab and DJ/producer Chief Xcel – and their EP *A2G* was choc-full of delights. The lyrical dexterity of Gift of Gab is astonishing, displayed to maximum effect on the track 'Alphabet Aerobics' (produced by Cut Chemist) whilst the title track is a hypnotic, piano-based tour-de-force of abstract expressionism.

84
AISHA
DEATH IN VEGAS
CONCRETE
OTHER SINGLES 1999: DIRGE
NEPTUNE CITY

Iggy Pop acts as guest lyricist and vocalist on this single by British dance/rock outfit, Death in Vegas; he gives us a mesmerisingly deadpan performance, portraying a psychically-damaged murderer who is in confessional mode. Swirling all around his voice we hear coffin-nailing beats, a guitar so fuzzy that it is suggestive of an overloading electric chair and also an organ that is pumping out a groovily churning jazzy riff, containing all the theatrical menace of a *Hammer Horror* classic.

83
ALL N MY GRILL
MISSY ELLIOTT
GOLDMIND
OTHER SINGLES 1999:
SHE'S A BITCH; YA DI YA

A superbly futuristic production – courtesy of Timbaland – provides the backdrop for Missy Elliott to deliver a song concerned with cutting a feckless, no-good lover out of her life and exerting her feminine power. Ably assisted by an emotional vocal performance from Nicole Wray, who ad-libs around Missy Elliott's commanding lead, there is also time for a rapping cameo from Outkast's Big Boi. I was never a huge fan of the R&B/rap hybrids that were dominating the airwaves at the time, but 'All n My Grill' is certainly a cut-above the vast majority of them.

82
YALLA YALLA
JOE STRUMMER
& THE MESCALEROS
MERCURY

Although Joe Strummer's career had meandered somewhat following the demise of The Clash (where, for the most part, his adoption of the role of rebel rocker was a defining and guiding principle), 'Yalla Yalla' was a thrilling demonstration of the talent that Strummer possessed… and it definitely stands comparison with most of his more popular work. It is a loosely thematic song that stands in opposition to those who seek to legislate against other people's personal freedoms. Musically, it is rather low key; a bubbling synth groove and a steady back-beat are all that Strummer requires in order to summon up his eloquent passion in support of those without a voice. As he sings – occasionally veering-off on thrilling tangents – he alludes to hip-hop and reggae culture and sees no boundaries or barriers between people; we all share the same problems, and together we are stronger is, once again, his consistent and unifying message.

81
NEW YORK CITY BOY
PET SHOP BOYS
PARLOPHONE
OTHER SINGLE 1999: I DON'T KNOW WHAT YOU WANT BUT I CAN'T GIVE IT ANY MORE

The steady procession of high-quality Pet Shop Boys hits continued with this ode to disco culture which contains a Village People-style chorus, strings courtesy of Vincent Montana Jr. from Salsoul Orchestra and a sample from Donna Summer's version of 'MacArthur Park'. The song celebrates the coming-out and sexual awakening of the titular 'New York City Boy' who is on the cusp of discovering the exciting club culture that he will soon throw himself into in a glorious, hedonistic rush towards new pleasures.

80
GET DIS MONEY
SLUM VILLAGE
INTERSCOPE
OTHER SINGLE 1999: CLIMAX

Following his death in 2006, James Dewitt Yancey, aka Jay Dee and J Dilla, would come to be regarded as a genius figure in hip-hop circles – but at this point in time, when he was still part of Detroit trio Slum Village, his talent was only known to the cognoscenti. Debut single 'Get Dis Money' clearly displays the prodigious production skills of J Dilla; he employs a sample from Herbie Hancock's 'Come Running to Me' to create a spacey and meditative vibe, and then, along with rappers T3 and Baatin, they consider the dilemma of having no money with which to chase their dreams… they are poor and they want to get paid…

79
PRETTIEST THING
THE CREATURES
SIOUX
OTHER SINGLE 1999: STAY

The previous single release by The Creatures had been 'Stay', a sombre and intense response to the death by suicide of Siouxsie Sioux's friend, Billy McKenzie of The Associates. For 'Prettiest Thing', the intensity level remains high, but there is also a sense of brooding malevolence in the whispered vocal and voodoo-ceremony style percussion. The lyrics contain disturbing and violent imagery and they hint at a possessiveness that has gone way past any normal boundaries of decency and morality.

78
I SEE YOU BABY
GROOVE ARMADA FEATURING GRAM'MA FUNK
JIVE ELECTRO

Groove Armada were a British duo operating in the electronic dance field, and they were nothing if not eclectic. Their previous single, 'At the River', had been a subtle and summery jazz homage, whereas 'I See You Baby' is a risqué, robo-funk dance number with more than a touch of Benny Hill-style sauciness conveyed via the "Shakin' that ass" refrain. Although this isn't chic in the manner of Air or Daft Punk – more Blackpool than Eiffel Tower perhaps! – it does cover similar ground stylistically, and it is undeniably a fantastically fun dance record.

77
SUPERFREAKY MEMORIES
LUNA
JERICHO

'Superfreaky Memories' is a song about looking back with wistful fondness at more dissolute times… days of scoring and taking drugs, then nodding and hanging out. It is a rather beautiful song with a fuzzy softness to its sound. Dean Wareham half-sings and half-speaks his way through the astute lyric that is a truthful portrayal of the way in which love can exist even during the most damaging periods of our lives.

76
ONCE AROUND THE BLOCK
BADLY DRAWN BOY
XL

In the guise of Badly Drawn Boy, Damon Gough from Bolton came along with this melodic and very appealing single. With his wispy beard and wooly hat, Gough was portrayed as being some sort of shambling hobo in the folk tradition, but 'Once Around the Block' is actually a breezy, baroque pop number with stylistic similarities to Love's seminal *Forever Changes* album, or perhaps the 1960s American group The Left Banke. Whatever the comparison may or may not be, Gough croons his way through the song with a confident ease, whilst the little musical flourishes make for a most stimulating listen.

75
OUT OF THE BLUE
SYSTEM F
ESSENTIAL

System F was an alias used by Dutch DJ/producer Ferry Corsten and here, with 'Out of the Blue', he creates a very European slice of exceptionally speedy hard trance music that also contains stately neo-classical themes, as well as the requisite horn and whistle breakdowns that are guaranteed to raise pulses on the dance-floor.

74
SWASTIKA EYES
PRIMAL SCREAM
CREATION

This provocatively titled release was a speedy excursion into techno territory for Primal Scream, and it was issued as a single containing two different mixes of the same track; the Chemical Brothers interpretation hurtles like a runaway train, detouring into dub territory and downgrading Bobby Gillespie's vocal to mere background noise amidst the carnage of the rhythmic rush. On the other hand, the Jagz Kooner version is more restrained and it contains much more group instrumentation, as well as placing Gillespie's voice higher in the mix to reveal a lyric that rails against illusions of democracy and justice.

73
COLD BLOODED OLD TIMES
SMOG
DOMINO
OTHER SINGLES 1999: LOOK NOW; HELD

A chugging Velvet Underground-style riff is surely one of the most joyous sounds in contemporary music, and here we have a very fine example – augmented only with a hand-clap rhythm and a smidgen of honky-tonk piano – which provides the rather jaunty accompaniment for a downbeat Bill Callahan to deliver a very skilfully composed lyric that references the emotional fall-out of some distressing, but unspecified domestic incident. This truly marvellous single came from the equally marvellous Smog album *Knock Knock*, and it became a surprise radio hit following its exposure as part of the soundtrack to the movie *High Fidelity*.

72
NA FE THROW IT
ROUND FIVE FEATURING TIKIMAN
MAIN STREET

'Round Five' was just one of multiple aliases adopted by German duo Mark Ernestus and Moritz Von Oswald, and this particular track also features regular contributor Tikiman on vocals. 'Na Fe Throw It' is a trippy and spacey, down-tempo techno/dub excursion, but Tikiman's rootsy and reggaefied vocals provide the flesh, blood and soulfulness that is juxtaposed amidst the hypnotic and soothing, head-nodding machine grooves.

71
THE DAY THE WORLD WENT AWAY
NINE INCH NAILS
INTERSCOPE
OTHER SINGLE 1999: WE'RE IN THIS TOGETHER

An ever-so-quiet drone is interrupted by a pounding, distorted and brutal guitar riff which suddenly stops dead. Then the drone continues and the voice of Trent Reznor is introduced, singing in his gnarled and gravelly voice about pursuing a path towards some kind of redemption, which he can never reach because his hopes – indeed is entire world – keep slipping away. When the voice ceases, the drone continues, until, with even more force, the brutal riff returns, but louder and more raggedy, buzzing wildly like the sound you might hear if you pushed your head into a wasps' nest. Finally, following the addition of some wordless voices, the tumult once again stops dead and this incredibly dynamic track has reached a suitably dramatic conclusion.

70
HEART COOKS BRAIN
MODEST MOUSE
MATADOR
OTHER SINGLE 1999: NIGHT OF THE SUN

This British-only release – originally released as a track on 1997 album *The Lonesome Crowded West* – seems to be about the age-old conflict between logic and emotion. Although metaphorically colourful and thought-provoking, the song is lyrically abstract and elusive, while musically the song is a medium-paced push-and-pull shuffle; there is a nagging guitar line which shouts-out for attention whereas the bass is grounded and pacifying. Admittedly, singer Isaac Brock does have one of those Marmite voices, but here, his angsty yowl is excellently well-judged.

69
HOLD ON
TOM WAITS
ANTI

As with so many Tom Waits songs, this one (co-written with his wife Kathleen Brennan) is, in essence, a vignette… a short-story set to music that is acted-out with Waits himself in the central role. 'Hold On' is a gentle lamentation on the trials and tribulations of life in general – but here concentrating specifically on the disintegration of a marriage due to high-expectations leading to broken dreams and disillusionment. Waits is the stoical narrator of the sorry tale who steadfastly refuses to give in and stop dreaming and believing – "Hold on" he urges. This bruised, romantic figure remains resolute in his confidence that things can be repaired through sheer force of will. Taken from the album *Mule Variations*, this song is infused with the blues… and nobody else can sing the blues with quite the style of Tom Waits.

68
I'D LIKE THAT
XTC
COOKING VINYL
OTHER SINGLE 1999: DREAM THEATRE

At this point XTC were no longer hit-makers, but they were still expert purveyors of intelligent and tuneful pop records that were often heart-warming delights… and 'I'd Like That' is exactly one of those. This gorgeously melodic song (written by Andy Partridge) is an unashamed, McCartney-esque love song – played predominantly on acoustic guitar – which features some dreamy vocal harmonies, and the track is given a charming rustic feel by virtue of the Wiltshire twang evident in Partridge's love-lorn croon.

67
CARROT ROPE
PAVEMENT
DOMINO
SPIT ON A STRANGER

'Carrot Rope' was the closing track on *Terror Twilight* – the final Pavement album – and thanks to John Peel, it received substantial radio airplay which built-up demand for what would prove to be the band's last single and highest UK chart placing. It meant that, happily, Pavement went out on a deserved high-note, because 'Carrot Rope' is an enchanting, irresistibly charming and eccentric song, that is also extremely catchy and uplifting.

66
SING IT SHITFACE
EDAN
BISCUITHEAD RECORDINGS

Edan is an alternative hip-hop artist from Rockville, Maryland, and here he uses lightweight, family-friendly music as a disarming backdrop to a skilful, scabrous and very funny verbal tirade. His whining, bratty rapping style is similar to that of the no more talented, but much more famous, Eminem. Although he would go on to collaborate with MF Doom and Cut Chemist, Edan remains an underground artist, and since the early 2000s – apart from some private pressings – he has only re-appeared once, in 2018, for a collaborative album with Homeboy Sandman.

65
SVEFN-G-ENGLAR
SIGUR RÓS
FAT CAT

'Svefn-G-Englar' was the nine-minutes and sixteen-seconds long debut single from Sigur Rós, and the title was taken from an Icelandic pun which mixes "sleepwalkers" with "sleep angels". As it drifts along dreamily, this stunningly beautiful and atmospheric piece of music is close to being an ambient track, but the gritty, distorted guitars lurking menacingly beneath the surface, provide at least a hint of darkness. The floaty vocals are ethereal and haunting, and with this record, the Sigur Rós sound was at once established, so almost straight away, their name became a reliable signifier of high-quality.

64
CONCRETE AND CLAY
KEVIN ROWLAND
CREATION

'Concrete and Clay' had been a 1960s hit for Unit 4 + 2, and Kevin Rowland included it on his album of cover versions, *My Beauty*, which was an affectionate and fascinating journey through the songs that had affected – and helped to mould – the future Dexys Midnight Runners front-man. His version of 'Concrete and Clay' was chosen as a single, and to coincide with its release, Rowland's latest new image was revealed; he appeared feminised and was wearing a mini-skirt. This was all too much for both the media and his previous fan base; those who did not ignore him, chose to ridicule instead. Rowland received next-to-zero support and so the single stiffed, as did the album… but those who did choose to listen were rewarded with a superb take on a very fine song. Like the original, Rowland gives the song a South American style treatment, incorporating Latin percussion and flamenco guitar, and he sings with great feeling; his voice, which had always been superb, was now better than ever. If he had presented himself in a more conventional way, the single would almost certainly have been on heavy rotation across the airwaves… and most probably a huge hit. But Rowland, always a maverick, chose the brave and honest path; by showing the world exactly where he was at, he paid a really heavy price… for the next decade, his career nose-dived towards oblivion.

63
STILL D.R.E.
DR. DRE FEATURING SNOOP DOGG
AFTERMATH

Dr. Dre had not been idle; he had produced both Snoop Dogg and Eminem's genre-defining debut albums, but he hadn't released any music under his own name since 1992. Feeling pressure to produce a hit, he recruited Jay-Z to ghost-write the lyrics for 'Still D.R.E.' – which was an accurate portrayal of Dre's street-level world-view – and, as Snoop Dogg himself commented, he did the job "flawlessly". The beats too were mesmerising, and as Dre and Snoop swapped rhymes at the mic, their chemistry was evident. When the track was completed, it was obvious they had a hip-hop anthem on their hands… so for Dr. Dre, his return was an unqualified triumph.

62
THE JAG
THE MICRONAUTS
SCIENCE

The Micronauts was an alias used by Cristophe Monier and 'The Jag' is a quirky slice of electronica with more than just a hint of disco flavouring introduced via samples taken from 'Make it Last Forever' by Inner Life, and a slowed-down sample of Joyce Sims's version of '(You Make Me Feel Like) A Natural Woman'. There is a strong sense of listening to disco music that comes from another dimension of space and time, and when combined with the electronic beats and bleeps, the effect is both eerie and inspired. In addition to the great music, there is also a visual element courtesy of an arresting and arty video film directed by Gregg Araki, making the whole package a totally fabulous creation.

61
NORTHERN LITES
SUPER FURRY ANIMALS
CREATION
OTHER SINGLE 1999:
FIRE IN MY HEART

This irresistible song (about the weather!) came from the ever idiosyncratic Super Furry Animals;

it is played in a cheery manner with a psychedelic, surf-style approach, replete with calypso steel drums and middle-of-the-road harmonies. Audacious in a way that only only a truly experimental outfit can be, this is yet another great pop record from a band who refused to cynically design their music to pander to audience tastes; instead, they did as they pleased, and happily found that what they created just happened to coincide with what the people wanted to hear.

60
BUTTONED DOWN DISCO
CLINTON
MECCICO

Side-stepping the pressing issue of how to follow-up the mega success of 'Brimful of Asha', two of Cornershop's principal members, Tjinder Singh and Ben Ayres, concentrated on their side-project, the more dance orientated Clinton. Their single, 'Buttoned Down Disco', owed its title to a long-running nightclub, and it is a playful and funky mix of horns, bleeps, hand-claps and sampled female vocals, all coming together to create a superbad groove for post-rock pre-millennials.

59
THEM THAT'S NOT
J-LIVE
LONDON

Copping a lazy jazz groove from 'All But Blind' (an Eddie Russ track from 1974), after four bars J-Live lets rip with a mega-quick, but supremely cool rapped vocal, fully displaying his oral dexterity, story-telling skills and humorous take on the life that he leads. This outstanding and totally fresh effort was a unique approach to the hip-hop form.

58
SEXX LAWS
BECK
GEFFEN

Not allowing himself to be manœuvred into a stylistic cul-de-sac, Beck undertook a sonic overhaul with the provocatively titled 'Sexx Laws', which melds a 1960s boogaloo rhythm with marching band horns and a bluegrass banjo solo – there is not a guitar in sight! Musically, this is big, brassy and bold, matched by an unrestrained vocal, with Beck singing about non-conformity in carnal affairs – the abandoning of taboos and stereotypical roles. Although it went unsaid, the implication is, of course, that this freeing of the mind from conventional patterns of behaviour is to be encouraged in non-sexual areas of our lives too.

57
I SURRENDER
DAVID SYLVIAN
VIRGIN
OTHER SINGLE 1999: GOD-MAN

After six-years without a single, David Sylvian released this quiet and reflective delight – a nine-minutes and twenty-five seconds jazz-infused piece. The song winds its way through numerous verses that express a renewed, and almost spiritual commitment to love, all of which are enhanced by Sylvian's beautiful singing voice... and the icing on the cake is a memorable flugelhorn solo from the masterful Kenny Wheeler.

56
ECHO'S ANSWER
BROADCAST
WARP

'Echo's Answer' is a gorgeous and understated meditative piece that incorporates elements of 'Nocturne' by Benjamin Britten. Minimalism is the key word here, but the melody is carried by Trish Keenan's girlish vocal timbre, and this quiet, yet powerful, piece of music stimulates the senses in a most captivating way.

55
NATIONAL EXPRESS
THE DIVINE COMEDY
SETANTA
OTHER SINGLE 1999:
THE POP SINGER'S FEAR OF THE POLLEN COUNT

'National Express' is a sharply-observed song concerning a trip taken with the long-distance coach company of the title. At the time, it was attacked by trendy socialists in the music press for being a sneering side-swipe at the working classes, when actually it was nothing of the sort. It is, in fact, a jaunty musical ride alongside a wide variety of other people – a sort of musical equivalent to the cinematic "kitchen sink" dramas of the 1960s – in which an illustrative tranche of human life is represented as co-passengers in this piano-led piece of clever, tuneful pop.

54
HIP-HOP
DEAD PREZ
LOUD
OTHER SINGLE 1999:
THEY SCHOOLS

Dead Prez were a well-schooled and politicised duo from New York who explored themes that other hip-hop acts were reluctant to touch, simply because they were anti-capitalist advocates working within a scene where the acquisition of wealth was perceived to be of prime importance. 'Hip-hop' is a single with a very sharply-pointed message that is aimed squarely at the hip-hop community at large; it tackles issues such as soundalike tracks by fake gangsters, the appalling treatment of women and the abuses of the recording industry. Although the themes discussed are all serious, their presentation is nothing less than joyous. The track features a wobbly and distorted synth bass riff along with crisply rapped vocals and a beautiful, unforgettably simple chorus.

53
HOT TOPIC
LE TIGRE
WIIIJA

Following the demise of Bikini Kill, singer and writer Kathleen Hanna formed the no-less socio-political Le Tigre – though rather than serve-up the full-frontal punk rock approach of the former band, this new ensemble were much more eclectic and playful, opting for a lo-fi electronic sound that was friendly and danceable. 'Hot Topic' was the group's first release and it trots along briskly rather than gallops; 1960s-style girl-group backing vocals are a prominent feature, along with fuzzy guitar accompanying the frisky beat whilst Hanna sings complimentary lyrics about strong female role models from the world of art.

52
THE TEMPLE
DESTROYER
ENDEARING

Destroyer are a band from Vancouver led by Dan Bejar; in 1995 they had released an album in cassette format, but 'The Temple' was their first single. It is played mostly as a piano vamp, over which, in a highly stylised, near yelping voice, Bejar sings cryptic verses which lead into a chorus that proclaims there is joy in being barred from the temple – and additionally we are twice treated to wonderful, counter-intuitive fuzzy guitar solos that give an extra kick to an already fascinating and individualistic release.

51
THIS IS YOUR LIFE
DUST BROTHERS
BMG

The Dust Brothers were a pair of musician/producers who came to prominence by helping The Beastie Boys create the layered and sample-heavy classic album *Paul's Boutique*, before working with, amongst others, Beck and The Rolling Stones. They were then engaged by film director David Fincher to score his cinematic version of the Chuck Palahniuk novel *Fight Club*, and 'This Is Your Life' is taken from the soundtrack to that film. It features lead actor Brad Pitt delivering a spoken monologue, which is set to a moody piece of rumbling electronica – with a devastating bass line at its core – and trip-hop beats that are not a million miles away from the sound of Massive Attack. All-in-all, this packs a real wallop.

50
THURSDAY'S CHILD
DAVID BOWIE
VIRGIN
OTHER SINGLE 1999:
THE PRETTY THINGS ARE
GOING TO HELL

'Thursday's Child' finds David Bowie – and co-writer Reeves Gabrels – opting for a smooth, mellow sound that is embellished with string effects to complement the wistful lyric that Bowie laconically conveys concerning a man who is looking into his past and despairing at his lack of achievement; he contemplates an equally bleak future before finally meeting somebody who gives him a renewed sense of purpose and optimism. Inspired by children's stories and the well-known rhyme that tells us "Thursday's child has far to go", this was a subtle and reflective mini-gem.

49
GET INVOLVED
RAPHAEL SAADIQ FEATURING Q-TIP
HOLLYWOOD

Raphael Saadiq was described by music critic Robert Christgau as "The pre-eminent R&B artist of the 1990s" and a glance at his production credits is enough to corroborate that accolade. Formerly, he had been a member of a production collective called The Ummah, alongside D'Angelo, Ali Shaheed Muhammad, J Dilla and Q-Tip, and it was with the latter that Saadiq put together 'Get Involved', which was first aired on animated TV show *The PJ's*. The track obtains its strutting soulfulness from Philly classic 'I'll Always Love My Mama' by The Intruders, but it builds upwards from that base to create something really fresh and unique; a modern twist is applied by incorporating elements of hip-hop and R&B, all mixed together in a seamless, joyous flow.

48
EXPO 2000
KRAFTWERK
EMI

The organisers of the *Hanover Expo 2000* world fair had hoped to engage Kraftwerk to do a one-off concert to open the event; the group were not able to comply with that request but they did provide a vocoderised voice singing 'Expo 2000'. Liking the sound of this snippet, the band elected to compose a full song based around it. This turned out to be Kraftwerk's first new music since 1986, and that fact alone was sufficient to arouse a good deal of interest. In the event, the finished track was no mere novelty record – it is melodically very strong and infused with the sense of classicism that had been a constant in the music of Kraftwerk for decades past. Admittedly, it didn't break any new ground as the world had effectively caught-up with these incredible innovators; but nevertheless, it was wonderful to once again hear potent new sounds from this group who had been such trailblazing sonic pioneers.

47
(YOU DRIVE ME) CRAZY
BRITNEY SPEARS
JIVE

Surely designed as a sound-alike to previous mega hit '... Baby One More Time'... except that '(You Drive Me) Crazy' is even more insanely addictive. This is a sugar-rush of a track; every element from Britney's heavily treated vocal to the grinding dance/rock riff hits the sweet-spot. The teen-appeal was immediately obvious and undeniable... but as a pop music loving adult, I had to ask "Why deny myself the pleasure?" This is classic dumb pop – and speaking as someone who had grown-up with T.Rex and The Sweet as part of my school-day soundtrack, it was almost like old-times again...

46
ROCK N ROLL (COULD NEVER HIP-HOP LIKE THIS)
HANDSOME BOY MODELING CLUB
TOMMY BOY
OTHER SINGLES 199:
THE TRUTH; METAPHYSICAL; MAGNETIZING;
THE PROJECTS

Handsome Boy Modeling Club was a conceptual hip-hop duo consisting of Dan the Automator and Prince Paul, who adopted the fictional identities of Nathaniel Merriweather and Chest Rockwell respectively. They worked with numerous guest vocalists and released brilliant, satirical mind-food that was of greater cultural than chart significance. However, they could also produce records that were just pure fun, and 'Rock 'n' Roll (Could Never Hip-Hop Like This) is unequivocal evidence of that fact. It is put together via obscure 1970s rock band samples to create a sludgy, Black Sabbath-type riff of genius simplicity; this is then combined with hip-hop beats and repeated assertions of the fact that "Rock and roll could never hip-hop like this"... and insofar as this proclamation goes, they were most certainly not mistaken!

45
WATERPARK
ROYAL TRUX
DOMINO

Taken from their album *Veterans of Disorder*, this outing was as straightforward and orthodox as Royal Trux ever got. It is a belligerently sleazy boogie-woogie record with a hay-wire guitar sound and a spat-out, tobacco-chewing vocal that indicates an extreme, hostile and brattishly bad attitude. A trip to the 'Waterpark' with this dangerous duo might not hold much appeal – but the sound they make in issuing the invitation is fantastic.

44
HE TOOK HER TO A MOVIE
LADYTRON
INVICTA HI-FI

Ladytron were an electro band who took their name from a Roxy Music song title; they came from Liverpool and 'He Took Her to a Movie' was their first record release. It is seemingly written from the point-of-view of an individual who is part of a love-triangle... but the least loved and most needy of the three. Delivered with deadpan style – and melodically similar to 'The Model' by Kraftwerk – this nevertheless has enough individuality and quirkiness to make it a very attractive and impressive debut.

43
GENIE IN A BOTTLE
CHRISTINA AGUILERA
RCA

After appearing on TV show *The Mickey Mouse Club* – and therefore following in the footsteps of Justin Timberlake and Britney Spears – Aguilera had been groomed for pop stardom over a number of years. 'Genie in a Bottle' was the first single from Aguilera's debut album and it deservedly pitched her into the high-end of charts worldwide and established her as a talented singer who was able to convey adult themes with a convincing level of maturity. The record has a rumbling R&B groove, a killer chorus and a lyric that suggests a sexual awakening; this was pop music gold of the finest quality.

42
I TRY
MACY GRAY
EPIC

The distinctive voice of Macy Gray – in combination with an organically rendered soul-groove and a lyric full of painful longing – was phenomenal and absolutely refreshing; this was a sound that had largely gone out of fashion since the time that Al Green stopped having hit records. To achieve such alchemy is a difficult trick to pull off, but it was successfully accomplished here and 'I Try' is a really magical record.

41
ECHO
KRISTIN HERSH
4AD

Besides leading Throwing Muses since the early 1990s, Hersh had simultaneously kept up a solo career, and here we have 'Echo' which expresses a range of contradictory emotions with a stark lyric that is sung with unerring clarity; maybe the subtext of this song is the notion that nothing in life is without complications, and these complications can really mess with the head – or maybe it isn't that… it doesn't really matter since each individual's take is equally valid. What is certain is the impressive musicality of the track, which alternates in the quiet/loud/quiet again pattern, that when performed as skilfully as this example is, first lulls and then jolts the listener, as it moves from music-box prettiness to full-throttle guitar noise.

40
TOUCH SENSITIVE
THE FALL
ARTFUL

Even in trying times The Fall were still capable of pulling metaphorical rabbits out of hats and turning them into magical singles such as this. Basically, it is a garage-rock stomper – composed by Julia Adamson – and it has a chanted "Hey, hey, hey" backing vocal that runs throughout like lettering inside Blackpool rock, while Mark E. Smith throws down a typically snarky vocal dismissing all those who considered him too old and drunk to still be relevant. Combative to the very end, this shows The Fall coming out fighting after receiving near knockout blows… and it was a record that turned the tide in their favour once again.

39
REVOLUTION ACTION
ATARI TEENAGE RIOT
DIGITAL HARDCORE
OTHER SINGLE 1999: TOO DEAD FOR ME

Atari Teenage Riot were a ferocious and often thrilling proposition; their mix of punk rock, electronics, visceral noise and screamed-out slogans was never likely to endear them to a mass audience – but I loved to listen to them… in small doses. 'Revolution Action' sounds like a scorching, malevolent collision between Public Enemy and Einstürzende Neubauten, as Alec Empire rages against the abuse of power by people in authority.

38
FLAME
SEBADOH
DOMINO

As miraculous as it may seem, Sebadoh really did have a UK hit single with 'Flame', which reached number thirty with a bullet. It has an ultra simple groove, riding along on just one riff and one rhythm; if sounds were feelings, this would be the exhilarating sensation of bouncing up and down, high above a swimming pool on a highly sprung diving board. Lou Barlow, in mid-register, delivers a lyric that seems to me to be about a person declining the promptings of another to engage in hard-drug usage; I may well be misinterpreting here, but the message could be something to the effect of "You can do whatever you choose and I won't judge you… but I don't want to do as you do, and my no means no".

37
MY FEELING
JUNIOR JACK
NOISE TRAXX

Belgium-based Italian Vito Lucente was the man behind the Junior Jack pseudonym, and his first single was 'My Feeling', an infectious, irrepressible excursion into house music territory. Apart from a dubby vocal section, the beat is constantly repeated; it never flags, never drags and never runs out of steam. This is relentless, good-time dance music that is seasoned with euro-disco stylings to create a near-perfect party record.

36
NO OTHER BABY
PAUL MCCARTNEY
PARLOPHONE

Paul McCartney returned to his roots with *Run Devil Run*, a rock-and-roll cover versions album from which 'No Other Baby' was chosen as a single. The song was originally recorded, in skiffle-style, by Dickie Bishop & the Sidekicks in 1957, whereas McCartney's version is consummate, laid-back rock-and-roll deluxe. The guitar, bass and drums are treated with an approximation of Sun Studio echo, while McCartney's vocal performance is both upfront and superb; truly he was just as brilliant a rock-and-roll singer as Little Richard, Jerry Lee Lewis or Elvis Presley. 'No Other Baby' is a superlative recording that wouldn't have been out of place on *With The Beatles* or *Beatles For Sale*.

35
SALTWATER
CHICANE FEATURING MÁIRE BRENNAN
XTRAVAGANZA

This is epic, uplifting trance, courtesy of English composer/musician Chicane who uses the ethereal voice of Clannad singer Máire Brennan to highly impressive effect, as well as employing vocal elements (sung in Gaelic) from that band's hit record 'Theme from Harry's Game'. This is best listened to in the unedited version, when it feels like a transportive journey to an elevated state of mind.

34
RUN ON
MOBY
MUTE
OTHER SINGLES 1999:
WHY DOES MY HEART FEEL SO BAD?; BODYROCK

Because he used a prominent vocal sample from the gospel hymn 'Run On For A Long Time' – as recorded in 1949 by Bill Landford and the Landfordaires – Moby was accused of exploiting impoverished artists; up to a point, Moby himself agreed that this was true, though he also argued that he was shining a light upon – and awakening interest in – music that would otherwise be gathering the dust of neglect. On this latter point, I emphatically side with Moby… and besides, it should also be pointed out that there is a lot more to the record than just that particular sample; the song is very skilfully put together and mixed into a joyous, madcap piano-vamp that jumps, bounces and grooves.

33
THE RUBETTES
THE AUTEURS
HUT

As mentioned previously, The Auteurs songwriter Luke Haines was somewhat misanthropic in his world-view; amid the nostalgia boom instigated by horrible Britpop acts, Haines was sufficiently triggered to respond with a sarcastic swipe via this vicious parody of a nostalgia song. But here, he hones in not on the 1960s acts who happened to be in vogue, but rather the hapless and extremely lame 1970s hitmakers The Rubettes – who were, ironically, a nostalgia act themselves. The titular hook from their signature tune 'Sugar Baby Love' is appropriated here, and although The Rubettes themselves are never mentioned in the lyric, masturbation is alluded to as something dreadful going on beneath the bed covers. All-in-all, this is delicious satire with very sharp claws.

32
YOU DON'T KNOW ME
ARMAND VAN HELDEN FEATURING DUANE HARDEN
FFRR
OTHER SINGLE 1999:
FLOWERZ

Here, American studio musician Armand Van Helden used sampling to create a looped backing track, and then invited collaborator Duane

Harden to write some lyrics and do the singing; the spectacular result is a track of relentless energy, full of musical hooks, that gets even more of a wow factor thanks to Harden's gritty vocal repudiation of other people's negativity towards him. This lit up dance-floors like a firework display, and it sounds equally good coming out of a transistor radio; in short, an ageless, classic chart-topper.

31
EVERYTHING IS EVERYTHING
LAURYN HILL
RUFFHOUSE

This was written by Lauryn Hill to express her concern about the social injustice suffered by inner-city ghetto youth; she sees how negativity can destroy young lives and encourages philosophical thought as a way of side-stepping the traps and mistakes that so many fall into, and also as a method of focussing on rising above desperate situations. The song, pitched as a raw soul number with hip-hop elements, features a piano vamp – played by future hit-maker John Legend – which is central to its inventive, rhythmic signature; it also demands a strong vocal that is, nevertheless, still sufficiently nuanced to express empathy, anger and compassion… of course, Lauryn Hill effortlessly delivers on that score.

30
SPANISH DANCE TROUPE
GORKY'S ZYGOTIC MYNCI
MANTRA

With its melding of acid-tinged folk, lovely melodies and Tijuana-style brass, the sweetly sung 'Spanish Dance Troupe' could not have been made by anybody other than Gorky's Zygotic Mynci. The mix of violin, Spanish guitar and woodwind instruments is typically idiosyncratic, managing to sound simultaneously childlike and profound. Gorky's had the uncanny knack of making strange and mysterious music that still functioned perfectly well as sunny pop.

29
SCI-FI WASABI
CIBO MATTO
WARNER BROTHERS
OTHER SINGLES 1999:
SPOON; WORKING FOR VACATION; MOONCHILD

The Japanese duo of Yuka Honda and Miho Hatori imagine their lives in New York to be comparable to life inside a video game, and the lyrics for 'Sci-fi Wasabi' find them cycling around the city attempting to relate and feel compatible. This track also finds them experimenting with hip-hop; they rap over a simple beat and growling electronic noise, and there are additional vocals by Duma Love. As ever, Cibo Matto avoid stereotypical manœuvres, and they leave us with a deliciously joyful sound, full of boundless energy.

28
GET UP
SLEATER-KINNEY
KILL ROCK STARS
OTHER SINGLE 1999: A QUARTER TO THREE

Tackling the big issues of life and death – with all the attendant feelings of lust and desire – Sleater-Kinney opine that they will live without inhibition and any notions of shame. Over a swirling, dizzying guitar and bass riff, accompanied by gut-thumping drums, the song is delivered with two distinct voices; one cool and matter-of-fact, the other wired and expressive. This is a track with huge momentum, impossible to ignore and easy to love.

27
ERASE/REWIND
THE CARDIGANS
POLYDOR
OTHER SINGLE 1999:
HANGING AROUND

Although my favourite Swedish band is definitely Abba, my second favourite has to be The Cardigans, who shared the Abba-esque knack of producing near-perfect pop records, seemingly on demand. 'Erase/Rewind' slows things down considerably from previous monster hit 'My Favourite Game', as it is played at leisurely pace, and although there is a hauntingly beautiful melody, there is also an undeniably chilly edge to proceedings. Perhaps it is the ice-pick percussion, combined with the clipped clarity of Nina Persson's vocal and the glacial quality of the synths that sends a shiver down the spine; there is something distinctly unsettling about the antiseptically clean sound, as if the group had been recording under laboratory conditions.

26
PRAISE YOU
FATBOY SLIM
SKINT
OTHER SINGLES 1999: RIGHT HERE, RIGHT NOW; BUILD IT UP - TEAR IT DOWN

To construct the monumental big-beat anthem that is 'Praise You', Norman Cook (aka Fatboy Slim) used six samples; most prominently, he used a vocal sample from American civil-rights activist Camille Yarbrough's 1975 record 'Take Yo' Praise', though he also weaved his head-spinning sound thanks to samples located on audio equipment records and a Walt Disney soundtrack, as well as a piano riff and drums from tracks by The Steve Miller Band and Tom Fogerty respectively. Despite the complexity, the whole piece was put together so skilfully that the essence of the Camille Yarbrough song remained fully intact, and consequently 'Praise You' functions brilliantly as a hedonistic dance track… but one that is profoundly imbued with a deep emotional quality.

25 LIGHTERS ON MY DRESSER
DJ DMD FEATURING LIL' KEKE AND FAT PAT
EASTWEST
OTHER SINGLE 1999:
GO BACK HOME

Texan hip-hop producer DJ DMB had put together a rhythm utilising a sample from R&B track 'Nite and Day' by Al B. Sure it was simple, but highly potent, and with further input from rappers Lil' Keke and Fat Pat they dropped a proverbial bomb... the aftershocks of which were heard within hip-hop for many years to come. The title and subject matter of '25 Lighters' is derived from the way that dealers would pack cleaned-out BIC lighters with drugs in order to disguise their transactions. Lil' Keke and Fat Pat have contrasting styles – the former is doleful and the latter quite sharp – but they work together extremely well, and southern hip-hop was very well represented by this collaborative classic.

24
SHE'S LOSING IT
BELLE AND SEBASTIAN
JEEPSTER

Taken from Belle and Sebastian's 1996 album *Tigermilk*, the funny but tender 'She's Losing It' takes a look at Chelsea, a girl who has suffered an abusive past and is so full of anger that she treats the male narrator of the song as a punch bag. Eventually Chelsea meets Lisa, who helps her to feel better, and in the end she concludes that "Inch for inch and pound for pound, who needs boys when there's Lisa around". The song is short and sharp, but the brevity means that not a single word is wasted. Musically, we hear a minimal, almost skiffle-like strum with dabs of colour added by nice and cheery trumpet playing.

23
HEY BOY HEY GIRL
THE CHEMICAL BROTHERS
FREESTYLE DUST
OTHER SINGLES 1999:
ONLY 4 THE K PEOPLE;
LET FOREVER BE;
OUT OF CONTROL

'Hey Boy Hey Girl' is an incredibly intense, psychedelic trip of a record; it starts-off as a hyper-anxious trance-track before exploding into a monstrous, big-beat raver that fizzes like a shaken bottle of Lucozade. The track features a vocal sample from hip-hop classic 'The Roof is on Fire' by Rock Master Scott & the Dynamic Three, which is skilfully transformed into an unforgettable and devastatingly effective hook. At that time UK dance music was in an incredibly healthy state and The Chemical Brothers possessed the remarkable combination of being both artistically credible and commercially unstoppable.

22
PUMPING ON YOUR STEREO
SUPERGRASS
PARLOPHONE
OTHER SINGLES 1999:
MARY; MOVING

There were often hidden depths to the music of Supergrass that were not evident on the surface; here, there are hints of classical music in the chord progressions, and lyrically, the influence of Spanish poet Manuel Machado can be heard. The band assimilate these elements into a piece of seemingly simple, energetic, guitar-driven pop, with the strut and swagger of The Rolling Stones or David Bowie very much attached. 'Pumping on your Stereo' is a very accomplished piece of work, albeit the song's mega-sized chorus is subject to a minor act of self-sabotage as the group cheekily sing "Humping on your stereo". – Supergrass were most definitely not precious, and in fact this lack of pretention served them very well and proved to be a most endearing attribute.

21
YOU GET WHAT YOU GIVE
NEW RADICALS
MCA
OTHER SINGLE 1999:
SOMEDAY WE'LL KNOW

New Radicals were a Los Angeles band centred around singer/writer/producer Gregg Alexander, with only keyboardist Danielle Brisebois as a further full-time member. The ultra radio-friendly 'You Get What You Give', with its hybrid rock/soul sound, was the group's first single – but before the release of their second, they would permanently disband, being tired and bored of touring. 'You Get What You Give' has a chugging, rhythmic charm and a supreme chorus that really soars… but if one has to be critical, it feels lyrically quite smug and self-congratulatory with its clichéd criticisms of society, and the closing lines about Beck, Hanson, Marilyn Manson and Courtney Love being fakes who deserve an ass-kicking are, unfortunately, pretty crass.

20
TURN AROUND
PHATS & SMALL
MULTIPLY

With more emphasis on the funky part of the equation, 'Turn Around' was a funk/house track that manages to tickle both dancing and smiling muscles at the same time. Hailing from Brighton, Phats and Small sampled vocals from the first verse of Toney Lee's 1982 disco hit 'Reach Up' and applied them to an irresistible rhythm that went round and around to dazzling and dizzying effect. To listen to 'Turn Around' feels akin to riding a Ferris wheel at the happiest, gaudiest and brightest funfair imaginable.

19
YOU'RE SO LEWD
REATARDS
EMPTY

From Memphis came The Reatards, fronted by Jay Reatard; they released albums with titles such as *Teenage Hate* and *Grown Up, Fucked Up*. Their music was very much of the no-frills variety, and they played in a gonzo garage-rock style. They were totally un-PC and deliberately aimed to provoke reaction by holding up a mirror to the gross behaviour, obsessions and attitudes of a bratty and trashy teenage America. 'You're so Lewd' is a neanderthal-sounding song about loveless teenage sex with a girl whose parents are oblivious to what their sweet child gets up to.

It is a hard, fast and extremely raw record that really plays it dumb but is still terrifically exciting.

18
KING OF SNAKE
UNDERWORLD
JUNIOR BOY'S OWN
OTHER SINGLES 1999: JUMBO; BRUCE LEE

Released in a dizzying array of versions, 'King of Snake' makes use of the bass line from Donna Summer's 'I Feel Love', something that inevitably gifts the track a huge amount of energy and momentum. Around the bass line, dazzling trance sounds slither and pulse; the track becomes a living entity… breathing and moving. When Karl Hyde adds his voice to proceedings, it is shaman-like, inspired; he seems possessed, whipping up a storm with his fervour and supplying an unpredictability that pushes the track into extreme *Heart of Darkness* territory.

17
BETTER OFF ALONE
ALICE DEEJAY
VIOLENT
OTHER SINGLES 1999: BACK IN MY LIFE

Alice Deejay was the name given to a Eurodance project led by DJ Jurgen. In 1997, an instrumental version of 'Better Off Alone' was recorded and released, only to disappear without trace. Two years later, having been left by his romantic partner, DJ Jurgen began experimenting with lyrics that related to the break-up. Singer Judith Pronk was recruited to provide vocals for the Alice Deejay project, and so it was that a newborn version of 'Better Off Alone' was issued. Melodically it is very strong, combining Eurodance sounds with a commercial, trance-feel, all topped-off with Pronk's excellent performance of what, in truth, is a mere sketch of a lyric, wrapped around a captivating hook line.

16
MICHAEL
ROY DAVIS JR.
NUPHONIC

Chicago house spawned a host of talented big names, and although Roy Davis Jr. is not so well known, he wrote and produced a series of excellent tracks. His best known single was 'Gabriel', but in terms of quality, 'Michael' was at least its equal. The song calls out to a winged archangel for direction and deliverance – although many people presumed it must be a tribute to Michael Jackson. The track flows on an easy, rhythmic groove and it is punctuated by horns and voiced with tenderness and a just a little hint of vulnerability. Seven minutes of an unchanging, understated rhythm can easily drag, but somehow the seven minutes of 'Michael' are soul-cleansing and over much too soon.

15
PIANO LESSONS
PORCUPINE TREE
KSCOPE

Porcupine Tree were a progressive rock band led by Steven Wilson;

personally, I find much of their music to be unpalatably po-faced, but 'Piano Lessons' is definitely the exception that proves the rule. The song operates on two levels: lyrically, it is a scabrous attack on the lack of integrity of the pop music industry, and its shameless promotion of talentless, manufactured celebrities, whilst musically, it is itself a wonderfully constructed piece of pop, based on a piano riff and swoon-worthy guitar effects, topped by Beach Boys-style vocal harmonies and the kind of beautifully ornate psych-pop sounds that The Left Banke and Kaleidoscope were experimenting with in the late 1960s.

14
WINDOWLICKER
APHEX TWIN
WARP

This begins with exaggerated lounge-porn muzak, before rapid, syncopated beats are introduced and a warped, wordless voice comes to the fore as the rhythm alters to a walking-pace shuffle. Thus far, listening to this record gives the listener a somewhat queasy feeling… similar perhaps to drunkenly lurching from one corner of a room to another, while simultaneously vomiting. Then we reach the final section of the track which consists of a sinister, malevolent and unmercifully grinding riff. Aphex Twin was once more pushing his music to extremes, and with 'Windowlicker', everything clicked, leading not only to an impressive creative triumph, but also a commercial hit.

13
SANDSTORM
DARUDE
NEO

Toni-Ville Henrik Virtanen began making music in his late-teens, utilising technical advances in computer programs in order to make recordings at home. He turned out happy hardcore and Eurodance tracks (using aliases such as Position 1 and Rudeboy) but when, in 1999, he made a demo of 'Sandstorm' – something of a stylistic departure – he required a new name… and he went with Darude. The track itself soon came to the attention of JS16, who co-produced a version that he released on his 16 Inch label in Finland. From that point onwards the song caught fire and swept across Europe and America; it is trance music but in an uncontainably epic form – a jaw-dropping, euphoria-inducing bomb to drop upon a dance floor that is capable of creating mayhem. In dance parlance, this is a complete banger… and beyond that, it is simply a masterpiece.

12
RE-REWIND (THE CROWD SAY BO SELECTA)
ARTFUL DODGER
FEATURING CRAIG DAVID
RELENTLESS
OTHER SINGLE 1999:
MOVIN' TOO FAST

Artful Dodger were a UK garage duo from Southampton, and – in collaboration with then unknown singer Craig David – they emerged from the underground garage scene of pirate radio and specialist clubs to conquer the hearts and minds of a much wider audience. The track is underpinned with stuttering, jittery beats and there is a devastatingly simple bass line that acts as a musical hook. Craig David rides along with the rhythm and his pleasant voice glides over the harsher beats to create a contrast that is effective in helping people to access a sound that, to uninitiated ears, can appear to be alien and unfathomable.

11
TENDER
BLUR
FOOD
OTHER SINGLES 1999:
COFFEE AND TV;
NO DISTANCE LEFT TO RUN

Reeling from his break-up with ex-Elastica singer Justine Frischmann, Damon Albarn – along with his Blur bandmates – wrote 'Tender' which acknowledges both the pain of parting and the forward-looking hope of finding new love. It is a song of warmth and consolation, with a hymn-like quality that is enhanced by the employment of The London Community Choir, who add their voices to those of Albarn and Graham Coxon. Mid-paced and majestic, this track has an ebb and flow that is convincingly suggestive of the multiple highs and lows that are experienced in matters of the heart.

10

NO SCRUBS

TLC

LAFACE

OTHER SINGLES 1999:

UNPRETTY; DEAR LIE

The female vocal trio TLC came from Atlanta, Georgia, and at the time of writing, they remain one of the highest-selling girl-groups of all-time. 'No Scrubs' was perhaps their most iconic single; written by former Xscape members Kandi Burruss and Tameka Cottle – with further contributions from producer Kevin Briggs and TLC member Lisa "Left Eye" Lopes – the song slaps back hard at the misogyny prevalent within the R&B and hip-hop communities with which TLC were associated. The term "scrubs" was derogatory slang used to describe an unattractive man of small means, who lacks the intellect to get their life together. Rozonda "Chilli" Thomas, usually a secondary vocalist, was given the lead for 'No Scrubs' and her excellent performance fully vindicates that decision; she sounds both decisive and strong. The track is introduced with acoustic guitars which re-appear occasionally to pierce the electronic washes of sound and beats that basically carry the song. At the end, Lopes provides a rapped coda to this fabulous track that conclusively affirmed the enduring quality of its performers.

9

1ST MAN IN SPACE

ALL SEEING I

FFRR

OTHER SINGLE 1999:

WALK LIKE A PANTHER

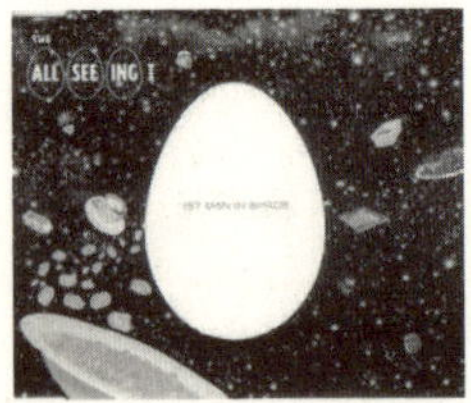

How I loved this single! I played it, played it and played it again… and every single time it filled me up to the brim with deep joy. All Seeing I co-wrote the track with Jarvis Cocker, who provided lyrics that demystify the glamorous image of space travel, as we hear the protagonist stating that "Space is cold, home is colder" as he floats about, alone with his thoughts in the vast nothingness of empty space. Here, All Seeing I play a chugging brand of electronic rock that owes much more to Status Quo than it does to Kraftwerk, while Cocker plays guitar and Phil Oakey puts the icing on the cake by singing in his unmistakable, almost blank style that leaves no room at all for cod hysteria. This is absolutely fantastic stuff, and just writing about it makes me want to hear it once more… in fact, I'm off right now to play it again!

8

SAY MY NAME

DESTINY'S CHILD

COLUMBIA

OTHER SINGLES 1999:

BILLS BILLS BILLS; BUG A BOO

Working as co-writers with Rodney Jerkins, Fred Jerkins III and LaShawn Daniels, the four members of Destiny's Child were displeased with the approach being taken by producer Rodney Jerkins, who – inspired by the 2-step garage music he was hearing in London – was taking the track into areas the girls were uncomfortable with. There's "too much stuff" going on, opined Beyoncé Knowles… until they got to hear the final mix; at that point, they knew their complaints had been wrong and they had on their hands a truly classic record. Lyrically, 'Say My Name' has the protagonist phoning a lover she suspects of infidelity and challenging him to use her name; he hesitates to do so and she believes this is because he doesn't want his new lover to know who he's talking to. The musical accompaniment cleverly accentuates the dynamics of the lyrical content, with syncopated drums, wah-wah guitar licks and inspired, synthesised strings intelligently incorporated. Knowles contributes a devastatingly good lead vocal and the wonderful harmonies added by Kelly Rowland, LeToya Luckett and LaTavia Roberson are peerless.

7

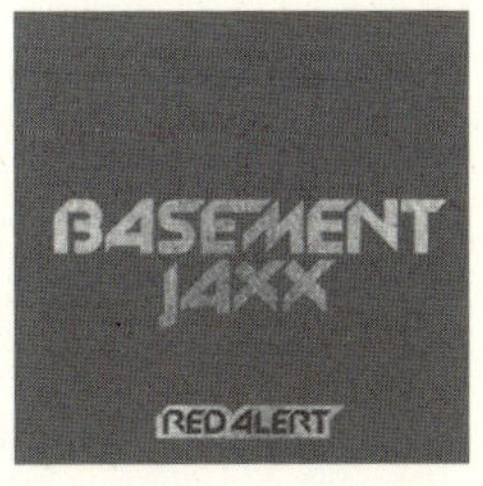

RED ALERT

BASEMENT JAXX

XL

OTHER SINGLES 1999:

JUMP N SHOUT; RENDEZ-VU

'Red Alert' was the first single taken from *Remedy*, the debut album by Basement Jaxx. It features biting vocals from Blu James that give the track some real soulfulness; as for the music, it is devastatingly good. It falls under the house umbrella, but there is a strong P-Funk influence; the elastic bass line pulverises while spacey-noises whizz all around it, and in general there is a ton of stuff going on… but it is all quite superbly layered and mixed. The groove is never once compromised and the excitement level remains sky-high throughout the entirety of the track.

6

BEAUTIFUL STRANGER

MADONNA

MAVERICK

OTHER SINGLE 1999:

NOTHING REALLY MATTERS

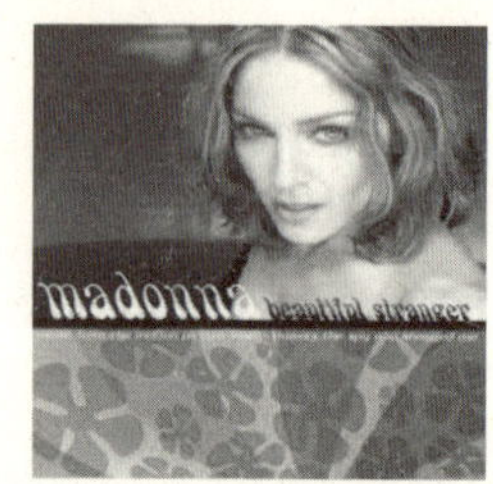

In combination with William Orbit, Madonna wrote and produced 'Beautiful Stranger' for inclusion on the soundtrack of the film *Austin Powers: The Spy Who Shagged Me*. This was something of a stylistic departure for Madonna, but one that paid huge dividends during what was yet another imperious phase of her career. 'Beautiful Stranger' is a heavily ornate, psychedelic rock song with disco leanings, perhaps owing just a little bit to Love's seminal *Forever Changes* album in terms of inspiration. The drums are high in the mix with reverberating guitars also prominent, while the lyrics address a romantic infatuation that comes with a hint of danger. Madonna's delivery is compelling and she sings with evident relish. So, in a recording era in which keyboards and computers were largely supplanting the guitar, Madonna had rejected the new orthodoxy to deliver a guitar-driven pop classic.

5

SHE TALKS TO RAINBOWS

RONNIE SPECTOR

KILL ROCK STARS

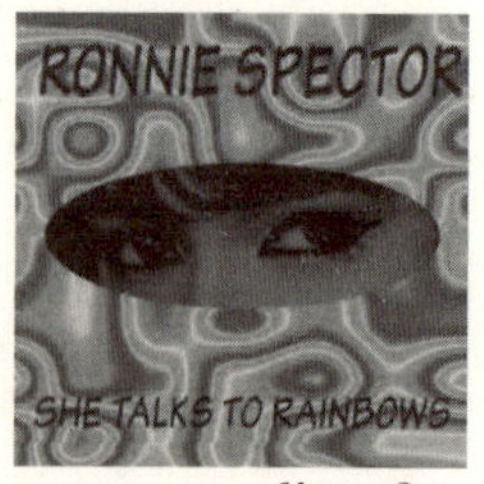

To pretty much everybody else, Ronnie Spector was a relic of a bygone era – she hadn't had a solo record released in twelve years – but to Joey Ramone she remained iconic and a very significant part of his musical DNA; he managed to get her a record deal and accompanied her into the studio as co-producer of a five track EP. The selected songs were all substantial (including Johnny Thunders

'Can't Put Your Arms Around a Memory' and Brian Wilson's 'Don't Worry Baby') and Spector totally inhabits each one, breathing fire and life into all of them. But the title track was especially fabulous; it was a late-period Ramones song from their album *¡Adios Amigos!* It is a beautiful, wistful song and Spector fills it with warmth; her voice is battered and bruised but her dignity remains intact and she is brave enough to reveal her vulnerability. Her journey through life had often been harsh, but she still remained a mesmerising singer, and over an acoustic strum, her voice rises magisterially, expressing compassion, empathy and wisdom. The release of the EP was low-key and without fanfare, but it was a significant artistic triumph and a reminder of two wonderful talents… surely more was to come? But by this time, Joey Ramone was terminally ill and would die only eighteen-months later, leaving only this EP as conclusive evidence of a quite brilliant collaboration.

4

RACE FOR THE PRIZE

THE FLAMING LIPS

WARNER BROTHERS

OTHER SINGLE 1999:

WAITING FOR A SUPERMAN

'Race for the Prize' was a single taken from The Flaming Lips album *The Soft Bulletin*, which saw them finally achieve the commercial and artistic breakthrough that led to them receiving the love and recognition they so richly deserved. Riding the zeitgeist was producer Dave Fridmann who, whilst working with The Flaming Lips, was simultaneously working with Mercury Rev; this inevitably led to some overspill of ideas and a degree of similarity in the two bands' sounds. 'Race for the Prize' is a thought-provoking song, worthy of some critical examination; it looks at two scientists who are working side-by-side in order to develop the atomic bomb. They are tireless in their work and share the aim to finally end the war through the use of this terrible weapon, which they hope will then irrefutably display the futility of continuing to fight. Their motivation is pure and they are depicted as being "Only human, with wives and children"… but as we all know to our great regret, to err is to be human; we make horrible mistakes and misjudgments. In the case of the bombs dropped upon the civilian population in Hiroshima and Nagasaki, we are forced to ask the question “Did the ends justify the means?”. The awful ambiguity between the desire to bring peace and the horror of what the bomb actually did to innocent people is evident in the bittersweet presentation of the song, delivered in a plaintive manner by Wayne Coyne, accompanied by a jumping piano motif and whirling synthesisers. This very humane song approaches the situation from an unusual angle – the scientists as individuals are treated with compassion – which ingeniously hammers home a stark warning about the consequences of using science as a force for destruction.

3

MY NAME IS

EMINEM FEATURING DR DRE

AFTERMATH

OTHER SINGLES 1999:

ROLE MODEL; GUILTY CONSCIENCE

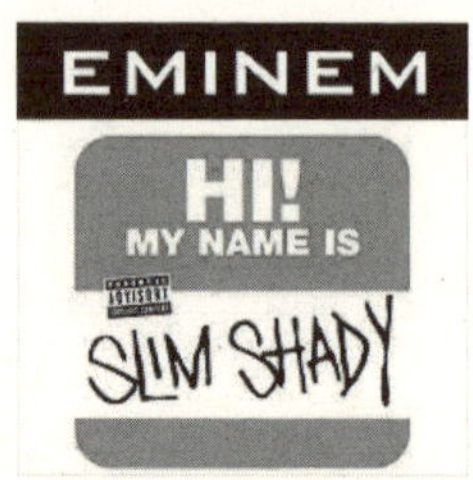

Following the failure of his 1996 debut LP *Infinite*, which was either ignored or dismissed as inauthentic, Eminem allowed his disappointment to fester and his demons led him towards methadone and alcohol abuse; he was filled with a darkness that ultimately culminated in a suicide attempt. As a consequence, his lyrics became angrier and increasingly sarcastic and he created the alter ego Slim Shady, in a move not dissimilar to David Bowie’s invention of the Ziggy Stardust character. Developing the Slim Shady persona allowed him to say things that Eminem might not have been able to say, because Slim Shady was an uncensored and reckless wildcard. The *Slim Shady* EP of 1987 introduced this Frankenstein’s monster to the world and it was heard by Dr Dre who was sufficiently impressed to make working with Eminem a priority mission. The groundbreaking *Slim Shady* LP would be the direct result of this collaboration and the first single taken from it was ‘My Name Is’. It is built-up using a prominent bass line sample and almost psychedelic keyboards borrowed from Labi Siffre’s ‘I Got The…’, amusingly played by Siffre’s backing musicians of the time, who just happened to be Chas and Dave! However, the track seems to leap-out and grab you by the throat, not letting go until the mix of cartoon violence and attacks on hypocrisy and the bubble of stardom are completed; it is funny as hell, but very pointedly so. Eminem raps in a brattish whine and uses numerous pop-culture references as he holds up a mirror to society and displays its horrible underbelly for all to see. This music was wildly exciting, unique and eccentric, and so the rise and rise of Eminem very quickly became unstoppable.

2

CAUGHT OUT THERE

KELIS

VIRGIN

In 1997, the eighteen-year old Kelis got her first singing gig as a backing vocalist on a track by Gravediggaz; this in turn led to work with Pharrell Williams and Chad Hugo (aka The Neptunes) who helped her find a solo record deal and acted as producer. Her first single release was the attention grabbing 'Caught Out There', which is built upon a jumpy and jittery rhythm track that had been previously offered to, and rejected by, Busta Rhymes. Kelis bounces her honeyed voice across the beats as she articulates her disappointment and frustration towards a cheating lover; at first she is measured and in control, but the burning fuse is short and… in a flash, all her pent-up anger is unleashed – "I hate you so much right now", she cries out, as a raw, emotional and primal rage consumes her. This is startling stuff to say the least; it is so visceral that it rocks you back on your heels and forces the listener to take a metaphorical step backwards in the face of the righteous fury that Kelis is transmitting.

1

HOLES

MERCURY REV

V2

OTHER SINGLES 1999: OPUS 40;

DELTA SUN BOTTLENECK STOMP

'Holes' was the fourth single extracted from the masterful album *Deserter's Songs*, produced – with great empathy – by Dave Fridmann, Jonathan Donahue and Aaron Hurwitz. This was the moment when Mercury Rev, from the depths of despair, summoned up all of their available musical craft and mixed it up with lots of emotion and fresh ideas to create something truly magnificent and quite extraordinary. 'Holes' is a record that has deep significance in my life; I played it often and its fragile beauty, abstract lyrics and atmosphere of warm melancholy had a profound effect on my mother too. By then, she was in her mid-seventies and had little relish left for life… and yet she was captivated by 'Holes'; whenever she heard the song, there was evident joy in her demeanour, and I treasure the memory of her smiling as she immersed herself within it. Quite a song it is too – perhaps written as the band's intended swansong. Jonathan Donahue shares his ruminations on what amounts to a guided tour past a series of thoughts that are occurring inside his mind. The lyric, never repetitive, is a stream of consciousness addressing of Donahue's preoccupations, and there is no chorus. Structurally, the song is written as two very long verses; they are in different styles but performed with similar vocal intonation. The whole piece is taken at a slow and steady pace, with interweaving synthesisers forming the musical bedrock of the track. Between the verses, a synthesiser swirls as if to suggest a troubling thought resolving itself, and then, at the close of the second verse, a surprising, but perfectly judged trumpet solo takes us to the closing lines of the song, sung with a parched rasp in a state of seeming bewilderment – "Bands, those funny little plans that never work quite right". As the song slowly fades into nothingness and the magical spell is broken, we feel that the world, for better or worse, is waiting to be faced anew…